THE "WRITER'S BOOK"
BY SHERWOOD ANDERSON

A Critical Edition

by

Martha Mulroy Curry

The Scarecrow Press, Inc.
Metuchen, N.J.   1975

Library of Congress Cataloging in Publication Data

Anderson, Sherwood, 1876-1941.
    The "Writers's book".

    Bibliography: p.
    Includes index.
    1. Authorship. I. Curry, Martha Mulroy,
1926-   ed. II. Title.
PN145.A53 1975   808'.02   74-22088
ISBN 0-8108-0737-8

To my father
and mother

TABLE OF CONTENTS

INTRODUCTION

ACKNOWLEDGMENTS

I wish to express my gratitude to Mrs. Eleanor Anderson, who not only graciously gave her permission to edit the "Writer's Book" but also has proved a valuable friend and adviser. I wish also to thank Mr. Lawrence Towner, Director of the Newberry Library, Chicago, Illinois, for his permission to consult the Sherwood Anderson Papers and to edit the "Writer's Book." My special gratitude goes to Mrs. Amy Nyholm, former curator of the Sherwood Anderson Papers, and to the entire staff of the Special Collections Department at the Newberry Library. Finally, I wish to express my debt of gratitude to the late Edward L. Surtz, S.J., for the inestimable assistance he gave me in the preparation of this edition.

Gratitude is expressed to the following persons and publishers for permission to reprint selections from copyrighted material:

Appleton-Century-Crofts for American Fiction by Arthur H. Quinn (New York, 1936), pp. 657-58; and for Spokesmen by Thomas K. Whipple (New York, 1928), pp. 120-21 and 136.

The Bodley Head, Ltd. for "The Cornfields" in Mid-American Chants by Sherwood Anderson (London, 1918), pp. 11-12.

Charles Scribner's Sons for "Preface" to Plays: Winesburg and Others by Sherwood Anderson (New York, 1937).

Elsevier Publishing Company, Amsterdam, for the address before the Swedish Academy on December 10, 1930, by Erik Axel Karlfeldt, translated by Naboth Hedin and printed in Why Sinclair Lewis Got the Nobel Prize (New York: Harcourt, Brace and Company), p. 8, © The Nobel Foundation, 1931.

Maxwell Geismar for "Introduction" to Sherwood Anderson: Short Stories (New York: Hill and Wang, Inc., 1962), p. xi.

Harcourt Brace Javanovich, Inc. for Main Street by Sinclair Lewis (New York, 1920), pp. 177-78.

Granville Hicks for The Great Tradition, rev. ed. (New York: Crowell-Collier and Macmillan, Inc., 1935), pp. 229-30.

Houghton Mifflin Company for "Introduction" by Frederick O'Brien
in The Best Short Stories of 1929 (New York: Dodd, Mead
and Company, 1929), p. ix, and in The Best Short Stories
of 1933 (Boston: Houghton Mifflin Company, 1933), p. xvi.

Little, Brown and Company for Letters of Sherwood Anderson,
edited by Howard Mumford Jones in association with Walter
Rideout (Boston, 1953), pp. 5, 15, 22, 24, 45, 48, 48-49,
54, 59-60, 99-100, 102, 116, 154, 160, 167-68, 168, 174,
191, 194, 195, 201, 202, 216-17, 246-47, 263-64, 277-78,
286, 288-89, 305-306, 358-60, 380, 387-88, 395-96, 398,
445-46, and 463, copyright 1953 by Eleanor Anderson; and
for Miss Elizabeth by Elizabeth Anderson (Boston, 1969),
pp. 133-34.

Louisiana State University Press for Freudianism and the Literary
Mind by Frederick Hoffman, 2nd ed. (Baton Rouge, 1957),
p. 236.

William Morrow and Company, Inc. for Sherwood Anderson by Irving Howe (New York, 1951), pp. 151-52, copyright 1951 by
William Sloane Associates, Inc.

Partisan Review for Sherwood Anderson's Answer in "The Situation
in American Writing: Seven Questions (Part II)," VI (Fall,
1939), 104, © 1939 Partisan Review.

Princeton University Press for selections from Augusto Centeno,
The Intent of the Artist (copyright 1941, © 1969 by Princeton University Press), pp. 40-60, reprinted by permission
of Princeton University Press.

Random House for "Introduction" by Ernest Boyd to Winesburg,
Ohio by Sherwood Anderson (New York: The Modern Library, 1922), p. xv.

The Scarecrow Press for The Road to Winesburg by William A.
Sutton (Metuchen, N. J., 1972), pp. 20, 174, 191-92.

James Schevill for Sherwood Anderson: His Life and Works (Denver: University of Denver Press, 1951), pp. 282 and 349-
50.

Twayne Publishers, Inc. for Sherwood Anderson by Rex Burbank
(New York, 1964), pp. 111-12 and 118-19.

The University of Minnesota Press for Sherwood Anderson by Brom
Weber (Minneapolis, 1964), p. 34.

The University of North Carolina Press for Sherwood Anderson's
Memoirs: A Critical Edition, edited by Ray Lewis White
(Chapel Hill, 1969), pp. 27-28, 28-29, 245, 278, 346, 348,
349-50, 352, 354, 407-408, 414, 473, 486-87, and 491.

The Viking Press for Winesburg, Ohio by Sherwood Anderson
(copyright 1919 by B. W. Huebsch, Inc., 1947 by Eleanor
Copenhaver Anderson), pp. 19-20, reprinted by permission
of The Viking Press, Inc.; for "Introduction" by Walter Rideout to A Story Teller's Story by Sherwood Anderson (copyright © 1969 by The Viking Press, Inc.), reprinted by permission of The Viking Press, Inc.; and for The Liberal
Imagination by Lionel Trilling (copyright 1941, 1947 by Lionel Trilling), pp. 30-31, reprinted by permission of The
Viking Press, Inc.

A. P. Watt and Son, London, for "Introduction" to The Country of
the Blind and Other Stories by H. G. Wells (London:
Thomas Nelson and Sons, 1917), p. viii, reprinted by permission of the Estate of H. G. Wells.

Harold Ober Associates for excerpts from the following works by
Sherwood Anderson: Hello Towns! (New York: Horace
Liveright Publishing Inc., 1929), pp. 232, 308, and 327-28;
The Modern Writer (San Francisco: The Lantern Press,
Gelber Lilienthal, Inc., 1925), pp. 14 and 27-28; No Swank
(Philadelphia: The Centaur Press, 1934), pp. 25 and 96;
Sherwood Anderson's Memoirs [edited by Paul Rosenfeld]
(New York: Harcourt, Brace and World, 1942), p. 228;
Sherwood Anderson's Notebook (New York: Boni and Live-
right, 1926), pp. 143-44, 145, and 197-98; A Story Teller's
Story: A Critical Text, edited by Ray Lewis White (Cleve-
land: The Press of Case Western Reserve University,
1968), pp. 71-72, 92, 93-94, 226, 227-28, 241, and 259-
60; Tar: A Midwest Childhood: A Critical Text, edited by
Ray Lewis White (Cleveland: The Press of Case Western
Reserve University, 1969), pp. 5 and 7; "Foreword" to
Horses and Men (New York: B. W. Huebsch, Inc., 1923),
pp. xi-xiii; "Introduction" to Poor White (New York: The
Modern Library, 1926), p. vi; Answer in "The Situation in
American Writing: Seven Questions (Part II), Partisan Review, VI (Fall, 1939), 104; and for "Introduction" to Theodore Dreiser's Free and Other Stories (New York: Boni
and Liveright, 1918), pp. vi-vii.

The first page of Anderson's manuscript, "A Sermon. Half a Story."

INTRODUCTION

I. DESCRIPTION OF THE MANUSCRIPT
OF THE "WRITER'S BOOK"

In 1947 Sherwood Anderson's widow, Mrs. Eleanor Anderson, deposited in the Newberry Library in Chicago as a bequest the papers of her late husband. Mrs. Anderson's gift consists of manuscripts of published and unpublished works, letters between Anderson and his family and friends over a period of twenty-five years, fragments, sketches, and notes of unfinished works, as well as royalty statements, newspaper clippings, photographs, and a few of Anderson's own paintings. Since the original bequest, the Newberry Library has acquired by gift or purchase many more documents concerned with Sherwood Anderson. Its most notable recent acquisition is the manuscript of Winesburg, Ohio, purchased from Mrs. Eleanor Anderson in 1969.

At the present time the Sherwood Anderson Papers in the Newberry Library consist of 16,783 items. Mrs. Amy Nyholm, former curator of the Sherwood Anderson Papers, is responsible for the excellent organization of the Papers. The arrangement is in four sections: 1) outgoing letters, arranged chronologically; 2) incoming letters and material relative to Anderson, arranged alphabetically; 3) works by Anderson, arranged alphabetically; and 4) appendix, consisting, among other things, of art work, dust jackets, photographs, the diaries that Anderson kept from 1936 until his death, and several sealed boxes, to be opened only after the death of Mrs. Eleanor Anderson.

One of the manuscripts among Sherwood Anderson's "Works" is a holograph of 267 pages called the "Writer's Book." The manuscript is divided into seven sections and, except for the third section, is written on white, unlined paper, 8.5 by 11 inches. The third section is written on sheets from a tablet of lined, coarse white paper, 8.5 by 12.25 inches. Each section of the manuscript, except for one typewritten page, is written with a fountain pen in light-blue ink. The manuscript is not dated, but internal evidence, as we shall see, indicates that it was written in the middle and late 1930's, that is, during the last decade of Anderson's life.

At the time of Anderson's sudden death in Colon, Panama,

on March 8, 1941, he left three unfinished projects: his Memoirs,
on which he had been working intermittently from 1933; a new
volume of short stories; and, as Ray Lewis White calls it in his
"Introduction" to the critical edition of Sherwood Anderson's Memoirs, "a literary textbook essay for creative writing, 'The Writer's
Book' " (Chapel Hill: The University of North Carolina Press,
1969, p. xxxiv).   This "Writer's Book, " except for passages published by Paul Rosenfeld in the first edition of the Memoirs (New
York: Harcourt, Brace and Company, 1942), has remained in its
manuscript form among the Sherwood Anderson Papers at the Newberry Library until now.   The present is the first edition of the
"Writer's Book" in its entirety.   This edition also includes an Introduction, a Commentary of interpretative and biographical notes,
and a Textual Apparatus listing editorial changes and citing Anderson's revisions of the manuscript whenever they are decipherable
and are more than mere deletions of false starts of words.

       The manuscript of the "Writer's Book" is in good condition.
Except for the pages of Part III, written on the coarse sheets of
tablet paper now turning yellow, the paper of the manuscript is
still in fair condition.   The ink throughout the work has not faded.
Although Anderson's handwriting is, at first, very difficult to decipher, familiarity renders it legible.   The manuscript itself consists of two introductory pages and seven sections of unequal length.
The two introductory pages are a typewritten page which lists possible topics for inclusion and is entitled "The Book for Writer, "
and a handwritten foreword which is entitled "A Sermon.   Half a
Story. "   The seven sections which follow are: I, "Prelude To A
Story (Addressed to Story Tellers)"; II, "How to Write to a Writer"; III, "The Writer"; IV, "The Workman, His Moods"; V, "Notes
on the Novel"; VI, "Note--On Saving Ideas"; and VII, "Note. "

       At the beginning of the manuscript there is a piece of
brown wrapping paper, ten inches wide and two-and-a-half inches
long, on which is written in pencil in Anderson's hand: "Mss--
For Writer's Book/These have been copied. "   "Copied" most likely means "typed, " for frequently among the Sherwood Anderson
Papers there are both a holograph and a typed copy of the same
work.   As the Commentary explains, however, any copy that was
made of the holograph of the "Writer's Book" has been lost, except for four pages.   These pages are in pairs and were found by
the present editor in the boxes marked "Journal" among the
"Works" with the Sherwood Anderson Papers.   The first pair was
found in the "Journal" folder marked 1933 and is the same as the
first four and a half pages of Part II, "How to Write to a Writer"
(pp. 62/1-64/18 of the present edition).   The second pair was
found in the "Journal" folder marked 1937 and is the same as the
last four pages of Part V, "Notes on the Novel" (pp. 79/32-81/32
of the present edition).   On these typed pages long passages are
deleted and the titles of imaginary works are changed to titles of
actual works by Anderson.   Mrs. Eleanor Anderson told the present editor in an interview at Ripshin Farm outside of Marion, Virginia, on July 17, 1970, that the penciled deletions and substituted

titles are in Paul Rosenfeld's hand. Rosenfeld, however, never
published, either in the Memoirs or in The Sherwood Anderson
Reader (Boston: Houghton Mifflin Company, 1947), any of the material on the four typed pages. (See the critical notes to 62/1,
63/1-2, 63/27-64/18, and 79/32 for further information on these
typed pages.)

Anderson's only typewritten page in the manuscript, as the
note to 2/1-6 explains, seems to be quite independent of the rest
of the "Writer's Book. " The title is given as "The Book for Writer, " and the topics listed are not systematically followed in the
remaining sections of the work. All of the topics are discussed,
however, with the exception of one, namely, "Trilena White and
the successful novelist ... Has he contempt?" The topics that
are systematically developed in the "Writer's Book, " at least in
Part I, are the topics mentioned in the second introductory page,
"A Sermon. Half a Story. " Therefore, it seems that "A Sermon.
Half a Story" is the Foreword to Part I only, and not to the
"Writer's Book" as a whole.

As has been explained, the seven sections of the "Writer's
Book" are of unequal length. Part I, "Prelude To A Story (Addressed to Story Tellers), " 168 pages, is by far the longest and,
in many respects, the most personal. Here Anderson, undoubtedly
in the last years of his life, reminisces about his life and works:
about his mother, his father, his boyhood in small Ohio towns,
his youth as a laborer in Chicago, about his business careers in
Chicago and Elyria, Ohio, and about his struggle to establish and
maintain his literary reputation. The other six sections are con-
siderably shorter; and except for Part III, the only fictional section, they continue the reminiscent, autobiographical musings of
Part I.

Part II, "How to Write to a Writer, " thirteen pages, is a
humorous account of Anderson's reaction to the numerous letters
he received from aspiring writers. Part III, "The Writer, " ten
pages, is the only part of the "Writer's Book" that is a fictional
narrative. A later section of the Introduction and the note to
67/1-70/28 explain why the editor believes that "The Writer" is
an early version of Anderson's short story "Pastoral, " published
originally in Redbook (LXXIV [January, 1940], 38-39, 59), and
later published, in a revised version, in Anderson's Memoirs (ed.
White, pp. 222-30). Part IV, "The Workman, His Moods, " sixteen pages, tells of "rich glad times" (74/29), when Anderson
wrote A Story Teller's Story in Reno, Nevada; Tar: A Midwest
Childhood in a shed in a cornfield on a farm in Virginia; and unnamed works in "a tall old house in the old quarter of New Orleans" and in "a cheap hotel in Kansas City" (75/1-2 and 6).
Part V, "Notes on the Novel, " twenty-three pages, is similar in
two respects to the shorter Part VI, "Note--On Saving Ideas, "
nine pages. Both Parts V and VI deal with the development of
the imagination and encourage the free flow of thoughts and ideas.
Part V, however, speaks also about the place of sex in literature

and about the relationship between the novel and the short story.
Part VII, "Note," twenty-six pages, likewise treats the relationship between the novel and the short story. Nonetheless, even
though Anderson had intended in Part VII to speak of this relationship (see 89/26-29 and 91/19-21), he had "been carried away" by
the remembrance of "the glorious times in the life of the writer
of short tales" (89/28-29). "These glorious moments, these pregnant hours" (85/30-31) of intense creativity are Anderson's subject in Part VII, where he describes in detail the circumstances
surrounding the writing of three short stories: an unnamed story
written in a railroad station in Harrodsburg, Kentucky; "I'm a
Fool," written in the office of his Chicago advertising agency; and
"The Man's Story," written in Stark Young's apartment in New
York.

       Since Part III is a story and Parts II, IV, V, VI, and VII
are relatively straightforward accounts of various aspects of Anderson's literary career, they do not require a detailed analysis in
the Introduction.   Part I, on the other hand, is a more complicated piece of writing. If "A Sermon. Half a Story" is the foreword to Part I and not to the whole of the "Writer's Book," then
"A Sermon" (3/1-8) tells us that Part I "attempts to tell a new
story," and that the telling will show "the processes by which a
story begins in the mind of the story teller's." These processes
include "the resistance in him to its flow" and "the struggle he
has with himself." Part I will also show "what finally emerges,"
that is, the story itself. Thus "Prelude To A Story" is itself a
story, but a story told in such a way as to include the very processes, with their struggles and resistances.

       The "new story" that Anderson tells in "Prelude To A Story"
is the story of his attempt to write a salable short story for
"some magazine" because "I am needing money" (4/8). The scene
in which the story is laid is Anderson's farm, Ripshin, in southwest Virginia. The external action of the story takes place on an
afternoon when Anderson is writing in the cabin at the side of Ripshin Creek and later during the night, first by the bedside of his
sleeping wife, then on a hillside overlooking his house, and lastly
at a grassy spot near his cabin, the "black spot on the grass by
the creek where I had burned the attempt I had made to impose
my own will on the people of my imaginative world" (61/6-9).
This framework of external action, however, is a means Anderson
employs to tell several stories. The stories that take place in
Anderson's imagination as he tells the skeletal story are as much
a part of the story of Part I as the skeletal story itself. Also
integral to "Prelude To A Story" are Anderson's statements on the
craft of story writing.

       The "processes by which a story begins in the mind of the
story teller's" (3/4-5) constitute the first thirty-nine pages of
Part I. In the course of describing these "processes," Anderson
tells three stories. First, he begins the skeletal story of his attempt to write the salable magazine story. Secondly, he tells the

story that a friend, called both a scientist (6/15) and a judge
(21/19), told him about a secret love affair. Thirdly, he tells
the story of his youthful search for an ideal woman, called Cecelia,
but of finding a prostitute instead. These three stories are made
to come together, or, more accurately, to blend into one another
by means of Anderson's use of personal reminiscences.

For example, as Anderson starts the skeletal story he is
reminded by his literary agent, either Otto Liveright or Jacques
Chambrun (see the note to 4/4), that "large American magazines
are business ventures" (4/26-27). This remonstrance reminds
him of the poverty of his boyhood and youth and of his early "passion for writing" (10/1). His "passion for writing" had found expression in writing letters to "Cecelia, " his personification of the
ideal woman. As Anderson recounts his letter-writing to Cecelia,
he is reminded of many scenes from his days as a young laborer
in Chicago. He remembers most vividly a scene on a Sunday
morning when an old man led a white horse past three other men
and past an old, bald-headed woman standing by the curb. This
scene makes him remember his encounter with a prostitute on the
previous night. Finally, all of his memories make Anderson think
of the Winesburg story "Loneliness, " a story which "described a
little man in a room and what the imagined figures his fancy had
conjured up had come to mean to him" (14/19-22).

Just as reminiscence plays a role in structuring the progress of "Prelude To A Story, " so does contrast. For example,
Anderson contrasts the story that the judge told him in the moonlit meadow, which contained "certain so-called sordid touches"
(6/26), with the story that he is trying to write for the magazine,
a story in which "there must be nothing that will remind readers
of certain sordid moments, thoughts, passions, acts, in their own
lives" (7/9-11). He also contrasts the imaginary Cecelia with the
real prostitute. These contrasts heighten the absurdity of Anderson's struggle to write the salable story, as well as the absurdity
of his dream to find ideal beauty. Nonetheless: "It is by such
absurd dreams, always coming, always changing, that the imaginative young man lives. And, if he becomes in the end an American popular short story or novel writer, it is out of such dreams
he later builds his tales" (16/20-17/2). Finally, when Anderson
contrasts the real prostitute with the unreal Cecelia and says that
perhaps he can imagine the prostitute "the real Cecelia" (18/11-
12), he sums up one of the dominant themes of "Prelude To A
Story. "

Cecelia is imaginary and the prostitute is real, but to Anderson and to the "imaginative young men" (16/29-30) for whose
benefit he is writing, Cecelia is real; but the prostitute, the radio
announcers whose tone of voice she mimicks, the writers of magazine short stories, and all the artists who prostitute their art, are
unreal. After telling the prostitute's story Anderson asks the rhe-
torical question: "And why do I, here, as a part of the introduction to another tale I have wanted to write, why do I tell it here?"

(21/10-11). Anderson's answer is the rest of Part I. "When I
sat down to write the story, to which this rambling talk may serve
as a sort of introduction, I had something in mind, as I have already suggested, other than the story of the country boy who later
became a judge" (21/15-19). Anderson had in mind a story of an
afternoon of determined effort in his cabin to write a story that
would observe all the "don'ts" (23/22-24) imposed by the editors
of popular magazines and, by extension, by all the manipulators of
popular taste. The story of his struggle culminates in his night-
time adventure when he listens to the sounds of the stream that
runs through his mountain farm. After doing so, Anderson goes
to his cabin and, in the middle of the night, burns his manuscript.
Anderson's struggle ends with his determination "not to impose myself, to let the story I was trying to write write itself, to be
again what I had always been, a slave to the people of my imaginary world" (61/14-16).

The "Writer's Book" is a manuscript that Anderson did not
revise extensively. Although it contains some revisions that Anderson clearly made during original composition, it does not contain
the kind of revision that an author makes on subsequent rereadings
of his text. For example, at 3/3 Anderson originally started the
first sentence of "A Sermon" as follows: "Written by a ve." He
then canceled "by a ve" and continued the sentence: "for young
American story tellers by a veteran of the craft." Therefore, it
would seem that during the original composition, as soon as he
wrote "by a ve" he decided that a better position for the phrase
"by a veteran of the craft" would be later in the sentence. Also,
at 5/25-26 the manuscript reads: "When I got there to his town
there was a sudden illness." The cancellation of the first "there"
seems to indicate that as soon as Anderson wrote the word he decided to use the expression "there was a sudden illness" and re-
places the first "there" with the phrase "to his town."

On the other hand, some revisions may have been made
either during the original composition or sometime afterwards.
For example, at 5/21 Anderson originally wrote: "a man friend
had come one evening to my house." In the manuscript "to my
house" is canceled; "to me" is interlineated after "come"; and a
period is added after "evening." The revised sentence reads: "a
man friend had come to me one evening." The great number of
interlineated words, especially the long phrase written down the
right hand margin on page ninety of the manuscript (39/19-20 of
the present edition), could indicate that many revisions were made
on a subsequent rereading. It is the editor's opinion, however,
that the majority of the cancellations were made and interlineated
words written during the original composition. The reason for
this opinion is the fact that Anderson failed to correct many of his
inadvertent errors. Of course, Anderson, like all poor spellers,
did not notice his misspelled words; but if he had reread his manuscript for revisions he probably would have noticed that he wrote
"spendid" for "splendid" (5/15), "I rember" for "I remember"
74/32), and "grassed" for "grasses" (87/27).

The first fifteen pages of Part I have double pagination.
Centered at the top of the first page is the number 4. This number is canceled and to its right is written "(1)." The title "Prelude To A Story (Addressed to Story Tellers)" is squeezed in above
both numbers. Therefore, it seems that page 4 of another manuscript was changed into the first page of a new work. The double
pagination continues through page 15 of the manuscript and the two
paragraphs in the bottom half of page 15 are canceled. See the
Commentary, the notes to 4/3 and 8/30, and the Textual Apparatus
for further details. It is also probable that the first fifteen pages
have been revised more carefully than the remaining pages. For
example, the revision in the first sentence on page 4, the first
page of "Prelude To A Story" in the present edition, seems to have
been made to accommodate the adaptation of the older manuscript
to the purposes of the "Writer's Book." The original wording of
the opening sentence was: "On a certain day, in the early summer,
a year or two ago, I got a letter from my literary agent." In
order to move the time of the narrative further into the past, the
manuscript was revised to read: "On a certain day, in the early
summer, some years ago..." (4/3-4). Also, the last sentence on
page 4 shows another revision that was probably made to adapt the
original manuscript for use in "Prelude To A Story." Originally
the sentence read: "'But,' he said, 'you are always getting something into all your stories.'" In the manuscript as we have it
now, the period and quotation mark at the end of the sentence are
canceled and the words "that spoils the sale" are interlineated. It
now reads: "'But,' he said, 'you are always getting something
into all of your stories that spoils the sale.'" Furthermore, in
the opening fifteen pages Anderson caught a few, although not all,
of his inadvertent mistakes. For example, the manuscript at 4/19
originally read: "He smiles when he said it and I also smiles."
Anderson corrected the first "smiles" to "smiled," but he failed
to correct the second "smiles." Hence the manuscript reads: "He
smiled when he said it and I also smiles."

Another reason why the editor concludes that Anderson did
not read his manuscript for revision is the fact that it contains
several inconsistencies. The first notable inconsistency might
have occurred because the opening pages were taken from an earlier work. As has been mentioned, at 6/16 Anderson calls the
friend who told him his story an experimental scientist, but at
21/19 this scientist turns into a judge. Other inconsistencies are:
the grey horse of 15/10 becomes white at 15/17; Anderson, who
"went barefooted out of my house" (53/7) becomes shod: "I had
come out of my house wearing bedroom slippers" (59/23-24); and
the shed in the cornfield in which he wrote Tar, a shed with "no
doors and windows" (74/2), acquires both: "The stacks pushed
through the open windows, through the low doorway" (74/9-10).

The manuscript of Part I has many words added to it in
pencil. Close examination of the penciled words reveals that they
are of two kinds. First, Mrs. Eleanor Anderson had gone over
the first eighty pages of Part I and had written above Anderson's

words whenever they were illegible or misspelled. As the note
she left between pages 80 and 81 explains, she had read through
and clarified the manuscript as far as page 81 by December 15,
1950. The second kind of penciled remark on the manuscript of
Part I are words written in by Paul Rosenfeld. Rosenfeld, New
York music and literary critic, was a friend of Sherwood Anderson's from the early 1920's until Anderson's death in 1941. It
was to Rosenfeld that Mrs. Eleanor Anderson turned for help in
the monumental task of organizing her husband's papers after his
sudden death. Rosenfeld selected portions of Parts I, IV, and VII
of the "Writer's Book" for inclusion in his edition of Sherwood Anderson's Memoirs in 1942; and, when he brought out The Sherwood
Anderson Reader in 1947, he reprinted the portion of Part I that
he had included in the Memoirs. Therefore, it is not surprising
to find four times in the manuscript of the "Writer's Book," in
the margin near passages included in Rosenfeld's edition of both
the Memoirs and the Reader, the penciled word "Memoirs," which
is then erased, and the word "Reader" written over the erasure.
A page number which corresponds to the Reader pagination is also
written in. See the notes to 56/7, 59/17, 59/32, and 61/22,
which describe Rosenfeld's penciled comments.

Because of the disorganized state of the manuscripts of the
three "works in progress" that Anderson left at the time of his
death, it is now impossible to determine with certainty which manuscripts he intended to include in the "Writer's Book" and which
manuscripts he intended to include in his Memoirs. Nevertheless,
a five-page list of "Omissions" in a folder at the beginning of Box
2 of the manuscript of the "Memoirs" in the Sherwood Anderson
Papers at the Newberry Library helps determine which manuscripts
Anderson intended to eliminate from his Memoirs. In a section
called "Previous Cuttings" this list gives, sometimes in a slightly
different form, the headings of the handwritten foreword and four
of the sections of the "Writer's Book." The headings as listed on
the pages of "Omissions" are as follows: "Sermon--try to get a
good copy," "Notes on the Novel," "How to Write a Writer (end,)"
"On Saving Ideas," and "The Workman, His Moods." This list also includes "Sound of the Stream (few pages)." It would seem,
therefore, that the bulk of the manuscript of the "Writer's Book"
was taken from manuscript material of the "Memoirs" and set
aside to form Anderson's essay on creative writing.

Although it seems clear that Anderson cut several sections
from his manuscript of the "Memoirs," Paul Rosenfeld included
three of the sections when he brought out Anderson's posthumous
Memoirs in 1942. Rosenfeld also changed the titles of the sections.
For the title of Part I he turned to one of the headings under "Previous Cuttings"; he called it "The Sound of the Stream." Perhaps
"Sound of the Stream" was the title of the original manuscript
which Anderson adapted to form the opening fifteen pages of "Prelude To A Story." Diligent search through the Sherwood Anderson
Papers as they now stand, however, has uncovered no manuscript
called "Sound of the Stream." Nonetheless, comparing Rosenfeld's

"The Sound of the Stream" with Part I of the "Writer's Book"
leaves no doubt that Rosenfeld's "The Sound of the Stream" is "Prelude To A Story. "

Rosenfeld took great liberties as editor when he prepared
"The Sound of the Stream" for publication. As the very change in
title suggests, the whole tone and character of the work were altered by Rosenfeld's editing. Principally by his deletions, but also by his transpositions, Rosenfeld changed a work concerned with
Anderson's struggle to maintain his artistic integrity to a work
which describes Anderson's writing of stories amid the beauties of
his mountain farm in Virginia. For example, Rosenfeld did not
begin "The Sound of the Stream" with the passage about Anderson's
correspondence with his literary agent (4/3-5/20). Rather, he
brought forward from 57/27-59/10 the passage about the stream
that runs through Ripshin Farm. Thus the bucolic passage about
the stream and about the way it talked to Anderson was taken out
of its original context and made to provide the opening scene of
"The Sound of the Stream. "

At 27/22 Anderson speaks about a well-wisher who told him
that, if he tried to write for a popular audience, "You can clean
up. " Rosenfeld changed this expression to: "You can change"
(Memoirs, p. 435). This change in wording is indicative of all the
changes that Rosenfeld made. He seemed intent on "cleaning up"
Anderson's text by making three types of changes: by omitting
"sordid details, " by omitting passages about Anderson's business
and/or literary careers, and by "improving" Anderson's style.

It is ironic that Rosenfeld omitted what he evidently considered "sordid details" from a work in which Anderson emphasizes
the necessity of not omitting such details. The theme of "Prelude
To A Story" is that the artist must maintain his artistic integrity
in the face of the crass pressures exerted by the commercial aspects of popular literature. Furthermore, "Prelude To A Story"
is concerned also with the difficulties encountered by Anderson
when trying to establish and maintain his literary career at the
same time that he was compelled to support himself in the manufacturing or advertising business. Because the details about Anderson's business careers do not fit the pastoral tone of "The
Sound of the Stream, " Rosenfeld omitted most of them.

In addition to an expurgated version of Part I, Rosenfeld
also included in his edition of Anderson's Memoirs portions of
Part IV and practically all of Part VII. The last section of Rosenfeld's edition (pp. 503-507), is entitled "The Fortunate One" and
is made up of portions of Part IV, "The Workman, His Moods"
and portions of the final section of the manuscript of the "Memoirs."
The parts of "The Workman, His Moods, " however, that Rosenfeld
used in "The Fortunate One" are not used in the order in which
they are in the manuscript. The opening pages of "The Fortunate
One" were taken from 73/29-74/28 of "The Workman, His Moods, "
and the middle pages were taken from 71/18-72/31. The last

part of the "Writer's Book" that Rosenfeld included in his edition
of Memoirs is Part VII, entitled by Anderson simply "Note" and
by Rosenfeld "Writing Stories." Even though the title is changed,
Rosenfeld's version of Part VII is closer to the manuscript than
either of the other two parts he edited. In Part VII he cut con-
siderably less material and did not change the position of any of
the passages.

Therefore, since the "Writer's Book" has never been edited
or published in its entirety, since portions of it have been too
freely edited by Paul Rosenfeld in the 1942 edition of Sherwood Anderson's Memoirs, and since Ray Lewis White in his critical edition of the Memoirs in 1969 excluded it because he did not consider it a part of the original manuscript of the "Memoirs" (see
pp. xxxiv-xxxv), the present edition of the "Writer's Book" is presented to all readers of Sherwood Anderson's works.

II. AUTOBIOGRAPHICAL INFORMATION
CONTAINED IN THE "WRITER'S BOOK"

The "Writer's Book" is an autobiographical and literary essay on the craft of story telling and, as has been explained, is organized according to two principles typical of Anderson's writing.
First, Anderson is above all a story teller, and everything written
by him takes on the aspect of a tale. Secondly, Anderson tells
the autobiographical-literary story that is the "Writer's Book" by
means of a series of reminiscences. As he recounts a story related to his literary career, he digresses into many personal musings on happenings in his life. In the course of these reminiscences the reader gathers a great deal of information about Anderson, about his works, and about his literary theories.

Even though a brief biography of Anderson can be recon-
structed from the "Writer's Book," the reader must not expect Anderson to tell the literal "truth" about his life. We, the readers,
and not Anderson, must separate "fact from fancy." Anderson
tells us in the "Foreword" to his second autobiography, Tar: A
Midwest Childhood:

> I have a confession to make. I am a story teller
> starting to tell a story and cannot be expected to tell the
> truth. Truth is impossible to me. It is like goodness,
> something aimed at but never hit. (ed. Ray Lewis White
> [Cleveland: The Press of Case Western Reserve Univer-
> sity, 1969], p. 5.)

> All tale telling is, in a strict sense, nothing but lying.
> That is what people cannot understand. To tell the truth
> is too difficult. I long since gave up the effort. (Ibid.,
> p. 8.)

The greatest aid in our task of separating fact from fancy in Anderson's early years is the excellent study by William A.
Sutton, The Road to Winesburg: A Mosaic of the Imaginative Life of Sherwood Anderson (Metuchen, N.J.: The Scarecrow Press, Inc.,
1972). Our greatest aid in separating fact from fancy in Anderson's later years in his letters in the Sherwood Anderson Papers
at the Newberry Library. Many, but far from all, of these letters have been published in Letters of Sherwood Anderson, Selected
and Edited with an Introduction and Notes by Howard Mumford
Jones in Association with Walter Rideout (Boston: Little, Brown
and Company, 1953; New York: Kraus Reprint Company, 1969).

Anderson's biography as constructed from the "Writer's
Book" begins with a description of the families of his father and
mother. When speaking of his fear of poverty and old age, Anderson tells us that his father, "in his occasional sad moods" (50/28),
used to sing the popular late-nineteenth-century song, "Over the
Hill to the Poor-House" (50/32). Anderson then speaks of his
father's family: "The fear in him too, perhaps, came into him
from his father and his father's father and on, back and back, all
perhaps men who had lived as I had always lived--precariously"
(51/1-4). From Sutton's work (pp. 469-472), we know that Anderson's father's family did not live "precariously." Anderson's
great-grandfather was Robert Anderson, who, when he died on
February 9, 1841, left to his heirs 226 acres of land in Adams
County, Ohio, which were sold for $1,638. Sherwood's grandfather
was James Anderson, who died on May 11, 1886, and who also left
a substantial estate.

Sherwood's father, Irwin McLain Anderson, was born in
West Union, Ohio, on August 7, 1845, the son of James Anderson
and Isabella Bryan Huggins Anderson. Isabella Bryan Huggins was
a widow with two children when she married James Anderson.
James too had been married before and by his first wife had had
six children. He and Isabella had three more children, of whom
Irwin was the oldest. The large family of father, mother, and
eleven children lived on a farm outside West Union, apparently in
a happy and comfortable home (Sutton, Road to Winesburg, pp. 470
and 484-85).

Sherwood mentions also his mother's family in the "Writer's
Book." In the context of describing his mother as a "bound girl"
(39/3), Sherwood alludes to his grandmother; but later he virtually
admits that his picture of his grandmother is a highly imaginative
one: "If you do not like my picture, make your own. My own
mother and my grandmother is my own mother and grandmother"
(42/1-3). In the "Writer's Book" Sherwood also says: "my grandmother was married four times. Let us say that my mother's
father is dead and that her mother has her eye on a new husband.
The girl will be a handicap to her and so she has bound her out"
(42/12-16). In his autobiographical writings Sherwood was fond of
telling certain "myths" about his grandmother: that she was of
Italian ancestry, that she had been married four times, and that

she had "bound out" her daughter Emma when she wanted to enter
into a new marriage. Sutton's biography gives us facts that disprove these myths.

Margaret Austry, Sherwood's grandmother, was born in
Germany, probably near Berlin, on September 10, 1830, and came
to the United States when she was three or four years old. Margaret Austry, also spelled "Oystry" and "Ostracy, " married William H. Smith in Butler County, Ohio, on December 22, 1851.
Smith deserted Margaret in March of 1854, when their first daughter, Emma, was seventeen months old and two months before their
second daughter, Mary Ann, was born. Margaret was granted a
divorce on December 4, 1857. Sutton says that Margaret probably
supported herself and her two daughters by going into a family
with her children and doing the housework for room, board, and
perhaps a little money. Within a few years, however, Margaret
married for a second time. She married Lewis Maer, also spelled
"Myers, " on March 29, 1858. Maer and she had another daughter,
named Margaret, but the mother was left a widow with three young
children when Maer died of cholera in Oxford, Ohio, in September
of 1861. Margaret Maer lived until June 30, 1915, and never
married again (Sutton, Road to Winesburg, pp. 476-77).

Emma Smith, Sherwood's mother, was born October 1, 1852.
She probably was taken into families with her mother and her sisters after the father had deserted them and again after her mother
was left a widow by Maer's death. Since she was nine at Maer's
death, she may have left her mother and sisters at that time and
gone into a family on her own. Sutton quotes Miss Nellie Finch
of Oxford, Ohio, who says that Emma went into the home of James
I. Faris on a farm near Morning Sun, Ohio, "as soon as she was
able to work" (Road to Winesburg, p. 482). The arrangement with
the Faris family seems to have been rather loose and probably
very friendly and charitable. Certainly Emma Smith never lived
under the harsh system of indentured servitude. Emma left the
Faris family only after her marriage to Irwin Anderson on March
11, 1873. At the time of their wedding Emma was twenty-one and
Irwin was twenty-eight.

In the "Writer's Book" Sherwood speaks about a photograph
of his mother. "Her photograph, enlarged from an old daguerreotype and presented to me by my brother Karl, hangs above my
desk" (37/4-6). The editor saw this picture in Mrs. Eleanor Anderson's files during her visit to Marion, Virginia, on July 16,
1970. It is indeed a picture of a "very beautiful" (39/12) young
woman. At 37/7-8 Sherwood says that the daguerreotype "must
have been taken when she was twenty-two"; but at 39/9-11 he says,
"she might have been eighteen rather than twenty-two when it was
taken. " Since Sherwood conjectures that the daguerreotype was
taken in a studio "upstairs perhaps above my father's harness
shop" (37/10-11), Emma was more likely twenty-two or twenty-
three rather than eighteen. At eighteen she was not yet married;
but in 1874, when she was twenty-two, Emma and Irwin moved to

Camden, Ohio. Camden is in Preble County, and in the Directory
of Preble Co., Ohio, for 1875 we find I. M. Anderson listed as a
dealer in "Harness &c" (Sutton, Road to Winesburg, p. 496).

Sherwood, Irwin's and Emma's third child and second son,
was born in Camden, Ohio, on September 13, 1876. In the "Writer's Book" Sherwood speaks of Emma as "the mother of five
strong sons and two daughters" (37/4). The children that came
to Emma and Irwin were Karl, born January 13, 1874; Stella,
born April 13, 1875; Sherwood, born September 13, 1876; Irwin,
born June 18, 1878; Ray, born May 21, 1883; Earl, born June 18,
1885; and Fern, born December 11, 1890 (Sutton, Road to Winesburg, p. 494). Fern died in infancy, but the others lived to maturity. Karl, the eldest, was the last survivor of the family. He
died in 1956.

The trade in which Irwin was engaged before his marriage
was harness making. Immediately after their marriage Irwin and
Emma settled in Morning Sun, Ohio, but in the following year they
moved to Camden. Ohio directories indicate that he was in the
harness business in Camden from 1875 until at least 1879. Sometime around 1883 the Anderson family moved to Caledonia, Ohio.
Sutton thinks that Irwin at that time was still self-employed in his
own harness trade. About the same year, however, Irwin left the
harness business. For a time he worked in Mansfield, Ohio,
thirty miles from Caledonia, in the Aultman-Taylor factory, then
the largest manufacturer of farm-machinery in the country. According to Sutton, he worked there in the fall of 1883 and Emma
and the children did not follow him to Mansfield but kept their
residence in Caledonia. By the fall of 1884, however, the whole
family had moved to Clyde, Ohio. School records show that Karl,
Stella, and Sherwood attended the Clyde public school in the fall of
1884. When Irwin moved to Clyde he went back into the harness
business, but he no longer owned his own shop. In Clyde he
worked for Erwin Brothers, harness manufacturers and dealers.
Soon, however, Irwin "became a house painter" (37/12). It is
certain that by 1887 Irwin had abandoned the harness trade and
was, as the Directory of Clyde and Vicinity describes him, a
"House and sign painter." An Ohio directory for 1890-91 describes
him simply as a "painter" (Sutton, Road to Winesburg, pp. 496-
500 and 512-13).

In the "Writer's Book" Sherwood sums up his father's life
by saying that his mother saw "the failure in life of the man she
married" (40/4-5). In all of his autobiographical writings Sherwood pictures his father as a ne'er-do-well, lovable but completely
irresponsible. See, for example, A Story Teller's Story (ed. Ray
Lewis White [Cleveland: The Press of Case Western Reserve University, 1968], p. 5); Tar (ed. White, p. 173); and Memoirs (ed.
White, pp. 44, 81, and 274). Nevertheless, the diary that Irwin
kept in 1871-72, that is, during his twenty-sixth and twenty-seventh
years, shows him to be an industrious and conscientious worker
(the Sherwood Anderson Papers in the Newberry Library; see also

William A. Sutton's analysis of both Irwin's and Emma's diaries
in Appendix I of Tar, ed. White, pp. 219-30). Furthermore, during the years of his marriage Irwin seems to have been a hard
worker, although the incipient industrialization of the late nineteenth
century forced him to abandon the harness business and undertake
house and sign painting. Irwin's loss of his preferred trade may
have been one reason for his excessive drinking. The residents
of both Caledonia and Clyde whom Sutton interviewed remember
that Irwin was generally well liked, played in the band, and was a
grand story teller. They also remembered that he drank too much
or, as one resident of Caledonia put it, went "on a toot once in a
while" (as quoted in Sutton, Road to Winesburg, p. 499).

Immediately after Sherwood's summation of his father's life
as a "failure, " he comments that his mother became "a few years
after marriage, a washwoman" (40/5-6). In A Story Teller's
Story (ed. White, p. 63), in Tar (ed. White, p. 175), and in his
Memoirs (ed. White, pp. 28, 38, 67-68, and 156), Sherwood speaks
of his mother as washing the neighbors' clothes. Sutton's biography
does not verify Emma's specific job of washwoman, but it does
show that she worked hard to maintain her family in decent circumstances. In Camden, Caledonia, and Clyde she seems to have
been more highly respected than her husband. Nonetheless, Sherwood's emphasis in all of his autobiographical writings upon the
extreme poverty of his family is an exaggeration. Although the
family certainly lived in modest circumstances, it probably is not
true that he lived "through boyhood and into my young manhood,
in a very poor family" (9/17-18). Sutton's comment on the matter
is: "The soundest view of the position of the Anderson family in
Clyde seems to be that conditions, though at times difficult, were
seldom if ever desperate.... It was assuredly a hard life, but it
was not so hard that Sherwood's imagination could not harden it
still more" (Road to Winesburg, p. 20).

In the "Writer's Book" Sherwood speaks several times about
his work as a common laborer. At 9/23 he says that he worked
as a "factory hand." Probably the first time that he worked in a
factory was during his high school days in Clyde. Largely because
the family needed to have the boys, as well as the mother, supplement the father's meager salary, Sherwood dropped out of high
school, for the first time in March, 1892, and once for all in
February, 1893. Perhaps at both of these periods, and most certainly after February, 1893, he worked in the bicycle factory that
was Clyde's one attempt to enter into the industrialization of northern Ohio in the last decades of the nineteenth century (Sutton,
Road to Winesburg, pp. 21 and 26). In A Story Teller's Story
(ed. White, p. 148), Sherwood speaks about working in "a bicycle
factory where I was employed as an assembler."

In the "Writer's Book, " as well as in A Story Teller's
Story (ed. White, pp. 21 and 63), Tar (ed. White, p. 175), and
Memoirs (ed. White, p. 156), Sherwood attributes his mother's
early death to her laborious life. In the "Writer's Book" Sherwood

says that when the fear of old age and poverty came upon him, he "began thinking of my mother, who died of overwork at thirty-five" (37/2-3). He also remembers her as a "washwoman until her death from overwork and exposure while still so young" (40/6-7). Actually Emma Anderson died of "consumption" on May 10, 1895, when she was forty-two and Sherwood was eighteen (Sutton, Road to Winesburg, p. 507). By advancing several years the age at which his mother died and by lowering the age at which he was left motherless--"she died when I was young" (41/23)--Sherwood again exaggerates the hardships of his boyhood. It is interesting to note that in Sherwood's masterpiece, Winesburg, Ohio, Elizabeth Willard dies when she is forty-two and George is eighteen. A year after his mother's death George Willard leaves Winesburg, "going out of his town to meet the adventure of life" (New York: B. W. Huebsch, 1919, p. 302).

As it is in the fictional portrayal in Winesburg, so it was with the Anderson family in life. After the death of the mother the family drifted apart. Irwin left Clyde, settled in Indiana, and married Minnie Stevens in 1901. He had a sixth son, Harold, and died in an old soldiers' home in Dayton, Ohio, on May 23, 1919 (A Story Teller's Story, ed. White, p. 63n). Most probably it is Sherwood's recollection of his father's death that causes him to speak about "my fear of perhaps ending my days in the soldiers' home" (37/29-30). By 1896 Sherwood himself had left Clyde and was living with his elder brother Karl in the home of the Paden family in Chicago. Clifton Paden, born in Sandusky, Ohio, in 1874, grew up with Sherwood and Karl in Clyde, where his father had been mayor before his death in 1890. By the middle of the 1890's the Paden children, Jeanette, Carrie, Alexander, and Clifton, were living at 708 Washington Boulevard in Chicago and were taking in boarders (Sutton, Road to Winesburg, pp. 53-54). Clifton Paden became the Hollywood actor and producer named John Emerson, and in the "Writer's Book" Sherwood reminisces about the time when he and John Emerson "had both left our home town and were rooming in the same house in Chicago" (38/5-6).

Twice in the "Writer's Book" (12/30 and 15/8), Sherwood speaks about working in a cold-storage warehouse. He does the same in Memoirs (ed. White, p. 150). Jeanette Paden remembers that Sherwood rolled barrels in a cold-storage warehouse when he lived in the Paden home (Sutton, Road to Winesburg, p. 55); and Karl Anderson writes in "My Brother, Sherwood Anderson" (The Saturday Review of Literature, XXXI [September 4, 1948], 6): "Sherwood spent the next two years wheeling meat in and out of frigid vaults."

After his first two years in Chicago, Sherwood was rescued from the cold-storage warehouse by the Spanish-American War. On March 28, 1895, Sherwood had enlisted in Company I, Sixteenth Infantry Regiment, Ohio National Guards, known in Clyde as the McPherson Guards. When the United States declared war on Spain on April 21, 1898, Anderson had been working in the cold-storage

warehouse for little over a year.   On April 25, 1898, Company I
of the Ohio National Guards was called into active service.   Karl,
in "My Brother, Sherwood Anderson" (p. 7), says that Sherwood
wrote to him as he was going off to war: "I prefer yellow fever
in Cuba to living in cold storage in Chicago. "   Sherwood never
glamorized his reasons for going to the war.   In A Story Teller's
Story (ed. White, p. 169), he says that he enlisted "because I was
broke and could see no other way to avoid going back into a factory"; and in his Memoirs (ed. White, p. 169), he says: "By going off to war I was dodging a certain responsibility.   At home they
needed the little money I had been able to send home from my job.
My sister had pointed all of this out to me. "

     Sherwood and his company arrived in Cuba on January 3,
1899, six months after the armistice was declared.   On April 21,
1899, Anderson left Cuba.   He arrived in Savannah, Georgia, on
May 2, 1899, where Company I was discharged from federal service by May 24.   Sherwood was back home in Clyde on May 26
(Sutton, Road to Winesburg, pp. 72-73 and 77-79; Memoirs, ed.
White, pp. 166n, 191n, and 198n).

     During the summer after his return from the Spanish-Ameri-
can War, Sherwood worked on a threshing rig on the farm of Wallace Ballard, a good friend of Karl's (Sutton, Road to Winesburg,
p. 88).   In the "Writer's Book" Sherwood tells us that he "had
been a farm laborer" (9/22), but the summer on the Ballard farm
probably was the only time when he worked on a farm for any considerable length of time.   In the fall of the same year, 1899, he
entered Wittenberg Academy in Springfield, Ohio, to complete his
high school education.   He received his high school diploma in
June of 1900, when he was twenty-three years old.   Trilena White
(2/4), his English teacher at Wittenberg, exerted a strong influence on Anderson during his year at school and remained a friend
throughout his life.   In his Memoirs (ed. White, p. 334), Anderson ascribes to her the "challenge" behind his writing his first
published story, "The Rabbit Pen" (Harper's, CXXIX [July, 1914],
207-10).

     The number of times that Anderson in the "Writer's Book"
speaks about his work in the advertising business is well-nigh
legion.   For example, he tells us that even after he had published
his first books, "Winesburg and others, " he "had to go on for
years, working in an advertising place" (4/24-26).   We also hear
him complain that even though he "had got a good deal of recognition as a literary artist, " he "had been compelled to go on writing
advertisements" (47/5-10).   He also comments that "this advertising business is so filled with fakery that it is easy to cheat"
(48/10-12); and he proceeds to recount how he sometimes wrote the
advertisements required of him on the train going to his assignment and thus was able to waste three or four days in the new
town.

     Anderson's advertising career started in 1900 when, after

graduating from Wittenberg Academy, he went to work for the
Frank B. White Advertising Agency in Chicago. In 1903 the White
agency merged with the Long-Critchfield agency. Anderson worked
for Long-Critchfield until 1906, when he temporarily left advertising to go into business for himself in mail-order houses in Cleveland and Elyria, Ohio. He returned to Long-Critchfield in 1913,
and he stayed with the Taylor-Critchfield-Clague Company, as it
was subsequently called, until he closed out his last accounts in
1922. Since Anderson was with the Frank B. White agency and its
successor, the Long-Critchfield Company, between 1900 and 1906,
and with Long-Critchfield and its successor, the Taylor-Critchfield-
Clague Company, from 1913 until 1922, it is true that he was "for
ten, fifteen years an advertising writer, in a big Chicago advertising agency" (25/23-24).

In the "Writer's Book" Anderson speaks about "my wife,
my sons and daughters" (42/6). Actually Anderson was married
four times, and he had two sons and one daughter. His first wife
was Cornelia Lane, whom he married in 1904 when he was in the
advertising business in Chicago. Cornelia and Sherwood had three
children: Robert Lane Anderson, born August 16, 1907; John Sherwood Anderson, born December 31, 1908; and Marion Anderson,
born October 29, 1911. The eldest son, Robert, succeeded his
father as editor of the Smyth County News and Marion Democrat
and died in Marion, Virginia, in 1951. John Anderson lives in
Chicago and is on the art faculty of Kennedy-King College in Chicago. Marion is now Mrs. Russell Spear and lives in Madison,
North Carolina, where she and her husband edit the Madison Mes-
senger. Cornelia and Sherwood were divorced in 1915, two years
after Sherwood returned to Chicago and the advertising business.
After her divorce Mrs. Cornelia Anderson lived in Michigan City,
Indiana, where she taught school. She died in 1967 (interviews with
Mrs. Eleanor Anderson on July 17, 1970, and with John Anderson
on July 23, 1970).

In the "Writer's Book" Anderson speaks about his "passion
for writing" (10/1) during the "years of my early young manhood
working as a laborer" (9/21-22). Placing his first attempts at
writing so early in his life may be another of Anderson's exaggera-
tions, but his "passion for writing" certainly manifested itself during his first advertising career from 1900 to 1906. The earliest
writings that Anderson published were columns in the Long-Critchfield's house organ, Agricultural Advertising. The two columns
were "Rot and Reason, " which ran for ten months in 1903, and
"Business Types, " which ran for ten months in 1904. In October,
1903, Anderson also published an article entitled "A Business
Man's Reading" in the Bobbs-Merrill periodical The Reader. In
December of the same year he published a second article in The
Reader, this one entitled "The Man and the Book. " In these articles Anderson cites several authors whom the American business-
man should read: Socrates, Shakespeare, Stevenson, Browning,
Carlyle, Macaulay, and Samuel Johnson.

Two letters of Anderson corroborate the fact that he began his serious writing near the start of his advertising career in Chicago. In a letter written to his son John in April, 1927, Anderson says: "The fools who write articles about me think that one morning I suddenly decided to write and began to produce masterpieces. There is no special trick about writing or painting either. I wrote constantly for 15 years before I produced anything with any solidity to it" (Letters, ed. Jones and Rideout, p. 166). Since Anderson's first story, "The Rabbit Pen, " was published in 1914 and his first novel, Windy McPherson's Son, was published in 1916, Anderson may have started his serious writing about 1900. Anderson also wrote to his psychologist friend Trigant Burrow (see 77/27) in 1919, shortly after the publication of Winesburg, Ohio:

> Naturally I am very anxious to continue my work as a writer, but the truth is that I am rapidly approaching the time when I shall have to give it up. It begins to look as though, having made myself this tool of expression by infinite labor, I shall have to put it aside.
>
> The situation with me is one you will readily understand. For twenty years I have carried a double load, making my living as a writer of advertisements and trying always to steal as much time as possible for this other work. (Letters, ed. Jones and Rideout, p. 48.)

In the "Writer's Book" Anderson speaks about "the fifteen or twenty years during which I was in business as advertising writer, as manufacturer" (34/31-35/1). Since we have already spoken about Anderson's fifteen years in advertising, from 1900 to 1906 and from 1913 to 1922, we need now turn our attention to his manufacturing career in Cleveland and Elyria, Ohio. At 51/7-8 Anderson says: "for a time I left advertising and became a manufacturer"; and at 25/22 he writes: "once I even owned a factory. " Sutton informs us that on Labor Day, 1906, Anderson went to Cleveland to become titular president of The United Factories Company. The United Factories Company wanted to secure control of the mail-order business of several companies; and, because of his success with Long-Critchfield in soliciting mail orders, Anderson was asked to join the firm. The scheme of The United Factories Company failed, however, for two reasons: lack of unity among the factories and deceptive practices among the manufacturers. Anderson left the company at the end of the year for which he was hired (Road to Winesburg, pp. 151-55).

In 1907 Anderson established in Elyria, Ohio, his own mail-order business selling roof paint. He founded the Anderson Manufacturing Company, which sold a paint called "Roof-Fix, " a name coined by Anderson. In 1908 the Purcell Company of Lorain, Ohio, was absorbed by the Anderson Manufacturing Company. In November, 1911, a new company was formed, the American Merchants Company, which was to serve as merchandising outlet for the Anderson Manufacturing Company. On the surface everything seemed to be going well, but in truth Anderson was neglecting his

business and spending hours at night in writing.   By the time Anderson left Elyria in 1913 the Anderson Manufacturing Company
was heavily in debt and all of its assets had to be liquidated.   The
American Merchants Company, however, was salvaged and reorganized by Waldo Purcell, former owner of the absorbed Purcell
Paint Company (Sutton, Road to Winesburg, pp. 162-79).

   In the "Writer's Book" Anderson tells us, "I had found the
courage to walk away from my factory" (51/19).   "Courage" is the
important word here.   In A Story Teller's Story (ed. White,
pp. 215-36), and Memoirs (ed. White, pp. 20 and 238-53), Anderson also speaks of the way in which he turned his back on business
and redirected his career towards the arts.   The degree to which
Anderson's repudiation of business in 1912 was a conscious choice
of the life of the artist over the life of the businessman is a moot
question; but the fact that, at the age of thirty-six, Anderson
changed the course of his life cannot be gainsaid.   William A.
Sutton's Exit to Elsinore (Ball State Monograph Number Seven
[Muncie, Ind.:   Ball State University, 1967]) and his Road to Winesburg (pp. 181-99) are the best factual accounts of what happened to
Anderson when on November 28, 1912, he suffered a mental collapse, walked out of his office in Elyria, wandered about in a state
of amnesia for four days, and finally was hospitalized in Cleveland
on December 1.   After a period of recuperation in the hospital,
Anderson returned to Elyria, took care of some of the details connected with closing out his business, and left Elyria for good in
February, 1913.

   In the "Writer's Book" Anderson remarks: "Let us say that
a man begins writing at the age of thirty.   It is young enough"
(76/13-14).   If Anderson began his serious creative writing only
after he came to Elyria, he began it no earlier than the age of
thirty-one.   Once when he was changing trains in Elyria six years
after he had left the town, he wrote to Marietta Finley, later Mrs.
Vernon Hahn, a reader for the Bobbs-Merrill Publishing Company.
In the letter, dated December 8, 1916, Anderson says: "In my
second year here I began to write.   I wrote Windy and Marching
Men here and the writing saved me from insanity.   Night after
night I crept away to my room to write" (Letters, Newberry Library,
Reserved Box: Letters of Anderson to Mrs. Vernon Hahn; printed
in Sutton's Exit to Elsinore, pp. 41-43).

   It is now impossible to determine exactly which works Anderson wrote in Elyria.   It would seem that some of them were
set in a town he called Winesburg, Ohio.   In the "Writer's Book"
Anderson tells us: "I had attempted two or three novels set in a
mythical Winesburg, Ohio" (54/31-32).   We know from the holograph of Winesburg, Ohio with the Sherwood Anderson Papers at
the Newberry Library that eighteen of the Winesburg stories were
written on the back of sheets from a discarded novel also set in
the town of Winesburg.   The novel is called alternately "The Gold-
en Circle, " "Talbot the Actor, " and "Talbot Whittingham. " (See
the excellent discussion of the Winesburg, Ohio manuscript in Wil-

liam L. Phillips, "Sherwood Anderson's Winesburg, Ohio: Its Origins, Composition, Technique, and Reception" [unpublished Ph. D.
dissertation, University of Chicago, 1949].) In addition to this
discarded novel, there is a fragment of another novel called "Talbot Whittingham" set in the town of Mirage, Ohio. This fragment
has been edited by Gerald Nemanic in "Talbot Whittingham: An
Annotated Edition of the Text Together with a Descriptive and Critical Essay" (unpublished Ph. D. dissertation, University of Arizona,
1969). When Anderson returned to Chicago in 1913 he brought with
him several novels in manuscript form. They included novels that
subsequently were published--Windy McPherson's Son in 1916 and
Marching Men in 1917--and novels that never saw publication--
"Mary Cochran" and two different works called "Talbot Whittingham. "

     We have already seen that Anderson went back to the ad-
vertising business when he returned to Chicago. Business and
money-making, however, were no longer his dominant concerns.
In Chicago he became closely associated with some of the writers,
critics, and newspapermen of the "Chicago Renaissance": Carl
Sandburg, Edgar Lee Masters, Ben Hecht, Floyd Dell, Margery
Currey, and Margaret Anderson. This group of artists and literary friends whetted Anderson's "passion for writing"; and it was
when he was living with the "Little Children of the Arts" (see
Memoirs, ed. White, pp. 346-50) in a boarding house at 735 Cass
Street, now Wabash Avenue, that he wrote most of the stories that
became Winesburg, Ohio. It was also through this group of friends
that Sherwood met Tennessee Mitchell, sculptress, musician, and
piano teacher, whom he married in 1916.

     In addition to many aspects of his writing career, Sherwood
alludes also to his painting in the "Writer's Book": "A good many
years ago, I painted" (41/7-8). By the time Sherwood returned
to Chicago from Elyria, his brother Karl was a successful commercial painter. In 1913 Karl introduced Sherwood to the Margery
Currey-Floyd Dell art colony at Fifty-Seventh Street. Although
painting remained no more than an avocation throughout his life, in
1920 Sherwood gave a one-man show at the Radical Book Shop in
Chicago; and in the following year he had a show at The Sunwise
Turn book store in New York (James Schevill, Sherwood Anderson
[Denver: University of Denver Press, 1951], pp. 83-84 and 133-
34). Furthermore, judging from his letters written in Reno in
1923 and 1924, Sherwood did a good deal of painting during the
year he spent in Reno waiting for his divorce from Tennessee.
The editor saw several of Sherwood's paintings during her visit to
Mrs. Eleanor Anderson's home in Marion, Virginia: two water
colors, one a landscape and one an abstract design; two chalk
sketches, a front view and a profile of a black man's face; and
one pencil drawing of the hills and the road leading to Ripshin
Farm.

     Although Anderson's books did not easily gain a large read-
ing public in the United States, they were "translated into many

languages" (23/15). They have been translated into Chinese, Czech, Danish, Finnish, French, German, Greek, Hebrew, Hungarian, Italian, Japanese, Korean, Norwegian, Polish, Rumanian, Russian, Slovenian, Spanish, and Swedish. Anderson, who always complained about the slow reception of his works at home, spoke about his translations in a letter written on June 24, 1924, to Alfred Stieglitz, photographer and art critic: "I have good news and bad news. In America, Horses and Men has sold hardly at all. On the other hand my books actually [have] begun to be published in Europe. Sweden has bought Poor White. The Russians are publishing three.... I shall have, apparently, a European success" (Letters, Newberry Library, 1924).

In the "Writer's Book" Anderson speaks about "so much of the world seen" (39/21-22). One of the reasons Anderson undertook the first two of his three European trips was to further his "European success." In 1921 he, Tennessee, and Paul Rosenfeld visited France and England; and in the winter of 1926-27 he, Elizabeth Prall (his third wife), and his son John and his daughter Marion visited the same two countries. The motive inspiring his third trip to Europe was other than literary. In 1932 he went to Amsterdam as a member of the American delegation to the leftwing World's Congress Against War. Finally, his last voyage overseas, this time to South America on an unofficial goodwill tour for the State Department, ended suddenly and tragically in his death at Colon, Panama, in March, 1941, just four days after his embarkation from New York.

In Part IV, "The Workman, His Moods," Anderson describes the conditions under which he wrote several of his works. He speaks of writing A Story Teller's Story "in Reno, Nevada. I was getting a divorce from a woman" (72/32-73/1). He also says: "The woman loved another man. She wanted me to divorce her" (73/2-3). Evidence shows, however, that Tennessee probably was not in love with another man--she never remarried after her divorce from Sherwood--and that it was Sherwood, and not she, who wanted the divorce. Sherwood had met Elizabeth Prall in New York in the Lord and Taylor bookstore which she managed, and in the spring of 1923 he left Tennessee and took up residence in Reno in order to obtain a divorce. Once in Reno he repeatedly wrote back to Tennessee in Chicago, as well as to many of his friends, asking that Tennessee be reasonable and not oppose the divorce. Sherwood did not expect to receive opposition from her because, at the time of their marriage, they had agreed to enter into what they regarded as a "new" or "liberated" marriage, one in which both partners retained their independence and even separate residences. Nonetheless, Tennessee opposed the divorce. Sherwood had to stay in Reno a whole year, negotiating from afar with Tennessee, with his friends, notably Ferdinand Schevill, professor of history at the University of Chicago, and with his Chicago lawyer, Clarence Darrow. Sherwood finally was granted the divorce on April 4, 1924. In the same month he married Elizabeth Prall (Letters, Newberry Library, 1923-24).

In September, 1924, Sherwood and Elizabeth moved to New
Orleans. It was at this time that Sherwood started to lecture in
order to supplement the money earned by his writings. He wrote
to Ferdinand Schevill that lecturing "will be better than being an
ad man and stealing spoons" (Letters, Newberry Library, 1924).
In the "Writer's Book" Sherwood gives the impression that only
once did he have to go on a lecture tour. He says that while he
was building his stone house on his farm in Virginia he was obliged
"once ... to stop building for four months while I went delivering
silly lectures to get more money" (53/32-54/2). In actual fact
Sherwood went on several lecture tours from 1924 until the early
1930's. His begrudging attitude toward the necessity of lecturing
is well reflected in the "Writer's Book, " as well as in the following letter to his biographer Nathan Bryllion Fagin, written on
September 30, 1929: "I am afraid I can't be encouraging about
the lecture. I have given the vice up. When broke it is a way
to become unbroke, but it is dreadful. Most ways of making money
are. A man cannot escape a rather dirty feeling of exhibitionism"
(Letters, Newberry Library, 1929).

It was while Anderson was living in New Orleans that he
wrote <u>Dark Laughter</u>, his one "novel that had sold" (26/22). Although he mentions it by name only at 32/32-33/1, he also speaks
about it and its publisher, Horace Liveright, at 26/21-26, 51/8-
18, and 51/24-52/1. In these passages Anderson betrays an ambivalent attitude toward Horace Liveright, his publisher from the
time he left Ben Huebsch in 1925 until Liveright's death in 1933.
Although Anderson says that Liveright came to his rescue when he
was down to his last hundred dollars (51/9-10), that Liveright
enabled him to buy his beautiful mountain farm (26/27-28 and
51/30), and that Liveright was "very tender" towards him (51/15),
Anderson also admits that Liveright "plunged on me" (26/24) and
"exploited me" (51/24). The exploitation seems to be explained
by the fact that Liveright bought advertisements in newspapers
and on placards on streetcars (26/24-26 and 51/24-26). The real
difficulty, however, rests not with Horace Liveright but with the
American public: "People in America do not buy books. They do
not buy anything. Everything is sold to them" (51/27-29).

Since Anderson was dissatisfied with Ben Huebsch's promotion of his books, he signed a contract with Horace Liveright on
April 11, 1925. The contract included the stipulation that Anderson give Liveright one book a year and that Liveright pay Anderson $100 a week for five years, assuring Anderson of an income
of a little over $5000 a year. Anderson's royalty was fifteen per-
cent on all books sold and ten percent on Modern Library editions.
By 1927, however, Anderson was finding it difficult to produce a
book-length work each year, and the weekly advances from Liveright were turning into a source of embarrassment, then of annoyance, and finally of debt. In 1927, Anderson had to ask Liveright to stop payments (Letters, Newberry Library, 1925-27).

A number of pages in the "Writer's Book" (43/10-46/15)

are concerned with Anderson's writing of a manifesto that he called
"I Accuse." He says that he wrote it "some five or ten years
ago ... I was living in New Orleans at the time" (43/10-11); and
he gives the occasion that called forth this accusation of his fellow
writers: "I had been in the evening to the movies and had seen a
picture written by a man of talent who had once been my friend,
and having seen it had been shocked by what seemed to me a terrible selling out of all life" (43/11-15). These words seem to indicate that Anderson wrote "I Accuse" in New Orleans about 1926,
but it is the opinion of the editor that he is referring to the 1931
sound version of Theodore Dreiser's An American Tragedy and that
Anderson is fusing in his memory two events.

In a letter to John Emerson written from New Orleans on
April 5, 1925, Anderson refers to the large sums of money that
Dreiser was receiving for movie rights to his books. He comments:
"Dreiser, for example, was recently offered twenty thousand for
movie rights to The Genius" (Letters, Newberry Library, 1925).
In 1926 Paramount Studios, then called Famous Players, bought
the rights for a silent version of An American Tragedy. The studio must have had second thoughts, however, and it was not until
1930 that Paramount finally decided to produce a sound version.
On January 2, 1931, Dreiser signed a contract with Paramount for
$55,000. When the film was completed Dreiser was displeased
with it and sued Paramount for what he considered a distortion of
the novel (W. A. Swanberg, Dreiser [New York: Charles Scribner's Sons, 1965], pp. 369-378).

In the "Writer's Book" Anderson might easily be telescoping
a night in New Orleans in 1926 when he heard that Dreiser had
been offered a large sum of money for the silent movie rights to
An American Tragedy and a night in San Francisco when, after
Dreiser's lawsuit, he might have seen the sound version of An
American Tragedy. We know from "You Be the American Zola"
in Memoirs (ed. White, pp. 542-45) that Anderson visited San
Quentin Prison in 1932 and that he was annoyed when "Tom Mooney," an alias for Thomas J. Zechariah, convicted of murder in
1917 and pardoned in 1939, told him: "I'm the American Dreyfus.
You be the American Zola." Thus the sound version of An American Tragedy, the visit to Tom Mooney in San Quentin, and the remembrance of news received in New Orleans about Dreiser and
movie rights--all might have coalesced to form the passage about
"I Accuse" in the "Writer's Book."

In addition to fusing two events concerning Dreiser and
movie rights, Anderson might also be fusing his several attempts
to write a manifesto called sometimes "I Accuse" and sometimes
"J'Accuse." Mrs. Eleanor Anderson told the editor during her
visit to Ripshin Farm on July 16, 1970, that Sherwood several
times during his life wrote such a manifesto. Sherwood says the
same thing in a typewritten fragment in Box 2 of the manuscript
of his "Memoirs" at the Newberry Library. The fragment reads
in part:

> Several times in my life I have begun the writing of a
> kind of manifesto, addressed to American writers, and
> after all, the man who writes for the theatre is a writer;
> makers of plays, of novels, writers of short stories for
> popular magazines, journalists, we are all in the same
> boat. How many times have I begun the writing of this
> manifesto, putting at the top of the page the words "I
> Accuse." I have never been able to go on because I
> have been unable to convince myself that my own hands
> were clean. (p. 9.)

In a letter written to Laura Lou Copenhaver, his wife Eleanor's
mother, Anderson describes one of these manifestos. Writing
from San Francisco, sometime after April 8, 1932, he speaks
about a finished novel, probably Kit Brandon, and "another book to
be called I Accuse--this already nearly done since I have been out
here--an indictment of all our crowd--writers, painters, educators,
scientists, intellectuals in general" (Letters, ed. Jones and Rideout, p. 258).

The "I Accuse" mentioned in this letter seems to be the
manuscript "J'Accuse" in the Sherwood Anderson Papers at the
Newberry Library. The manuscript is written on stationery from
many different hotels, but mainly from "The Clift" in San Francisco. It is an indictment of "the mob of us, in America, educators,
thinkers, painters, tale-tellers, professional men, scholars, scientists, all of us always hedging. We are presumed to be men of
brains, of talent. We want to lead" (p. 26). The "J'Accuse" manuscript differs from "I Accuse" as described in the "Writer's
Book" in three important respects. First, in "J'Accuse" Anderson
includes himself in his accusations: "wanting to whiplash myself a
bit" (p. 18). Secondly, he speaks out against "all the world of us
here in America who are always pretending to ourselves we are
leaders" (p. 19). Thirdly, he mentions Theodore Dreiser and his
movie version of An American Tragedy by name: "Mr Dreiser
going to court, after selling his boy Clyde of An American Tragedy
into the talkies.... A second and greater American Tragedy because Mr Dreiser is a true man" (p. 127). In the version of "I
Accuse" described in the "Writer's Book," however, Anderson ex-
cludes himself from his indictment of writers who are guilty of
"the continual selling out of the imaginative lives of people" (44/28-
29) because "there had been no offers. I had not been tempted"
(45/22). Secondly, in "I Accuse" Anderson limits his indictment
to actors and literary men: "American actors, American writers,
who, having had a quick and often temporary success on the New
York stage, or who, having written a novel or a story that had
caught the popular fancy, had rushed off to Hollywood" (43/23-27).
Thirdly, in "I Accuse" Anderson mentions none of these writers
and actors by name. He simply says that "many of them [were]
my personal friends" (44/11-12). Therefore, it probably is true
that Anderson destroyed the version of "I Accuse" referred to in
the "Writer's Book": "I tore up what I had written" (45/5).

Even though the version of "I Accuse" as described in the "Writer's Book" was more limited in scope than the extant manuscript "J'Accuse," Anderson's discussion of it provides him with the occasion for his most explicit statement of the theme of Part I: "And do you not understand that the complete selling out of the imaginations of the men and women of America by the artists of the stage, by the artist story tellers, is completely and wholly an acceptance of whoredom?" (44/6-9).

After Horace Liveright "sold" Dark Laughter to the American public, Anderson was able to buy a farm in Grayson County, Virginia. He bought the farm from Mrs. Barbara Miller for $1450, making his downpayment of $50 on September 15, 1925. The first building that Anderson had erected on the farm was a cabin in which he could do his writing. It was built during the winter of 1926. On May 1, 1926, Sherwood and Elizabeth moved from New Orleans to Ripshin; and while their new stone house was being built, they lived in a barn converted into a dwelling and called the "green house." The large stone house, of which Sherwood was so justifiably proud and of which he speaks so lovingly in the "Writer's Book," was built from the late spring of 1926 until the late summer of 1927 (Letters, Newberry Library, 1925-27). It was at Ripshin that Sherwood wrote the "Writer's Book": "I live in the country on a farm and in the house built by my one successful book" (30/9-10).

When speaking of Ripshin, Anderson, as is his wont, liberally mixes fact with fancy. At 26/27-32 he says: "I had got some money and had built with it a house in the country, but when it was built I couldn't live in it for some five years. The publisher had plunged on me but I had played him false. The next book I sent him was, alas, a book of verse. I couldn't expect him to plunge on that." At 53/30-54/2 he writes: "For two years and while the house was building, all the money made for me by Horace Liveright going into it, myself once having to stop building for four months while I went delivering silly lectures to get more money, I had done no writing." The facts of the case, however, are slightly different.

As has been said, the stone house at Ripshin was built in little more than a year. It was started in the late spring of 1926; by the late summer of 1927, although work on it was not entirely finished, Sherwood and Elizabeth were living in it. Sherwood is quite accurate, however, when he says that "all the money made for me by Horace Liveright" (53/31-32) went into Ripshin. During 1926 Dark Laughter netted $8000 for Anderson, but he wrote to Ferdinand and Clara Schevill: "Cost of all buildings, farm, etc., about $10,000" (Letters, Newberry Library, 1926). He also informed Roger Sergel: "We have about got a house. Our debt on it, all told, may be $4,000, a stone house with a barn & a tenant house, also a cabin for me" (Letters, ed. Jones and Rideout, p. 160). Furthermore, the "book of verse" that Anderson "couldn't expect him to plunge on" (26/31) was A New Testament, which

Liveright published in 1927. It was not, however, the "next" book
that Anderson sent to him; in 1926 Liveright had published Sherwood Anderson's Notebook and Tar. Since none of these three
books was financially successful, even though Anderson did not
have to "stop building for four months," he did have to go "delivering silly lectures" (54/1-2). Finally, it is not true that "for two
years and while the house was building" (53/30-31) Anderson "had
done no writing" (54/2).

During the two years between the downpayment on his farm
and the completion of his stone house, Anderson continued to work
on his writing, although it is true that these years represent a low
ebb in his creative productivity. Nonetheless, he kept on trying to
write. He did what he advises writers to do in Part VI: "A man
should write and throw away. Write and throw away again" (84/15-
16). At this time in his life Anderson was trying to write, among
other things, the novel he called alternately Another Man's House
and Other People's Houses, a novel with Talbot Whittingham once
again as the protagonist. This novel was later destroyed. Nevertheless, just as it is true that Anderson did a good deal of writing
that did not satisfy him during the time of the building of Ripshin,
he also did some excellent writing. For example, he wrote the
final revision of "Death in the Woods." Chapter XII of Tar represented one version of the story, and in the September after its publication Anderson published in American Mercury (IX, September,
1926, 7-13) a revised version. The final version of the story,
published as the title story in Death in the Woods (1933), his fourth
collection of short stories, is virtually the same as the 1926 magazine version (see William Vaughn Miller, "The Technique of Sherwood Anderson's Short Stories" [unpublished Ph.D. dissertation,
University of Illinois, 1969], pp. 245-46).

Anderson's writings in the first years of the 1930's show
his interest in socialism and communism. The "Writer's Book,"
on the other hand, indicates that by the middle and late 1930's
Anderson's political and economic views had changed. For example, in Part I Anderson speaks against writers who write "so-
called proletariat stories" (44/19). The passage 44/12-24 speaks
ironically about the "radicals" who write for "causes," especially
"the overthrowing of capitalism, the making of a new and better
world" (44/23-24). In the context of telling us about writing "I
Accuse," Anderson declares that writing for "causes" is not a
remedy for, but rather a cause of, suffering. The true remedy
for the suffering of the world is in the hands, not of the economists, but of the creative artists: "the most bitter suffering, does
not come primarily from physical suffering. It is by the continual
selling out of the imaginative lives of people that the great suffering comes. There the most bitter harm is done" (44/27-30). In
Part VI, where Anderson speaks against literature with "a good
proletariat angle" (83/9), he again uses an ironic tone: "We are
to be saved by communism, or socialism, or fascism, or by this
or that" (83/7-8). The ironic tone shows that the "Writer's Book"
was written in the later 1930's when, after the policies of Frank-

lin Roosevelt and the New Deal started to alleviate much of the
misery of the depression years, Anderson turned away from the
socialism and communism that had attracted him in the late 1920's
and early 1930's.

In 1933 Anderson married for the fourth time. He had divorced Elizabeth Prall in 1932, and on July 6, 1933, he married
Eleanor Copenhaver. He speaks of Eleanor frequently in Part I of
the "Writer's Book." He describes her as "certainly a patient
woman ... has she not lived for years with me?" (32/20-21). In
the course of his description of one sleepless night during the time
he was trying to force himself to write a salable short story,
Sherwood speaks about standing at the foot of the bed in which his
wife lay sleeping. He says: "there is something grows very close
between people who have lived long together, who have really
achieved a marriage" (53/2-4). In actual fact, Eleanor and Sherwood were married for only eight years; but with Eleanor, Sherwood finally achieved a marriage that was lasting and happy.

The last bit of autobiographical information that the reader
can glean from the "Writer's Book" is the picture of Sherwood in
the last years of the 1930's, living in his beautiful mountain home:
"My house is in a little valley amid hills in the state of Virginia,
far west in Virginia, in a sweet land of stars, softly rounded
mountains and swift running mountain streams" (46/18-21). Ripshin Farm is twenty-two miles outside Marion, Virginia. Two
streams run through the property. At the point where Laurel
Creek and Ripshin Creek meet, the motorist turns off the county
road onto the Anderson farm. A bridge over Ripshin Creek takes
him to the stone house, its walled flower garden, and its apple
orchard (see 33/1 and 53/16-17). On the other side of the bridge,
"across the road from my house and hidden away under trees by
a little creek" (56/21-22), is "a log cabin by a stream in which,
on ordinary occasions, I work" (33/2-3). The reader of the "Writer's Book" can envision Anderson writing his text "for young American story tellers" (3/3) in this cabin.

III. THE "WRITER'S BOOK" IN RELATION
TO ANDERSON'S OTHER WORKS

Internal evidence indicates that the "Writer's Book" is one
of Anderson's late works, undoubtedly written in the last decade of
his life. In it he reminisces about many of his other works. He
describes the manner in which he wrote several of his books and
stories, including Winesburg, Ohio, A Story Teller's Story, Tar,
"I'm a Fool" and "The Man's Story." He also gives his interpretation of the critical reception given to such works as Winesburg,
Ohio, Many Marriages, A Story Teller's Story, and "There She Is,
She Is Taking Her Bath." Lastly, he passes judgment on some of
his works: Winesburg, Ohio, Poor White, Many Marriages, "The

Untold Lie, " "Paper Pills, " "The New Englander, " "I'm a Fool, "
"The Man's Story, " "Death in the Woods, " and "Brother Death. "

Although the manuscript of the "Writer's Book" is not dated,
various indications point to the years 1933 to 1939 as the time of
composition.   The first indication is the piece of brown wrapping
paper which precedes the manuscript.   On this piece of paper is
written in pencil in Anderson's hand: "Mss--For Writer's Book /
These have been copied" (1/1-2).   As has been mentioned, a
search through all of the Sherwood Anderson Papers at the Newberry Library resulted in finding only four typed pages.   All four
were found with the manuscript of Anderson's "Journal. "   The first
two pages are copies of the opening four and a half pages of Part
II and were found in the folder marked 1933; the other two pages
are copies of the last four pages of Part V and were found in the
folder marked 1937.   The editor thinks that it is reasonable to assume that Part II, "How to Write to a Writer, " was written in
1933 and that Part V, "Notes on the Novel, " was written in 1937.

Perhaps all seven sections of the "Writer's Book" were
written at different times.   Since Part III, "The Writer, " appears
to be an early version of the story that finally became "Pastoral, "
printed in the Redbook in 1940 and in a slightly revised form in
Anderson's Memoirs in 1942, it seems likely that Part III was the
first part written.   It may even have been composed quite early
in Anderson's career.   This editor feels that it is not representa-
tive of the writing that Anderson did in the 1930's, the kind of
writing that we find in his Memoirs and in the rest of the "Writer's Book. "   It may have been included in the "Writer's Book" in
order to provide an example of Anderson's usual method of writing
short stories: "I have never been one who can correct, fill in,
rework his stories.   I must try and when I fail must throw away.
Some of my best stories have been written ten or twelve times"
(28/12-15).   Later he confesses: "I have seldom written a story,
long or short, that I did not have to write and rewrite.   There
are single short stories of mine that have taken me ten or twelve
years to get written" (85/2-5).   "The Writer" is one of Anderson's
stories that "has not yet come to life" (28/22).   It came to life
only later as "Pastoral. "

If we assume that Part III was written early in Anderson's
writing career and that Part II was written in 1933, we know from
internal evidence that Part IV, "The Workman, His Moods" was
written after 1933.   In Part IV Anderson not only alludes to
"Brother Death, " a story written in 1933, but he speaks also about
the difficulty he has in working in his cabin on the hilltop amid the
beauty afforded by the magnificent view.   The work cabin on the
top of the highest hill of the property was the first building that
Anderson had constructed at Ripshin.   Although it is not true, as
we have seen, that he "never wrote anything up there that I could
bear printing, " it is true that he "had to give up the cabin on the
hilltop" (72/13-15).   Mrs. Eleanor Anderson remembers that during the summer when Louis Gruenberg collaborated with Sherwood

on a projected opera, that is, during the summer of 1933, they
worked together in the cabin on the hilltop. The last event that
Mrs. Eleanor Anderson connects with the cabin on the hilltop was
the bringing of a piano to Gruenberg up the narrow, winding road
that led to the cabin. Later, realizing that he was not working
well in the hilltop cabin, Sherwood had each log numbered and the
cabin moved, log by log, down the hill to its present location by
the shores of Ripshin Creek (interview at Ripshin on July 17,
1970).

We have noted already that Part V, "Notes on the Novel, "
may have been written in 1937. Therefore, it seems that the
chronological order of composition of the sections of the "Writer's
Book" is: Part III, early in Anderson's writing career; Part II,
1933; Part IV, sometime after 1933; Part V, 1937. It is impossible to ascertain when the brief Part VI was written, but internal
evidence indicates that Part I was composed between 1937 and
1939. Perhaps Part I, "Prelude To A Story, " was the last section
written, and possibly at the time of its composition Anderson con-
ceived the idea of cutting some sections originally intended for his
Memoirs and of grouping them with "Prelude To A Story" in order
to form his textbook for young writers. Anderson begins a letter
written on August 27, 1938, to George Freitag, an aspiring writer
who had asked for advice: "It sometimes seems to me that I
should prepare a book designed to be read by other and younger
writers" (Letters, ed. Jones and Rideout, p. 403).

Several remarks made by Anderson in "Prelude To A Story"
point to a year late in the decade of the 1930's as the date of composition of Part I. For example, in speaking of "I Accuse, " Anderson tells us that he wrote it: "some five or ten years ago ...
I was living in New Orleans at the time" (43/10-11). If we add
ten years to 1926, the year Sherwood and Elizabeth left New Orleans for Ripshin, we have an indication that he wrote "Prelude To
A Story" in 1936; if we add five years to 1932, the year he wrote
"J'Accuse" in San Francisco, we have the year 1937 as the date of
composition of "Prelude To A Story. " Of course, we must always
keep in mind Anderson's disregard for the accuracy of dates.

A clear indication of the date of Part I is Anderson's remark: "after twenty-five years of writing, some twenty to twenty-
five books published" (23/12-13). It is safe to assume that the
"writing" referred to is Anderson's short stories and novels.
Therefore, by adding twenty-five years to the date of his first published story, "The Rabbit Pen, " in Harper's in 1914, we arrive at
the year 1939 as the date of composition of "Prelude To A Story. "
By 1939 Anderson had published exactly twenty-five books. For a
list of these titles see the note to 23/12-13 and the Bibliography.

Perhaps the clearest single piece of evidence for dating the
composition of "Prelude To A Story" is Anderson's comment: "even
as I write these sentences I can hear the thump, thump of a dasher
in a churn and know that our Ruby is on the back porch of our

house churning the milk from our cow into butter" (32/11-14).
Ruby Sullivan Barker worked for the Andersons for different periods of time from 1933 or 1934 until her marriage in 1940. In a
letter she wrote to the editor from Roanoke, Virginia, on August
24, 1970, she verified many of the facts Sherwood mentions in the
description of his Virginia farmhouse. Her letter says in part:

> I did work for the Andersons at Ripshin for a few years.
> There was no electricity during those years. The
> butter was churned by hand....
> About 1933 or '34 I worked at Ripshin as a baby sitter
> for some of the Anderson guests. I do not recall their
> names at this time.
> In the years that followed I helped out with the house-
> keeping and cooking for two or three years....
> Then for about the years of 1937 thru 1939, I worked
> for the Andersons with my younger sister, Charlotte,
> helping me for about one year. She was married at the
> age of 16. Then I was assisted by Miss Faye Price for
> the last years I worked for Mr. and Mrs. Anderson.
> The last year I worked was 1939. I was married in the
> spring of 1940, and was unable to be at the farm that
> year.

Although Paul Rosenfeld, in the Table of Contents to The Sherwood
Anderson Reader, assigns 1940 as the date of "The Sound of the
Stream," Ruby Sullivan's letter makes it clear that Part I of the
"Writer's Book" could have been written no later than 1939.

   The "Writer's Book" is undoubtedly one of Anderson's last
works, and in it he looks back upon his writing career. For example, he describes the circumstances under which he wrote several of his novels and short stories. He says, as he does in many
of his writings, that he wrote the Winesburg stories in a boarding
house: "In the Winesburg series of short stories, written in just
such a rooming house as I have described" (14/12-14). From his
letters written in 1915 and 1916, we know that his address was
735 Cass Street, Chicago. Cass Street is now Wabash Avenue,
and the boarding house that stood at that address no longer exists.
A parking lot now covers the site. Anderson's description of the
boarding house is given in the note he appended to the manuscript of "Winesburg," presumably when he found it in a box of
of old papers in 1938. The note reads:

> At the time these stories were written the author was
> employed as a copy writer in a Chicago advertising agen-
> cy and the paper is no doubt that used for roughing up
> advertisements. It is likely the stories were written two
> or three times, in the writer's room, in a rooming house
> in Cass Street in Chicago, or in hotels as he traveled
> about, visiting clients of his employers. (The Sherwood
> Anderson Papers, Newberry Library, Chicago.)

Later in Part I Anderson says that both Poor White and Winesburg were written "in a Chicago rooming house" (28/1-2). This statement is erroneous. Poor White was begun and nearly completed when Anderson was in New York in the fall of 1918, working on his "sinecure" in John Emerson's movie company (see Memoirs, ed. White, p. 407). He finished it in the winter of 1920 in Fairhope, Alabama.

To discuss in chronological order Anderson's account of writing his stories, we must turn next to Part VII. "Note" describes "these glorious moments, these pregnant hours" (85/30-31) when a short story is written in one absorbing burst of awareness and inspiration. "Note" discusses the manner in which Anderson wrote three short stories: an unnamed story written in a railroad station in Harrodsburg, Kentucky; "I'm a Fool," written in his Chicago advertising office; and "The Man's Story," written in Stark Young's apartment in New York.

As the note to 86/2 explains, there is reason to believe that the unnamed story could be "Nobody Laughed" or "The New Englander." "Nobody Laughed" is a story that was published for the first time by Paul Rosenfeld in The Sherwood Anderson Reader. In the Table of Contents the story is labeled "1939, unpublished." It is possible that the first version of this story was written in 1916. There is in the Sherwood Anderson Papers in the Newberry Library a typewritten copy of a fragment of one of Anderson's earliest stories. The fragment, dated December 15, 1916, seems to be an early draft of "Nobody Laughed" because, before it breaks off abruptly at the end of page 3, the fragment tells of Tom, seventy-five, who cures warts, and his crippled wife of thirty. The opening scene is laid in "the railroad station in a small Kentucky town" (typewritten copy of the fragment housed in the University of Chicago Libraries, the Hi Simon Papers; the editor is indebted to Mark Shore of Harvard University for calling this fragment to her attention).

Stronger evidence points to "The New Englander" as the story that Anderson refers to in Part VII (86/2-88/14). In A Story Teller's Story Anderson speaks about writing a section of Poor White and "The New Englander." He says: "I remember ... how at a railroad station at Detroit I sat writing the tale of Elsie Leander's westward journey, in The Triumph of the Egg, and missed my own train--these remain as rich and fine spots in a precarious existence" (ed. White, p. 155). "The New Englander" was first published in the Dial, LXX (February, 1921), 143-58, and was reprinted in The Triumph of the Egg, Anderson's second volume of short stories. Anderson's memory when he was writing the "Writer's Book" could have confused Harrodsburg with Detroit; or, if the story referred to is "Nobody Laughed," he could have confused "a summer night" (86/14) with December 15.

Regardless of which story Anderson wrote one summer evening "when I was still a writer of advertisements" (86/3), he gives

in "Note" a vivid picture of the circumstances under which he
wrote: "A hunch had come to me and I had bought a yellow tablet
of paper at a drugstore as I walked to the station. I began writing on a truck on the station platform. . . . The great passion had
come upon me" (86/6-12). Anderson goes on to speak of the mixture of intense awareness of his surroundings coupled with an intense concentration on the task at hand. Such periods of awareness and concentration are "the rich moments" (88/6) in a writer's
life, the moments when a writer enters into "the land of the Now"
(87/15).

        Anderson's description of writing the other two stories also
speaks of his utter absorption in the task of writing and, at the
same time, his intense awareness of external circumstances. With
the words, "I was in a big business office, surrounded by many
people" (88/19-20), Anderson starts his description of writing "I'm
a Fool." In addition to telling about the awareness and concentration characteristics of all creative work, he also confesses the way
he hedged when he was supposed to be writing advertisements: his
fellow workers "discussed with me the work in which I was engaged,
or rather the work in which I was presummed to be engaged"
(88/24-25). Anderson makes it clear that he turned to the writing
of "I'm a Fool" when he became disgusted with the kind of writing
required of him in his office: "Here I am, condemned day after
day to write advertising. I am sick of it" (88/27-28); "I am a
man of talent and they will not let me practice the art I love"
(88/20-32). Twice in Memoirs Anderson also speaks about the
writing of "I'm a Fool." In one place he asserts he wrote it after
he had been given "an assignment to write certain advertisements
of pills to cure people's bound up bowels"; in the second place he
maintains he wrote it after "I was given the assignment to write
the advertisements for the manufacturer of commercial fertilizer"
(ed. White, pp. 122 and 432). "I'm a Fool" was originally published in the Dial, LXXII (February, 1922), 119-29; it was reprinted in Anderson's third volume of short stories, Horses and
Men (1923).

        Anderson introduces his description of writing "The Man's
Story" with these words: "There was the day in New York City
when I was walking in a street and the passion came to me. I
have spoken of how long it sometimes takes to really write a
story. You have the theme. You try and try but it does not come
off. And then one day, at some unexpected moment, it comes
clearly and sweetly" (89/30-90/4). In Part I (57/3-7) Anderson
had alluded to the circumstances under which he wrote this story,
but in Part VII (89/30-92/6) he goes into much greater detail.
Likewise in Memoirs (ed. White, pp. 434-35) he describes the
writing of "The Man's Story." In all these accounts the circumstances are the same: Anderson had written it in Stark Young's
apartment in New York; he had been trying to write it for several
years; he had created it in one burst of creative energy sustained
throughout the day; he had thrown each sheet on the floor as he
finished it; and, although Stark Young had left a bottle of whisky

with Anderson, he had not felt the effects of the drink until the story was finished. Anderson concludes his account in the "Writer's Book" by saying: "At least at the moment, my story, written thus, seemed very beautiful to me. As it happens I have not reread the story for years, but I have a kind of faith that something of the half mystic wonder of my day in that apartment still lingers in it" (92/2-6). In an interview with the editor on June 5, 1969, Mrs. Eleanor Anderson said that Sherwood always maintained that "The Man's Story" was his favorite among all his "favorite" imaginary children. "The Man's Story" was first published in the Dial, LXXV (September, 1923), 247-64, and reprinted in Horses and Men.

In Part I, immediately after Anderson briefly refers to writing "The Man's Story" in a mood of total absorption, he adds: "I had written my A Story Teller's Story in such a mood, day after day passing as in some delicious dream, and my Many Marriages" (57/7-9). Anderson might be referring to Many Marriages also in the passage in Part IV when he speaks about writing "with joy [in] a certain room in a tall old house in the old quarter of New Orleans" (74/32-75/2). It was during the winter and, although there was no heat and he had to write clad in his overcoat (75/3-5), he remembers this time as one of the "rich glad times" of intense creativity. Because of the fondness with which Anderson always speaks of Many Marriages and because it seems to have been one of the works he wrote with comparative ease, Anderson probably is referring to the house at 708 Royal Street, New Orleans, and to the winter of 1922. He is probably not alluding to the house at 540-B St. Peter Street, where he lived when he wrote Dark Laughter in the fall and winter of 1924. Although Dark Laughter was his one novel "that had sold" (26/22), Anderson never once in the "Writer's Book" gives it praise or speaks about the joy and ease with which it was written. Many Marriages, on the other hand, was a work that was always close to Anderson's heart. It was published by Huebsch in 1923.

In two other places in the "Writer's Book" Anderson speaks of the ease with which he wrote A Story Teller's Story. In Part I he says that it "flowed out of my fingers as the water in the mountain stream before my cabin, where my mother's picture hangs on the wall above my desk, runs down to a river" (38/26-29); in Part IV he gives a long account of writing A Story Teller's Story when he was in Reno in 1923 waiting for his divorce from Tennessee: "I began to write joyously.... Every morning I awoke singing.... I wrote until I was exhausted, slept, wrote again. I wrote a book called A Story Teller's Story, a very gorgeous book. It is a gay book, a laughing book. The days marched past in splendor" (73/7-13).

Many of the letters that Anderson wrote from Reno, however, give evidence to disprove that A Story Teller's Story was written with such joy and ease. It seems true that a good deal of material "flowed out of my fingers"; but, as Anderson wrote to Otto Liveright in September, he had to "revise it rigidly" (Letters,

Newberry Library, 1923). In the spring of the same year he had
written to Paul Rosenfeld: "In the meantime I work--rather intensely. As for the actual work that creeps out from under my
pen--I can't be sure of it yet.... As a matter of fact I've written
a good deal--have plowed straight on thinking to go back and balance and weigh what I have done a little later" (Letters, Newberry
Library, 1923).

        Anderson also describes the manner in which he wrote
Tar: A Midwest Childhood. He explains that it was written in the
midst of a cornfield in "a low shed that had formerly, I believe,
housed pigs" (74/1-2). During their first summer in the Blue
Ridge country of Virginia, Sherwood and Elizabeth had stayed on
the farm of the John F. Greear family. The "young boys in the
family" (73/31-32) were John, Joshua, David, Philip, and Solomon.
Mr. David Greear, who died in Roanoke, Virginia, in 1973, told
the editor in an interview on July 17, 1970, that the house in which
Sherwood wrote Tar was an abandoned tenant house, not a hog
house. He said that it stood on the edge of the cornfield, and he
confirmed Anderson's statement (74/4-7) that he, David, and his
brothers cleaned it out so that Sherwood could use it for his writing.

        When Sherwood says that "a madness of writing had seized
me" (74/8-9) in working on Tar, he is incorrect if by "madness"
he means great joy and facility. If, on the other hand, by "madness" he means that he worked hard and long over Tar, the expression is accurate. The letters that he wrote while working on
Tar attest to the labiousness of his task. For example, he wrote
to W. Colston Leigh of the Leigh Lecture Bureau towards the end
of July: "As I wrote you before, I am an erratic cuss about my
writing. The book on which I have been at work all summer has
been a failure until just now. At last it is going well" (Letters,
Newberry Library, 1925). Anderson hoped to finish the book before he had to return to New Orleans at the end of the summer, but
he did not. He wrote to Otto Liveright on September 1: "During
the month up in the country I wrote about 50,000 words on the
Childhood book but threw away about half of it when I came home as
not quite up to what I wanted" (Letters, Newberry Library, 1925).
Anderson finally completed Tar in time to have chapters serialized
in the Woman's Home Companion from June, 1926, to January, 1927.
Tar was published as a book by Horace Liveright in 1926.

        The last time in Part IV that Anderson speaks about the
"rich glad times" (74/29) when a writer works well, he does not
name a specific work. He simply remembers "a cheap hotel in
Kansas City. Prostitutes came there.... I was inside my room.
I was in a clean mood. I was working" (75/6-10). As Anderson's
letters tell us, from January to March, 1933, he stayed at the
Hotel Puritan in Kansas City, Missouri. His letters from this hotel comment on the ironic character of its name. For example,
he confides to Ferdinand Schevill in a letter written on March 2:
"I am in a rather tough little hotel here.... Poker games in nea-

by rooms and ladies of the night often laughing in the hallways. "
In the same letter he remarks: "Then I wrote a new story--the
last one in the book [Death in the Woods], when you see it--called
'Brother Death' that I think will make the book" (Letters, ed.
Jones and Rideout, p. 278). Therefore, it is reasonable to assume
that the work referred to in Part IV is "Brother Death. " In Part
I Anderson mentions "Brother Death" by name (54/10). It is one
of the four stories to which, he says, a friend compared the beauty
of his house at Ripshin. The only publication that "Brother Death"
had during Anderson's life was as the concluding story in his fourth
volume of short stories, Death in the Woods, published by Liveright in 1933.

     In addition to describing the composition of several works,
in the "Writer's Book" Anderson also gives his reactions to their
critical reception. He retells, as he does in many places, his interpretation of the circumstances surrounding the publication of
Winesburg, Ohio. Anderson tells us that Winesburg was "two
years selling the first five thousand; and all the stories of the
book, previously published in the smaller literary magazines, had
brought me in a total of eighty-five dollars" (25/30-26/1). He
repeats that Winesburg was two years selling five thousand copies
in Memoirs (ed. White, p. 22) and in a letter to N. Bryllion Fagin
(Letters, Newberry Library, 1927). He cites the figure of eighty-
five dollars also in Memoirs (ed. Rosenfeld, p. 288; omitted in
White's edition) and in a letter to George Freitag written on August
27, 1938 (Letters, ed. Jones and Rideout, p. 404). The "smaller
literary magazines" in which the Winesburg stories appeared were
Masses, Little Review, and Seven Arts. Of these three, only
Seven Arts paid.

     In the "Writer's Book" Anderson goes on to declare that
Winesburg "had brought me, when published, some literary recognition but also much bitter condemnation. " He explains the condemnation by saying that the stories were called "filth" and "the
book spoken of, by most of the literary critics, as a kind of literary sewer" (26/4-6). When Anderson says that the publication
of Winesburg brought him "some literary recognition, " he is not
acknowledging the fact that most of the critical opinion was favorable (see the note to 26/2, which documents this fact). Furthermore, at the time of Winesburg's publication, Anderson himself
acknowledged its favorable reception. For example, he wrote to
Trigant Burrow on September 15, 1919: "Have you read my new
book, Winesburg? The book has been getting rather remarkable
recognition even from those who have fought me before" (Letters,
ed. Jones and Rideout, p. 48). He also admitted in a letter to
Waldo Frank written in December: "I get constant and beautiful
reactions from Winesburg (Letters, Newberry Library, 1919).

     Therefore, "most" critics did not condemn Winesburg.
Nonetheless, throughout his life Anderson repeated the story of the
charges of filth and sex-obsession that were leveled against it.
See, for example, Hello Towns! (New York: Horace Liveright

Publishing Inc., 1929, p. 244), Memoirs (ed. White, pp. 22-25
and 349-50), and the letter to George Freitag written on August 27,
1938 (Letters, ed. Jones and Rideout, pp. 405-406). Perhaps the
reason why Anderson, in later years, remembered the adverse
criticism given to Winesburg more than its enthusiastic reception
is the fact that the charge of sex-obsession hurt him deeply. He
reveals this in a letter to Van Wyck Brooks written in August,
1920:

> It did hurt, though, when I found you also rather tak-
> ing Winesburg, for example, as a sex book. ˙ It got under
> my hide a bit. I'm usually thick-skinned.
>   To me it seems a little as though one were permitted
> to talk abstractly of things, to use scientific terms re-
> garding them, in the new dispensation, but when one at-
> tempts to dip down into the living stuff, the same old
> formula holds. A really beautiful story like "Hands,"
> for example, is--well, nasty. God help us! Dozens of
> men have told me privately they knew Wing Biddlebaum.
> I tried to present him sympathetically--taboo. (Letters,
> ed. Jones and Rideout, pp. 59-60).

When Anderson in the "Writer's Book" claims that this kind
of condemnation of Winesburg was given "often by critics who, after some ten or fifteen years, began to praise it highly" (26/6-7),
he is repeating once again the largely imaginary story of the way
Floyd Dell and Henry Mencken first rejected and later praised the
Winesburg stories. In his Memoirs (ed. White, pp. 22-25 and
349-50) and in the Freitag letter (Letters, ed. Jones and Rideout,
pp. 404-405), Anderson gives the same story and mentions Dell
and Mencken by name. Mencken, however, praised Winesburg at
the time of its publication in articles in the Chicago American and
in his Smart Set, even though he never saw fit to publish any of
the Winesburg stories in Smart Set. Floyd Dell published three
Winesburg stories--"The Book of the Grotesque," "Hands," and
"The Strength of God"--in Masses in 1916. After the book's publication he wrote in an article called "American Fiction" in Liberator
(II [September, 1919], 47) that Winesburg was "a magnificent collection of tales." William Phillips in his dissertation, "Sherwood
Anderson's Winesburg, Ohio," quotes a letter that Dell wrote to
him on December 12, 1948. Dell claims that there was "no truth
at all" to Anderson's story that Dell rejected the Winesburg stories
when he first saw them. Dell explains: "The origin of that delusion was the fact that some of the later Winesburg tales were
submitted to vote at an editorial meeting or meetings and were
voted down by the editors. S. A.'s paranoid self-pity turned this
into a conspiracy with me as villain" (p. 148n). Dell also disavows
his alleged mistreatment of Anderson in "How Sherwood Anderson
Became an Author," a review of Anderson's Memoirs, which appeared in New York Herald Tribune Books (April 12, 1942, pp. 1-
2), and in "On Being Sherwood Anderson's Literary Father," Newberry Library Bulletin (V [December, 1961], 315-21). Evidence
is not lacking, however, to support Anderson's contention that Dell

did not fully appreciate at least one Winesburg story when he first
saw it.   In a letter to Waldo Frank written on December 14, 1916,
Anderson speaks of "Loneliness, " the story "concerning Enoch Robinson. " "Loneliness" was never published in a magazine prior to
its appearance in Winesburg, Ohio.   Anderson comments to Frank:

> I am glad you liked the story "Mother" and that you
> are going to publish it.   Damn it, I wanted you to like
> the story about Enoch Robinson and the woman who came
> into his room and was too big for the room.
> There is a story every critic is bound to dislike.   I
> can remember reading it to Floyd Dell, and it made him
> hopping mad.   "It's damn rot, " says Floyd.   "It does
> not get anywhere. "
> "It gets there, but you are not at the station, " I re-
> plied to Floyd, and I think I was right.
> Why do I try to convince you of this story?   Well, I
> want it in print in Seven Arts.   A writer knows when a
> story is good, and that story is good.   (Letters, ed.
> Jones and Rideout, p. 5.)

In Part I (54/23-55/32) Anderson tells also the story of his
correspondence with the Reverend Arthur H. Smith concerning
Winesburg.   The Reverend Mr. Smith, pastor of the Wicker Park
Methodist Church in Chicago, but a native of Winesburg, Ohio,
wrote a small book called An Authentic History of Winesburg,
Holmes County, Ohio, Including a Winesburg Who's Who (Chicago:
n. p. , 1930).   In this book, under the heading "A Few Side Notes, "
Smith comments on Anderson's Winesburg, Ohio:

> If you have been disturbed because of Sherwood Ander-
> son's book, "WINESBURG, OHIO" (a burlesque) and re-
> sented it as an insult and a slander on our home town,
> it will put your mind to rest in perfect peace if you will
> remember that Mr. Anderson did not know that there was
> such a town as Winesburg, Ohio, when he wrote his book
> which, by the way, is well worth reading.   The imaginary
> town he writes about is a much larger town and has a
> railroad.   Where he got the name is not known.   But
> "we (of our actual beloved Winesburg) should worry. "
> (p. 70.)

On June 1, 1932, the Reverend Mr. Smith wrote Anderson a letter,
and Anderson answered Smith with a letter on June 6, 1932.   Both
of these letters are printed in the "What Say" column of the Smyth
County News for July 7, 1932.   In Anderson's letter to Smith he
objects to Smith's use of the word "burlesque" and tells Smith
many of the things that he says in the "Writer's Book. "   For example, he informs Smith that Winesburg was first condemned and
called "filthy" but that later it was praised and "translated into almost all of the European languages. "   When comparing the people
of the real Winesburg, Ohio, with the people of his "mythical"
town, Anderson says: "Do not be offended if I say that I hope that

the real people of the real Winesburg, Ohio, are at bottom as decent and have as much inner worth" (Archives, Virginia State Library, Richmond). See Anderson's recollection of this statement as given in 55/17-19.

In Part V Anderson speaks about the critical reception given to either the Winesburg stories or the stories of his second volume of short stories, The Triumph of the Egg. Reminiscing about a time when he "was called sex-obsessed. When almost every story I put forth was condemned as nasty" (77/8-9), he remarks: "I remember a particular period. It was after the publication of my Triumph of the Egg and I was living in a Chicago rooming house" (77/17-19). Although Anderson may have written some of the stories that appeared in The Triumph of the Egg when he was living at 735 Cass Street, he had moved away from this rooming house by the time the stories were printed in magazines between 1918 and 1921 and by the time the book was published by Huebsch in 1921. Nevertheless it is interesting to note that within a year of the book's publication, that is, in January of 1922, Paul Rosenfeld wrote in an article called "Sherwood Anderson":

> Anderson has to face himself where Freud and Lawrence, Stieglitz and Picasso, and every other great artist of the time, have faced themselves: has had to add a "phallic Chekhov" to the group of men who have been forced by something in an age to remind an age that it is in the nucleus of sex that all the lights and the confusions have their center, and that to the nucleus of sex they all return to further illuminate or further tangle. (Dial, LXXII [January, 1922], 35.)

Incidentally, although most critics of Anderson, and Anderson himself in his Memoirs (ed. White, p. 451), attribute to Rosenfeld the coinage of the phrase "the phallic Chekhov," in a letter written prior to Rosenfeld's article Anderson attributes the coinage to Van Wyck Brooks. Anderson tells Rosenfeld in October, 1921:

> Brooks, I believe, once called me "the phallic Chekhov." I really do not believe I have a sex-obsession, as has so often been said. I do not want to have, surely. When I want to flatter myself, at least, I tell myself that I want only not to lose the sense of life as it is, here, now, in the land and among the people among whom I live. (Letters, ed. Jones and Rideout, p. 78.)

In the "Writer's Book" Anderson speaks also about the reception given to Many Marriages, published by Huebsch in March, 1923. He calls it a "terribly misunderstood book that some day-- when the world has again passed out of our dark age of belief that life can be remade on a sounder and happier basis by economic professors--will come into its own" (57/10-13). Anderson cannot resist slurring propaganda literature, but his prophecy that Many Marriages will someday "come into its own" has not been fulfilled.

The fault probably is not the readers' and critics' "misunderstanding" of the novel as much as Anderson's inability, as Rex Burbank explains, "to condense his material, to tighten the structure of the book, and to examine the nature and consequences of his themes and the assumptions behind them" (Sherwood Anderson [New York: Twayne Publishers, Inc., 1964], p. 112). When speaking about John Webster, the novel's protagonist, Burbank adds: "In the absense of any discernible dialectic or narrative conflict, Webster's supposedly sophisticated ideas about life and sex become the maunderings of a terribly ignorant man, and his symbolic act of psychic and physical rebirth is reduced to absurdity" (p. 112).

Nonetheless, Many Marriages was always a favorite work of Anderson's. He wrote to Ulrico Hoepli of the Casa Editrice Libraria Ulrico Hoepli in Milan on June 5, 1937, that, although Dark Laughter was his best seller and Winesburg, Ohio the book most acclaimed by critics, "I think that I myself am fondest perhaps of another called Many Marriages, but this may be only true because the book, when published, was very generally abused by the critics" (Letters, ed. Jones and Rideout, p. 380). Anderson mentions the footsteps of John Webster, "the naked man in the room with his daughter in Many Marriages" (59/4-5), as one of the sounds that spoke to him from the stream on the night that he heard sounds from his "real" and "imaginative" lives.

Since Anderson calls Many Marriages "another terribly misunderstood book" (57/10), he implies that the book he has just been discussing, A Story Teller's Story, was also misunderstood. Earlier in Part I Anderson had said that A Story Teller's Story was "a book that has never had the audience it deserved but that will have" (38/30-31). As in the case of Winesburg, Anderson is overlooking the fact that most critics were favorable to A Story Teller's Story when it was published by Huebsch in 1924. For example, Lloyd Morris in "The Education of Sherwood Anderson" (New York Times Book Review, October 12, 1924, pp. 6, 22) compares A Story Teller's Story favorably with The Education of Henry Adams and goes on to comment:

> In its widest application, as a whole challenge to our life to justify itself ideally, Mr. Anderson's autobiography is a book which should be read by every intelligent and reflective American. In its narrow application, as the story of the development of an American writer, it will exercise a compelling fascination upon those who, like Mr. Anderson, are seeking to give our life adequate esthetic expression. (Ibid., p. 22.)

Lloyd Morris' recommendation that "every American" should read A Story Teller's Story goes further than Anderson's observation that it is a book "that every young writer should read" (38/29-30). When work on A Story Teller's Story was nearing completion Anderson wrote to Ferdinand and Clara Schevill: "There is a chance to say something that will mean something to some younger Sherwood Anderson some day" (Letters, Newberry Library, 1923).

The passage from 30/16 to 31/27 contains an amusing account of the difficulty Anderson experienced in trying to sell to a magazine "There She Is, She Is Taking Her Bath." Anderson writes: "Once a magazine called Pictorial Review paid me seven hundred and fifty dollars for a short story. I had given the story the title 'There She Is, She Is Taking Her Bath,' but after the story had been got into type and illustrations made for it, the editor of the magazine grew doubtful" (30/16-21). According to Anderson, the editor liked the story well enough but objected to the title. Anderson suggested a new title, "Roll Your Own," which, of course, was rejected; and the story was never published. Anderson, however, guessed the real reason behind the story's rejection: "Alas, as in so many of my stories, there was a businessman made to appear a little ridiculous. And I am quite sure that may be the reason that so many of my stories have not sold" (31/23-27).

Several letters written at the time Anderson was trying to sell "There She Is, She Is Taking Her Bath" confirm the facts related in the "Writer's Book." He wrote to Jerome and Lucile Blum early in 1923: "Luck comes along. A magazine has paid $750 for the story about the jealous husband" (Letters, ed. Jones and Rideout, p. 91). Anderson was anxious to get the stories that were to be published in Horses and Men printed in magazines before the fall publication of the book. Therefore, he wrote to Otto Liveright on April 25: "Also, Otto, try to get Pictorial to use the story they have before October--as I would like to include it in the book" (Letters, Newberry Library, 1923). Otto Liveright wrote back on July 13: "Mr. Vance [Arthur Turner Vance, editor-in-chief of Pictorial Review] is trying to publish THERE SHE IS, SHE IS TAKING HER BATH in the November number of Pictorial Review which is released October 15th. He cannot promise it definitely as there is so much pressure from the Circulation Department. He will know surely in a month and I have spoken to Mr. Huebsch about it. He will be able to hold the book open until Vance answers definitely" (Letters, Newberry Library, Incoming, Otto Liveright to Anderson, 1923). Anderson wrote back to Liveright on July 24: "About the Pictorial. That is good news. I've a notion the Circulation objection is the title. If it is tell them to give the story another title. I won't care. I can't see what else there is objectionable" (Letters, Newberry Library, 1923).

"There She Is, She Is Taking Her Bath" was never given another title and was never published in Pictorial Review or in any other magazine. Furthermore, Horses and Men had to go to print without it. Before it was published in Anderson's last volume of short stories, Death in the Woods, it appeared only in The Second American Caravan: A Yearbook of American Literature, edited by Alfred Kreymborg, Lewis Mumford, and Paul Rosenfeld (New York: The Macaulay Company, 1928), pp. 100-111. In the "Writer's Book" Anderson uses this recollection to draw a moral: " 'You

are just a little too apt, Sherwood, my boy, to find the businessman a little ridiculous, ' I have told myself" (32/2-3).

In addition to speaking about the composition of his works
and the reception accorded them, Anderson in the "Writer's Book"
gives his opinion of several of his books and stories. Winesburg,
Ohio he says is "the book by which, if I am remembered at all
once I am dead, I will be best and with the most affection remembered" (40/11-13). He speaks also about three individual Winesburg stories. He merely mentions the story "Loneliness": "I described a little man in a room and what the imagined figures his
fancy had conjured up had come to mean to him" (14/20-22). He
makes evaluative statements about "Paper Pills" and "The Untold
Lie." In Part VI, "Note--On Saving Ideas, " as he is explaining
that writers should not be "clinging to ideas" (83/6), he alludes
to "Paper Pills": "It is a story that should be read by every
young writer" (83/3-4). In Part I Anderson includes "The Untold
Lie" as one of the four stories which he says a friend told him
were as beautiful as his stone house at Ripshin (54/10-11). There
is implicit praise of another Winesburg story in the fact that Doctor Parcival is listed as one of the loved ones of his "imaginary"
life whose footsteps sound on the bridge over Ripshin Creek (59/4).
Doctor Parcival, the unsuccessful doctor in "The Philosopher, "
tells George Willard: "Everyone in the world is Christ and they
are all crucified" (Winesburg, Ohio, p. 48).

Poor White, the book published the year after Winesburg,
also receives Anderson's praise in the "Writer's Book. " In Part
I he lists several books in which he takes pride: "my Winesburg,
Ohio, my Triumph of the Egg, [my] Horses and Men"--all volumes
of short stories. The list continues: "and two or three novels,
among them Poor White, a novel that had been put into the Modern
Library" (48/20-23). Anderson had published two novels, Windy
McPherson's Son and Marching Men, before Poor White, and he
published four novels afterwards, Many Marriages, Dark Laughter,
Beyond Desire, and Kit Brandon. Most critics agree with Ander-
son's estimate that Poor White is his best novel. For example,
Horace Gregory selected it as the only novel included in The Port-
able Sherwood Anderson (New York: The Viking Press, 1949).
William Phillips in "Sherwood Anderson's Two Prize Pupils [Faulk-
ner and Hemingway]" (The University of Chicago Magazine, XLVII
[January, 1955], 9-12), Lionel Trilling in "Sherwood Anderson"
(The Liberal Imagination [New York: The Viking Press, 1950],
pp. 22-33), and Frederick J. Hoffman in "The Voices of Sherwood
Anderson" (Shenandoah, XIII [Spring, 1962], 5-19), all agree that
Poor White is Anderson's best novel. In the "Writer's Book" Anderson mentions for a second time that Poor White was put into
the Modern Library, this time coupling it with Winesburg, Ohio
(27/31-28/1). He includes its protagonist, Hugh McVey, in his
list of loved ones who spoke to him from the stream (59/1).

We have already noted that Anderson includes his second
and third volumes of short stories in the list of works of which he

is proud. Stories from both volumes are praised also in the "Writer's Book." The four stories mentioned at 54/10-11 include "The New Englander," published in The Triumph of the Egg. "The New Englander," as has been explained, may be the unnamed story written in Harrodsburg, Kentucky, which Anderson discusses in Part VII. The two stories named in Part VII are stories that were published in Horses and Men. "I'm a Fool" is called "a very beautiful story" (89/4). In addition to listing "The Man's Story" with the three other stories at 54/10-11, Anderson calls it "a beautiful, a significant story" (91/32) and believes that it contains a "half mystic wonder" (92/5).

We have already spoken about Anderson's contention that both Many Marriages and A Story Teller's Story are "terribly misunderstood" (57/10). At 73/11-12 he describes A Story Teller's Story as "a very gorgeous book"; and in a similar but expanded statement he calls it "a really gorgeous book, one of the best that ever came out of the pen I here hold in my hand" (38/25-26).

Anderson's last book of collected short stories, Death in the Woods, contains two stories which are generally considered among his finest. They are the first and the last in the volume, "Death in the Woods" and "Brother Death." "Death in the Woods" receives high praise in the "Writer's Book": "Some of my best stories have been written ten or twelve times, and there is one story, 'Death in the Woods,' a magnificent tale, one of the most penetrating written in our times, that was ten years getting itself written" (28/14-18). "Brother Death," written specifically as a companion piece for the title story, was composed in the Hotel Puritan in Kansas City and is probably the work referred to in Part IV where Anderson speaks about writing well in "a cheap hotel, in Kansas City" (75/6). "Brother Death" heads the list of "beautiful" stories that Anderson compares to his house at Ripshin (54/10).

The last work mentioned in the "Writer's Book" is "Brother Death." This allusion, another indication that Part IV was written after 1933, lends support to the theory that all sections of the "Writer's Book," except Part III, "The Writer," were written between 1933 and 1939.

IV. THE "WRITER'S BOOK" AS AN EXPRESSION OF ANDERSON'S CRITICAL THOUGHT

The "Writer's Book" contains many of Anderson's theories about writing and some opinions of his fellow writers. One of the main themes of the "Writer's Book" is the struggle that the artist must wage in order to maintain his integrity in the face of the allurements of success and the pressure to sell his works to the New York stage or to Hollywood. Anderson insists also that the artist must remain independent of both adulatory and adverse criticism, an independence which he himself never completely attained. A second major theme of the "Writer's Book" is the writer's fidelity to the imaginative life. Anderson believes that the life of "fancy" is as important as the life of "fact." In addition to presenting these two themes, the "Writer's Book" comments also on the creative process. It shows "Anderson at work," striving to achieve "form" in his novels or "grasping whole" the ideas which become his short stories. One of the most important aspects of the "Writer's Book" is the insight it provides regarding Anderson's theory of the short story. It gives two descriptive definitions of the short story, speaks about the difference between the short story and the novel, and describes Anderson's usual method of writing his stories.

The main theme of Part I, "Prelude To A Story," can be expressed as the author's struggle to maintain his artistic integrity in the face of pressures exerted by the manipulators of popular taste. This central theme finds expression in Anderson's attitude towards "the mythical thing we call 'success' " (29/23). The context of this remark is his attempt to convince "our young American writers" (29/16) that they will always have to struggle to maintain their integrity because the mythical thing called "success" is ever present to entice them to the pursuit of money or fame. In Part V, "Notes on the Novel," Anderson also tells these young writers: "often enough the failure, the attempt of the young inexperienced writer who has at least the intent of the sincere worker, is worth more than all of the great successes, the slick books that slide so easily over all of the reality of lives" (81/28-32). In Part VI, "Note--On Saving Ideas," Anderson asserts: "It seems to me that the real purpose of all this writing is first of all to enrich the writer. It isn't surely to get fame, recognition" (84/13-15). In Part VII, "Note," he insists again: "What nonsense to mourn that we do not grow rich, get fame" (91/17).

All of these reflections on success lead Anderson to take a stand: "Let me remain small, as obscure a figure as possible" (49/23-24). There can be no doubt that Anderson was sincere when he made this and similar statements. For example, he wrote to Burton Emmett on December 6, 1928: "I mean I really do not need or desire enhancing of prestige. I am like Shaw, about money, have already more 'prestige' than is good for me. My God--hasn't my poor soul been messed with by all the critics from Dan to Beersheba?" (Letters, Newberry Library, 1926). The very frequency of statements of this kind, however, leads the reader to suspect that Anderson is covering a hurt. In the "Writer's Book" he can recognize such facts as: "my name up as one of the outstanding American writers of my day" (23/13-14); "I have had a profound effect upon the art of short story writing" (31/30-31); and "I had brought new life into American story telling" (47/8-9). Nevertheless, throughout his life Anderson felt that his work was not sufficiently or correctly appreciated. Perhaps the truest statements about his attitude toward criticism occur in the later sections of the "Writer's Book." In Part II, "How to Write to a

Writer, " Anderson asserts in humor and irony, but, one suspects, also in truth: "I like only those critics who praise my work. I am, like most writers, inclined to think all others fools" (64/32-65/2). On the opening page of Part VII he admits: "For years I have had my wife go over all criticisms of my work. 'I can make myself miserable enough, ' I have said to her. 'I do not want others to make me miserable about my work. ' I have asked her to show me only the more favorable criticisms" (85/11-15).

Anderson's ambivalent attitude towards criticism is reflected also in his ambivalent attitude towards the mass media. Throughout Part I, when he describes his struggle to write a salable short story, he pretends to disdain writing for the movies: "At that time the movies had just become a gold mine for writers. 'Take it on for a time, ' my friends were saying to me" (27/18-22). Likewise in his account of writing "I Accuse, " Anderson lashes out against writers who, after an initial success, "had rushed off to Hollywood" (43/26-27). At 45/8-13 Anderson speaks of a trip to Hollywood. In this passage he compares the little offices in the movie studio to the offices in his advertising agency and implies that the writing done in the movie studio is no more creative than the writing done in the advertising office. Even though Anderson admits that "I had even written, two or three times, to agents in New York or Hollywood" (45/18-19), he concludes by stating that he could not include himself in "I Accuse" because: "There had been no offers. I had not been tempted" (45/22).

The truth seems to be that Anderson would have been very happy to sell some of his works to the movies and to have had some of his works dramatized for the stage. A good example of his uncertain attitude toward the film and stage is a letter to Roger Sergel, in which he refers to his novel Kit Brandon, published by Scribner's in 1936. Anderson quotes George Nathan as saying that Kit Brandon was "movie sure-fire" and continues: "So, you see, I may be getting an offer and if I do I will take it, not, of course, going near their damned Hollywood" (quoted in Paul P. Appel, ed., Homage to Sherwood Anderson, 1876-1941 [Mamaroneck, N.Y.: Paul P. Appel, Publisher, 1970], p. 195).

Three years earlier there had been some negotiations between Anderson and Paul Muni about collaboration on a movie, and seven years before that Gilbert Seldes had approached Anderson about the movie rights to "I'm a Fool. " Anderson's interest in the movies was paralleled by an interest in the stage, as his letters, especially in 1932 and 1933, show. H. S. Kraft, a freelance writer in New York at the time, wanted to collaborate on a movie or a play, and Louis Gruenberg came to Ripshin in the summer of 1933 in the hope of adapting one of Anderson's works into an opera (Letters, Newberry Library, 1926 and 1932-33; see also Letters, ed. Jones and Rideout, pp. 279-80, 282-85, and 288-89). All these efforts, however, came to naught.

As Anderson himself tells us in the "Writer's Book" (43/25-

28), he was anxious to have Winesburg, Ohio dramatized. Eventually three dramatic versions were made: one by Anderson, one by Christopher Sergel, and one by Gerry Morrison (Sherwood Anderson Papers, Newberry Library). Anderson's own dramatization was produced by the Hedgerow Theatre, Moylan-Rose Valley, Pennsylvania. The play had its premiere on June 30, 1934, and was in the Hedgerow Theatre repertoire for three years. This version of the play was printed in Plays: Winesburg and Others (New York: Charles Scribner's Sons, 1937). The other plays that make up the volume are dramatizations of three short stories: "The Triumph of the Egg, " "Mother, " and "They Married Later. "

Another theme that runs through Part I of the "Writer's Book" is the theory that "the unreal is more real than the real, that there is no real other than the unreal" (43/2-4). In this context Anderson also says: "There is a sense in which it may be said, of any imaginative writer, that anything he says of the past, of people known in the past, is a lie. It is a lie and not a lie. As I have already said, in an introduction to another book [Tar], it is only by the lie that we arrive at truth" (40/17-23). For Anderson, artistic creation is a blending of facts and the artist's intuitive understanding of these facts. For example, if Anderson's imagination sees the photographer's studio where his mother's picture was taken as being above his father's harness shop (37/10-11), Anderson the artist is perfectly free to put it there, wherever the facts may put it. If Anderson the artist "creates" an Italian grandmother for himself, to him "it is a true picture" (41/30-31).

Since Anderson believes that the imagination of the creative artist is free to mingle the "facts" of the real world with the "fancy" of the imaginative world, he holds, on a different but no less important level, that the artist must be "true" to his imaginative world. One of the most explicit statements of this belief expressed outside the "Writer's Book" is in "Man and His Imagination, " published in The Intent of the Artist, edited by Augusto Centeno (Princeton, N.J.: Princeton University Press, 1941, p. 45):

> It seems to me that the obligation of the writer to the imagination is pretty obvious. I am, to be sure, speaking of the writer as a story teller. There is the obligation to himself, to his own imagination, its growth, what he does to it, the obligation to the imaginations of other people, and there is the third and perhaps most important obligation. The writer in his creative mood is creating figures of people, to be true imaginary figures, and there is the writer's tremendous obligation to these imaginary figures. I think this is the most important of all the obligations. It is the obligation least understood. It is, I think the thing to talk about. It is the obligation too often forgotten by our professional writers.

In the "Writer's Book" Anderson comments on all three as-

pects of this obligation. First, the artist's obligation to his own
imagination is the main theme of the whole of Part VI, "Note--On
Saving Ideas, " just as it is the purpose behind Anderson's constant
inveighing in Part I against what he calls the prostitution of art.
Secondly, the writer's obligation to the imaginations of other people
is emphasized in the passage in Part I where Anderson describes
writing "I Accuse": "It is by the continual selling out of the imaginative lives of people that the great suffering comes. There the
most bitter harm is done" (44/28-30). Thirdly, Anderson's attitude towards "the most important" of the obligations, the obligation
to the characters of his imagination, is shown throughout Part I in
Anderson's struggle with the temptation to write the salable story.
It reaches a climax when Anderson, speaking of the characters of
his story, says: "They are just people and the people of our imaginations are as important to us as the real people in the flesh about
us. To sell them out, as is always being done, in the imaginative
world is as low and mean a trick as to sell people out in so-called
real life" (55/27-31).

The "Writer's Book" contains many of Anderson's statements
on the creative process. It shows Anderson in the actual task of
writing. For example, Anderson describes himself sitting at his
desk, trying to write a story that his literary agent can sell to one
of the popular magazines. He becomes "interested, absorbed, often a little in love with these characters" (8/13-14). As he writes
the story based on the tale told him by a friend in the moonlit
meadow, the friend "had disappeared. There is a new man, coming to life, here, on this paper, under my hand" (8/19-21). It
is this new man who tells the writer: " 'There is a certain morality involved, ' he says. 'Now you must tell everything, put it all
down' " (8/25-26).

Just as Anderson insists that everything "true" to his characters must be told, he also believes, as has been said, that the
literal truth can sometimes be abandoned. Anderson uses the comparison between the real prostitute and the unreal Cecelia, as well
as his ironic statement that perhaps in the darkness of her room
he can imagine the prostitute to be "the real Cecelia" (18/11-12),
to point up the fact that art depends on "absurd" and "unreal"
dreams: "There is this dream world in which we live in this intimacy with beauty. To the more imaginative young man, and perhaps also young woman, for them I cannot speak, the dream sometimes grows more and more intense. The very power of concentration that is characteristic of the artist man makes his dream
constantly more and more real" (14/6-12). A little later Anderson insists: "Do not deny it, you imaginative young men. It is
by such absurd dreams, always coming, always changing, that the
imaginative young man lives. And, if he becomes in the end an
American popular short story or novel writer, it is out of such
dreams he later builds his tales" (16/29-17/2).

Even though the artist blends truths from both his real and
his imaginative worlds, his stories must be grounded in his own

experiences. In Part I Anderson comments on the fact that most
beginning writers start with autobiographical novels: "And it is so
they should begin too. First the learning to use the experiences,
the moods and hungers of your own life, and then, gradually, the
reaching out into other lives" (29/11-14). In Part II Anderson returns to this idea. He deprecates a superficial "self-expression"
(64/3) that urges some people to write, but he also insists, by
means of a tale about an inspiring woman writer, that authors
must write about the things they know. After reading the woman's
manuscript Anderson suggested that "if she felt she must be a
writer, she write about people she knew something about, whose
lives did a little touch her own experiences" (64/19-21). The gist
of Part II is that the creative artist is simply that, and not an
editor or a critic: "He is not at all anxious to impose his judgment on others" (64/30-31). Anderson adds: "in the end every
writer must be his own critic. There is something in a man that
tells him when he has hit the mark at which he aimed" (65/3-5).

In Part IV Anderson stresses the fact that "the work before
you when you sit at your desk does demand some control" (71/15-
17); but in Parts V and VI he speaks against "a tendency to be
economical, to save" (76/7-8). Both Parts V and VI develop Anderson's theory that creative writing is hindered more by over-
control than by lack of control. Part V begins with the idea that
in a novel "fatness, richness, does not depend upon bulk. There
is such a thing as richness of suggestion" (76/2-4). Part VI begins with the words: "What strikes you about many writers is a
certain thinness, poverty" (82/2-3). Both of these sections go on
to consider an important aspect of the creative process, namely,
the development of the imagination in order to free thoughts and
ideas and to allow them to "flow" (84/16) and produce rich work.
Note, for example: "There was never a novelist lived who did not
write, in imagination, ten, a hundred novels for every one he actually puts down in ink. He is always doing it, always taking such
flights. He is trying to select, choosing and rejecting" (79/11-15);
and "There should be a continual flow, a stream, thoughts of others
flowing through you, feelings of others flowing through you. This
saving of your little two-for-a-penny ideas, your feelings, only
dams the flow" (84/8-12).

We have already had occasion to comment on Anderson's
description of the "rich glad times" (74/29) of intense creative ac-
tivity. One of the factors that enters into the writer's ability to
write well at such times is the acuteness of his senses. Speaking
of the unnamed story written in Harrodsburg, Kentucky, Anderson
implies that a writer can work well only if "all of your senses
[are] curiously awake" (86/23). Similarly, he confesses that as
he was writing "The Man's Story" in Stark Young's apartment, he
was "very conscious of everything going on in the street below, of
a little cigar store on a corner, men going in and coming out,
feeling all the time that, were I not at the moment engaged with a
particular story, I could write a story of any man or woman who
went along the city street, feeling half a god who knew all, felt

all, saw all" (90/22-27). The conclusion that Anderson presents
to the reader, therefore, is: "It is absurd to save ideas. Throw
them away. What a man wants, what we all want, is a full rich
life, to feel more, see more, understand more" (82/31-83/2).

In Part V, "Notes on the Novel, " Anderson makes frank
avowals of the difficulties encountered in writing novels. First,
there is the problem of sustaining a theme. Anderson speaks
about the difficulty the novelist has in concentrating on a central
theme through the long time required to write a novel, through "all
the changing circumstances of a life" (81/1-2). Secondly, there is
the problem of characterization. Anderson admits that often for
the novelist: "Some minor character in his novel begins suddenly
to run away with his book. " Invoking the simile of "a general
trying to manage a vast army during a battle, " Anderson concedes
that, in addition to making the characters "alive and real, " the
novelist "must think his way through their relations to each other"
(81/10-15). These reflections lead Anderson to say that the novelist "must orchestrate his work, give it what is called 'form' "
(81/16). Perhaps Anderson is partially concurring in the oft-repeated criticism that his novels are lacking in "form. "

Some of Anderson's published works and letters give us insight into what he understood by "form" in art. First of all, he
admits in a letter written to Jerome Blum in 1926 that he has difficulty achieving form in his novels. The novel he is speaking
about in the letter, called either "Another Man's House" or "Other
People's Houses, " was never published. He remarks to Blum:

> I got started on a new novel--a rather delicate busi-
> ness--then checked my start, started again--checked
> again, etc. It will come off eventually and it may be
> that this present start will get somewhere.
> Anyway am working on it every day and that is fun.
> It's the old business of trying to get too much into one
> book and getting it messed up. The simple direct form
> of the thing only seems to emerge for me after a lot of
> sweating. I put doodads all over the house and then have
> to go around and knock them off. (Letters, Newberry
> Library, 1926.)

In 1930 Anderson wrote to the aspiring painter Charles Bockler.
He spoke about form in painting as well as in prose:

> I think it would be a great mistake to waste any time
> at all thinking of "form" as form. It is one of the things
> artists, and most of all half-artists, babble of when their
> minds are most vacant.
> Form is, of course, content. It is nothing else, can
> be nothing else. A tree has bark, fiber, sap, leaves,
> limbs, twigs.
> It can grow and exist and not grow in the soil of your
> own being. It is so with women too.

The great thing is to let yourself be the tree, the sky,
the earth. Enter into your inheritance. It is difficult
and can only happen rarely, as between man and woman.
My meaning is that life is not so separated from art.
How often I go away from the presence of talking artists
into the street, the field.
What I want is there. If I go in and come out clean,
even now and then, in the end these same people who say
I have no form will be prattling of the "form" in my
work. (Letters, ed. Jones and Rideout, p. 202.)

In "A Note on Realism" Anderson explains what he means by
saying "form is content":

The life of reality is confused, disorderly, almost always without apparent purpose, whereas in the artist's
imaginative life there is purpose. There is determination
to give the tale, the song, the painting Form--to make it
true and real to the theme, not to life. (Sherwood Anderson's Notebook, pp. 75-76.)

In A Story Teller's Story, while speaking against the "formula"
story with its "Poison Plot," Anderson writes:

What was wanted I thought was form, not plot, an altogether more elusive and difficult thing to come at. (ed.
White, p. 255.)

In certain moods one became impregnated with the seeds
of a hundred new tales in one day. The telling of the
tales, to get them into form, to clothe them, find just
the words and the arrangement of words that would clothe
them--that was a quite different matter. (Ibid., p. 257.)

The words used by the tale teller were as the colors
used by the painter. Form was another matter. It grew
out of the materials of the tale and the teller's reaction
to them. It was the tale trying to take form that kicked
about inside the tale teller at night when he wanted to
sleep. (Ibid., p. 261.)

Even though Anderson often did not achieve in his novels
the form desired, these quotations describe well the kind of form
that he attained in his short stories. Therefore, some statements
of Anderson's in the "Writer's Book" are disconcerting to those
who recognize his greatest contribution to American literature to
be in the genre of the short story. For example, in Part V, after
citing H. G. Wells' simile that writing a short story is like running to a fire but writing a novel is like taking an afternoon stroll,
Anderson continues: "A man writes a novel as he takes an afternoon stroll only in his imagination. The actual physical feat of
writing either a long or a short novel is another matter" (80/27-
30). Furthermore, immediately after saying that novelists must

"orchestrate" and give "form" to their work, Anderson declares:
"It is not for nothing that we honor the novelists above the simple
story tellers.   The novel is the real test of the man" (81/17-18).
It is disappointing to hear Anderson, one of the acknowledged
masters of the short story, succumb to the popular notion that the
novel is superior to the short story.   Undoubtedly, as he is at
pains to show, the physical feat of writing the longer work is
greater than that of writing the shorter work, but the test of artistic worth is not judged by length or physical exertion expended.
Anderson's biographer Brom Weber gives one explanation why he
persisted until the end of his life in his attempts to write novels:

> It was not merely the pressure of publishers, as well
> as readers and critics, which pushed Anderson toward
> the novel against his natural inclination to work in short
> forms.   Anderson shared the erroneous cultural belief
> that a novel is qualitatively as well as quantitatively
> more valuable than a short work.   Had he been a young-
> er man in the late 1910's and early 1920's, it is possible
> that he might have been able to develop the lyrical novel,
> a delicate form that would have best utilized his talents
> as it did those of Virginia Woolf, his admirer.   But he
> had insufficient time in which to work slowly and perfect
> his art in every form.   (Sherwood Anderson [Minneapolis:
> University of Minnesota Press, 1964], p. 34.)

The last three sections of the "Writer's Book" contain several statements regarding short story writing.   First of all, they
include two descriptive definitions of the short story.   In Part VI
Anderson says: "The writing of the short story is a kind of explosion" (80/22).   This statement is similar to a remark he made in
a letter to Ben Huebsch written on November 12, 1919.   He tells
Huebsch that the Winesburg stories came "all at one sitting, a distillation, an outbreak" (Letters, Newberry Library, 1919).   In a
letter to Paul Rosenfeld written from Reno in late 1923 or early
1924, he praises what the Chinese call "the short stop":   "The notion was to touch something off and then let it complete itself in
the reader" (Letters, Newberry Library, 1924).   Anderson's second
descriptive definition of the short story is found in Part VII: "The
short story is the result of a sudden passionate interest.   It is an
idea grasped whole as one would pick an apple in an orchard"
(85/26-28).   This definition reminds the reader of a paragraph in
the Winesburg story "Paper Pills--concerning Doctor Reefy, " a
paragraph which explains both Anderson's theory of the grotesque
and his method of writing in Winesburg, Ohio.   After explaining
that Doctor Reefy's story is a curious one, Anderson continues:

> It is delicious, like the twisted little apples that grow in
> the orchards of Winesburg....   On the trees are only a
> few gnarled apples that the pickers have rejected.   They
> look like the knuckles of Doctor Reefy's hands.   One
> nibbles at them and they are delicious.   Into a little
> round place at the side of the apple has been gathered

> all of its sweetness.   One runs from tree to tree over
> the frosted ground picking the gnarled, twisted apples and
> filling his pockets with them.   Only the few know the
> sweetness of the twisted apples.   (Winesburg, Ohio,
> pp. 19-20.)

When Anderson maintains that a short story "is an idea
grasped whole as one would pick an apple in an orchard, " and when
he speaks about "single short stories of mine that have taken me
ten or twelve years to get written" (85/3-5), he is commenting on
both his theory and his practice of short story writing.   The author
does not actually take ten or twelve years to write a story, but a
story sometimes takes ten or twelve years "to get written. "   Anderson again uses the passive voice when he says: "Some of my
best stories have been written ten or twelve times" (28/14-15).
Rewriting does not mean that Anderson was "one who can correct,
fill in, rework his stories" (28/12-13), nor is he one who can
"linger over sentences" (85/5).   Even though he does not literally
mean that "all of my own short stories have been written at one
sitting" (85/28-29), he does mean that the final version was often
written in one burst of creative energy when, in definitive form,
the idea for the story was finally "grasped whole. "

As has been explained, when praising "Death in the Woods, "
Anderson admits that it was "ten years getting itself written"
(28/17-18).   A holograph in the Sherwood Anderson Papers at the
Newberry Library called "The Death in the Forest" has attached
to it a note in Mrs. Eleanor Anderson's hand.   The note reads:
"Early version of short story Death in the Woods. "   This holograph
is printed in an appendix to William Vaughn Miller's dissertation,
"The Technique of Sherwood Anderson's Short Stories" (pp. 259-68),
and in an appendix to Ray Lewis White's critical edition of Tar
(pp. 231-36).   The second known version of "Death in the Woods"
was printed as Chapter XII of Tar, and the third version, greatly
revised, was published in American Mercury in September of 1926.
Since the story that appeared in American Mercury is virtually the
same as it appeared in Death in the Woods, the final version of
the story was written most probably in 1926.   Therefore, if the
story was "ten years getting itself written, " the holograph "The
Death in the Forest" in the Sherwood Anderson Papers was written
about 1916, at the time Anderson was writing his Winesburg stories.

Even though Anderson in the "Writer's Book" speaks quite
often about the novel and the short story, he is unable to formulate
an adequate theory on the relationship between the two forms.   He
admits this inability in two places in Part VII.   He confesses that
in this concluding section he had not originally intended to speak
about the writing of three short stories: "I had intended, when I
began to write, to speak of the great gulf that separates the two
arts" (89/26-27).   After he describes writing his three stories,
he again admits: "I had started here to speak of the relationship
of the story to the novel but have been carried away" (91/19-21).
Anderson is a creative artist, not a theorist, and he cannot trans-

late into theory what he intuitively understands and practices as an artist.   He comes nearest to articulating a theory of short story writing when he ascribes to H. G. Wells the statement that writing a short story is like a man running to a fire while writing a novel is like the same man taking an afternoon stroll (80/23-26), but he ends this passage with the statement: "The actual physical feat of writing either a long or a short novel is another matter" (80/29-30).   The "other matter," the real difference between short story writing and novel writing, is never explained.

Therefore we are forced to say that Anderson could never arrive at a satisfactory theory regarding the essential difference between the short story and the novel.   Nevertheless, he can lay claim to an outstanding accomplishment: the creation of a wholly new art form in American letters.   In "Waiting for Ben Huebsch" in Memoirs (ed. Rosenfeld, p. 289), he writes:

> I have even sometimes thought that the novel form does not fit an American writer, that it is a form which had been brought in.   What is wanted is a new looseness; and in Winesburg I had made my own form.   There were individual tales but all about lives in some way connected. By this method I did succeed, I think, in giving the feeling of the life of a boy growing into young manhood in a town.   Life is a loose flowing thing.

Since the question whether Winesburg, Ohio is a series of short stories or a novel is still debated by critics, it is well to see what Anderson himself says about his masterpiece.   In the "Writer's Book" he always speaks of Winesburg as a series of stories, never as a novel.   For example, note the phrases: "Winesburg series of short stories" (14/13), "the Winesburg series of stories" (14/19), "all the stories of the book" (25/31), "the Winesburg tales" (27/31), "your Winesburg stories" (45/27), "the Winesburg stories" (54/31), and "my Winesburg series of stories" (83/2-3).   Furthermore, at 48/20 he lists Winesburg as a volume of short stories, along with The Triumph of the Egg and Horses and Men, and not as a novel; and at 85/17-25 he uses Winesburg as an example to substantiate the critical opinion that he is "best at the short story."

In letters of Anderson's written in the year of the publication of Winesburg, he speaks of it as a hybrid form.   For example, writing on November 12, 1919, to Ben Huebsch, he compares his unsuccessful and unpublished "Mary Cochran" to Winesburg: "In its final form it will be like Winesburg, a group of tales woven about the life of one person but each tale will be longer and more closely related to the development of the central character."   To Hart Crane on November 19, he remarks: "I shall later have another book of stories grouped into a semi-novel form"; and to Waldo Frank, sometime after December 4, he states: "Out of my necessity I am throwing the Mary Cochran book into the Winesburg form, half individual tales, half long novel form" (Letters, Newberry Library, 1919).

   In "Waiting for Ben Huebsch, " omitted in Ray Lewis White's
critical edition of Anderson's Memoirs, Anderson speaks about the
Winesburg stories as follows: "The stories belonged together.   I
felt that, taken together, they made something like a novel" (Memoirs, ed. Rosenfeld, p. 289).   Anderson does not call Winesburg a
hybrid form, however, in White's critical edition of the Memoirs.
There, as in the "Writer's Book, " Anderson consistently calls it a
series of short stories:

> So I invented a figure I called George Willard and about
> his figure I built a series of stories and sketches called
> Winesburg, Ohio. (Memoirs, ed. White, p. 22.)

> Later, when I had become a writer and had written and
> published books, I wrote and published a book of tales,
> called Winesburg, Ohio. (Ibid., p. 177.)

> He [Jacques Copeau] was, at that time, particularly in-
> terested in a book of tales I had written and that I had
> called Winesburg, Ohio. He said the tales had excited
> him. (Ibid., p. 362.)

> I had myself written, in my Winesburg tales, the story
> of a woman who seemed to me a rather fine mother.
> (Ibid., p. 409.)

> When he [Hemingway] began to write he began with the
> short story and I had already published my Winesburg,
> Ohio. I had published also my Horses and Men and my
> Triumph of the Egg. (Ibid., p. 462.)

> At the time I was being published by Ben Huebsch who
> had taken my Winesburg stories after they had been kicked
> about in several publishing houses. (Ibid., p. 490.)

   When, in the course of the "Writer's Book, " Anderson gives
his opinion of some of his contemporaries, he also gives expression
to his critical theory.   As has been noted already, Anderson probably is referring to Theodore Dreiser, although he does not mention
him by name, in the passage in Part I concerning "I Accuse. "   Anderson mentions Dreiser by name in Part V.   He alludes to the
prose poem that he wrote about Dreiser (76/21-25), published originally in the Little Review (III [April, 1916], 5-6).   This poem in
a slightly revised form was printed at the beginning of Horses and
Men, dedicated to Dreiser.   After mentioning the poem, Anderson
goes on to speak of the "nerve force, of patience, of courage"
(76/29-30) with which Dreiser met the vicissitudes attendant on the
publication of Sister Carrie.   When speaking of the reaction of the
public to Sister Carrie, Anderson links himself with Dreiser as a
man who also was accused of being "sex-obsessed" (77/8).   In ex-
onerating Dreiser of this charge, Anderson implicitly exonerates

himself.   Anderson calls Dreiser "the man I consider the pioneer,
the father of so much later American writing" (79/21-22).   Dreiser
"did not, as he was accused of doing, overemphasize sex. . . .   The
truth is that Mr Dreiser simply put sex back into our sexless literature.   He gave sex a normal place in the lives of the people of
whom he wrote.   He gave all of our American writing a new health"
(79/22-29).

Anderson's championing of the cause of his lifelong friend
Theodore Dreiser leads him into a discussion of Sinclair Lewis.
Lewis was the first American to be awarded the Nobel Prize for
Literature (1930).   In the "Writer's Book, " as in his Memoirs (ed.
White, p. 536), Anderson thinks Dreiser, rather than Lewis, should
have been given this distinction.   The reason for Anderson's pref-
erence of Dreiser over Lewis is the contention that Dreiser "is a
man who has always been tender about life, all kinds of American
life, in the poor and in the rich, in the healthy and in the deformed, and Mr Lewis is very seldom tender" (79/32-80/3).   In
comparing Main Street unfavorably to Sister Carrie, Anderson summarizes his attitude towards Sinclair Lewis: "Lewis' doctor shaking the ashes out of his furnace becomes the symbol of all life"
(80/10-11).

Another contemporary of Anderson's who comes in for small
praise in the "Writer's Book" is Somerset Maugham.   In describing his struggle to write a salable short story, Anderson recounts
that one afternoon he picked up Maugham's Of Human Bondage.
He mentions, but does not quote, a paragraph from Of Human
Bondage which, by implication, upholds the obligation which an artist has to the integrity of his art and which, perhaps, scorns
money-making.   Anderson concludes his remarks on Maugham:
"Well, Maugham, by his writing and by his plays after his Of Human Bondage, had got rich" (56/14-15).   Judged by Anderson's
"myth" that the artist is poor and the businessman is rich, Maugham
falls short of the true artist.

Since Anderson's "lifelong friend John Emerson" (37/32)
was not a fellow artist but only a movie actor and producer, he is
not condemned because he became rich nor because he "married
that charming little woman Anita Loos and went to live in Hollywood" (38/3-4).   Emerson is even included in the group of "old
friends" (59/15) whose voices speak to Anderson from Ripshin
Creek and mingle with the voices of loved ones from his imaginative life.   In addition to John Emerson, the friends from Anderson's real life include Carl Sandburg, Ben Hecht, and Maurice
Long.

Long was the owner of a large laundry in Washington, D.C.,
who, with Fred O'Brien, is described in "Two Irishmen" in No
Swank (Philadelphia: The Centaur Press, p. 33) as "the two best
story tellers I ever knew. "   Fred O'Brien, mentioned at 82/4 as
the author of White Shadows on the South Seas, is perhaps the
"Fred" of 58/28, whose footsteps Anderson hears on the bridge

over Ripshin Creek.

Another of Anderson's close friends mentioned in the "Writer's Book" is Gertrude Stein. After Anderson confesses that he is not the kind of writer who can "linger over sentences, " he adds: "It is true that Gertrude Stein once declared I was one of the few American writers who could write a sentence. She spoke, I think, of passionate sentences" (85/7-10). Anderson is alluding to The Autobiography of Alice B. Toklas, in which Gertrude Stein writes: "Gertrude Stein contended that Sherwood Anderson had a genius for using a sentence to convey a direct emotion, this was in the great american tradition, and that really except Sherwood there was no one in America who could write a clear and passionate sentence" (Selected Writings of Gertrude Stein, ed. Carl Van Vechten [New York: Random House, 1946], p. 218).

Anderson first became acquainted with Gertrude Stein's writings when his brother Karl brought to his boarding house at 735 Cass Street a copy of Tender Buttons, published in 1914. Tender Buttons, and later Three Lives, exerted a great influence on Anderson's prose style (see A Story Teller's Story, ed. White, pp. 260-63). Anderson met Gertrude Stein for the first time when he went to Europe in 1921. They renewed their acquaintance when Sherwood returned to Europe in 1926-27, and they remained close friends. In an interview with the present editor on June 5, 1969, Mrs. Eleanor Anderson affirmed that both Theodore Dreiser and Gertrude Stein were two of Sherwood's best and most loyal friends until his death in 1941.

V.   THE PRESENT EDITION AND ITS PROCEDURES

Since the purpose of this edition is to make available to readers Sherwood Anderson's "Writer's Book, " the basic editorial principle guiding all decisions is for the presentation of an accurate, readable text, the text as Anderson most probably would have presented it if he had had time to prepare it for publication. Therefore, five kinds of changes are introduced into the text. First, spelling is standardized. Second, necessary words omitted by Anderson are supplied in brackets. Third, inadvertent errors in handwriting are corrected. Fourth, glaring grammatical errors that impede easy reading are corrected; otherwise, Anderson's grammar is allowed to stand. Last, many changes are made in punctuation, even though the basic principle is to retain Anderson's highly individualistic punctuation whenever compatible with clarity.

Anderson's spelling is standardized, but his occasional British spelling, for example, "defence" (2/5), "enamoured" (21/27), and "armour" (73/25), is retained. When Anderson omits a word clearly called for by the context, the word is supplied in brackets. Greater clarity and readability, not an attempt to "improve" Anderson's style, are the criteria for these additions. For example: "He may think me one [of the] anarchists" (33/9-10); and "no one thinks [about] what is really going on in the room" (83/27-28). What the editor considers inadvertent errors in handwriting are, for the most part, silently corrected. For example, "her two room" (18/18) is changed to "her two rooms"; and "suggester" (17/4) is changed to "suggested." Because some grammatical errors of Anderson's are considered both inadvertent slips in handwriting and hindrances to easy reading, they are corrected. For example, "Your heart jump" (41/1) is changed to "Your heart jumps"; and "I, who had always love the piles of clean white sheets" (24/25-26) is changed to "I, who had always loved the piles of clean white sheets." On the whole, however, Anderson's grammar is allowed to stand.

In the manuscript of the "Writer's Book" there are five instances of complicated, grammatically imperfect sentences: 29/22-27, 31/6-10, 37/32-38/7, 49/25-50/3, and 51/5-18. In the first three cases, in the interest of clarity, superfluous words in the manuscript are omitted. In the last two cases the editor omits nothing but suggests in the Textual Apparatus another reading. There are, furthermore, two passages (25/22-26/1 and 30/21-25) in which the editor divides a long sentence into two: in the first case by changing a comma to a question mark and deleting a parenthesis (25/27); in the second case by capitalizing "And" after a question mark (30/22).

Undoubtedly the most numerous decisions concern Anderson's punctuation. Even though a fundamental rule guiding the editing of the "Writer's Book" is to retain punctuation wherever possible, clarity and readability often take precedence over strict adherence to Anderson's practices. Furthermore, changes in punctuation, unless they are significant enough to be mentioned in the Textual Apparatus, are made silently. For example, since Anderson often omits terminal punctuation at the end of sentences, periods, exclamation marks, and question marks are supplied when necessary. On the other hand, since Anderson occasionally uses British spelling, no period is added when Anderson, in imitation of British usage, writes "Mr" and "Mrs" without a period. Titles of books are underscored, with the exception of "Winesburg" when used as an adjective, as in "Winesburg series of short stories" (14/19). Quotation marks, when missing, are supplied for titles of stories and articles. Missing quotation marks in direct quotations are supplied, and Anderson's unnecessary quotation marks are omitted. When Anderson has a quotation within a quotation he sometimes encloses it in single quotation marks and sometimes in double quotation marks. His practice is made consistent by always using single quotation marks. Another practice of Anderson's that is made consistent is the placement of quotation marks in relation to periods and commas. All periods and commas are placed inside the quotation marks. Furthermore, when Anderson omits apostrophes in the possessive case, these apostrophes are supplied.

The colon and the semicolon, uncommon in any of Anderson's manuscripts, do not appear in the manuscript of the "Writer's Book." For the sake of clarity, however, the colon is added three times and the semicolon even more often. For example, Anderson's comma after "come" is changed to a colon in the sentence: "Bills come: so many pounds of grass seed for a field, a ton of lime, a new plow" (30/10-12). In the four lines, 76/22-25, the period after "it" in the sentence which gives the title of a poem Anderson wrote to Theodore Dreiser is changed to a colon: "I called it: Heavy heavy lies over thy head"; and the period after "poem" is changed to a colon in the sentence which follows: "Here is the poem: (Copy poem)." The semicolon is introduced into compound-complex sentences when, in the opinion of the editor, the large amount of internal punctuation in the independent clauses makes it necessary to demarcate the independent clauses clearly. For example, Anderson's comma after the word "life" in the following sentence is replaced by a semicolon: "We want passionately the luxuries of life; the things we produce, our books, paintings, statues, the songs we make, the music we make, these are all luxuries" (52/9-12).

Anderson uses the comma to help express his thought and to regulate the rhythm of his sentences, not consciously to follow arbitrary rules. Academic rules of punctuation did not interest Anderson, and he never mastered them. What he strove to write were simple, clear, readable sentences, and the editor tries to be true to his intent and style. One practice of his, however, that is consistently changed is to bring the comma which he puts after "and" and "but" to its usual position in front of these conjunctions. For example: "I have breakfasted in the room, but in the morning I cannot set to work until everything is in order" (71/6-8). Also, the reader often expects a pair of commas where Anderson has only one. The second comma is added whenever the editor judges that smooth reading requires it. For example, the comma after "hoped" is added in the following sentence: "At least he thought, or hoped, he was meeting her in secret" (21/30-31).

Although Anderson most probably did not reflect upon the difference between a restrictive and a nonrestrictive clause or phrase, the editor's decision about omitting the first or adding the second of a pair of commas is often determined by this difference. Very often Anderson puts a comma at the beginning of a restrictive element in a sentence. Since he does not follow the clause or phrase by another comma and since the sense of the sentence is clearer if the first comma is omitted, the editor leaves it out. For example, commas are omitted after "artist" and "doctor" in the following sentences: "She had an artist who works in wood build a desk for him" (75/13-14); and "Lewis' doctor shaking the ashes out of his furnace becomes the symbol of all life" (80/10-11). On the other hand, the following sentence provides an example of a nonrestrictive clause that needs the second of a pair of commas added after "words": "I, who am a lover of words, must use them for this purpose" (47/32-48/1).

In most instances, Anderson's indentation, unorthodox as it might be, is allowed to stand. Just as he has reasons for his highly individualistic punctuation and sentence structure, he also intends his paragraphs--short, abrupt ones or long, rambling ones --to regulate the movement of his thoughts and emotions. Therefore, Anderson's indentation is respected. One unusual practice of his is to start a new paragraph when the speaker in a conversation starts a new sentence. This practice, too, is respected, except in one case. The dialogue at 84/1-3 is not clear if, as in the manuscript, the two sentences uttered by the first speaker are put into separate paragraphs. Therefore, in the present text they are put into the same paragraph; and the third sentence of the dialogue, spoken by the other speaker, is reserved for the new paragraph:

> "What a dull evening. I notice that you had very little to say."
> "A dull evening?"

Although this is the only case in which Anderson's opening of a new paragraph is not respected, there are several instances in which the present text commences a paragraph where Anderson has no indentation. The reason behind these changes is mainly typographical. For example, at the beginning of "A Sermon" and "Prelude To A Story" (3/3 and 4/3), Anderson does not indent the opening words. The appearance of pages 3 and 4, it is hoped, justifies making the change. There is, furthermore, one instance (70/5) where indentation is added not for typographical reasons but for clarity. It is consistent with Anderson's usual practice of starting a new paragraph whenever a new quotation is introduced, and it makes for clearer reading, if the judge's statement, "I am ashamed that I am so short," is made to start a new paragraph.

The "x's" that Anderson uses to break his text into sections are retained. Usually Anderson uses three "x's," although in a few cases he uses four. The three periods which Anderson often has in his manuscripts are retained in the present text. These three periods are not ellipsis marks. There is only one instance in which the present editor omits words from Anderson's manuscript and indicates this omission by three periods. As the Commentary and the Textual Apparatus explain, three periods are substituted for the words "with whom, when" and for the comma after "town" in the sentence which in the manuscript begins: "My lifelong friend John Emerson, with whom, when we were both boys in the same small town," (37/32-38/1). In the present text this sentence commences: "My lifelong friend John Emerson ... we were both boys in the same small town ..." In a few other cases, also, the editor has supplied three periods when either clarity or Anderson's style calls for them. For example, in order to make Anderson's punctuation consistent as well as to clarify the meaning, in the following sentence three periods are substituted for a comma after "enough": "A protest having come from the office ... 'You have put in time enough' ... I showed the man the advertisements written on the train" (49/2-4).

The editor emends the wording of the text in nine places.
"Lugs" is changed to "dugs"; that is, an archaic word for "ears"
is changed to a synonym for "udders," clearly called for by the
context: "she is a woman with great breasts, like cows' dugs"
(15/15-16). "Wom" (22/26) is emended to read "woman," and
"fakiness" (48/11) is emended to read "fakery." In two cases the
editor construes what looks like "jole" to read "joy" (57/14 and
60/10). In the sentence which begins: "If there is something in
a writer's work that really touches you, makes your life a lit
richer" (65/8), the editor emends "lit" to "bit," assuming that it
is more probable that Anderson failed to notice he wrote "l" for
"b" rather than that he failed to notice he wrote "lit" for "little."
The name "Jane Emerison" is emended to read "John Emerson"
(59/3) because no research uncovered the existence of a Jane
Emerison, whereas John Emerson was a lifelong friend of Anderson's. "Passion" (86/22) is emended to "passing" in the sentence:
"You are, as you are not at other times, aware of all going on
about you, ... of happenings along a street, of people passing,
the expression of faces, ..." (86/19-22). Lastly, "glories" (89/28)
is emended to read "glorious" in the following sentence: "I have
been carried away by this remembering of the glorious times in
the life of the writer of short tales" (89/27-29).

As has already been said, the holograph of the "Writer's
Book" contains some corrections, additions, and deletions made in
Anderson's own hand, apparently during its original composition.
All corrections and additions have been incorporated into the text,
with the original wording given in the Textual Apparatus. Deletions,
unless they seem important for an understanding of the text, are
silently omitted. This practice seems warranted by the fact that
in the first editing of the "Writer's Book" prepared by the present
editor ("The 'Writer's Book' by Sherwood Anderson: A Critical
Edition," unpublished Ph.D. dissertation, Loyola University of Chicago, 1972), the critical apparatus at the foot of the pages of the
text indicates every single change introduced into the text by the
author or by the editor, as well as all deletions, even of indecipherable letters and words, made by Anderson himself. Since the
purpose of this edition is to present an accurate and readable text,
and since the dissertation is available to anyone desirous of the
complete textual history of the manuscript, the present edition offers a "clear text," unencumbered by textual footnotes. All textual
changes of importance, however, are recorded in the Textual Apparatus appended to the text.

Mss--For Writer's Book

These have been copied

1

THE BOOK FOR WRITER

Literary flirtation.

How books carry on in the mind...

Trilena White and the successful novelist... Has he contempt?

A defence of critics.   5

How the writer feels about his own books.

A Sermon.

Half a Story

Written for young American story tellers by a veteran of the craft, its purpose to show the processes by
which a story begins in the mind of the story teller's, the   5
resistance in him to its flow, the struggle he has with himself and what finally emerges.   The sermon to go at the
front of a book in which he attempts to tell a new story.

Prelude To A Story--

(Addressed to Story Tellers)

On a certain day, in the early summer, some years
ago, I got a letter from my literary agent. It may be that
I had been writing to him. He had certain stories I had   5
sent him to sell.

"Can't you, sir, sell one of the stories to some
magazine? I am needing money."

He answered my letter. He is a sensible man,
knows his business.   10

"I admit that the stories you have sent me are good
stories.

"But," he said, "you are always getting something
into all of your stories that spoils the sale."

He did not go further but I knew what he meant.   15

"Look here," he once said to me, "why can't you,
for the time at least, drop this rather intimate style of
yours?"

He smiled when he said it and I also smiled.

"Let us say, now, that you are yourself the editor   20
of one of our big American magazines. You have yourself
been in business. When you first began to write, even
after you had published some of your earlier books, Winesburg and others, you had to go on for years, working in
an advertising place.   25

"You must know that all of our large American
magazines are business ventures. It costs a great deal of
money to print and distribute hundreds of thousands of
magazines. Often, as you know, the price received for
the magazine, when sold on the newsstand, does not pay   30
for the paper on which it is printed."

"Yes, I know."

"They have to have stories that please people."

"Yes, I know."

We had stopped to have a drink at a bar. But a
few weeks before he had written me a letter. "There is   5
a certain large magazine that would like to have a story
from you.

"It should be, let us say, a story of about ten
thousand words.

"Do not attempt to write the story. Make an out-   10
line, I should say a three or four page outline.

"I can sell the story for you."

x   x   x

I had made the outline and had sent it to him.

"It is splendid," he wrote. "Now you can go ahead.   15
I can get such and such a sum."

"Oho!" The sum mentioned would get me out of my
difficulties.

"I will get busy," I said to myself. "In a week I
will dash off this story." Some two or three weeks before   20
a man friend had come to me one evening. He is a man
to whom I am deeply attached.

"Come and walk with me," he said, and we set out
afoot, leaving the town where he lived. I had gone to the
town to see him but when I got to his town there was a sud- 25
den illness in his house. The man has children and two of
them were in bed with a contagious disease.

I stayed at a hotel. He came there. We walked
beyond the town, got into a dirt road, passed farm houses,
dogs barked at us. We got into a moonlit meadow.   30

We had walked for a long time in silence. At the
hotel I had noticed that my friend was in a tense excited

mood.

"You are in some sort of trouble. Is it the children?
Has the disease taken a turn for the worst?"

"No," he said. "The children are better. They are
all right."   5

x   x   x

We were in the moonlit meadow, standing by a fence,
some sheep grazing nearby, and it was a delicious night of
the early summer. "There is something I have to tell to
someone," he said. "I wrote to you, begged you to come   10
here."

My friend is a highly respected man in his town.

He began talking. He talked for hours. He told me
a story of a secret life he had been living.

My friend is a man of fifty. He is a scientist. He   15
is employed, as an experimental scientist, by a large manufacturing company.

But, I might as well confess at once that I am, as
you the reader may have guessed, covering the trail of my
friend. I am a man rather fortunate in life. I have a good   20
many men friends. If I make this one an experimental
scientist, working for a large manufacturing company, it
will do.

His story was, on the whole, strange. It was like
so many stories, not invented but came directly out of life.   25
It was a story having in it certain so-called sordid touches,
strange impulses come to a man of fifty, himself in the
grip of an odd passion.

"I have been doing this.

"I have been doing that.   30

"I have to unload, to tell someone.

"I have been suffering."

x   x   x

My friend did unload his story, getting a certain relief, and I went home.

The letter came from the agent. I made the outline
of the story that was pronounced splendid by my agent.   5

But what rough places I had smoothed out!

"No, I cannot say that such a figure, holding such
a respectable place in my life, did that.

"There must not be anything unpleasant. There must
be nothing that will remind readers of certain sordid mo-   10
ments, thoughts, passions, acts, in their own lives.

"If I am to get this money, and, oh, how I need it!"

x   x   x

I am no Shakespeare but did not even Shakespeare
write a play he called As You Like It?   15

"When you are writing, to please people, you must
not touch certain secret, often dark, little recesses that
are in all humans.

"Keep in the clear, man. Go gayly along.

"It will be all right to startle them a little.   20

"You must get a certain dramatic force into your
story."

But that night the man, upon whose story I have
based the story I am about to write, was, as he talked,
simply broken. He even put his face down upon the top   25
rail of the fence, there in that moonlit meadow, and cried,
and I went to him. I put my arms about his shoulders,
said words to him.

"This passion, that has come to you at this time in
your life, that now threatens to tear down all you have so   30
carefully built up, that threatens to destroy the lives of

others you love, will pass.

"At our age everything passes."

I do not remember just what I did say to him.

      x   x   x

But I was at my desk.   5

"Never mind him. Use, of the story he told you,
only so much as will perhaps a little startle, without too
much shocking, your readers.

"You know very well how badly you need this money."
These the sentences I had begun saying to myself.   10

      x   x   x

And so I began to write, but alas!

Our difficulty is that as we write we become interested, absorbed, often a little in love with these characters
of our stories, that seem to be growing here, under our   15
hand.

I have begun this story, taking off, as it were, from
the story told me in the meadow by my friend but now, as
I write, he has disappeared.

There is a new man, coming to life, here, on this   20
paper, under my hand. He seems to be here, in this room
where I work.

"You must do me right now," he seems to be saying
to me.

"There is a certain morality involved," he says.   25

"Now you must tell everything, put it all down.

"Do not hesitate. I want it all put down."

      x   x   x

And so, there is all of that money I so needed, gone
out of the window.   30

There is a series of letters, concerning a story to be
written, that lie here on my desk. I have had them brought
to me from my files.

"If you are to write the story for us it would be well
for you to keep certain things in mind.   5

"The story should be concerned with the lives of
people who are in what might be called comfortable circumstances.

"Above all, it should not be too gloomy.

"We want you to understand that we do not wish, in   10
any way, to dictate to you."

       x   x   x

I sit at my desk, reading over the above letter. "It
is true," I say to myself, "that I was once in business."
For years I was employed as a writer of advertisements, in   15
an advertising agency. Having been born into and having
lived, through boyhood and into my young manhood, in a very
poor family, I had for a long time what I presume might be
called "the American dream." I dreamed of getting rich,
or at least well-to-do, of living in a big house, having an   20
assured income. I had spent the years of my early young
manhood working as a laborer, had been a farm laborer, a
factory hand, lived as such men do in little rooms, often in
cheerless enough streets. As I sit here this morning writing, scenes, smells, sights of that time in my own life   25
come back to me. I see myself in a room in a house in a
street in a factory town. I am sitting at my window looking
out. I have got, at a second-hand furniture store, an old
kitchen table and at a stationery store some tablets of white
paper. Even at that time, and although I had not then begun   30
to think of myself as a writer, such a thing as authorship
being seemingly as far away from me as the stars in the

sky at night, I had nevertheless this passion for writing.
Like my man of the story of certain phases of a human life
I have here written, in this book, I took it out in writing
letters.   I used to get names out of newspapers or out of
books, borrowed at the public libraries.   I began a letter,   5
"Dear Cecelia."

I wanted to tell Cecelia of certain impressions, certain feelings about life, I had been having.

But who was Cecelia?   How old was she?   What did
she look like?   10

It was not difficult for me to evoke the figure of
Cecelia.   Although, as a young workman, not skilled in any
one trade and therefore never very well paid, I was compelled to live always in some poorer section of the town or
city where I was employed, I did, usually, have one good   15
suit of clothes, a presentable hat, presentable shoes, I
could put on for a Sunday afternoon's or an evening's walk.

I walked in some rich or well-to-do section of town
and there, on a wide street, under trees, I had seen a
young woman walking.   20

She was tall and slender.   She walked with easy
grace.   She had a somewhat dark, so-called "olive" skin--
not the green but the ripe olive--but not that either--

"Her skin is of the color of the soil, in a certain
field, seen from a distance, from a freight train, on which   25
I was once bumming my way to a new town and a new job,"
I told myself.

She had dark eyes and very fine glistening black hair.

So I wrote to her.   I called her Cecelia.   I began to
tell her stories of workmen beside whom I worked, of   30
dreams that came, of people seen, of the hours of sleepless
loneliness that sometimes came at night.

Of the noises at night in the rooming house, where I
had my room.

I always made my Cecelias a bit older than myself.
Let us say I had reached the age of twenty-four. I made
her a woman of thirty.   5

It is true that these thoughts of Cecelia led sometimes into lascivious thoughts. What young man has not had
them about some imagined woman? I stopped thinking of her
eyes, the broad forehead, the finely shaped nose and chin,
her graceful stride as she walked under the trees and thought   10
instead [of] holding her two shapely breasts in the palms of
my hands, of her lips, of her shapely thighs.

Then I could not write to her. I could not sleep.
Sometimes, when such thoughts came, I had to leave my
room. I walked for hours in the street. I went into sa-   15
loons and drank. I wanted to get drunk. "I'd better get
drunk, " I told myself.

        x   x   x

I have spoken of scenes, looked at from the windows
of rooms, in workingmen's rooming houses. I have told   20
how these keep coming back to me.

I see, in fancy, in such a reminiscent mood, a certain street intersection. It is in a Middle-Western American city. It is a Sunday morning in a section of the city
where a great many workers live.   25

Go down along this street, a block, two blocks, and
there is a large brick factory, facing the street, where,
every day, hundreds of thousands, it may be even millions,
of loaves of bread are baked. There is a row of small
mean-looking, unpainted houses facing it, and on hot sum-   30
mer nights men and women, the men in their shirt sleeves
and the women, for the most part, in soiled, Mother-

Hubbardish-looking dresses, sit on the steps while their
children play, fight and quarrel in the street.

And on summer nights, there are young men, very
like myself no doubt, at least some of them, walking up and
down. Some of them are young roughs, others quiet gentle   5
fellows.

Are they imagining their own Cecelias?

Very likely they are.

On the street, in one of the houses, upstairs in the
house, where she has taken two rooms, there is a woman   10
lives. She is, I'd say, thirty-two. She has blond hair.

But perhaps it was not originally blond. She may
have had it bleached.

Her eyes are dark and there are dark patches under
her eyes. The eyes look tired.   15

She is a prostitute and the women, married to workers, who sit on the steps before the houses, do not speak
to her when, in the evening, she comes down the stairs
from her rooms to begin her evening's walk in the street,
but usually she does not come down early. She has two   20
children, both girls, one five and the other three; and before she sets out for her evening's work, to practise her
old, old profession, she must get them into their bed and
asleep. They sleep in one of the two rooms she rents. She
uses it also as a kitchen but there is a little bed in a cor-   25
ner, hidden behind a curtain. The curtain is made of a bed
sheet, arranged on some wires she has strung up.

But how do I know all of this?

I shall have to tell you. One night, after work, in a
certain cold-storage warehouse, where butter and eggs were   30
stored, some half dozen blocks from the house where I had
my own room, after dining at a cheap workingmen's res-

taurant ... I remember that on that evening a drunken young
workingman came in there ... he seemed under the impression that the place was a bar ... he kept asking for whiskey.

"But we do not sell any kind of intoxicating drink.
This is a restaurant, a place to eat, " the waitress kept say-   5
ing.

She was a tall woman and heavy and walked with a
limp, and more than once, when I had dined there, I had
wondered why she didn't try to get a job that would let her
work sitting down.   10

"So many hours, every day, spent standing and walking on the poor crippled foot, " I had thought. I did not look
at her when she brought my food. "Why look? Why make
yourself unhappy by looking?" I said to myself.

On that night the drunken young man kept insisting.   15

"Hell, you got it in here, I know you have, " he kept
saying. He sat at a little table pleading with the waitress
of the crippled foot. He said his mother was always hiding
his whiskey from him. "I get a bottle. I take it home.
Well, I hide it good but she finds it.   20

"I do not swear at her because she is my mother
and a man should respect his mother but you are not my
mother, " he said to the waitress, but presently, other
workers coming in to dine, she gave him no more attention
but waited on [us] others while he sat, amusing the other   25
workers by declaring over and over that he would not move
until he got his drink.

"And they can't throw me out. I'm strong. Just let
them try it, " he kept declaring.

        x   x   x   30

And so, on that night I dined and went to my room.
I began writing to some Cecelia, describing to her the

events, the thoughts and feelings of my day, but, presently ...

It began. Desire raged in me. Who has not seen
such young men as I was then wandering restlessly in city
streets at night?   5

But it is not lust alone that drives us forth. There
is this dream world in which we live in this intimacy with
beauty. To the more imaginative young man, and perhaps
also young woman, for them I cannot speak, the dream
sometimes grows more and more intense. The very power   10
of concentration that is characteristic of the artist man
makes his dream constantly more and more real. In the
Winesburg series of short stories, written in just such a
rooming house as I have here described--

In a city rooming house, where often you do not know   15
the others in the house--sound of the footsteps of girls and
women on stairs at night. Women are undressing in nearby
rooms. A young girl begins to sing softly.

In the Winesburg series of stories, in the story
"Loneliness, " I described a little man in a room and what   20
the imagined figures his fancy had conjured up had come to
mean to him.

              x   x   x

But I was speaking of myself, in such a room. I
spoke of writing long letters to a woman I had named Ce-   25
celia and then of growing weary of writing and sitting by my
window.

It is a Sunday morning, after a hot night. There is
a small delicatessen a few doors down the street, beyond
the corner, and on Sundays people go there for food. The   30
windows of the store are dirty and it is run by a German
in a dirty white apron. Often I wonder if he never has it

washed.

Frowsy-looking women are going into the store.
They look tired and bleary-eyed. There are two men standing at the corner, their backs against a building, and a
third who sits at the curb, his feet in the street. He has   5
got drunk during the night before and is still drunk.

And then, from out of the street along which I go to
work ... there is a cold-storage warehouse along that street
and I am employed as a laborer there ... along the street
comes a man leading an old grey horse.   10

The horse is lame. It goes painfully along. The
three men and a fat woman with bare feet thrust into bedroom slippers that are run down at the heels, a soiled
dress and with grey hair that is twisted into an ugly little
knot at the back of her bald head ... she is a woman with   15
great breasts, like cows' dugs ... these all stare at the old
white horse being led along the street by a little old man
with a white beard.

And all of this scene fixed, to stay until death, sharp
as an etching, in the mind of a young man sitting in a win-   20
dow in a room in a rooming house.

Why?

I have spent my life wondering why.

x   x   x

I have spoken of the prostitute in the nearby street.   25
On the night before the day when I saw the old white horse
in the street, I had grown profoundly restless. I had been
writing one of my Cecelia letters and could not write any
more. I undressed and got into bed but could not sleep. I
got up and dressed, went down into the street.   30

It was very late and the streets in the section of the
city where I then lived were now almost deserted.

"But where am I going?" I asked myself.

I would walk and walk and at last would grow weary.
On more than one such night I had walked until daylight
came, trying to quiet my restless longing.

But what did I hope?   5

For what did I hunger?

I am sure that young men, the restless young men
out of the ranks of whom we are to get the artists of the
future, will understand.

Yes, it is true, I was hungry for a woman but I did   10
not want just any woman. Such dreams as imaginative young
men have, become at times absurd. As he walks restlessly
about, as I was doing that night, he will come suddenly upon
his Cecelia, and she, out of some divine impulse, will
recognize at once that he ...   15

There may be some accident happen. She was in a
car that was wrecked, was thrown stunned to the sidewalk,
even here, in this dark dismal street, and her companion,
an older man, it would have been her father, who was driving the car, was killed.   20

Our young man springs forward. He puts his ear to
her breast. She is still alive. He hails a car, takes her
into his arms, accompanies her to a hospital.

He is in the car, holding her thus, and suddenly, as
the car he has hailed passes a street light, she opens her   25
eyes.

She looks into his eyes and at once, by a kind of
magic, she recognized in him ...

But why go on? Do not deny it, you imaginative
young men. It is by such absurd dreams, always coming,   30
always changing, that the imaginative young man lives.

And, if he becomes in the end an American popular

short story or novel writer, it is out of such dreams he
later builds his tales.

x   x   x

I was in the street, walking as suggested, but a few
doors from my own rooming house, when that prostitute   5
spoke to me.

She was standing in the narrow hallway of the house
in which she had the rooms. It had been a bad night for
her, little or no trade coming her way, and she had, as I
later knew, just run up to her room to see that her children   10
were safe.

She had come softly down a flight of dark stairs and
was just about to step out again, into the street, to again
walk a certain number of blocks, looking about ... there
was a street, several blocks away, on which there were   15
several saloons ... there were some small dance halls ...
she would go there.

One more round and she would give it up for the
night. She saw me coming along and spoke to me.

"Hello. Won't you come here?"   20

When she spoke in the street thus she had a rather
soft voice, but, as I later found out, it was not her natural
voice. She was like the people who, nowadays, speak to
all of us over the radio ... she had cultivated a special tone
for her work in the streets as the radio announcers cultivate   25
a special tone for their work on the air.

"Hello. Come here. Come here."

I had stepped toward her. I stood looking at her.
Her figure was dim, there in the half light. She began
speaking quickly. There was a little whine in her voice.   30

"I'll give you a good time," she said.
She seemed to be pleading with me.

x   x   x

And what was I thinking?

I hardly know but I am quite sure that in a moment, when I had decided, on a sudden impulse, that I would accompany her up the stairs ... there must have been a kind of clutching. It must have been that I was like one who has climbed to the top of a tall tree and has fallen. I clutched at branches as I fell.

"If I do not look too closely at her.

"It may be that the room to which she will take me will be dark. I can close my eyes. I can imagine her the real Cecelia."

Do we not all, and often, tell ourselves such desperate nonsense?

She had said quickly that the charge would be two dollars and that day I had drawn my pay. I went after her up the stairs.

I was in one of her two rooms, in the one facing the street.

There was no light in there but there was a light, seemingly behind a curtain in her other room. There was light that seemed to come into the room over the top of the curtain. There was light on the ceiling of the room but the floor of the room was dark.

The floor of the room was a dark pit and I sat on the edge of her bed and gazed down into it.

She was undressing.

"Aren't you going to get ready?" she asked, and without looking up at her I took off my coat.

I held it in my hand. I looked up at her. I had not spoken to her. In that light, as she started to come toward me, perhaps to collect her money, I saw that her figure

... she was now partly undressed ... her figure was slender.

When she asked if I was not going to get ready her
voice was harsh. She came toward me. She had on some
sort of short shirt, or waist, that came to her navel but all   5
the lower part of her body was naked.

I saw that she had slender hips. She had straight
legs.

"She must be quite young, " I thought.

"I wonder how many others she has been with to-   10
night. "

    x   x   x

She had taken a step toward me, to collect, no doubt,
her money, but suddenly stopped. In the room behind the
curtain a child had screamed and I had jumped to my feet.   15

And now she was running, passing the curtain that
divided her two rooms, and I had followed her. I saw her
part the curtain made from the bed sheet. There was a
narrow bed with the two children and one, the older of the
two, was sitting upright in the bed.   20

The child had a look of terror on her face.

    x   x   x

Was it because I had come in there with her mother?

I stood behind the mother as she took the child into
her arms.   25

"Now, now. What is it?" she was saying to the
child.

And now her voice was really soft.

But the child, had it, as by some subtile impulse,
felt me in the place?   30

I decided that it was not me, that I had not frightened

the child.

"It has had a bad dream, " I thought. I stood thus,
my coat in my hand, behind the mother, who held the child
against her breasts.

"Now, now. There, there, " she kept saying, speak-   5
ing softly, and my hand, fumbling in my pocket, had taken
out a bill.

It was a five-dollar bill and I thrust it into the
woman's hand. I did not speak to her, had not as yet
spoken to her, and as I put the bill into her hand she said   10
nothing.

There was no look of surprise or gratitude in her
eyes. Her eyes were very tired. She was one who could
no longer be surprised.

"And what kind of a one is this, who, while I am   15
standing here, as he can see, with a frightened child in my
arms, comes in here to me, pushes money into my hand?

"Is it that he cannot wait until I have quieted the
child?"

I do not know what she thought, but in the flying mo-   20
ment, before I turned away, went down the stairs and along
the street and back to my room, not having exchanged a
word with her, I knew her story.

I knew it as well as though she had talked to me for
hours, knew that she had been a girl, perhaps a waitress,   25
in such a restaurant as the one in which I went for my food,
and that she had married a man, a worker like myself, who,
after her two children were born, had lost his job.

He had become discouraged and blue, had tramped
from place to place, seeking a job, as I myself had done.   30

And at home there were the two babies always crying and the wife frightened.

He had run away, deserted her.

"And now, how am I to support myself, and feed the babes?

"I cannot go, all day, to a factory or to wait on people in a restaurant.   There is but one trade I can prac-   5
tise."

x   x   x

A simple tale, one of a thousand, [that] every man who has eyes to see and ears to hear may pluck out of life.

And why do I, here, as a part of the introduction to   10
another tale I have wanted to write, why do I tell it here?

"He might have spared us that," I can hear the reader, who by chance has picked up my book, saying to himself.

But to that I have something to say.   When I sat   15
down to write the story, to which this rambling talk may serve as a sort of introduction, I had something in mind, as I have already suggested, other than the story of the country boy who later became a judge.   I have told how, as I stood with him in a field, a friend talked to me of a turn   20
in his life that threatened to destroy the position he had achieved in his community.   The friend cried like a small boy.   He had got a sudden passion for a woman of his town, the sort of thing always happening in towns.   "Three years ago," he said to me, "there was another man here, a   25
friend, a man as I am of standing in our community, who did what I am doing now.   He became enamoured of a wo-man here, the wife of a friend, and began to meet her se-cretly.

"At least he thought, or hoped, he was meeting her   30
in secret.

"He did as I have been doing.   In the evening, when

darkness came, he got into his car. She had walked out
along a street and in some dark place along the street he
picked her up. He drove with her out along little side
roads, went to [a] distant town, but soon everyone knew.

"And how I blamed him. I went to him. 'What a   5
fool you are being,' I said.

"'Yes, but I cannot help it. This is the great love
of my life.'

"'What nonsense,' I said. I pleaded with him, quarreled with him, but it did no good. I thought him an utter   10
fool and now I am being just such another."

                    x   x   x

I had taken the man, with whom I talked in the field,
[and] his story as the bases for the story I was to write for
one of the popular magazines, had made an outline which   15
was approved. I began to write.

To be sure I could not bring into my story any of the
rather sordid details, happenings, so likely to come into
such affairs. I had to lift it out of that. Just what I did,
in making the outline for the story I was to write, I can't   20
remember except that it was another case of myself, in my
room, a young laborer, with my dream of my Cecelia and
of what I actually found when, growing restless and weary
of dreams I went into a city street to find my Cecelia in
the flesh.   25

And what I found was the woman with the two babes,
deserted by her husband, driven to the desperate expedient
of making her living, getting food and clothes for her babes
in an old and terrible trade.

And there I was, on the dark stairs, following her   30
up into her two poor rooms, refusing to look at her, hoping
to find her rooms above also dark.

"In the darkness I can make myself believe she is
Cecelia." How much of life is like that? It is in the
movies, in the theatre, in our magazines, in our novels.

But what does it do to those of us who feed the
dream?   5

Is the dream necessary? Is there not something, in
the actuality of life, even now, in our own day, in our own
towns and cities, that is better and richer?

     x   x   x   x

When I sat down to write the tale, for which I had   10
made an outline, being in bitter need of the money it might
bring, being always, after twenty-five years of writing,
some twenty to twenty-five books published, my name up as
one of the outstanding American writers of my day, my
books translated into many languages, after all of this being   15
always in need of money, always just two jumps ahead of
the sheriff, I was determined.

"Well, I will do it. I will. I will."

For a day, two days, three, a week, I wrote dogged-
ly, with dogged determination.   20

"I will give them just what they want." I had in
mind the "don'ts." I had been told, it had been impressed
deeply upon my mind, that, above all things, to be popular,
successful, I must first of all observe the "don'ts."

"Don't make the people, of your story, do this or   25
that."

"Be careful of what you make them say."

A friend, another American writer, came to see me.
He mentioned a certain, at present, very popular woman
writer.   30

"Boy, she is cleaning up," he said.

However, it seemed that she, one who knew her

trade, was safe, occasionally slipped.

It may be that here, in telling of this incident, that
I have got the story of what happened to the woman writer
confused with many such stories I have heard.

However, it lies in my mind that the writer was mak-   5
ing, for the movies, an adaptation of a very popular novel
of a past generation.   There was a child that began eating
candy before breakfast in the morning and was reproved by
the mother.

"Put that stuff aside.   It will ruin your health. "   10

Something of that sort must have been written.   It
was unnoticed, got by.

What, and with the candy people spending millions in
advertising!   What, the suggestion that candy could ruin the
health of a child, candy called "stuff"!   15

My friend told some tale of a big damage suit, of
indignant candy manufacturers.

"Why, there must be thousands of these 'don'ts,' " I
said to myself.

"It would be better, in your story, if your people be   20
in what might be called comfortable positions in life. "

I had got that sentence from someone.   I wrote it
out, tacked it up over my desk.

And so I wrote for a week and there was a great
sickness in me.   I, who had always loved the piles of clean   25
white sheets on my desk, who had been for years obsessed
with the notion that someday, by chance, I would find myself suddenly overtaken by a passion for writing and would
find myself without paper, pencils, pens or ink so that I
was always stealing fountain pens and pencils from my   30
friends, storing them away as a squirrel stores nuts, who,
upon going for even a short trip away from home always

put into my car enough paper to write at least five long
novels, who kept bottles of ink stored in all sorts of odd
places about the house, found myself suddenly hating the
smell of ink.

There were the white sheets and I wanted to throw   5
them all out at the window.

Days of this, a week. It may have gone on for two
weeks. There were the days, something strangely gone out
of life, and there were the nights. Why, I dare say that
to those who do not write, or paint, or sculp or in any way 10
work in the arts, all of this will seem nonsense indeed.

"When it comes to that, " they will be saying, "our
own work is not always so pleasant.

"Do you think it's always a joy to be a lawyer,
wrangling over other people's ugly quarrels in courts, or   15
being a doctor, always and forever with the sick, or a factory owner, with all this new unrest among workers, or a
worker, getting nowhere, wearing your life out for the profit
of others?"

      x   x   x   x   20

"Yes, I know. I have thought of all that, " I answer.
Haven't I been also a worker? Once I even owned a factory.
Was I not for ten, fifteen years an advertising writer, in a
big Chicago advertising agency, going every day to the office,
and this even after I had written and published several books, 25
hating the place as I might have hated living in a pest house,
my books not selling--so-called literary kudos coming? My
Winesburg, Ohio was written at that time, and although it
has now become a textbook for story writers in schools and
colleges, it was, when published, two years selling the first 30
five thousand; and all the stories of the book, previously
published in the smaller literary magazines, had brought me

in a total of eighty-five dollars. It had brought me, when
published, some literary recognition but also much bitter
condemnation. Strange to think now that the stories of the
book should have been called, at the time, filth, the book
spoken of, by most of the literary critics, as a kind of   5
literary sewer, and this often by critics who, after some
ten or fifteen years, began to praise it highly, asking often
why I did not keep on writing in the same mood. "I knew,
when I first read it, that it was a great book, one of the
greatest of our times, " said a certain famous literary critic,   10
myself, although I did not remind him of it, remembering
that when I had taken the unpublished stories to him ... we
young writers were all looking up to him at the time ...
[he] had dismissed the book with a wave of his hand. "They
aren't even stories at all, " he had said. "They are nothing.   15
I advise you to throw them away. "

     x   x   x

  But, my dear reader, there is something curious
about the practise of an art. You take my own case.
There I was, as I have pointed out, after the years of writ-   20
ing, some fame got ... I had, some years before, written
a novel that had sold ... there was a publisher who suddenly decided that I was what he spoke of as "an undeveloped
property. " He plunged on me, spent money for newspaper
advertising. For a time I even saw my picture, staring   25
down at me from placards in city streetcars.
  I had got some money and had built with it a house
in the country, but when it was built I couldn't live in it
for some five years. The publisher had plunged on me but
I had played him false. The next book I sent to him was,   30
alas, a book of verse. I couldn't expect him to plunge on
that. Books, like everything else in America, are sold,

not bought, but I had myself been an advertising man.   I
knew that no amount of advertising would sell my experimental, half mystic verse.

x   x   x

So there I was, having what is called literary fame.   5
I was no longer young.   "Presently I will be old.   The pen
will fall from my hand.   It will come the time of long afternoons sitting in the sun, or under the shade of a tree.   I
will no longer want to write.   It may be that I will have my
fill of people, their problems, the tangle of life, and will   10
want only to look at sheep grazing on distant hillsides, to
watch the waters of a stream rolling over rocks, or just to
follow with my aging eyes the wandering of a country road
winding away among hills, " I thought.

"It would be better for me to turn aside, make   15
money now.   I must.   I must. "

I remembered the advice always being given me when
I was a young writer.   "Go in for it, " my friends said.   At
that time the movies had just become a gold mine for writers.   20

"Take it on for a time, " my friends were saying to
me.   "You can clean up.   Get yourself a stake.   Make
yourself secure and then, when you are quite safe, you can
go ahead.   Then you can write as you want to write. "

"It may not have been good advice then but it is   25
now, " I said to myself.   Formerly, when I was writing all
of my earlier books, I was very strong.   I could work all
day in the advertising place or in the factory I once owned.
I could go home to my rooms.   I took a cold plunge.   Always, it seemed to me, there was something that had to be   30
washed away.   When I was writing the Winesburg tales and,
later, the novel Poor White, both now to be had at a low

price, in The Modern Library, I was living in a Chicago
rooming house.

I was in the advertising place and on Saturdays we
got off at noon.   I went to my room.   I undressed.   It
seemed to me that I wanted, more than anything else in the   5
world, a great washing.   I stood naked in my room and
there was also a bathroom.   "I must wash myself.   I must
wash the floor of my room, the chair in which I am to sit,
my desk."   Sometimes I even washed the walls of the room.
There was a debauch of scrubbing.   I scrubbed myself.   10

At that time I couldn't get tired and often, after
working all day, I wrote all night.   I have never been one
who can correct, fill in, rework his stories.   I must try
and when I fail must throw away.   Some of my best stories
have been written ten or twelve times, and there is one   15
story, "Death in the Woods," a magnificent tale, one of the
most penetrating written in our times, that was ten years
getting itself written.

I had to approach and approach.   I was like a lover
patiently wooing a woman.   I wrote and threw away, wrote   20
and threw away.

"No, it is not there.   It has not yet come to life,
throw it away.   Wait.   Wait."

                    x   x   x

"But while you are waiting ...   It was all right to   25
wait and wait when you were young, when you could work
all day and write all night, but now ..."

                    x   x   x

I have spoken of the days of trying.   An odd thing
happens to a man, a writer.   Perhaps I am saying all of   30
this, not at all for those who do not write, but for the

young American writers.   Nowadays they are always coming
to me.   They write me letters.   "You are our father," they
say to me.

    "One day I picked up a book of stories of yours, or
it was one of your novels, and a great door seemed to   5
swing open for me."

    There are such sentences written to me by young
writers in letters.   Sometimes they even put such sentences
into the autobiographical novels with which almost all new
writers begin.   10

    And it is so they should begin too.   First the learn-
ing to use the experiences, the moods and hungers of your
own life and then, gradually, the reaching out into other
lives.

           x   x   x   15

    And so I am addressing here our young American
writers, the beginners, but what am I trying to say to them?

    Perhaps I am only trying to say that the struggle in
which we are engaged, in which any man or woman who
turns to any one of the arts must always be engaged, has   20
no end, that we in America have, all of us, been led into
a blind alley.   We have always before us, we keep before
us, the mythical thing we call "success," but for us, there
is, there can be, no success, but while this belief in the
mythical thing called "success" [is] running among us, al-   25
ways in the minds of others about us, we will be in danger
of inoculation by it.   I am trying to prove all of this to you
by showing here how I, a veteran now among you, for a
long time thinking myself safe from the contagion, was also
taken with the disease.   30

        x   x   x   x

And so I sat in my room, trying and trying.

I was in one of my frightened moods. Soon now my
money would all be gone. I am a man who has always had,
in the matter of finance, a line that, when crossed, I begin
to tremble. Anything above five hundred dollars in [the]   5
bank has always seemed to me riches but when my bank
account goes below that amount the fears come.

Soon I shall have but four hundred dollars, then
three, two, one. I live in the country on a farm and in the
house built by my one successful book. Bills come: so   10
many pounds of grass seed for a field, a ton of lime, a
new plow.

Great God, will I be compelled to return to the advertising agency?

I have three or four short stories in my agent's   15
hands. Once a magazine called Pictorial Review paid me
seven hundred and fifty dollars for a short story. I had
given the story the title "There She Is, She Is Taking Her
Bath, " but after the story had been got into type and illustrations made for it the editor of the magazine grew doubt-   20
ful. "We are doubtful about the title, " he wired, "Can't
you suggest another?" And I replied, saying, "Roll Your
Own, " but got from him a second wire saying that he didn't
think that title fitted the story, and in the end [he] never
published it.   25

"Will he be demanding back my seven hundred and
fifty dollars?" I asked myself, knowing nothing of my own
legal rights, but then a thought came, a very comforting
thought.

"He may demand but how can he get it?" I had   30
spent the money for an automobile, had got a new overcoat,
a new suit of clothes.

"Just let him try. What can he do? I am dust-
proof, " I muttered, but I had misjudged the man. He must
really have been a splendid fellow, and in the end and without protest and after some four or five years, he sent the
story back to me, saying nothing at all of all that money   5
given me for it. He said, if I remember correctly, that he
personally liked the story, in fact thought it splendid, a
magnificent achievement, etc., etc., also that he had always
greatly admired my work, but that the story did not really
fit into the tone of the magazine. There was in it, as I   10
now remember, a little businessman, timid and absurdly
jealous of his wife. He had got it into his head that she
was having affairs with other men and had determined to
have it out with her, but when he had worked himself up to
it and had rushed home, always fearing he would lose his   15
courage on the way, it happened that he arrived invariably
just as she was taking her bath. A man couldn't, of course,
stand outside the door of a bathroom, his wife splashing in
the tub, and through the door accuse her of unfaithfulness.

        In my story the wife was, to be sure, quite innocent;   20
as a detective he hired to watch her assured him, she was
as innocent as a little flower ... if I remember correctly
that was the expression used ... but, alas, as in so many
of my stories, there was a businessman made to appear a
little ridiculous.   25

        And I am quite sure that may be the reason that so
many of my stories have not sold. Why, I am told there
are men, and women, who receive, for a single short story,
as much as a thousand, fifteen hundred, even two thousand
dollars. I am also told that I have had a profound effect   30
upon the art of short story writing.

        "And so, what's wrong?" I, more than a hundred

times, ask myself but at last I came to a conclusion.

"You are just a little too apt, Sherwood, my boy, to
find the businessman a little ridiculous," I have told myself.

There is a man comes to the door of my house. He
is selling electric washing machines but we live in the   5
country and our house is not wired. In the evening we use
the old-fashioned coal oil lamps. We rather like them. We
live in a hill country and most of our land is covered with
trees, and trees are always dying so we burn firewood in
our cookstove and in our fireplaces. We have no electric   10
stove, no electric irons or churns, and even as I write
these sentences I can hear the thump, thump of a dasher in
a churn and know that our Ruby is on the back porch of our
house churning the milk from our cow into butter.

My wife had explained all of this to the man, a tall   15
strong-looking fellow, but he had been taught a certain patter regarding the advantages of an electric washing machine
and, having got started, could not stop. All of this in a
nearby room, and as the man talks I can, in fancy, see my
wife, certainly a patient woman ... has she not lived for   20
years with me? ... standing at the open door. She is
being very polite and even kindly and does not interrupt the
man who goes on and on. He must, he feels, even though
the making of a sale is under the circumstances impossible,
go on to the end of it, get it all off; and when at last he   25
finishes, and having been told again, for the third or fourth
time, that we have no electricity, I see him going away,
past the window of the room where I sit writing, a curious
baffled look on his face.

"What, no electricity?" he is saying to himself. He   30
stops and looks back. Our house is quite large. It is of
stone. It is a very beautiful house. My novel Dark Laugh-

ter built it for me. It built also a walled garden. It
planted flowers. It built a log cabin by a stream in which,
on ordinary occasions, I work.

"Can such a place be without electricity? It is
against the law. It is not done.   5

"There is something queer about these people. It
may be they are foreigners."

"He may even belong to an organization to advance
the teaching of Americanism. He may think me one [of the]
anarchists. Very likely he does," I think. I am amused,   10
as I so often am, by the world of business. There is a
strong-looking country boy, who should be plowing fields or
cutting down trees but who had read an advertisement.

"Be a salesman. Rise in the world," the advertisement said. It told of a young man, out in Iowa, who was   15
out of a job. He worked in a small factory in his town but
it closed. His picture is in the paper. He had just married, had gone into debt for furniture for his house and was
desperate, but he became a salesman and, at once, began
making three hundred dollars a month.   20

And so this other country boy, with a little case of
samples in his hand, is at our door. He wants to sell ex-
tracts, or perfumed toilet soap, and he also has got a
patter. He is a shy boy and does not look at my wife. He
looks at the ground, as he stands there, by the door, say-   25
ing rapidly and in a half-frightened voice the words he has
taught himself, and my wife, a sudden surge of sympathy
sweeping through her, buys a bottle of extract.

It is later discovered to be an imitation. It is vanilla. It is synthetic vanilla.   30

"Oh, the world of business!

"How wonderful!

"How wonderful!"

x   x   x

"Yes, and there is just your trouble, my boy. The
businessman, as he is represented in our fiction, as he
must be represented, is, above all things, a shrewd and   5
knowing man. It would be better to represent him as very
resolute, very courageous. He should have really what is
called 'an iron jaw.' This is to indicate resolution, courage,
determination.

"And you are to bear in mind that, earlier in life,   10
he was an athlete. He was a star football player, a triple
threat, whatever that is, or he was on the crew at Yale.

"He is older now but he has kept himself in trim.
He is like the first Roosevelt, the Teddy one. Every day
he goes to his club to box. The man who is to succeed in   15
business cannot ... keep that in mind ... let himself grow
fat. Do not ever make him fat, watery-eyed, bald. Do not
let him have a kidney complaint.

"The trouble with you," I told myself, "is just the
years you spent in business"; and I begin to remember the   20
men, hundreds of them, some of them known quite intimate-
ly, often even sensitive fellows, at bottom kindly, puzzled
as I was puzzled, always breaking out into odd confessions,
telling intimate little stories of their loves, their hopes,
their disappointments.   25

"How did I get where I am? What brought me here?

"This is something I never wanted to do. Why am I
doing it?"

Something of that sort and then also, so often, something naive, often wistful and, alas, a little ridiculous.   30

I could not shake off the fact that, in the fifteen or
twenty years during which I was in business, as advertising

writer, as manufacturer, five men among my personal acquaintances had killed themselves.

So there was tragedy too, plenty of it.

x   x   x   x

"But, my dear fellow, you must bear in mind that   5
this is a country ruled by business. Only yesterday, when
you were driving on the highway, you saw a huge sign.
'What is good for business is good for you,' the sign said.

"So there, you see, we are a great brotherhood."

x   x   x   10

All of this above, said to myself, over and over.
"Now you are below the line, the five hundred dollar line.
Keep that in mind."

There were these days, my struggle to write in a
new vein, being persistently cheerful, [to] let nothing reflect-   15
ing on the uprightness, the good intent, the underlying courage of business creep into my story.

"Above all, do not put into your story a businessman
who is by chance shy, sensitive, even neurotic, who does
occasionally ridiculous things. Even if, at bottom, the   20
fellow is quite lovable, do not do that."

"But, you see, my man is not in business. I have
made him a judge."

"But, you fool, don't you see ... my God, man, a
judge!"   25

"Is there not also a pattern, a mould, made for the
judge?"

x   x   x

And so you see me arguing, fighting with myself,
through the days, through the nights. The nights were the   30

worse.

"But can't you sleep, my dear?"

"No, my darling, I cannot sleep."

x   x   x

"But what is on your mind?"   5

You see, I cannot tell her. She would rebel. She would begin talking about a job. "We can give up this house, this farm," she would say. "You are always spending your money on it," she would add. She would call attention to the absurd notion I have that, in the end, I can   10 make our farm pay. We would get into an argument, myself pointing out that it is a dishonorable thing to live on land and not work constantly to make it more productive.

"It would be better for me to surrender everything else before my love of the land itself," I would say, and   15 this would set me off. As she is a Southern woman I would begin on the South, pointing out to her how the masters of the land and [of] the slaves of the Old South, claiming as they did an aristocratic outlook on life, had been nevertheless great land destroyers; and from that I would go on, de-   20 claring that no man could make claim to aristocracy who destroyed the land under his feet.

It is a favorite subject of mine and it gets us nowhere.

"I think I have been smoking too many cigarettes," I   25 said and she agreed with me. She spoke again, as she had so often, of her fear of the habit-forming danger of a certain drug I sometimes take; but--"You had better take one," she said.

And so I did but it did not help.   30

"But why should you be afraid?" I asked myself. Even after I had taken the drug I was wide-awake and remained so night after night.

"But, man, you will not starve." I began thinking of
my mother, who died of overwork at thirty-five, having been
the mother of five strong sons and two daughters.   Her
photograph, enlarged from an old daguerreotype and pre-   5
sented to me by my brother Karl, hangs above my desk.
She sits there ... the photograph must have been taken when
she was twenty-two ... in one of the uncomfortable chairs
that used to be in all small-town photographers' studios ...
the studio would have been in a small and stuffy room, up-   10
stairs perhaps above my father's harness shop ... this before he lost his shop and became a house painter ... and I
can in fancy see the photographer, a thin man of forty-two,
a little dirty, with stained fingers and a three-days' growth
of beard on his thin cheeks.   15

He would have been unmarried, a small-town fairy,
an unconscious one, always furtively eyeing small boys in
the street but always fighting down the impulse to entice one
of them into the dark studio.

But these are thoughts my mother would never have   20
had.   Modern knowledge of the queer tangled lines of sex
in all of her had not yet come to America.   There was no
Freud, not _____ _____.   She knew only that the photographer
was a Baptist and that he never missed the Sunday morning
preaching or the Sunday school.   25

It was an intense relief to me, during those days and
nights, when I was trying so valiantly to write the kind of
story I did not want to write, one that would bring me in a
pot of money, taking away my fear of perhaps ending my
days in the soldiers' home.   30

"You were once a soldier.   You can always go live
in the soldiers' home."   My lifelong friend John Emerson

... we were both boys in the same small town ... who was
one of the founders and the first president of The Actors'
Equity Society, who married that charming little woman
Anita Loos and went to live in Hollywood, used to tell me,
after we had both left our home town and were rooming in   5
the same house in Chicago, that I would end up in the
soldiers' home. I went off to the Spanish-American War,
and when I came back he gave me a new nickname. He
called me Swatty, explaining that a Swatty was an old soldier
sitting in the yard before a soldiers' home. "You will end   10
your days there. You have no sense of money. If you got
any you would quickly lose it, blow it in. You will sit in
the shade of a tree, in the yard before the soldiers' home.
You will be telling lies and playing checkers with other old
Swatties as you sit there, your hair and teeth gone. You   15
will make a perfect old Swatty."

                    x   x   x

     I have spoken here of my mother because I am writ-
ing of a time when the fear of coming poverty and old age
was strong on me, and her figure came back sharply into   20
my mind because she never knew anything else but poverty
and, I'm sure, was not afraid.
     "But look what you have had [that] she never had,"
I told myself. In a book of mine, A Story Teller's Story,
a really gorgeous book, one of the best that ever came out   25
of the pen I here hold in my hand, a book that flowed out of
my fingers as the water in the mountain stream before my
cabin, where my mother's picture hangs on the wall above
my desk, runs down to a river ... a book that every young
writer should read, a book that has never had the audience   30
it deserved but that will have ... in that book I told a story,
a true one, of my mother's acquiring cabbages to feed us

by a trick she played on small-town boys out throwing heads
of cabbage at doors of houses to celebrate Halloween.

"My mother was a bound girl, bound out by her
mother as a child to work in the kitchen of a farmer, having, in the agreement made in an earlier America in such   5
cases, the privilege of going to school, for a few months
each winter, in some country schoolhouse." She would have
walked there, a girl child, very pretty ... in the daguerreotype, taken later, when she was a young woman ... she
might have been eighteen rather than twenty-two when it was   10
taken ... that hangs where my eye always catches it when
I raise my eyes from my writing, she is very beautiful.

The privilege of a few months each winter at a country school, a new dress and a pair of shoes once a year.
When she was eighteen ... or could it have been at six-   15
teen? ... she would have been given a hundred dollars with
which to make her start in life.

What a comfort to think of my mother and of her
life, rather than the characters in the absurd story I was
trying to force myself to write, comparing it with my own,   20
the privileges given me she never had, so much of the
world seen, men and women of distinction met, friends
made ... who in all America had been so rich in friends as
myself? ... little surges of tenderness for her running
through me, as always when I thought of her.   25

In actuality I knew so little of her. I had always
been making up stories about her. I began doing it again.
I saw her, a girl child, being taken to the house of the
farmer where she was to serve, half a slave, half free.

"And why am I not trying to tell her story rather   30
than the one I am telling?

"But you would get into it so much that would make

it seem sad, a tragedy, and they do not want that, " I answered myself.

"But was her life, for all its years of poverty, of
hardships endured, seeing the failure in life of the man she
married, becoming, but a few years after marriage, a   5
washwoman until her death from overwork and exposure
while still so young, washing other people's dirty clothes to
feed and clothe the boys and girls that had come out of her
delicate body, was her life an unhappy one?"

It was a question I couldn't answer. I had dedicated   10
to her the book by which, if I am remembered at all once
I am dead, I will be best and with the most affection remembered, my Winesburg, Ohio.

"To my mother--

"Whose shrewd observations etc. "   15

But was she shrewd? Did she make such observations? It is entirely possible she did not. There is a
sense in which it may be said, of any imaginative writer,
that anything he says of the past, of people known in the
past, is a lie.   20

It is a lie and not a lie. As I have already said, in
an introduction to another book, it is only by the lie that we
arrive at truth.

Perhaps there is no such thing as truth. This I
know, that having, long ago, seen for the first time my   25
wife, my brothers, any friend with whom I may be at all
intimate, I never see any of these people again. Something
gets between me and them. My imagination goes to work
on them. There is, for example, a woman loved, even
tenderly and dearly loved. Today, at such and such an   30
hour, you walk into a room where she sits or stands. Or
she is walking across the room, coming toward you.

How altogether lovely. Your heart jumps. You are near to tears.

And then, in an hour, or the next day, you see the same woman and pass her unnoticing. It is with women as with paintings; their beauty comes to you only at moments, when you are prepared to receive and also when it has become alive in them. Formerly, a good many years ago, I painted, and when I had finished a painting I hung it on the wall at the foot of my bed.

I wanted to look at it when I awoke in the morning and at odd moments during the day. You see crowds of people going through picture galleries. What dumb expressions on their faces. There may be beautiful paintings in the room through which they walk. They are uncomfortable. It must be the inner feeling that there is something false in what they are doing that makes them say such stupid things. They use expressions they have read in books about painting or that they have heard others say. You want to shout at them, saying--"Go away. You are poisoning the air of this room. There may be beautiful paintings here but how can I see them while you are here?"

I will return, however, to my mother of whom, in actuality, as she died when I was young, I knew so little but of whom I have written so much. The truth is that I have seen something of my mother in every woman I have loved and in every woman of whom I have written, and could, I'm sure, still write for years, without exhausting the theme. In fancy I have seen her, a hundred times, going with her mother, who is, in my picture--some of my brothers have often told me it is false but to me it is a true picture--who are you, more than myself, to say what my mother, or my grandmother, her mother, is like?

("If you do not like my picture, make your own.   My own mother and my grandmother is my own mother and grandmother, " I have said.)

And when it comes to that, I have created for myself, out of my own thoughts, my own feelings, also my   5
brothers, all of my friends, my wife, my sons and daughters, all of the men and women I have loved in the past; all the men and women I now love are being constantly, day by day, re-created in me.

So, whether to others the picture is true or false,   10
there is my mother, a girl child, being taken by her mother, who wants to get rid of her ... my grandmother was married four times.   Let us say that my mother's father is dead and that her mother has her eye on a new husband. The girl child will be a handicap to her and so she has   15
bound her out.

My mother goes into the strange house, a little shy, rather awkward and frightened, and I see her crying with loneliness and homesickness in her bed at night.   She is to become a beautiful woman but her beauty, under the hard-   20
ness of her whole life, is to fade quickly; but I, in turn, am to live, over and over, every moment of her loneliness. I am to see and feel, in a thousand different ways, all the events of her life, the courtship of the man who became my father, her going to live with him.   I have even felt and   25
could, if challenged, describe vividly my own birth, the coming of the birth pains, the room in which my mother is lying; I can see my father running along a street in an Ohio village to fetch the doctor.   The doctor came in a buggy and I can see the buggy and the horse, a great bony grey   30
beast.

But why go on?   We story tellers, and I am writing

all of this solely for story tellers, all know, we must know,
it is the beginning of knowledge of our craft, that the unreal is more real than the real, that there is no real other
than the unreal; and I say this here, first of all, I presume,
to reestablish my own faith, badly shaken recently by an ex-   5
perience gone through, and a little, because I am a veteran
story teller, to strengthen the faith in other and younger
American men.

x   x   x   x

I remember that once, some five or ten years ago   10
... I was living in New Orleans at the time ... I had been
in the evening to the movies and had seen a picture, written
by a man of talent who had once been my friend, and having
seen it had been shocked by what seemed to me a terrible
selling out of all life; and having got out of the movie   15
theatre and into the street, I went along, growing constantly
more and more angry, so that when I got to my room I sat
down at my desk and wrote for the rest of the night, and
what I wrote was a kind of American "I ACCUSE."

I had written the words "I ACCUSE" at the head of   20
the first of a great pile of sheets on the desk before me,
and as I wrote that night, I called the roll. I made a
great list of the names of American actors, American writers, who, having had a quick and often temporary success
on the New York stage or who, having written a novel or a   25
story that had caught the popular fancy, had rushed off to
Hollywood.

There was the temptation and I knew it must be a
terrible one ... five hundred, a thousand a week.

"I will do it for a time. I will store up my money.   30

"When I have got rich I will be free."

"But, my dear fellow, you would not advise a woman,

let us say a beautiful girl of eighteen, such a girl, say, as
my own mother, who never had, during her whole life, any
money with which to buy gowns, the trappings that so enhance a woman's beauty--you would not advise her to get
these things by going on the street?   5

"And do you not understand that the complete selling
out of the imaginations of the men and women of America,
by the artists of the stage, by the artist story tellers, is
completely and wholly an acceptance of whoredom?"

I had written all of this, very bitterly, on a certain   10
night in New Orleans, naming men who had done it, many
of them my personal friends. A good many of them were
also radicals. They wanted, or thought they wanted, a new
world. They thought that a new world could be made by de-
pending on the economists ... it was a time when the whole   15
world was, seemingly, dominated by the economists. A
new world was to arise, dominated by a new class, the
proletariat. A good many of them had turned to the writing
of so-called proletariat stories. It was the fashion.

"If I go to Hollywood, write drivel there, get money   20
by it, and if I give that money to the cause?"

"But, please, what cause?"

"Why, to the overthrowing of capitalism, the making
of a new and better world."

x   x   x   25

"But, don't you see that what you are doing ... the
suffering of the world, the most bitter suffering, does not
come primarily from physical suffering. It is by the continual selling out of the imaginative lives of people that the
great suffering comes. There the most bitter harm is done." 30
I accuse.
I accuse.

I had accused my fellow artists of America, had
named names. I wrote for hours and hours, and when I had
finished writing, had poured out all of the bitterness in me
brought on by the picture I had seen, I leaned back in my
chair and laughed at myself. I tore up what I had written.   5
    "How can you accuse others when you yourself have
not been tempted?"
    Once I had gone to Hollywood, being in California,
to see a friend working in one of the great studios; and as
we walked through a hallway in one of the buildings, row   10
after row of little offices, like the offices we used to sit in,
in the advertising agency, names of writers I knew, one of
the writers came out to me.
    "And have they got you too?"
    "No," I said, "I am just looking about."   15
    "Well, they have not got you yet but they will get to
you."
    I had even written, two or three times, to agents in
New York or Hollywood.
    "Cannot you sell, to the pictures, such and such a   20
story of mine?"
    There had been no offers. I had not been tempted.
    "Let us say," I remarked to myself, that night in
New Orleans, after the outbreak of writing against others,
accusations hurled at their heads, "that you had been of-   25
fered ... let us be generous ... let us say twenty-five
thousand for the use of one of your Winesburg stories, or
for that matter for the whole series.
    "Would you have turned the offer down? If you did
such a thing everyone who knew you and who knew of your   30
constant need of money would call you a fool. Would you
do it?"

I had to admit that I did not know and so, laughing
at myself, I was compelled to tear up, to throw in the
wastebasket the thousand of words of my American "I AC-
CUSE. "

        x   x   x   5

"You were, on that night in New Orleans, asking
yourself whether you, the pure and holy one, would have the
courage to turn down an offer of twenty-five thousand just to
let someone sentimentalize one of your stories, twist the
characters of the stories about; and now here, for a few   10
hundred, because you are again near broke, because you
are beginning to fear old age, an old age perhaps of poverty,
you are at work doing the thing for which you were about to
publicly accuse others and doing it for a few hundred dollars. "   15

        x   x   x

The above thought jumping into my head at night, I
got out of bed. My house is in a little valley amid hills in
the state of Virginia, far west in Virginia, in a sweet land
of stars, softly rounded mountains and swift running mountain   20
streams; and that night, the moon shining and sending so
bright a path of light through an open door into the room
that I thought a lamp must have been left burning in a nearby room, I went to look.

I returned to the room where my wife lay, curled   25
into a little ball at the bed's edge, the light coming through
the door falling on her face.

And why had I not told her of the struggle going on
in me?

Was it because I really wanted to fight it out myself?   30
It was an old, old struggle and my life had been filled with

compromises. All of my life to do what I myself wanted to
do, not to turn aside, to go on and on with my own work,
paying little attention to criticism, had been my central
passion. During the long years--some ten, twelve, even
fifteen of them--when, after I had got a good deal of recog-   5
nition as a literary artist, my books translated into many
languages, articles and new books written about my work,
men beginning to say that I had brought new life into American story telling, I had been compelled to go on writing advertisements to get clothes, food, the right to space within   10
the four walls of a room where I could sit at a desk to
write at night.

There had been times during those years when, having been given some assignment ...

That night in the room, in the moonlight, standing at   15
the foot of the bed in which my wife lay sleeping, having
stepped into the next room to see that no lamp had been left
burning there and having returned, I thought of a certain
assignment on which I was once sent to an Illinois town.

I was to write advertisement for a certain medicine   20
to aid in the evacuation of the bowels of the constipated; and
on the particular day, having arrived in the town and having
gone to the office of the man who was growing rich by selling the medicine, I sat listening while he talked.

"There is one point I want you to emphasize. It is   25
the softness of the stools."

He had talked on and on. A small man he was with
a great nose, a small puckered mouth and a grey ashen
complexion.

"So, here I am, an artist, and I must sit listening   30
to this. I must go sit at a desk writing words about men
and women in privies. I, who am a lover of words, must

use them for this purpose. "

That day I had stood the man's talk as long as I
could and had then excused myself. He had wanted to give
me his ideas of what the advertisements should be like but
I had told him he had better not.   5

"I had better go out, walk about town and think, " I
said, and leaving his office I had walked to the edge of town
and going into a small wood had vomited.

I had, however, written the advertisements. After
all, I had sometimes thought, during those years, this ad-   10
vertising business is so filled with fakery that it is easy to
cheat. I did not have often to write of people's bowels, and
on more than one occasion, having been sent thus to some
town, to write perhaps a dozen, two dozen advertisements,
I wrote them all on the train, going to the town.   15

However, I did not show them. "Your problem is a
very serious one, " I said to the manufacturer. "I will have
to give it thought. " All during the later years of my experience as advertising writer, having already written and
published my Winesburg, Ohio, my Triumph of the Egg,   20
[my] Horses and Men and two or three novels, among them
Poor White, a novel that had been put into the Modern Library, the manufacturers I served as scribbler, having
heard or been told by some salesman from our office that I
had published books, that my stories were published in high-   25
brow magazines, there was a certain awe of me I could
take advantage of.

"I will have to give your problem thought. " Naturally
I had not shown him the advertisements already written.

"I shall have to walk about alone, go into your fac-   30
tory, wander about the streets.

"It is my way of courting sin. "

And more than once I had thus gained several days,
and when at last, a protest having come from the office ...
"You have put in time enough" ... I showed the man the advertisements written on the train coming to his town, he
was always enthusiastic.   5

"I tell you it pays to take your time," he invariably
cried, and I had gained all that time. I had quit once or
twice, thinking it would be better and healthier for me to
make my bread by physical labor, but it had not worked.
In the factories in that time I was compelled to work ten   10
hours a day, almost always on my feet all day; and when,
after such a day, I went to my room and sat at my desk,
trying to write, I fell asleep.

So I had returned to and had stayed at the advertising writing. By being frugal and careful with my money I   15
could, at least once in two years, take a few months off.
There had been a legend created about me ... it still goes
on ... that I was a particularly clever writer of advertisements; and once or twice it had been proposed to me that,
if I would let myself be what was called "staged," the im-   20
pression built up that I was an advertising genius, huge
prices being charged for my services, I could grow rich.

"But no. It is bad enough as it is. Let me remain
small, as obscure a figure as possible," I had said to myself when resisting these proposals. It had been my thought   25
all along that, if I could keep what I called "an honest
mind," helping others in the making of money by the creating of often false notions of values but all the time knowing
just what I was doing, not continually lying to myself as
most of the others about me ... and these often quite lov-   30
able men ... some of whom I liked intensely, even loved
... were constantly doing, some of them even occasionally

begging of me ... this would happen when we were in our
cups and I had broken forth, saying that we were all whores
... not to talk so.

"Don't, " they said.   "I have to go on as I am.   I
have a wife and children.   If you must think such thoughts   5
keep them to yourself. "

                    x   x   x

I was standing as I have described, at the foot of the
bed in which my wife lay sleeping.   I had told her nothing
of the new temptation that had come to me.   She was one   10
who, like my mother, would have gladly worked herself into
the grave as my mother had done, rather than that I should
be trying to do what I had been trying to do.

And what was this fear that had come upon me, the
fear of old age, an old age of poverty?   15

But you will not starve.   At the worst you will have
more than your mother ever had during her whole life.
You will wear better clothes, eat better food.   You may be
even able to retain this beautiful house a book of yours
built.   20

I stood that night by my wife's bed, having this argument with myself, the whole matter being one that will interest only other artists, realizing dimly, as I stood thus,
that the fear in me that night, of which my wife knew
nothing ... it would have shocked her profoundly to be told   25
of it ... the fear perhaps came up into me from a long line
of men and women ... I remembered that night how my
father, in his occasional sad moods ... he was, most of the
time, rather a gay dog ... used to go sit in the darkness
of our house in a street of workingmen's houses and sitting   30
in there, the rest of us grown suddenly silent, sing in a
low voice a song called "Over the Hill to the Poor-House. "

The fear in him too, perhaps, came into him from
his father and his father's father and on back and back, all
perhaps men who had lived as I had always lived--precarious-
ly.

And, if it had not happened that, twice in my life, I   5
was comparatively rich so that I could indulge a passion for
luxurious living, once for a few years when for a time I
left advertising and became a manufacturer, and again when,
on the streets of New Orleans, when I was down to my last
hundred dollars [and] I had met that strange figure among   10
American publishers, Horace Liveright, the man among
American publishers to whom justice has never been done,
a strange figure of a man, physically very handsome, often
toward certain people to whom he took a fancy ... I was
one of them ... very tender, toward others a sadist, loving   15
to hurt or humiliate them, a bold gambler, a Don Juan, who,
like all Don Juans, could not love any one woman and must
therefore have many women ...

I had found the courage to walk away from my factory,
throwing aside the opportunity before me to make much   20
money, telling myself that I was through with all idea of
moneymaking forever, and after a few years had walked into the arms of Horace.

And he had exploited me. Pages of advertising had
been taken in newspapers. I had seen my picture looking   25
down at me from placards in city streetcars.

"Why, of course your books can be sold. People in
America do not buy books. They do not buy anything.
Everything is sold to them, " he had said to me.

He had got my beautiful house for me, my mountain   30
farm. He had given me the privilege of buying paintings to
hang in my house, beautiful beds to lie in, beautiful chairs

to sit in.

It is what gets a man. In the artist there must always be this terrible contradiction. If he be an artist he is
a sensualist. If I myself had not been an artist, pouring
the vast energy buried away in me into work, I would have   5
given my life to lusts. It is only by work, by the intensity
of concentration necessary to produce any work of art having its own life, that I have escaped a life of lust.

There is this contradiction in all of us. We want
passionately the luxuries of life; the things we produce, our   10
books, paintings, statues, the songs we make, the music
we make, these are all luxuries.

We want luxuries, for who but his fellow artists can
really love the work of the artist, while at the same time
knowing, deep down in us, that, if we give way to this pas-   15
sion for the possession of beautiful things about us, getting
them by cheapening our own work, all understanding of
beauty must go out of us.

"And so, why all this silly struggle? Why this ab-
surd fear?"   20

On the night, after some weeks of trying, as I have
here described, to write a story that would be a sure seller,
that would bring in money by which I could live comfortably
another year, making the characters in my story all, at
bottom, approved people, the judge in my story such a man   25
as people think a judge is--he being a judge ... people in
my story, as had been suggested to me, all, to use the
words that had been used in describing a publisher's need,
all "in what might be described as in comfortable circumstances in life, " the people of my story constantly struggling   30
to break out of the world into which I had been trying to
force them, a struggle going on between them and me too--

after all of this and leaving the moonlit room where my wife
lay asleep ... there is something grows very close between
people who have lived long together, who have really achieved
a marriage ... as I had stood at the foot of the bed in
which my wife lay I had seen little waves of pain run across   5
her sleeping face as waves run across a lake in a wind ...

　　　After all of this I went barefooted out of my house,
clad in my pajamas ... they are of silk ... my wife insists
on buying them for me with money she herself earns ... she
is constantly, persistently buying me expensive shirts, ex-   10
pensive ties, shoes, hats, overcoats ... I speak here of
poverty, but on a hook in a closet off my sleeping room
there are dozens [of], perhaps even a hundred, ties that
have cost at least three dollars each.

　　　Absurdity and more absurdity. What children we   15
are. I went and stood by an apple tree in the orchard back
of my house and then, going around the house, climbed a
little hill where I could see the front of the house.

　　　"It is one of the most beautiful houses in all America, " I said to myself, and for a time that night I sat ab-   20
sorbed, forgetting entirely the absurd struggle that had been
going on in me for a week, for two weeks, my eye following the line of the wall rising out of the ground and then
following along the roof. "Oh, how perfect the proportion
and there is where the beauty lies. "   25

　　　Only a few of the many people who had come to visit
me had been able to realize the extreme beauty of my
achievement in building the house. It was true that there
had been an architect who had made the drawings for me
but I had not followed the drawings. For two years and   30
while the house was building, all the money made for me
by Horace Liveright going into it, myself once having to

stop building for four months while I went delivering silly
lectures to get more money, I had done no writing. It
didn't matter. A friend had once walked up the hill with
me, to sit with me on the top of a cement tank that went
down into the ground, where I sat that night in my pajamas,   5
it also being a moonlight night, and had said that my house
was as beautiful to him as a poem. "Cling to it, " he said.
"Live all the rest of your days in it. " He went on at
length, saying that the house was as beautiful as my story
"Brother Death. " He named three other stories, "The Un-   10
told Lie, " "The New Englander" and "The Man's Story. "
"It has the quality they have. "

He said that and I wriggled with pleasure, enjoying
his praise of the beauty of my house more than any praise
I had ever got from my writing.   15

x   x   x

I was on the hill alone, at night, in the moonlight,
my wife sleeping in the house below. She knew nothing of
the absurd fear of old age, trembling feet going down stair-
ways, trembling hands trying to hold the pen, through which   20
I had been passing. I had been trying to force the people
of my imaginative world into a world dictated by others, by
people who did not know my people. As I sat up above my
house that night I remembered suddenly some letters that,
a few years before, had passed between me and a certain   25
man of God.

He was a preacher--whether Methodist, Baptist or
Lutheran I have forgotten--and wrote to me from Winesburg,
Ohio.

There was then really such a town. Before writing   30
the Winesburg stories I had attempted two or three novels,
set in a mythical Winesburg, Ohio, and one day had got

from a friend a little book that listed, so he said, the
names of all of the towns of the state.

There was no Winesburg and I was delighted. As it
turned out the little book listed only towns on railroads, but
that I did not know.   5

The preacher in the real Winesburg had written a
history of the town, as I gathered a small German community, devoted I hoped to the raising of the grape, and in it
had mentioned my book. He had assured the people of the
town that I had never been there. He was quite sure I did   10
not intend to reflect on the people there. He wrote me a
letter, speaking of all this and sending me his little book,
and I was indignant. At once I sat down and wrote him a
hot letter. What did he mean by suggesting that, had I
really been in Winesburg, had I really written of the people   15
there as I had written of the people of my mythical town,
the stories would have brought shame to them? "If the
people of your real Winesburg are a third as decent as the
people of my Winesburg, you should be happy and proud."

I had said something of that sort to him for, all   20
during my life as a writer, I had not minded when some of
the critics had condemned me for my stories ... when the
Winesburg stories were published there had been a great
outcry about filthiness in me ... I had been called a filty-
minded man, but any condemnation of any of the people in   25
any of my stories I had always deeply resented.

"They are just people and the people of our imaginations are as important to us as the real people in the flesh
about us. To sell them out, as is always being done, in
the imaginative world is as low and mean a trick as to sell   30
people out in so-called real life," I had for years been saying to myself.

"And now you yourself are doing it.

"Coward!"

              x   x   x

On that night I jumped up from the tank top and
walked down the hill past my house and to a bridge over a   5
stream and stood still arguing with myself.

"But I have a right now to put money first." I began to think of a paragraph read that afternoon in an early
novel by Somerset Maugham. It was Maugham's <u>Of Human</u>
<u>Bondage</u> and I had picked up the book during the afternoon   10
and it had fallen open at a certain page.

Put in Maugham's paragraph.

Maugham had said

Well, Maugham, by his writing and by his plays,
after his <u>Of Human Bondage</u>, had got rich.   15

"He is right. I have got to begin now thinking of
money. I have got to begin making money," I had said to
myself, after reading the paragraph. I had, that afternoon
and after reading the above paragraph, put the book back
into its place on my shelves and had returned to my cabin,   20
across the road from my house and hidden away under
trees by a little creek. I had been trying to write, going
heavily and laboriously at the task, much in the half-des-
perate mood in which I formerly wrote advertisements; but,
the words refusing to flow, I had given up for the day.   25

I had, however, gone back at it. "I will. I will.
These people of my story shall behave as I wish. For
years I have been a slave to these people of my imagination
but I will be a slave no longer. For years I have served
them, and now they shall serve me." In the past, when I   30

was at my desk writing, I had often sat for hours, a kind
of quiet joy in me, unconscious of the world of reality about
me. Once I had written for ten hours, throwing the sheets
on the floor as I filled them. I had done ten thousand words
at a sitting, and had the house in which I sat that day caught   5
fire I am sure I would have known nothing of it until the
fire had burned the coat off my back. I had written my A
Story Teller's Story in such a mood, day after day passing
as in some delicious dream, and my Many Marriages ...
another terribly misunderstood book that some day--when   10
the world has again passed out of our dark age of belief that
life can be remade on a sounder and happier basis by economic professors--will come into its own.

There had been this happiness, this [joy] of the mind,
of the body, in sitting, my pen racing over page after page   15
of white paper, myself, as people about me saw and felt
me, having no existence, the self, for the time, completely
gone; but now, on that afternoon, I had sat, determined, as
it were fighting my own people, determined to make them
at last my subjects.   20

And in that mood I had covered many, many pages.
It had been bitter laborious work but I had done it. I had
on that afternoon at last understood what had been meant by
writers who told me they hated writing, that they had to
force themselves to write.   25

                    x   x   x

And now I must speak [of] something else. I have
already mentioned that my house stands by a mountain
stream.

It is a stream of sounds, and at night, ever since I   30
had completed the building of my house and had moved into
it, the stream had talked to me.

On how many nights had I lain in my bed in my
house, the doors and windows that faced the stream all open
and the sounds coming in.

The stream ran over rocks. It ran under a bridge
and somewhere I have written telling how, on dark nights,   5
the sounds change and become strangely significant.

There was the sound of the feet of children running
on the floor of the bridge. A horse galloped, soldiers
marched. I heard at night the footsteps of old friends, the
voices of women I had loved.   10

There was a crippled girl with whom, when I was a
young workman, I had once made love, in the rain, under a
bush in a city park. She had cried and I had been puzzled
as to whether her sobs had been sobs of joy because of the
exquisite pleasure I had got from her slender little body or   15
of sorrow that our joy was such a passing thing. The
crippled girl had one leg shorter than the other, and as I
had walked to her home with her, that night in the rain ...
her home being in a street of peculiarly ugly apartment
buildings, run up cheaply for the Chicago World's Fair and   20
afterwards and later occupied by employees of a Chicago
streetcar company ... the girl I had begun flirting with on
a streetcar and had later followed along a street until, after
a hesitating refusal she had let me walk with her, had told
me that her father was a streetcar conductor ...   25

I had heard the haunting sound of her feet, the curious broken rhythm on the bridge over the stream by my
house at night--the voices of Fred, of Mary, of Tom, of
Ester and a hundred others, loved and lost in what I called
my real life and, always, above these voices [and] the   30
sound of the footsteps of these, the sound also of the footsteps and the voices of those of my imaginative world.

The long slow stride of Hugh McVey. These mingled,
let us say, with the footsteps of Carl Sandburg, or Ben
Hecht. My friend John Emerson or Maurice Long walking
beside my Doctor Parcival. The naked man in the room
with his daughter in Many Marriages soft beside the foot-   5
steps of some dear one in the life I had led away from my
desk.

These sounds from the stream whispering to me,
sometimes crying out, through many nights, making nights
alive.   10

And there I was, on this other night, clad in my pajamas and standing in silence on the bridge over the stream
and there again were the sounds. The sounds crept into
me, invaded me. I heard again the sob of that crippled
girl. I heard the voices of old friends. The sounds went   15
on for a time and then, of a sudden the sounds all changed.

There were no more voices, only laughter. The
laughter began. It increased in volume. It seemed to become a roar.

"Why, the very stream is laughing at me, " I cried   20
and began to run along the country road that goes past my
house. I ran and ran. I ran until I was exhausted. I ran
up hill and down. I hurt my bare feet. I had come out of
my house wearing bedroom slippers but I had lost them. I
ran until I was out of breath, exhausted. I had hurt one   25
of my feet on a sharp stone. It bled. I am trying to set
down here the story of a real if absurd experience. I
stopped running that night at the brow of a low hill, after
all not far from my house ... a man of my age, who has
spent so much of his life at a desk, who has smoked so   30
many hundreds of thousands, it may be even millions of
cigarettes, does not run far.

I ran until I was exhausted and then, hobbling along, as once a crippled girl in Chicago had hobbled sobbing beside me in a rain-swept Chicago street I went back along the road along which I had been running and to my cabin by the creek.   5

I let myself into my cabin, and getting the manuscript on which I had been at work I took it out to a little open grassy place beside the stream, and sitting there on the grass I burned it page by page.

The burning took a long time but it was a joy. It   10
was, I knew, an absurd performance and that I was, as all such men as myself must ever be, a child, but later as you see I have wanted to write of it, to see if in words I can catch the mood of it.

"It will be a joy to other writers, other artists, to   15
know that I also, a veteran among them, am also as they are, an eternal child, " I thought.

I did all of this, as I have here set it down, going at great length as you will see, to catch the mood of it, to give it background and then, being very careful with my cut   20
foot I went back to my house and to my bed.

However, I went first to the bathroom. I put disinfectant on the cut on my foot and my wife awoke.

"What are you doing?" she asked me, speaking sleepily; and, "Oh, I just got up to go to the bathroom, " I   25
said. And so she slept again, and before again getting into bed I stood for a time looking at her asleep.

"I dare say that all men, artists and others, are, as I am, children at bottom, " I thought and wondered a little if it were true that only a few women among all the millions   30
of women got, by the pain of living with us, a little mature.

x   x   x

I was again in my bed and I thought that the voices
in the stream by my house had stopped laughing at me and
that again they talked and whispered to me; and on the next
morning, my shoe hurting my foot so that when I was out
of my wife's sight I hobbled painfully along, I went to my   5
cabin and to the black spot on the grass by the creek where
I had burned the attempt I had made to impose my own will
on the people of my imaginative world.   I began to laugh at
myself.

It had, I thought, been an absurd and silly experi-   10
ence through which I had passed, but God knows, I told myself, I may have to pass through it again, time after time.
I was, I knew as I sat down at my desk that morning, determined again not to impose myself, to let the story I was
trying to write write itself, to be again what I had always   15
been, a slave to the people of my imaginary world if they
would do it, making their own story of their own lives, my
pen merely forming the words on the paper ... I knew that
what I had been through, in such an absurd and childish
form, letting myself again be a victim to old fears, was   20
nevertheless the story of like experiences in the life of all
artists, no doubt in all time.

How to Write to a Writer

I am sure my own experience is that of all writers
who have been a long time at the trade. We are all constantly receiving letters from younger writers and from those
who aspire to become writers.   5

Young writers are wanting us to read their manuscripts. It puts a man in a difficult position. The common
practise is to write declaring that you want only a frank
honest opinion.

"Shall I go on trying or shall I quit?"   10

I received recently a letter from a young woman.
She had, she said, a passionate desire to be a writer.

However, she hadn't much time. She had to work
for a living.

"There is a young man who has taken a fancy to me   15
and I am fond of him. Naturally, he wants me to go out
with him in the evening. To do it I must give up my writing. Will you read my manuscript and tell me whether you
think my talent is great enough to risk losing him for the
sake of going on with my art?"   20

There are schoolteachers who have got an idea.
They are teaching children of eight. They give to each pu-
pil the name and address of an author.

"I am a little girl, eight years old, and you are my
favorite author. Will you write me a letter, telling me the   25
history of your life?"

A man walks up and down. He becomes profane.
He cannot well be angry with an eight-year-old child. He
would like to get his hands on that schoolteacher, box her
ears, shake her until the teeth fell out of her mouth.   30

A common practise among young writers, addressing

older ones, is to discuss his books. "Your story 'The Lost
Millionaire' is my favorite, " he says. "I think it is the
best of all your books. "

    Oh, you do, eh?

    And who, will you tell me, asked your opinion?   5

    Naturally, you are a good deal annoyed. The writer
who has written many books is in a good deal the same
position as the mother who has had many children. You
do not go to such a mother asking her which of all her
children is her favorite. You do not tell her which is your   10
favorite. At best, you see, the writer has to put up with
the professional critics. Often they are men he knows.
Aside from their work, as critics, he likes them very well.
He knows that most of them are harassed troubled men.
There are some of them, a good many, who must write of a   15
new book every day. He realizes that it is a paralysing
task. It makes him shudder to think of it but at least he
can be sympathetic ...

    But these volunteer critics!

    "I would like you to read my manuscript. I think   20
that 'Stung by a Bee' is by far the best story you ever
wrote. You are my favorite author. Recently I read a
story of yours in some magazine. I thought it rather thin.
It may be you are getting old. I was talking to a man who
said that you were about worn out. I do admire you so.   25
Please be perfectly frank with me about my own work. "

    It seems to me that most of the young writers who
write to older ones, who send them manuscripts, have no
real interest in writing. They have a great desire to be
writers. They think of the life of the writer as very ro-   30
mantic. He is a fellow who can go freely from place to
place. He does not have to ring a time clock. Nowadays

employment is hard to get.

　　And there is a great yearning for what is called
"self-expression." It is a yearning a great many women
seem to have. I had, some two or three years ago, a
letter from such a woman. She was the wife of a friend.   5

　　"I have written this story and you must read it."
It was, I thought, a rather highfalutin story. It happened
that I knew quite well the circumstances of the woman's life.
In her story, it seemed to me she had gone skyrocketing
off into space. I told her so. I rather gave her down the   10
river.

　　"So she wants frankness, an honest opinion. Well,
she shall have it."

　　Of course I lost her friendship. I had been, before,
a welcome guest in her house but that was at an end. She   15
wrote to me saying that while she appreciated my taking my
valuable time to read her story she had not expected to be
insulted. She said she hadn't realized I was so stuck on
myself. I had suggested that, if she felt she must be a
writer, she write about people she knew something about,   20
whose lives did a little touch her own experiences, and she
answered saying that she thought it impertinent of me to
pretend that I knew anything of her experiences in life.

　　"You think you know everything. You think you are
the all-wise. You make me tired," she wrote.   25

　　As a matter of fact I think it nonsense for the younger writer to send his manuscript to the older, more experienced writer. What I am after in my work you may not
be after.

　　The writer is not an editor. He is not at all anxious   30
to impose his judgment on others. I think that I am like
most other writers. I like only those critics who praise

my work. I am, like most writers, inclined to think all
others fools.

And, in any event, in the end, every writer must be
his own critic. There is something in a man that tells him
when he has hit the mark at which he aimed. This running   5
about to others, really asking them to reassure us, gets us
nowhere. If there is something in a writer's work that
really touches you, makes your own life a bit richer, even
perhaps reveals something of yourself to yourself and you
have the impulse to write thanking the man, that is some-   10
thing else. There is something fine in that. Writers are
often terribly depressed. There are long periods in the lives
of even veteran writers when all they have ever written
seems rather nonsense, when they feel themselves utter
failures; and very often during such periods a letter re-   15
ceived, that does not put the writer on the spot, does not
ask him to pass judgment on the work of another at a time
when he cannot pass judgment on his own work, that does not
ask him to suddenly become not a writer but a critic, but
that gives him in his black period a word of praise, may   20
lift him up. It may put him back on his feet when one of
his own failures has put him down for the count. It is a
very thoughtful, a very splendid thing to do for the writer
whose work has pleased you a little. It is about the only
excuse for writing to a writer you do not personally know.   25

I have got a letter from a man. He has read a
story of mine.

"Your story hit me where I live, " he says. "It gave
me something I wanted. "

The man who wrote the letter did not give an address.   30
He did not send a manuscript to be read. It was impossible
to answer his gracious letter.

"And that, " I thought, "is the way to write to a writer."

The Writer

The impulse to write must be in many people. In a
certain town a judge told me a story. There was a certain
doctor in the town, a rather small man, the judge said.
One of the sort of men, he said, you would never notice if   5
you met him in the street. He was very devoted to his profession, studied constantly, read all of the medical journals.
He had a little round bald head with a bulging forehead,
pale blue eyes, a small nose turned sharply up at the end
and a small puckered mouth. He was married and had   10
three children.

His wife and daughters were a good deal involved in
the social life of the town. They went to card parties, to
the country club, to dances, but he didn't go. He said he
was too busy. When he wasn't out seeing his patients he   15
sat in his office.

There was a drugstore in the building where he had
his offices, and in the drugstore a certain woman worked.
She was tall and handsome. She had red hair. She had
been married but her husband had died. Her name was   20
Agnes Riley.

The doctor began to write her letters although he
never mailed one of them, never gave one of them to her.

When it began he addressed her as Mrs Riley. He
spoke of having been in the drugstore about a prescription.   25
He had noticed that she had a cold. He prescribed a remedy.

Then in another letter, really in a series of letters,
he spoke to her of little happenings of his day. A Mrs
Snodgrass had been in his office.   30

"She thinks she has ulcers of the stomach but it is

all nonsense. There isn't a thing in the world wrong with
her. However, I didn't tell her so. I gave her some medicine that will do no harm. "

He spoke of other patients. He had been driving in
the country. The little man had a great love of nature.   5
Sometimes he went many miles out of his way to drive along
a certain stretch of country road. He grew bold as he
wrote. After he had written some ten or twelve of the
letters ... they grew longer and longer ... he no longer
called her Mrs Riley. He called her "Agnes, " and then   10
"dear Agnes, " and finally "my adored one. "

It was a chance for the little doctor to spill something out of himself. Often he sat in his office writing until two or three in the morning. The judge, who told me
the story, had read all of the letters.   15

He had begun after a time to speak of Agnes Riley's
hair, her eyes ... the most beautiful eyes in the world he
said ... of her figure, how straight and fine it was, of the
way she walked.

"When I see you walk it makes my heart dance with   20
joy. "

He began telling her stories of his own boyhood, of
what a trial it had been to him to be small. "I have always been homely, " he said. "When I was still a young
boy I passionately wanted the little girls in school to be at- 25
tracted to me. They never were. "

He used to dream at night that he had grown suddenly tall and handsome. He told Agnes about that. After he
began writing the letters he never went into the drugstore,
didn't dare, he said.   30

"I am afraid I will suddenly fall on my knees at
your feet, kiss the hem of your skirt. "

He knew to the minute when she went home to her
lunch, when she returned, when she came in the morning,
when she left the store at night. He could see her from
his office window.

"I was ten miles away. I was with a patient who   5
was desperately ill. I shouldn't have left but I did." He
described a desperate drive over muddy roads. "I missed
seeing you in the morning. I was fixing a farmer's broken
leg. He fell out of a haymow. I didn't think I could live
through the afternoon if I didn't see you at noon." There   10
was a little stretch of street through which she passed,
going to and from the store. "The wall of the baker blocks,
cuts you off," he wrote. As she went past the front of an
A & P grocery and a hardware store she was to him, he
said, like a young birch tree dancing in the wind. When he 15
saw her thus he thought of hummingbirds, the ruby-throated
kind, suspended above flowers in a beautiful garden. He
thought of the wind, playing in ripe yellow wheat. In one
of the letters he told her of the time when he was a medical student and went, at night, to the door of a house of ill 20
fame. He had been unable to enter. He said he began running along a street. It was raining. "I fell. I broke my
nose. That is what gives it such a funny angle."

The doctor continued writing the letters for several
years. He grew passionate. He grew reminiscent. He   25
made little sketches of his patients. He said that sometimes, when he went into his house, late at night, when he
was in a little hallway at the front of the house, he stood
for a time. "There is a light and I turn it out," he said.
"It seems to me that I can feel you coming along the hall-   30
way toward me." He said that sometimes the impression
of her presence was so real, so vivid, that he stood for a

long time trembling so that he couldn't walk to his own
room.

"My wife speaks to me.   She calls to me and I can't
answer."

"I am ashamed that I am so short," he wrote.   5
"Sometimes when you come to me thus in the darkness, you
kiss me and, oh, how delicious your lips, but I am terribly
ashamed that to kiss my lips you have to lean down."

The little doctor died.   He was killed in an accident
in his car.   It may have been when he was driving furiously   10
to get to his office, to see Agnes as she left the store to
go to her lunch.   He was on a clay road and his car skidded.
It rolled down a hill and he was killed.   The judge said that
the little man had always been kind and faithful to his wife.
He had been an indulgent father.   He had saved money.   He   15
left his family comfortably fixed.

And as for Agnes Riley, she knew nothing about it
all.   A lawyer who had charge of his estate had found the
letters and had brought them to the judge.   The judge said
that he and the lawyer spent several evenings reading them.   20

"It made us a little ashamed to do it but we did it,"
he said.   "It is strange," the judge said, "but as we read
we had, both of us, the same feeling.

"We mentioned it," he said, "after we had burned
the letters."   25

"And what did you feel?"

"We both felt," he said, "as though it had been ourselves writing the letters."

The Workman,

His Moods

I dare say that every writer has his own idiosyncrasies. For many years of my own life, as writer, I have
lived in rooming houses or in the cheaper kinds of hotels.   5
I have had to work in the same room where I slept. Often
I have breakfasted in the room, but in the morning I cannot
set to work until everything is in order. All traces of the
breakfast must be put out of sight. The bed must be made.
The life you lead in bed, alone or with another, is a dis-   10
tinct life widely separated from your daytime life. It must
be put away. During your hours in bed your imaginative
life is beyond your control. The fancy roams free. It is
up to all sorts of tricks. It may be true, as certain scientists contend, that it can teach you much, but the work   15
before you when you sit at your desk does demand some
control.

I went to the country and having a little money built
a cabin on a high hill and every morning I climbed the hill.

"Oh, what a magnificent view. " The few people who   20
climbed the hill to my cabin all went into ecstasies. "What
a place in which to work.

"You should do magnificent work up here. "

I did nothing. Day after day I climbed the hill. The
hills, going away into the distance, were like the waves of   25
a vast sea. Clouds floated across the hills. Little fragments of clouds crept down into hollows in the hills. My
eye could follow a pale-yellow dirt road that wound around
and up over hills. Horses in a distant hilltop pasture stood
silhouetted against a pale blue sky.   30

I sat on some steps before my cabin and the hours

passed. Nature, so on parade, was too much for me. Nature seemed to be mocking me, laughing at me. The hills
laughed. Trees on a nearby hill thumbed their noses at
me. I kept going back to the cabin on the hilltop. Formerly, when I first began to write, I used to tell myself that a   5
good test, for anything I had written, would be to try reading it aloud in a cornfield. I thought of going into a silent
wood, of standing under tall trees, my manuscript in my
hands, reading to the trees.

    "If I am not too much ashamed it should be a sign, "   10
I said to myself. The truth is that I had never tried the
experiment. It was one of my poetic notions.

    I am always having them. I had to give up the cabin
on the hilltop. I never wrote anything up there that I could
bear printing.   15

    I have had times of being very pagan. It has seemed
to me that formerly, when man believed in wood gods, rain
gods, in fairies dancing in the grass, in giants living in
castles hidden in mountains, life must have been richer. I
have tried to recreate these. When I have been living in   20
the country and have gone to my place of work at night ...
usually in some isolated building I have lighted candles and
carried them outdoors.

    I put the candles under two trees. I went indoors
and sat at my desk near a window. I prayed to the old   25
gods. I dare say I got a certain satisfaction out of these
fantasies but they did not help my work. There was some
difficulty. I had got together certain characters. How did
this woman, created in my imagination, affect the life of
this man? I had got lost in some maze and wanted the old   30
gods to come back and lead me out of the maze.

    I was in Reno, Nevada. I was getting a divorce

from a woman. I rented a little house in a row of many little houses. I had very little money. The woman loved another man. She wanted me to divorce her.

My surroundings were all very commonplace. There were no friends near. A part of the time I had to cook my own food, make my own bed, clean my own little house.

I began to write joyously. I forgot the woman who loved another man. Every morning I awoke singing. Often I ate no breakfast. I cleaned my house hurriedly, sat at my desk. I wrote until I was exhausted, slept, wrote again. I wrote a book called A Story Teller's Story, a very gorgeous book. It is a gay book, a laughing book. The days marched past in splendor. The rather sordid business of getting a divorce under our absurd American laws did not bother me. All during my time in that strange town I was far away from the town. It is true that occasionally I went out among people. The life about me was all a little feverish. I went on drinking parties, went to dances. Among men and women, all up to the same thing, all, for the time, rather self-conscious, all feeling themselves cut loose from the respectable associations of their former lives, there is a new recklessness. Women are being bedded with strange men, men with strange women, and I dare say, during my time there, I had opportunities too.

I was, however, incased in an armour. I was, for the time, a writer, nothing more. I was very happy, very strong, very moral.

x   x   x

I was in the country, having taken a room in the house of a certain family. There were many children. There was no place to work. There were young boys in the family.

There was a low shed that had formerly, I believe,
housed pigs. It had no doors or windows. It stood in the
midst of a cornfield.

The boys cleaned it and I helped. We shoveled dirt
from the floor until we got down to the hard clean clay. 5
We whitewashed the walls.

I moved my desk in there. I could not stand erect.
While I worked in that place ... again a madness of writing
had seized me ... the corn about me grew tall. The stacks
pushed through the open windows, through the low doorway. 10
A broad green corn leaf lay across the corner of my desk.

I wrote a book of childhood, an American childhood.
It was in that place that a certain sentence came into my
head. I thought that if, after my death, there were any who
wished to do me honor they would honor me, not for what I 15
had written but for the full rich life I have lived. I thought
I would like to be known as one man who had never saved,
never provided for the morrow, as a man who had wished
only to live in the Now.

"Life Not Death Is The Adventure," I wrote. "When 20
I am dead I wish someone would carve that sentence on a
stone and put it over my grave," I thought.

As a writer I have had endless miserable days.
Black gloom, having settled upon me, has often stayed for
days, weeks and months, and these black times have always 25
been connected with my work.

I have been too lustful. I have wanted to create
constantly, never stopping.

And then have come these rich glad times. It is, it
seems, for the writer, for any artist, impossible to create 30
the conditions, the place, the associations under the influence of which he will work best; and I remember with joy

a certain room in a tall old house in the old quarter of New
Orleans.

It was winter and there was no heat.   There was a
cheap and ugly brass bed.   I had to sit at my desk clad in
a heavy overcoat.   My feet were cold.   5

I remember a cheap hotel, in Kansas City.   Prostitutes came there.   They brought men up an elevator and
along a hallway past my door.

I was inside my room.   I was in a clean mood.   I
was working.   10

I remember places where all was prepared for me
and I did nothing.   I could not work.

I knew a poet who married a very rich woman.   She
had an artist who works in wood build a desk for him.   Oh,
how beautiful and expensive the desk at which he was to   15
sit.   How beautiful the room in which the desk sat.   He
showed it to me.

We looked into each other's eyes.   He loved the woman and she was deeply in love with him.   He knew, as I
did, that at the desk in the room he could do nothing.   He   20
could not sing, could not work, could not be joyous in that
place, at that desk.   We did not speak of the matter but
went quickly out of the room into a street.

"Well, good-bye, " I said but he did not answer.   He
turned from me and hurried away.   He could not bear my   25
knowing what he himself knew.

Notes on the Novel

A novel may be thin or fat but fatness, richness,
does not depend upon bulk. There is such a thing as richness of suggestion. The mind, the imagination, of the reader is sent off into new and unexplored fields. Or the famil-   5
iar is made more familiar. I have a notion that as a man
goes on writing novels there is a tendency to be economical,
to save. Few of us are really rich in invention. We try
to use, over and over, the same situations, put them in a
new way. We have learned to write by much writing and   10
begin to depend upon our ability to elaborate to write fine.
A certain swift movement is lost.

Let us say that a man begins writing at the age of
thirty. It is young enough. For some reason men in America, if they mature at all ... many never do ... mature   15
later in life than does the European. I have my own notion
as to the reason. We still here live in a new land and it
seems that the practise of the arts begin only after a nation,
a people, have rather spent the vigor that expresses itself
in physical accomplishment. And then too artists beget   20
artists. Once I wrote a little prose poem to Mr Theodore
Dreiser. I called it:

Heavy heavy lies over thy head.

Here is the poem:

(Copy poem)   25

It will be apparent to the young writer what I am
here trying to say. Mr Dreiser, when he began writing
his novels, must have been a very strong man. There was
in him a great reserve of nerve force, of patience, of courage. We have all heard the story of the fate of his Sister   30

<u>Carrie.</u> There must have been a period of several years
after that happened when the man stood rather stunned, unable to go on.   When a man has written of life, in another,
beautifully and tenderly and the reaction to his work is only
abuse.   When people speak of his work as brutal and ugly   5
there comes this stunned feeling.   I know all of this from
my own experience, of which I have already spoken.   There
was, for me also, a period when I was called sex-obsessed.
When almost every story I put forth was condemned as nasty.
People who read my books began to write me letters abus-   10
ing me.   Sometimes I got as many as a half dozen in one
morning's mail.

       I began to doubt myself.   There was a time when I
avoided people.   There was a kind of sickness.   I was being
pelted with filth and a stench arose from me.   15

       "There are so many saying it that it must be true, "
I began to tell myself.   I remember a particular period.
It was after the publication of my <u>Triumph of the Egg</u> and I
was living in a Chicago rooming house.

       I went into my room at night and in the darkness   20
knelt by a window and looked at the sky over the city.   Although I am far from a conventionally religious man I
prayed.

       "If I am, as so many say, unclean, make me clean. "
Sometimes I even walked crying in the streets at night.   A   25
great many of the letters coming to me were from women
and later a psychologist, Mr Trigant Burrow, then at
Johns Hopkins, told me that the letters of abuse thus sent
to me were but a perverted attempt on the part of starved
women to make love to me.   30

       If what the psychologist said was true it was some-
thing I did not want.   It is perhaps true that every man

who is by his nature an artist ... and there must be many,
many thousands of such men who never begin working in the
arts ... is also a lustful man.

He may even be a man highly sexed. He is fond of
women. He wants them. However, when he begins the   5
practise of an art he becomes absorbed. The energy, the
vitality in him makes a new channel. It flows away from
actual physical contact with women and he begins to enter
women in a new way. Balzac spoke of this. He had spent
a night with a woman. Bang went a chapter, he said.   10

There is the awakening of a new love. No woman
ever entirely absorbs the artist, and speaking for myself I
can recall that more than one woman, having known me,
having perhaps for a time been what is called "in love"
with me, has after a time begun to complain.   15

"I have been talking to you for an hour but you have
heard nothing of what I said. Outwardly you have seemed
to be giving attention to me but, all the time, you have been
far away.

"The truth is that I am nothing but dust under your   20
feet.

"You seem to me to be using me only as a way of
entry for your thoughts. Why not tell me of your thoughts?"

But how was I to tell her of my thoughts? Let us
say that the woman and I had been strolling in a city park.   25
We had been sitting together on a bench, let us say, in a
Chicago park and looking out over the lake.

People were passing up and down. There were old
men and old women, young men and women, people of the
middle age. A man's mind becomes fixed upon some one   30
figure in such a crowd or perhaps [upon] a couple.

There is a short slender man with a little black mus-

tache who is walking with a tall fair woman, and they are
speaking to each other rapidly, with a curious intensity.

You become lost in them. Your imagination goes to
work. Suddenly you are trying to reconstruct their lives.

You begin telling yourself the story of their two   5
lives. They have got suddenly into a quarrel. Yesterday
they were happy together, they loved, but now they are filled
with hatred.

Why? Why?

How can you pay attention to the woman who is sitting   10
with you? There was never a novelist lived who did not
write, in imagination, ten, a hundred novels for every one
he actually puts down in ink. He is always doing it, always
taking such flights. He is trying to select, choosing and rejecting. He may want terribly, in another mood, to win the   15
woman with whom he sits on the park bench, but when his
imagination is at work he keeps pushing her away. It needs
an extraordinary woman to forgive him, not to begin to hate
him.

But to return to the matter of sex in our novels.   20
Mr Dreiser, the man I consider the pioneer, the father of
so much later American writing, did not, as he was accused
of doing, overemphasize sex. Reread one of his earlier
novels now and you will be amazed. "Why all the fuss?
Why all of this calling of names?" you will begin asking   25
yourself. The truth is that Mr Dreiser simply put sex
back into our sexless literature. He gave sex a normal
place in the lives of the people of whom he wrote. He gave
all of our American writing a new health and I have always
believed that he, rather than Mr Sinclair Lewis, should   30
have been given the Nobel Prize. He should have been
given this recognition. He is a man who has always been

tender about life, all kinds of American life, in the poor
and in the rich, in the healthy and in the deformed, and Mr
Lewis is very seldom tender.   He has been a man too much
absorbed in himself, has done too much hating.   The first
book that established his fame was the novel Main Street.   5
If you have not read it for a long time reread it.   Then reread Sister Carrie.   In Sauk Centre there was never a base-
ball game, boys never went swimming, the circus never
came, lovers never walked in the moonlight.   It is all drab
and grey.   It is ashes.   Lewis' doctor shaking the ashes out   10
of his furnace becomes the symbol of all life.   There is no
coal, no fire, only ashes, and I have sometimes thought that
the worldwide recognition given Mr Lewis by the bestowal
of the Nobel Prize was more than half due to a desire on
the part of Europeans to see American life through Mr   15
Lewis' eyes.

And I do not mean to say that Mr Lewis has not
had his tender moments.   There are lovely spots in his
Arrowsmith, in his Babbitt.   I am speaking only of the general tone of his work.   20

x   x   x

The writing of the short story is a kind of explosion.
I think it was Mr H. G. Wells who once described the
writing of the short story by the figure of a man running to
a fire and the novel by the figure of the same man taking an   25
afternoon stroll.

But it is not as simple as that.   A man writes a
novel as he takes an afternoon stroll only in his imagination.
The actual physical feat of writing either a long or a short
novel is another matter.   30

There is his theme and he must hang on to it day
after day, month after month and often year after year.   He

must carry the theme within himself in all the changing circumstances of a life.   There will be, during the process of
the writing, birth and death.   He must perhaps move from
place to place.   He suddenly finds for himself a new woman,
begins to want her.   He is a poor man and must, in some   5
way, manage to make a living.   This applies particularly
to the young writer to whom I am addressing these remarks.
Publishers do not give young, unknown writers big advances.

    The man is constantly swept by all sorts of emotions
having nothing to do with the work in hand.   Some minor   10
character in his novel begins suddenly to run away with his
book.   He is like a general, trying to manage a vast army
during a battle.   It is not enough that he has made the
characters in his novel seem alive and real to us.   He
must think his way through their relations to each other.   15
He must orchestrate his work, give it what is called "form."
It is not for nothing that we honor the novelist above the
simple story tellers.   The novel is the real test of the man.
People are always saying there are too many people trying
to write novels but I do not think so.   I think the writing   20
of novels, when the job is sincerely undertaken, a noble occupation.   It is the giving to oneself a real challenge.

    And even when the novel does not quite come off, if
it have but few alive spots in it, there is something gained.

    There is inevitably, for the one who makes the at-   25
tempt, a good deal gained.   You cannot, even in a small
way, give yourself to the life about you in others without
gaining something for yourself; and often enough the failure,
the attempt of the young inexperienced writer who has at
least the intent of the sincere worker, is worth more than   30
all of the great successes, the slick books that slide so
easily over all of the reality of lives.

Note--On Saving Ideas

What strikes you about many writers is a certain
thinness, poverty. They speak of saving material. My
former friend, the Irishman Fred O'Brien, wrote a book
called <u>White Shadows on the South Seas</u>. He wrote another   5
book on the same theme, and then, I believe, a third. He
came to see me and we talked of it. He blamed the public.
He blamed the publishers. He spent several days with me.
He had been a newspaperman in China, in the Philippines.
He was a grand story teller. It seemed to me that, having   10
succeeded in the telling, in print, of one story, of a particular experience in an interesting and adventurous life, he
was afraid to venture further.

I was talking to another writer. He said ... "I am
asked by such and such an organization to write for them a   15
one-act play. I would like to do it. It is a worthy organization, doing good work in a good cause, but I cannot afford
to give out too freely my ideas. I must save them for my
own work."

I have heard many writers get off this sort of thing.   20
It has always shocked me. When men speak of the difficulties of telling a story truly, getting at the real meat of a
story, that is another matter; but this saving of ideas, of
so-called material, has always struck me as curiously niggardly.   25

And I think it is due to an utter misunderstanding.
Young writers are always being told that the way to learn to
write is to write and the saying is true enough, but it is
also true that the way to learn to use the imagination is to
use it.   30

It is absurd to save ideas. Throw them away. What

a man wants, what we all want, is a full rich life, to feel
more, see more, understand more. In my Winesburg series
of stories I wrote a story called "Paper Pills." It is a
story that should be read by every young writer. One of the
very poisonous things in life just now is that so many of   5
our intellectuals are clinging to ideas.

     We are to be saved by communism, or socialism, or
fascism, or by this or that. I send to my publisher a novel
and he writes me that it has "a good proletariat angle."

     What does he mean? I am not trying, when I tell   10
stories, to represent, to speak for the proletariat. To me,
as story teller, people are just people. It happened that all
of my own early life was spent among the poor. A man
gathers his sharpest impressions of life when he is young.
Most of my life I have written about small businessmen,   15
workingmen, etc., but that is accidental.

     But I was speaking of the development of the imagina-
tion. I said that what we all wanted was full rich lives. I
think it is only through the development of the imagination
that a man can be truly rich.   20

     You see several people sitting in a room. They are
engaged in conversation. Watch them. You will find most
of them eager, straining a little.

     "There is a conversation going on here and I am not
being heard."   25

     Several people begin talking at once. They are all
eager to be heard. No one listens. No one thinks [about]
what is really going on in the room.

     There are all sorts of subtile relationships, thoughts
passing back and forth, things thought, not said. People   30
are always saying one thing and meaning another. I come
with another man from such an evening spent with people.

"What a dull evening. I notice that you had very
little to say."

"A dull evening?"

I am surprised. I do not think that life is ever very
dull. I think that we dull our own imaginations by trying to   5
save our thoughts, our ideas. You cannot save thoughts,
ideas, feelings, by putting them in a savings bank. You
cannot put them out at interest. There should be a continual flow, a stream, thoughts of others flowing through you,
feelings of others flowing through you. This saving of your   10
little two-for-a-penny ideas, your feelings, only dams the
flow. Everyone knows that a man may be very rich without
a cent in his pocket. It seems to me that the real purpose
of all this writing is first of all to enrich the writer. It
isn't surely to get fame, recognition. A man should write   15
and throw away. Write and throw away again. The habit
of letting the thoughts and ideas that come to you flow
through your body, down your arm, through your hand to
the pen is a kind of housecleaning. Often enough, when
you get it out, on paper, you see how petty it is. The   20
great idea that you were clinging to, thus stopping the flow
of other ideas, amounts to nothing at all.

Note

I have seldom written a story, long or short, that I
did not have to write and rewrite.   There are single short
stories of mine that have taken me ten or twelve years to
get written.   It isn't that I have lingered over sentences,   5
being one of the sort of writers who say ... "Ah, to write
the perfect sentence. "   It is true that Gertrude Stein once
declared I was one of the few American writers who could
write a sentence.   She spoke, I think, of passionate sen-
tences.   Very well.   I am always pleased with any sort of   10
flattery.   I love it.   I eat it up.   For years I have had my
wife go over all criticisms of my work.   "I can make myself miserable enough, " I have said to her.   "I do not want
others to make me miserable about my work. "   I have
asked her to show me only the more favorable criticisms.   15
There are enough days of misery, of black gloom.

However, this has leaked through to me.   There is
the general notion, among those who make a business of
literary criticism and who have done me the honor to follow
me more or less closely in my efforts, that I am best at   20
the short story.

And I do not refer here to those who constantly come
to me saying, "Winesburg contains your best work, " and who,
when questioned, admit they have never read anything else.
I refer instead to an opinion that is no doubt sound.   25

The short story is the result of a sudden passionate
interest.   It is an idea grasped whole as one would pick
an apple in an orchard.   All of my own short stories have
been written at one sitting, many of them under strange
enough circumstances.   There are these glorious moments,   30
these pregnant hours, and I remember such hours as a man

remembers the first kiss got from a woman loved.

I was at the little town of Harrodsburg in Kentucky ... this when I was still a writer of advertisements. It was evening and I was at a railroad station--a tiny station as I remember it--and all day [I] had been writing advertisements of farm implements. A hunch had come to me and I had bought a yellow tablet of paper at a drugstore as I walked to the station. I began writing on a truck on the station platform. I stood by the truck writing. There were men standing about and they stared at me.

It did not matter. The great passion had come upon me and the men standing about, small-town men, loitering about the station, now and then walking past me ... the train must have been late but it was a summer night and the light lasted ...

There were crates of live chickens at the other end of the truck on which I rested my tablet. There is this curious absorption that at the same time permits a great awareness. You are, as you are not at other times, aware of all going on about you, of the color and shape of the clouds in the sky, of happenings along a street, of people passing, the expression of faces, clothes people wear ... all of your senses curiously awake ...

At the same time an intense concentration on the matter in hand.

Oh, that I could live all of my life so! Once I wrote a poem about a strange land few of us ever enter. I called it the land of the Now.

How rapidly they march! How the words and sentences flow, how they march!

It is strange, but now that I try to remember which of my stories I began standing by the truck at the little

railroad station at Harrodsburg, Kentucky, and ended riding
in the day coach of the train on my way to Louisville, I
remember only the station, each board of the station wall,
the places where the boards of the station wall had pulled
loose, nails pulled half out.   The tail feather of a rooster   5
stuck out of one of the crates.   Once later I made love to
a woman in the moonlight in a field.   We had gone into the
field for that purpose and she was grateful to me.   There
were some white flowers, field daisies growing in the field,
and she plucked one of them, "I am going to keep it to re-   10
member this moment, " she said.

       And so also did I pluck a feather from the tail of a
rooster at the railroad station at Harrodsburg.   I put it in
my hat.   "I will wear it for this moment, for this glorious
peep I am having into the land of the Now, " I said to my-   15
self.   I do not remember which of my stories I wrote that
evening but I remember a young girl sitting on the porch of
a house across a roadway.

       She was also wondering what I was up to.   She kept
looking across at me.   When I raised my eyes from the   20
paper on which I wrote so rapidly, she smiled at me.   The
girl ... she couldn't have been more than sixteen ... was
something of a slattern.   She had on a soiled yellow dress.
She had thick red hair.   In such moments as I am trying to
describe here the eyes see more clearly.   They see every-   25
thing.   The ears hear every little sound.   The very smell
of the roots of weeds and grasses buried down under the
earth seem to come up into your nostrils.

       The girl sitting on the porch of the house across the
road from the railroad station had heavy sleepy blue eyes.   30
She was full of sensuality.   "She would be a pushover, " I
thought.   "If I were not writing this story I could walk over

to her.

"'Come,' I could say to her. What woman could resist such a man as I am now, at this moment?" I said to
myself.

I am trying to give, in this broken way, an impres-   5
sion of a man, a writer, in one of the rich moments of his
life. I am trying to sing in these words put down here the
more glorious moments in a writer's life.

But I have gone far enough with the particular mo-
ment although I could go on for hours, describing in detail   10
a lumberyard along the street beyond the railroad station,
the features of two men standing by a pile of lumber and
talking earnestly. A thousand little details of the particular
scene could be put down.

Oh, glory, glory.   15

Oh, hail the land,,

the towns, the houses,

the people seen.

But my mind moves on to other such moments. I
was in a big business office, surrounded by many people.   20
Clerks and other fellow workers in the office where I was
employed walked up and down past my desk.

They stopped to speak to me. They gave me orders,
discussed with me the work in which I was engaged, or
rather the work in which I was presumed to be engaged.   25

I had been for days in a blue funk. I had been
drinking. "Here I am condemned day after day to write advertising. I am sick of it." I had been filled with self-
pity. No one would buy the stories I wrote. "I will have
to spend all of my life in some such place as this. I am   30
a man of talent and they will not let me practise the art I
love." I had begun hating the men and women about me,

my fellow employees. I hated my work. I had been on a
drunk. For several days I stayed half drunk.

I sat at my desk in the crowded busy place and wrote
the story "I'm a Fool." It is a very beautiful story. Can
it be possible that I am right, that the thoughts I now [am]   5
having, looking back upon the two or three hours when I
wrote thus in that crowded busy place, have any foundation
in fact? It seems to me, looking back thus on that poetical
morning, as I sat at my desk, in a long room where there
were many other desks, that a curious hush fell over the   10
place, that the men and women engaged in the writing of advertisements in the room, advertisements of patent medi-
cines, of toilet soaps, of farm tractors, that they all suddenly began to speak with lowered voices, that men passing
in and out of the room walked more softly. There was a   15
man who came to my desk to speak to me about some work
I was to do, a series of advertisements to be written, but
he did not speak. He stood before me a moment. He began speaking. He stopped. He went silently away.

   x   x   x   20

Do I just imagine all of this? Is it but a fairy tale
I am telling myself? The moments, the hours, in a writer's
life of which I am here trying to speak seem very real to
me. I am, to be sure, speaking only of the writing of
short stories. The writing of the long story, the novel, is   25
another matter. I had intended, when I began to write, to
speak of the great gulf that separates the two arts, but I
have been carried away by this remembering of the glorious
times in the life of the writer of short tales.

There was the day in New York City when I was   30
walking in a street and the passion came upon me. I have
spoken of how long it sometimes takes to really write a

story.   You have the theme.   You try and try but it does
not come off.

And then, one day, at some unexpected moment, it
comes clearly and sweetly.   It is in your brain, in your
arms, your legs, your whole body.   5

I was in a street in New York City and, as it happened, was near the apartment of a friend.

The friend was Mr Stark Young and I rang his bell.
It was in the early morning and he was going out.

"But may I sit in your place?"   10

I tried to explain to him.   "I have had a seizure."
I tried to tell him something of my story.

"There is this tale, Stark, that I have for years
been trying to write.   At the moment it seems quite clear
in my mind.   I want to write.   Give me paper and ink and   15
go away."

He did go away.   He seemed to understand.   "Here
is paper.

"And here is a bottle."

He must have left with me a bottle of whiskey for I   20
remember that as I wrote, that day, hour after hour, sitting
by a window, very conscious of everything going on in the
street below, of a little cigar store on a corner, men going
in and coming out, feeling all the time that were I not at
the moment engaged with a particular story, I could write   25
a story of any man or woman who went along the city
street, feeling half a god who knew all, felt all, saw all
... as I wrote hour after hour in Mr Young's apartment
and when my hand began to tremble from weariness I drank
from the bottle.   30

It was a long short story.   It was a story I called
"The Man's Story."   For three, four, five years I had been

trying to write it. I wrote until the bottle before me was
empty. The drink had no effect upon me until I had finished
the story.

That was in the late afternoon and I staggered to a
bed. When I had finished the story that at least one man,   5
Mr Ralph Church, now at Cornell University, a philosopher
there, a man whose mind I respected, once called the most
beautiful story he had ever read--when I had finished it I
went and threw myself on the bed. There were sheets of
my story thrown about the room. Fortunately I had num-   10
bered the pages. There were sheets under the bed in the
bedroom into which I went, blown there by a wind from the
open window by which I had been sitting, there were sheets
in Mr Young's kitchen.

I am trying, as I have said, to give an impression   15
of moments that bring glory into the life of the writer.
What nonsense to mourn that we do not grow rich, get fame.
Do we not have these moments, these hours? It is true
something is said of such times. I had started here to
speak of the relationship of the story to the novel but have   20
been carried away. I have long been wanting to write of
these moments, of these visits a writer sometimes takes
into the land of the Now.

On the particular occasion here spoken of I was on
the bed in Mr Young's apartment when, in the late after-   25
noon, he came home.

He had brought a friend with him and the two men
stood beside the bed in which I lay. It may have been that
I was pale. He may have thought that I was ill. He began
pulling at my coat. He aroused me.   30

"What has happened?" he asked; and, "I have just
written a beautiful, a significant story and now I am drunk, "

I replied.

     At least at the moment, my story, written thus,
seemed very beautiful to me. As it happens I have not reread the story for years but I have a kind of faith that
something of the half mystic wonder of my day in that apart-   5
ment still lingers in it.

COMMENTARY

The following short titles are used for the works most frequently cited in the Commentary. A Selected Bibliography is given at the end of the Commentary. When letters are quoted from the Jones and Rideout edition, that version, with spelling and punctuation standardized, is reproduced exactly, and the Jones and Rideout page number is given. When manuscripts are quoted, the Newberry Library's method of cataloging the Anderson Papers is indicated. For outgoing letters, that is, letters written by Anderson, the year of composition is given. For incoming letters, that is, letters written to Anderson, the writer and the year of composition are given. The manuscripts of Anderson's works are indicated simply by title. When Anderson's manuscripts are quoted, spelling and punctuation are standardized and errors are corrected according to the editorial practices followed in the text. When the text of the "Writer's Book" is referred to in the Commentary, only the page and line number are given. The title, "Writer's Book, " is assumed.

PRIMARY MATERIAL

Letters, ed. Jones and Rideout. Letters of Sherwood Anderson. Selected and Edited with an Introduction and Notes by Howard Mumford Jones in Association with Walter Rideout. Boston: Little, Brown and Company, 1953; New York: Kraus Reprint Company, 1969.

Letters, Newberry Library. Sherwood Anderson. Papers. Deposited in the Newberry Library, Chicago.

Memoirs, ed. Rosenfeld. Sherwood Anderson's Memoirs. [Edited by Paul Rosenfeld.] New York: Harcourt, Brace and Company, 1942.

Memoirs, ed. White. Sherwood Anderson's Memoirs. A Critical Edition. Newly Edited from the Original Manuscript by Ray Lewis White. Chapel Hill: The University of North Carolina Press, 1969.

Notebook. Sherwood Anderson's Notebook. New York: Boni and Liveright, 1926.

A Story Teller's Story, ed. White. A Story Teller's Story. A
    Critical Text. Edited with an Introduction by Ray Lewis White.
    Cleveland: The Press of Case Western Reserve University,
    1968.

Tar, ed. White. Tar: A Midwest Childhood. A Critical Text.
    Edited with an Introduction by Ray Lewis White. Cleveland:
    The Press of Case Western Reserve University, 1969.

SECONDARY MATERIAL

Fagin. Nathan Bryllion Fagin. The Phenomenon of Sherwood An-
    derson. Baltimore: The Rossi-Bryn Company, 1927.

Howe. Irving Howe. Sherwood Anderson. New York: William
    Sloane Associates, 1951.

Schevill. James Schevill. Sherwood Anderson: His Life and
    Works. Denver: University of Denver Press, 1951.

Sutton, Road to Winesburg. William A. Sutton. The Road to
    Winesburg: A Mosaic of the Imaginative Life of Sherwood An-
    derson. Metuchen, N.J.: The Scarecrow Press, Inc., 1972.

1/1-2. This page consists of a cut piece of brown wrapping paper,
ten inches wide and two to two-and-a-half inches long. The writing is in pencil in Sherwood Anderson's hand.

1/2. These have been copied. After long and careful search only
four typed pages of the "Writer's Book" have been found among
Anderson's papers. Therefore, it might be safe to assume that,
although a typed copy was made, the copy has been lost except for
two pairs of two pages each. These four pages were found in the
box marked "Journal, 1933-1940" in the Sherwood Anderson Papers
at the Newberry Library. The first two pages are typescripts of
the first four-and-a-half pages of Part II, "How to Write to a
Writer" (62/1-64/18), and the other two pages are a typescript of
the last four pages of Part V, "Notes on the Novel" (79/32-81/32).
See the notes to 62/1 and 79/32.

2/1-6. Note that the title is changed to "The Book for Writer"
and that the topics proposed are not systematically developed in the
body of the work. With one exception, however, the topics are
treated but in the manner outlined on page 3 rather than on page 2.

2/4. Trilena White. Since she is not mentioned again in the
"Writer's Book, " the question of her relationship to the successful
novelist and his contempt is the one topic listed on page 2 that is

not treated in the "Writer's Book." Trilena White was Anderson's
English teacher at Wittenberg Academy in Springfield, Ohio, during
the school year 1899-1900 when, at the age of twenty-three and
after his service in the Spanish-American War, Anderson returned
to school and received his high school diploma. Trilena White
had a powerful and lasting influence on Anderson. Schevill, p. 29,
quotes Anderson as saying: "She was the first woman who introduced me to real writers."

In his Memoirs, ed. White, p. 334, although he deliberately
confuses Wittenberg Academy with Wittenberg College because he
was ashamed that he finished high school at twenty-three, Anderson gives a clear picture of "an old friend, Miss Trilena White, a
school teacher with whom I had become acquainted when I was, for
a brief time, a student at Wittenberg College at Springfield, Ohio."
Anderson ascribes to Miss White the inspiration, or rather as he
puts it, the "challenge," behind his writing the first story he published, "The Rabbit Pen," Harper's, CXXIX (July, 1914), 207-10.
For other details about his writing "The Rabbit Pen," see the note
to 23/12-13.

A letter to Hart Crane, written from Chicago on December
3, 1919, and a letter to Mrs. Martha Keifer of Springfield, Ohio,
written on April 20, 1926 (Letters, Newberry Papers, 1919 and
1926), both speak of Trilena White and of Anderson's lasting friendship with her. Probably the last letter that Anderson wrote to
Trilena White was the one written on May 22, 1940, shortly before
her death (Letters, ed. Jones and Rideout, pp. 460-61).

3/1. A Sermon. As is explained in the Introduction, the "Memoirs" manuscript, Box 2, contains a list of "Omissions." Under
the caption "Previous Cuttings" is the heading: "Sermon--try to
get a good copy." There is no copy of anything called "Sermon"
in the "Memoirs" manuscript as it now stands, nor, to the present
editor's knowledge, in any of the Anderson Papers.

3/3-4. Written ... by a veteran. The manuscript reads: "Written p̷y̷ a̷ v̷e̷ for young American story tellers by a veteran of the
craft,..." Revisions of this kind indicate that Anderson probably
made them during the original composition, in this case as soon as
he realized that he wanted to put "by a veteran of the craft" later
in his sentence. They also might indicate that Anderson did not
reread the manuscript of the "Writer's Book" after original composition.

4/1. Prelude To A Story. This is the manuscript title of the
first and by far the longest part of the "Writer's Book." It is the
part that Paul Rosenfeld included with excessive editorial changes
under the title "The Sound of the Stream" in his edition of Sherwood Anderson's Memoirs, pp. 429-45, and reprinted in The Sherwood Anderson Reader (Boston: Houghton Mifflin Company, 1947),
pp. 356-373. The heading "Sound of the Stream (few pages)" is included under "Omissions" and "Previous Cuttings" in Box 2 of the
"Memoirs" manuscript, but nothing with this title is now in the An-

derson Papers.

Double pagination goes from page 1 to page 15 of the manuscript of Part I, "Prelude To A Story." Therefore, page 1 of the manuscript as we have it now, with two lines of title squeezed in at the top, seems to have been page 4 of something written earlier. The three missing pages, however, are now impossible to identify.

4/3. summer. The manuscript reading for this word is "sumer." Written in above Anderson's misspelling, in pencil in Mrs. Eleanor Anderson's hand, is the correction "summer." Throughout the first 80 pages of the manuscript of "Prelude To A Story," Mrs. Anderson writes in pencil above words that are misspelled or hard to decipher. See the note to 35/19, which comments on the last of these penciled words and on the slip of paper that Mrs. Anderson left with the "Writer's Book" manuscript between pages 80 and 81.

4/3-4. some years ago. The manuscript reads: "a̶ year̶ o̶r̶ t̶w̶o̶ ago." Since page 1 probably is page 4 of an earlier work, Anderson had to make this revision in order to move the time further into the past. The question of the date of composition of the "Writer's Book" is discussed in the Introduction.

4/4. my literary agent. In the 1920's Anderson's agent for his short stories was Otto Liveright, brother of Horace Liveright, his publisher from 1925 to 1933. See 26/22-24 and 51/11. Anderson wrote to Edmund Wilson from New York in August, 1922: "I have made an arrangement with Otto Liveright to handle my stories" (Letters, Newberry Papers, 1922), and to Roger Sergel from Reno in October, 1923: "If you have any short things you want to sell, I suggest you get into touch with Otto Liveright[,] 2 West 43rd St.[,] New York[.] He has done well for me as an agent" (Letters, ed. Jones and Rideout, p. 111). In 1929 Anderson entered into correspondence with the literary agent Jacques Chambrun about placing translations of his stories in foreign periodicals (Letters, Newberry Papers, 1929), and by 1937 Chambrun was handling all of Anderson's short stories. Anderson wrote to Marshall A. Best of the Viking Press in regard to the Redbook reprint of "I Want to Know Why": "Before I got your letter, I had already written to the literary agent, Jacques Chambrun, 745 Fifth Avenue, New York City, telling him to forward the Redbook check to you" (Letters, ed. Jones and Rideout, p. 383).

4/7-8. Can't you, sir, sell one of the stories to some magazine? Anderson's preoccupation with his personal financial problems and his concern over the adverse effect that financial considerations have on creative writing in America combine to form one of the main themes of the "Writer's Book." Anderson's essay "Man and His Imagination" in The Intent of the Artist, edited by Augusto Centeno (Princeton, N.J.: Princeton University Press, 1941), p. 48, asserts:

> Story telling, as we know it here in America has become
> too much the servant of the dollar. There is a constant
> corruption of the imagination always going on. The story
> teller, instead of being absorbed in human life, is made
> too much to serve, through our magazines, the radio
> etc., the purpose of selling some toothpaste or some
> hair invigorator and to do this successfully the story tell-
> er must never draw his audience too close to the strange-
> ness of life as we lead it.

4/14. that spoils the sale. An example of the kind of letter that
Anderson refers to here is the following from Otto Liveright written
on June 8, 1926. This letter also shows that Anderson was not,
as he sometimes made out to be, the helpless victim of business
machinations.

> DEATH IN THE WOODS is a fine story but one which I
> think all of the better-paying magazines will reject be-
> cause they will consider some of the relationships you
> mention as being illicit and, therefore, not pure as ivory
> soap for their readers.... What I would like to do is to
> offer it to Harper's who would, if they accept it, cancel
> one half of your one thousand indebtedness to them.
> Aside from Harper's, The Dial and American Mercury
> are the only possible magazines. Please instruct me
> immediately.
>
> I have had a long talk with [Donald] Freeman of Vanity
> Fair and am trying to get their price up. Other Vanity
> Fair contributors, including Hendrik van Loon, have told
> me what they receive and the price they offer you is far
> in excess of what they pay them. I shall let you know
> just as soon as I hear from them. (Letters, Newberry
> Papers, Incoming, Otto Liveright to Anderson, 1926.)

"Death in the Woods, " one of the acknowledged masterpieces among
Anderson's short stories (see 28/16-17 and the notes to 25/27 and
54/2), was rejected by Harper's but bought by American Mercury
for $350. It was published in September, 1926, pp. 7-13.

4/23-24. some of your earlier books, Winesburg and others. Before Anderson published Winesburg, Ohio in 1919 he had published
two novels, Windy McPherson's Son in 1916 and Marching Men in
1917, and a book of verse, Mid-American Chants, in 1918. See
the note to 23/12-13 for a list of all the books that Anderson had
published by 1938, a probable date for the composition of the "Writer's Book. "

4/25-26. for years, working in an advertising place. Having
completed his year at Wittenberg Academy, Anderson went to work
in 1900 for the Frank B. White Advertising Agency in Chicago. In
1903 the White agency merged with the Long-Critchfield agency.

Anderson worked for Long-Critchfield until 1906, when he temporarily left advertising to go into business for himself in mail-
order houses in Cleveland and Elyria, Ohio. He returned to Long-
Critchfield in 1913. He stayed with the Taylor-Critchfield-Clague
Company, as it was subsequently called, until he closed out his
last accounts in 1922. See Schevill, pp. 41 and 60; Dale Kramer,
Chicago Renaissance (New York: Appleton-Century, 1966), pp. 46-
48; and Letters, Newberry Library, 1919-1922. The most authori-
tative study of Anderson's life prior to 1913 is William Sutton's
Road to Winesburg.
        See 9/15-16 and 25/23-25, where Anderson also speaks
about his years in advertising. A letter that illuminates this period is one to Trigant Burrow (see 77/27 and its note), written from
Chicago early in 1919:

> I have had to come back to my grind here. It means
> working in an office eight hours a day at work in which
> I have no interest. Much of my energy is exhausted in
> that and in the effort to keep my outlook on life sweet
> and clear. Most of our artists give themselves up to
> protest and become in the end embittered and shrill. It
> is fortunate, however, that I have the constitution of an
> animal. I still rebound quickly and do manage to creep
> off into the world of the imagination.
> Proof is read for my next book, Winesburg, Ohio,
> and it has gone to press. I expect it will be published
> in March. The new book [Poor White], a novel, stands
> still for the present. It wants two or three weeks'
> steady writing yet and then a week or two for cutting to
> shape. I wonder how and where I am to get the time
> for that. (Letters, ed. Jones and Rideout, p. 45.)

4/26-27. our large American magazines are business ventures.
In a small book of criticism that he published in 1925, The Modern
Writer (San Francisco: The Lantern Press, Gelber, Lilienthal,
Inc.), Anderson says:

> As a natural result of the demand for standardization
> of taste and material desires came the modern magazine.
> The magazine with a circulation of a million or two mil-
> lion became not unusual. The real purpose, as everyone
> understands, was to create through advertising, a nation-
> wide demand for certain commodities. The magazines
> were business institutions run by business men with busi-
> ness ends in view. (p. 14.)
> I have tried to show you here that the popular maga-
> zines are but factories for efficient standardization of the
> minds of people for the purpose of serving the factories.
> I think they do not really pretend to be anything else.
> I am bringing no personal accusation against the fac-
> tory owner or the publishers of factory-made literature.
> They are business men and if I were a business man I

> would try to be a good one. I would try to make mon-
> ey.... Until the impulse for vast production of second-
> rate goods and the tendency to be satisfied with second-
> rate art wears itself out or people grow tired of it
> things will go on just as they are. (pp. 27-28.)

See also Memoirs, ed. White, p. 408, where Anderson says: "I
had found out that the magazines were, first of all and always,
business institutions."
     There are two indecipherable words canceled between "are"
and "business ventures." The present editor is slow to say what
canceled words are. At its best Anderson's handwriting is difficult
to decipher; it is particularly difficult under cancellations. Perhaps the second of the two canceled words was intended to be
"business," but written "buis." From this point on, no comment
will be made regarding indecipherable deletions.

5/2. stories that please people. Anderson believed, as he wrote
to his son John in the spring of 1927, "The object of art is not to
make salable pictures. It is to save yourself" (Letters, ed. Jones
and Rideout, p. 166). Nevertheless, he also had to support himself and his family by the sale of his books and stories. He wrote
to Otto Liveright on June 14, 1926: "Have just finished a short
story of a sort you should be able to sell to any magazine.
Nothing in it to scare anyone. Would like to get some real money
from this one" (Letters, Newberry Library, 1926).

5/6-7. a certain large magazine that would like to have a story
from you. "Large" or "popular" magazines that published stories
by Anderson in the 1930's and 1940's include:

> New Yorker: "Pop, " IX (May 27, 1933), 12;
>   "Off Balance, " IX (August 5, 1933), 12-14;
>   "Nice Girl, " XII (July 25, 1936), 15-17;
> Reader's Digest: "Discovery of a Father, " XXXV (Novem-
>   ber, 1939), 21-25;
> Redbook: "I Want to Know Why, " LXX (November, 1937),
>   38-41, 114 (originally published in Smart Set, LX
>   [November, 1919], 35-40);
>   "A Moonlight Walk, " LXX (December, 1937), 43-45,
>   100-104;
>   "Pastoral, " LXXIV (January, 1940), 38-39, 59 (see
>   the note to 67/1-70/28);
> Scribner's Magazine: "In a Strange Town, " LXXXVII (Janu-
>   ary, 1930), 20-25;
> Vanity Fair: "These Mountaineers, " XXXIII (January, 1930),
>   44-45, 94.

In the 1930's and '40's Anderson also published articles on litera-
ture and on social and political questions in these same magazines.
See the note to 48/25-26, where the "highbrow magazines" in which
Anderson published are listed.

5/13. This is the first occasion in which Anderson uses three or
four x's to mark a division in the text. Here the x's seem to be
used to indicate the passage of time, the time in which he worked
on the outline. As the text of the "Writer's Book" proceeds, however, the x's seem to be used arbitrarily to indicate breaks and
divisions of all kinds. Anderson frequently used three or four x's
in this manner in his writings at this time, as the manuscripts in
the Newberry Library collection of Anderson Papers show.

5/14. I had made the outline. A letter to Jacques Chambrun
written from Marion on July 2, 1938, well reflects the situation
that Anderson describes here in the "Writer's Book":

> I have your letter about the outline I made for the
> Redbook story. I am not altogether surprised. [The]
> truth is that, as it has turned out, I would have been un-
> able to deliver. I began working on the story and sud-
> denly realized that the story I wanted to write did not at
> all follow the outline I had made. I began to be inter-
> ested. What had happened is that I have been busily
> writing on the story, which I expect will turn out to be a
> novel, ever since I sent you the outline. I have already
> probably written 20 or 25 thousand words. And I, when
> your letter came, was just about to sit down and write,
> telling you the situation. The difficulty is that I am at
> present so absorbed in the story that has come out of
> the brief outline that for a long time I may not be able
> to do anything else. (Letters, ed. Jones and Rideout,
> p. 398.)

5/19-20. I will dash off this story. In "The Writer's Trade, " in
Hello Towns! (New York: Horace Liveright Publishing Inc.,
1929), a book that is a compilation of articles written for his two
weekly newspapers, Smyth County News and Marion Democrat, Anderson says:

> Writing is both a trade and an art. Ordinary writing,
> such as the writing of articles, newspaper stories, etc.,
> has little to do with art. I can see no reason why it
> should not be an honorable trade.
>   I see no reason why it should not be a fair trade to
> write clever plot stories for magazines. I am always
> wishing I could do it. (p. 321.)

5/21. friend had come to me one evening. The manuscript reads:
"friend had come to one^(to me) evening. to my house. " This revision
makes the interview more personal--"come to me" replacing "come
to my house"--and makes this sentence more in keeping with the
following sentence: "He is a man to whom I am deeply attached. "

5/25-26. when I got to his town there was a sudden illness. The manuscript reads: "when I got ~~there~~ to his town there was a sudden illness." This is the kind of revision that would seem to indicate that Anderson corrected his manuscript only during original composition. As Anderson was in the process of writing this sentence, he realized that the first "there" was awkward and repetitious.

5/32-6/1. <u>in a tense excited mood</u>. The manuscript reads: "in ~~an~~ ^a ^{tense}excited ~~tense~~ mood." The revision from "an excited tense mood" to "a tense excited mood" shows Anderson's concern with the rhythm of his sentences. Placing the monosyllabic adjective "tense" before the trisyllabic adjective "excited" gives a rhythm that suggests excitement. See 15/20-21 and its note for a discussion of Anderson's style.

6/6. This is the second occasion (see the note to 5/13) in which Anderson uses three <u>x's</u>, and again he uses them to indicate the passage of time. The <u>x's</u> are not used, however, to indicate that Anderson is going back to the principal "time" of the story, that is, to the "time" in which the agent is urging him to write a salable story. A more conventional use of the <u>x's</u> would be, perhaps, to use them for this purpose. For example, the next time they are used (7/1) they again indicate passage of time within the episode of the friend's telling Anderson his story; if they had been used two lines later, they would have indicated the movement back to the original fictive present, a movement back to the main story.

6/15. <u>He is a scientist</u>. Several inconsistencies in the manuscript of the "Writer's Book" indicate that it probably was not worked over by Anderson. One example is the "experimental scientist" and "experimental scientist, working for a large manufacturing company" of 6/16 and 21-22 who turns into a judge in 21/19. He remains consistently, however, a judge for the remainder of the story.

6/19-20. <u>covering the trail for my friend</u>. Since, as he frequently admits, Anderson could not or would not separate fact from fancy, he constantly writes of his friends while at the same time "covering the trail." See <u>Memoirs</u>, ed. White, pp. 278-81, where Anderson recounts the influence of a man he knew in Elyria, Ohio. "It was this man, whose name was Luther Pawsey (he is dead now so I may write of him with ease, and besides Luther Pawsey was not his name), with whom I began spending a good many hours together" (p. 280). Anderson says it was he "who first suggested to my mind the idea of being a writer" (p. 279). Sutton, <u>Road to Winesburg</u>, pp. 177-78, claims that Luther Pawsey was the name given to Perry S. Williams, Anderson's best friend in Elyria, although Pawsey differs from Williams in one important respect. When they were together in Elyria, Williams was surprised to discover that Anderson had aspirations to be a writer.

6/26. <u>certain so-called sordid touches</u>. Note Anderson's ironic overuse of the word "sordid" here and in 7/10-11, where he says he should not "remind readers of certain sordid moments, " and in 22/17-18, where he says he should not "bring into my story any of the rather sordid details, happenings. "

7/1. The three x's, if they had been held until after the next sentence--"My friend did unload his story, getting a certain relief, and I went home"--would have indicated a more definite division in the organization of the story. Anderson, however, uses these x's arbitrarily to indicate all kinds of divisions and breaks in the thought of the narrative. See the notes to 5/13 and 6/6. Therefore, subsequent use of the x's will be allowed to pass without comment.

7/9. There must not be anything unpleasant. The manuscript reads: "There must not be anything too unpleasant. " Note how the revision makes the thought stronger, implying that anything unpleasant would not sell.

7/10-11. certain sordid moments. See "An Apology for Crudity" in Sherwood Anderson's Notebook:

> To me it seems that as writers we shall have to throw
> ourselves with greater daring into life. We shall have
> to begin to write out of the people and not for the people.
> We shall have to find within ourselves a little of that
> courage. To continue along the road we are traveling
> is unthinkable. To draw ourselves apart, to live in little
> groups and console ourselves with the thought that we
> are achieving intellectuality is to get nowhere. By such
> a road we can hope only to go on producing a literature
> that has nothing to do with life as it is lived in these
> United States. (pp. 197-98.)

7/14. Shakespeare. Both William A. Sutton's monograph Exit to Elsinore and his Road to Winesburg give the text of Anderson's "Amnesia Letter, " written while he was wandering about in a state of nervous exhaustion for four days in 1912. See the note to 51/19, where this letter is discussed in the context of Anderson's dramatic departure from his paint factory in Elyria in 1912. In the "Amnesia Letter" Anderson uses the expression "to Elsinore" as a veritable refrain. Sutton comments:

> Anderson had a strong interest in Shakespeare and other
> highly-acclaimed writers. The symbol of Elsinore in the
> "amnesia letter" indicated more knowledge of literature
> than Anderson, who protected himself by claiming to be
> uneducated, normally would admit. (Road to Winesburg,
> p. 192.)

Mrs. Eleanor Anderson, in an interview with the editor at the Newberry Library on June 5, 1969, corroborated the fact that An-

derson had a deep and abiding love for Shakespeare. She said that
one of the books that he always took on trips, no matter how short,
was an edition of Shakespeare's sonnets.

7/16-17. you must not touch certain secret, often dark, little recesses. See The Modern Writer, p. 21, where Anderson says:
"To actually touch people's lives is the unforgivable sin. Both
thinking and feeling are dangerous exercises, and besides people
do not like them." See also "Man and His Imagination," p. 46,
where, in speaking of the publishers and editors who came to his
Chicago advertising agency to get stories written as if they were
ordering automobiles, he says: "Life was not to be touched too
closely, to disturb people or make them think. People did not
like being made to think, or to be disturbed." Despite the quotation cited in the note to 7/10-11, these two quotations, along with
the fact of Anderson's abiding love for Shakespeare, show that his
anti-intellectualism was, at times, a pose.

7/21-22. a certain dramatic force into your story. "Practical
handbooks" on how to write short stories proliferated in Anderson's
time. Many of the authors misunderstood the first critic of the
short story, Edgar Allan Poe, when in his criticism of Hawthorne's
Twice-Told Tales ("Hawthorne's 'Tales,'" Graham's Magazine,
May, 1842; reprinted in The Works of Edgar Allan Poe, ed. by
Edmund Clarence Stedman and George Edward Woodberry, VII
[Chicago: Stone and Kimball, 1895], pp. 30-31), he praised the
dramatic qualities of the short story because of its similarity, not
to the drama, but to the lyric poem. Consequently, the authors of
these handbooks insisted on imposing on the short story dramatic
"rules" supposedly deduced from the teachings of Aristotle. A
list of these handbooks would include:

> Harry T. Baker, The Contemporary Short Story: A Practi-
> cal Manual (Boston: D. C. Heath and Company, 1916);

> J. Berg Essenwein, The Art of Story-Writing (Springfield,
> Mass.: The Home Correspondence School, 1913);

> _____, Studying the Short-Story: Sixteen Short-Story
> Classics with Introduction, Notes and a New Labora-
> tory Study Method for Individual Reading and Use in
> Colleges and Schools (Springfield, Mass.: The Home
> Correspondence School, 1912);

> _____, Writing the Short-Story: A Practical Handbook
> on the Rise, Structure, Writing and Sale of the Modern
> Short-Story (New York: Hinds, Hayden and Eldredge,
> Inc., 1924);

> F. M. Perry, Story-Writing: Lessons from the Masters
> (New York: Henry Holt and Company, 1926);

Henry Albert Phillips, Art in Short Story Narration: A
   Searching Analysis of the Qualifications of Fiction in
   General, and of the Short Story in Particular, with
   Copious Examples, Making the Work a Practical Trea-
   tise (Larchmont, N.Y.: The Stanhope-Dodge Publish-
   ing Company, 1913);

_____, The Plot of the Short Story: An Exhaustive Study,
   Both Synthetical and Analytical, with Copious Examples,
   Making the Work a Practical Treatise (Larchmont,
   N.Y.: The Stanhope-Dodge Publishing Company, 1912);

Walter B. Pitkin, The Art and the Business of Story Writing (New York: The Macmillan Company, 1912);

Blanche Colton Williams, Short Story Writing: Reading with
   a Purpose, No. 64 (Chicago: American Library Association, 1930).

7/24-25. story I am about to write, was, as he talked, simply
broken. The manuscript reads: "story I am about to write here,
was, as he talked that night, simple broken." This revision is a
good example of a revision probably made during original composition. Anderson canceled "here" and the second "that night," realizing that this expression had already been used in the sentence
(7/23), but he failed to notice that he wrote "simple" for "simply."

7/26-27. and cried, and I went to him. The manuscript reads:
             cried
"and wept, and I went to him." One wonders why Anderson canceled "wept" and substituted "cried." "Weep" is from the Old
English "wēpan," "to shed tears"; "cry" is from the Old French
"crier," which in turn is from the Latin "quiritare," "to cry for
help (from a citizen)." (See Webster's Third New International
Dictionary of the English Language Unabridged, 1961.) Perhaps
Anderson wanted the word that suggested both weeping and crying
out for help.

8/7-8. a little startle, without too much shocking, your reader.
See also "Notes on Standardization" in the Notebook, p. 145:

   A magazine having a circulation of a million is in a
   rather ticklish position when it comes to handling any
   such matter as honest reactions to life. There are so
   many things the editors of all such magazines have to be
   careful about. All such basic human attributes as sex
   hungers, greed and the sometimes twisted and strangely
   perverted desires for beauty in human beings have to be
   let alone. The basic stuff of human life that all real
   artists, working in the medium of prose, have handled
   all through the history of writing has to be thrown aside.
   The writer is perpetually called upon to seem to be doing
   something while doing nothing at all. There is the per-

petual tragedy of unfulfilment.

8/12. I began to write, but alas! In a letter to the young painter
Charles Bockler on November 26, 1930, Anderson wrote:

> My situation is a bit absurd.
> This winter I have had opportunity to make perhaps
> $3,000 by doing articles for popular magazines, but
> couldn't do them. It seems to me that I will have to
> find a way other than writing to make my living. (Let-
> ters, Newberry Library, 1930.)

There is a similar statement in a letter to his friend Ferdinand
Schevill, Professor of History at the University of Chicago, written
about the same time:

> This winter I have had opportunity to make three or four
> thousand dollars, but can't make any of it. I'm becom-
> ing a nut. When I am offered money for anything, it be-
> comes spoiled for me. It doesn't matter so much, as I
> spend little.
> I've about concluded that it is wrong for me to go on
> thinking of myself as an artist at all. I can't be pro-
> fessional, it seems. On the other hand, I can't quite go
> to work at some commercial thing. (Letters, ed. Jones
> and Rideout, p. 229.)

8/20-21. a new man, coming to life, here, on this paper. In
"Man and His Imagination, " pp. 55-57, when speaking of his novel
Kit Brandon (New York: Charles Scribner's Sons, 1936), Anderson tells about a woman rum-runner he met while covering a smug-
gling trial in Virginia. As he started work on his novel, he
changed the woman completely into Kit Brandon, or rather, the
woman rum-runner disappeared and Kit Brandon came into being:

> What I am trying to say is that the new woman, the
> central figure, in my story no longer lived in the reality
> of her own life, but that she had a new life in this
> imaginative world. This is a matter that is a little dif-
> ficult sometimes to make people understand who are not
> writers. A book or story that comes alive, that really
> has form and substance, has its own life and it is right
> here that violence is so often done to the art of writing.
> (p. 57.)

8/25. a certain morality involved. In two letters, both written
from Marion, Virginia, but written ten years apart, Anderson
speaks about the morality involved in art. In the spring of 1929
he wrote to Dwight Macdonald, then a writer for Time, later an
editor of Partisan Review:

> When I saw you in New York, I said a little to you
> about the artist's life. I would like to see artists in

America become a bit more class-conscious. I would
like to see them become men of pride in their bearing.
I would like to see them quit kneeling down before
money and middle-class moral standards.
There must come someday real morality here. Towns
must be comprehended, lives, fields, rivers, mountains,
cities.
Everything is to be comprehended. Life here is loose,
unmoral, meaningless. (Letters, ed. Jones and Rideout,
pp. 192-93.)

On August 9, 1939, Anderson wrote to Carrow De Vries, poet and
short story writer:

Have you not often read a story where a character has
been made by the storyteller to do something you knew
the character could not do? We call it bad art. It is
more than that. It is a display of immorality.
What is needed among so-called artists is moral men
who will not do this violence to people in their imagined
world. That is what the world is seeking, a morality.
To my mind the place to find it is in an attitude, first
of all, to this imagined life. (Letters, ed. Jones and
Rideout, p. 446.)

See the notes to 44/28-29 and 55/29-30, which explain Anderson's
attitude toward "this imagined life."
One of Anderson's clearest statements about morality in art
is in a letter written to Norman Holmes Pearson in the fall of
1937. This letter, which links morality in art with form, is
quoted in the note to 81/16, which documents Anderson's attitude
towards form.

8/30. window. After this word Anderson canceled the rest of
page 15 of his manuscript. The canceled portion is given in the
Textual Apparatus. Page 15 also marks the end of the double
pagination of the manuscript (see the note to 4/1). It is hard to
determine why Anderson made this long cancellation. Most likely
it marks a new direction given to the manuscript. The original
manuscript could have had more pages describing the author's and
agent's visit to the bar, but with this cancellation Anderson turns
back to the story about his trying to write a salable short story
for a magazine.

9/7-8. comfortable circumstances. Two similar passages are:
"It would be better, in your story, if your people be in what might
be called comfortable positions in life" (24/20-21); "in what might
be described as in comfortable circumstances in life" (52/29-30).
In 52/28 the admonition about "comfortable circumstances" is called
"a publisher's need."

9/9. it should not be too gloomy. See 39/30-40/1, where Anderson asks himself why he does not tell his mother's story "rather

than the one I am telling." Then he answers, "But you would get
into it so much that would make it seem sad, a tragedy, and they
do not want that."

9/10-11. we do not wish, in any way, to dictate to you. One of
the stylistic devices Anderson uses throughout the "Writer's Book"
is irony. Much of the irony of this passage comes from the fact
that all of his life, and even after his death, Anderson had to contend with the over-editing of those who prepared his texts for publication. A case in point is Rosenfeld's editing of the Memoirs.
Rosenfeld jumps back and forth in Anderson's manuscript in order
to piece together the passage from Part I that he prints on pp.
431-33. Furthermore, after 9/10 he cuts twenty-eight pages of
the manuscript, that is, pp. 9/11 to 21/20 of the present edition.
It is as if Rosenfeld were dictating what Anderson should and should
not include in his text.

In regard to the question of the way business dictates to the
writer, see an article called "Why Men Write," published in Story,
VIII (January, 1936), 2-4, 103, 105:

> A good many do it for money. It seems such an easy
> way. It isn't so easy. I have never yet known one of
> our commercial writers who was very happy. There are
> too many concessions to be made. The businessmen who
> employ us are very stupid about it. They are arrogant.
> They make the most absurd demands and suggestions.
> (Typescript version, Newberry Library, p. 1.)

9/15-16. a writer of advertisements, in an advertising agency.
See 4/25-26 and 25/23-24 and their notes.

9/17-18. through boyhood and into my young manhood, in a very
poor family. Throughout Road to Winesburg Sutton maintains that
the Anderson family, although certainly in modest financial circumstances, did not live in extreme poverty. See especially pages 18-
20 and 502-505.

9/19-20. I dreamed of getting rich, or at least well-to-do, of
living in a big house. For a time this dream came true. In
Memoirs, ed. White, when speaking of the time he left his Chicago
advertising agency for his own business in Cleveland and later in
Elyria, he says:

> I had returned to Ohio where my youth had been spent.
> As a boy in a neighboring Ohio town I had been half a
> young hustler. Because of my eager hunger for jobs I
> had been called "Jobby Anderson." (p. 240.)

> I had got into the position described, the money begin-
> ning to roll in, my house on a good enough street. I
> would have a bigger and a finer house in a few years.
> (p. 241.)

Later, when Anderson left Elyria in 1913, he repudiated both the
dream and the reality.

9/22-23.   working as a laborer, had been a farm laborer, a factory hand.   There is a similar sentence in Memoirs, ed. White,
p. 198:   "I had been a laborer, a farm hand, a soldier, a factory
hand. "
        In regard to his farming experiences, in a letter to David
Karsner, in response to Karsner's request for information for his
article "Sherwood Anderson, Mid-West Mystic, " New York Herald
Tribune, Magazine Section, May 16, 1926, Anderson speaks of his
early jobs: "I sold newspapers, worked in the fields of nearby
farmers, went about to fairs with race horses, went with a threshing crew to thresh grain in the wheat harvest, worked in the cabbage and corn fields" (Letters, Newberry Library, April 5, 1926).
We know from Sutton's Road to Winesburg, p. 88, that during the
summer of 1899, after his return from the Spanish-American War
and before he entered Wittenberg Academy, Anderson worked on a
threshing rig on the farm of Wallace Ballard, a good friend of his
brother Karl.
        Anderson's experiences as a factory hand were more num-
erous and are easier to verify.   Sutton, Road to Winesburg, pp. 34-
35, speaking about the minimal industrialization of Clyde in the
late nineteenth century, attests to the fact that Anderson worked in
its bicycle factory.   In A Story Teller's Story, ed. White, Anderson speaks about working in the bicycle factory in Clyde (p. 148),
of working in a sheet-iron warehouse before he came to Chicago
(p. 100), and of later working in a Chicago warehouse (p. 156).
Appendix I of White's edition of A Story Teller's Story prints for
the first time "Sherwood Anderson's Earliest Autobiography, " a
publicity essay written in 1918.   In this essay, although he makes
himself much younger than he was and says that he worked more
years than he did, Anderson conveys the essential truth of his life
as a factory laborer in Chicago:

            When I was sixteen or seventeen years old, I came to
        the city of Chicago [actually he was eighteen or nineteen]
        and there made the most serious mistake of my life.
        For four or five years, I worked as a common laborer
        and got myself caught in that vicious circle of things
        where a man cannot swagger before his fellows, is too
        tired to think, and too pitifully ashamed of his appearance
        to push out into the world.   (p. 346.)

See also 12/30-31 and 15/8, where Anderson speaks about working
in a cold-storage warehouse.

9/23-24.   in little rooms, often in cheerless enough streets.
Throughout the early section of Part I Anderson is preoccupied with
the memory of living in rooming houses during his early years in
Chicago.   He mentions it in 11/1 and 20, 12/31-32, 13/31, 14/23,
17/5, 20/22, and 28/4.   See also 14/12-14, where he speaks
about writing Winesburg, Ohio in a rooming house, and 77/18-19,

where he says he lived in a rooming house after he published The
Triumph of the Egg. Documentation for the rooming house referred
to here (9/23-24) is given in the note to 38/5-6, where Anderson
speaks of living with John Emerson.

9/26-27. I see myself in a room in a house in a street in a factory town. Two other times in the early pages of the "Writer's
Book" Anderson writes sentences with a series of prepositional
phrases strung together. See the sentence near the end of this
same paragraph: "Like my man of the story of certain phases of
a human life I have here written" (10/2-3), and the sentence at
15/19-21: "... sharp as an etching, in the mind of a young man
sitting in a window in a room in a rooming house. " See also the
note to 15/20-21 on Anderson's style.

9/28-29. I have got, at a second-hand furniture store, an old
kitchen table. In A Story Teller's Story, ed. White, when speaking of living in cheap houses on side streets in Chicago, Anderson
says: "At a second-hand furniture store nearby you procure a
second-hand kitchen table and a cot and on the cot, when you are
not sleeping on it, you put a red Indian blanket" (p. 293). This
passage is in a section that is bracketed, indicating that Anderson,
or the editor or publisher, deleted the passage before the original
publication by Huebsch in 1924.

10/1. this passion for writing. Since Anderson places this writing in the "years of my early young manhood working as a laborer"
(9/21-22), he is referring to writing done before his two columns,
"Rot and Reason, " 1903, and "Business Types, " 1904, appeared in
the Long-Critchfield Advertising Agency's house organ Agricultural
Advertising, and before he wrote two articles which appeared in
The Reader, a Bobbs-Merrill periodical, "A Business Man's Reading, " October, 1903, and "The Man and the Book, " December,
1903. In A Story Teller's Story, ed. White, when speaking of a
time about two years after his mother's death--she died in 1895
when he was eighteen years old--Anderson says:

> It must have been about this time that my own imagi-
> native life began to take form. Having listened to the
> tales told by my father, I wanted to begin inventing tales
> of my own. At that time and for long years afterwards,
> there was no notion of writing. Did I want an audience,
> someone to hear me tell my tales? It is likely I did.
> There is something of the actor in me.
>   When later I began to write I for a time told myself
> I would never publish and I remember that I went about
> thinking of myself as a kind of heroic figure, a silent
> man creeping into little rooms, writing marvelous tales,
> poems, novels--that would never be published.
>   Perhaps it never went quite that far. They would have
> to be published sometime. My vanity demanded that.
> (pp. 71-72.)

In "Man and His Imagination" Anderson says:

> The first thing I ever wrote was a long book, of some
> several hundred pages, under the title, Why I Am a So-
> cialist. I must have written the book when I was seven-
> teen or eighteen years old. I had come upon the idea of
> socialism, the co-operative commonwealth, and, like
> most young men, having got the idea, I had, temporarily,
> the impression that I was the first man in the world it
> had ever come to. I wanted to explain it to all the world.
> I wrote and wrote feverishly. I do not know what ever
> became of the book. It got lost. Perhaps later I threw
> it into the fire. (p. 60.)

No copy of "Why I Am a Socialist" has ever been discovered. In
Memoirs, ed. White, p. 293, Anderson speaks of writing "Why I
Am a Socialist" at a much later date, when he was in business in
Elyria. He also speaks about writing and publishing a magazine,
called Commercial Democracy, during that same period. In regard
to Anderson's views on socialism, see the notes to 44/13-14 and
83/7-8; in regard to writing "Why I Am a Socialist" and Commercial Democracy, see the note to 51/7-8.

10/2-4. Like my man ... I took it out in writing letters. Anderson now turns his attention back to the friend who spoke to him in
the moonlit field, the man of 7/23-25 who is "simply broken" as
he tells the story of his secret love, the friend of 8/17-19 who
disappears so that the "new man" of 8/20 can take his place. But
Anderson seems to forget that he has not mentioned anything about
the friend's writing letters to his beloved. The fact of the letter
writing, however, links Part I to Part III, "The Writer." "The
Writer" relates a story that a judge (Anderson's scientist friend
here in Part I turns into a judge at 21/19) told him about a doctor
writing secret letters that he never sent to a woman named Agnes
Riley. See the note to 67/1-70/28.

10/11-12. It was not difficult for me to evoke the figure of Cecelia. Judging from the letters collected at Newberry Library,
certainly only a portion of Anderson's correspondence, Anderson
was a voluminous letter writer. In a letter to Marietta Finley,
later Mrs. Vernon Hahn, dated December 11, 1916, when Anderson speaks of "all this writing, " he is referring no doubt, in addition to his letters, to writing novels and stories. In the winter of
1916 he was writing the Winesburg stories:

> I am trying with all my might to be and remain a
> lover. All this writing is addressed to my beloved.
> I am writing these snatches of things to women, to all
> women, to one woman. I am telling her of my life, of
> a man actively engaged in the grim wrestle of modern in-
> dustrial life.
> The wrestler is myself. I tug and pull at my oppo-
> nent, Reality. Sweat rolls from me. Occasionally I cry

out with pain.
          My woman is made up of all the women in the world.
     She is no longer young nor is she old.   She is beautiful.
     You have something of that woman in you.   All women
     have.   (Letters, Newberry Library, Reserved Box 7:
     Mrs. Hahn's Letters from Anderson, 1916.)

10/13-14.   I was compelled to live always in some poorer section
of the town.   See A Story Teller's Story, ed. White, p. 154: "As
I was destined to live most of my life and do most of my work in
factory towns and in little ill-smelling, hideously furnished rooms,
freezing cold in winter and hot and cheerless in summer...."   Although Anderson certainly is exaggerating when he says: "live
most of my life and do most of my work," he did live in this kind
of surroundings when he first came to Chicago, probably around
1896, and until he enlisted in the Spanish-American War in 1898.
Again when he returned to Chicago after his year at Wittenberg
Academy and until his marriage to Cornelia Lane in 1904, he may
have lived in conditions similar to those described here in the
"Writer's Book."

10/25-26.   from a freight train, on which I was once bumming my
way to a new town.   See A Story Teller's Story, ed. White, p.
243: "One night, years before, when I was a young laborer and
was beating my way westward on a freight train, a brakeman had
succeeded in throwing me off the train in an Indiana town."

10/31-32.   hours of sleepless loneliness that sometimes came at
night.   The theme of loneliness is one that preoccupied Anderson
throughout his life.   In "Man and His Imagination," p. 47, he
says: "It is my belief that we Americans are, in spite of our
great achievements, an essentially lonely people, and this may be
true because we were, in the beginning, a transplanted people."
In the "Writer's Book" he explicitly mentions sharing his mother's
loneliness at 42/18-22, and he mentions the Winesburg story
"Loneliness" at 14/20.   Furthermore, the loneliness of the writer
striving to preserve his artistic integrity is a main theme per-
vading the whole of the "Writer's Book."   One of Anderson's greatest contributions to American literature is his portrayal of the
hidden beauty of the lives of the lonely, inarticulate, and frustrated.
One of the most beautiful expressions of this theme, as well as one
of Anderson's explanations of his theory of the "grotesque," is
found in the Winesburg story "Paper Pills--concerning Doctor
Reefy."   See 83/2-4 for Anderson's comment on "Paper Pills."
In Winesburg, Ohio Anderson says that Doctor Reefy's story is
curious:

          It is delicious, like the twisted little apples that grow in
          the orchards of Winesburg....   On the trees are only a
          few gnarled apples that the pickers have rejected.   They
          look like the knuckles of Doctor Reefy's hands.   One
          nibbles at them and they are delicious.   Into a little
          round place at the side of the apple has been gathered

all of its sweetness. One runs from tree to tree over
the frosted ground picking the gnarled, twisted apples
and filling his pockets with them. Only the few know the
sweetness of the twisted apples. (New York: B. W.
Huebsch, 1919, pp. 19-20.)

11/23-24. a Middle-Western American city. Most probably Anderson is referring to Chicago. He made Chicago his home in
1896-98, 1900-06, and 1913-23. The time he is referring to in
this passage is the period between 1896 and 1898 when he was
working as a common laborer in Chicago.

11/27-29. a large brick factory ... where ... millions, of loaves
of bread are baked. In Memoirs, ed. White, pp. 146-48, Anderson recounts an incident with a prostitute who has two small
children. She has one room with an alcove separated from the
rest of the room by a curtain. After Anderson leaves the prostitute's room, he walks the streets in shame, finds a purse in which
there are five one-dollar bills and some small change, returns to
the woman, and gives her the money. The incident starts:

> I remember sharply one such adventure. I had walked
> for hours through the night, too restless to go home and
> to bed. It is true that, at the time, I was doing hard
> laborious work all day but I was very strong.
> I was in a street of drab little frame houses clustered
> about a factory. As I remember the night there was a
> huge bakery where bread was made. There was an ele-
> vated railroad going through the street.
> A woman spoke to me and I followed her up a stair-
> way into a small dismal room. (p. 146.)

This incident is very similar, although much shorter, to the incident described at 11/26-21/6.

12/14-15. there are dark patches under her eyes. The manuscript reads: "there are dark ~~rings~~ ^patches^ under her eyes. " By sub-
stituting "patches" for the more usual word "rings, " Anderson emphasizes the woman's made-up, artificial appearance. A similar
idea is expressed by her bleached hair (12/12-13) and her unnatu-
ral voice (17/22-23). At 17/25-26 Anderson likens "the radio announcers [who] cultivate a special tone for their work on the air".
to the prostitute. Thus the artificiality and deception of the prostitute become images for the selling out of true art by commercial
writers. This theme is made explicit several times in the "Writer's Book, " for example, at 50/2 and, most fully, at 44/6-9:
"The complete selling out of the imaginations of the men and women of America by the artists of the stage, by the artist story
tellers, is completely and wholly an acceptance of whoredom. "

12/16. She is a prostitute. A three-page typescript, entitled
"Amateur Critic, " in Box 2 of "Memoirs" manuscripts at the New-

berry Library has many interesting similarities with the passage
in the "Writer's Book" concerning the prostitute. The typescript
tells about writing "I Want to Know Why" twenty years earlier;
this would date it about 1938. It also gives one more version of
writing "Hands." Also of interest are Anderson's reflections on
the connection between sensuality and the love of beauty (see 52/3-
18). The manuscript reads in part:

> A doctor who said he had made a deep study of the
> human mind spoke to me of one of my short stories. It
> was a story called "I Want to Know Why." I had written
> the story twenty years before [published in Smart Set,
> LX (November, 1919), 35-40, and in The Triumph of the
> Egg (New York: B. W. Huebsch, Inc., 1921)] and had
> difficulty selling it. One of the smaller literary maga-
> zines did finally publish it and paid me perhaps thirty
> dollars. Twenty years later one of the big popular mag-
> azines paid me five hundred for the privilege of reprint-
> ing it [Redbook, LXX (November, 1937), 38-41, 114]. It
> was the story of a young boy, passionately fond of
> horses....

> . . . .
> It is somewhat interesting, to the writer, to try to
> find, in his own experience, the source of such a story.
> There are these strange contradictions in every man.
> The man of science got from the story the notion that,
> sometime, in my early life, I had fallen deeply in love
> with a prostitute. He said that I, having discovered
> what she was, was terribly shocked and hurt. I think
> what did happen was that, having on some particular day
> written something solid, having been in such a glow, I
> found myself, later, perhaps on the same day, going to
> some prostitute.
> For example, I remember a day when I sat down at
> my desk, in a Chicago rooming house, to write. For
> several years I had been writing but nothing I had done
> satisfied me. I kept writing and throwing away but on
> that day I suddenly wrote the story called "Hands." It is
> in the Winesburg collection of stories. It wrote itself as
> water flows down hill. When I had finished, there it was.
> I never had to correct it, never touched it again [see the
> note to 85/28-29].

> . . . .
> And I think of another experience. It might well have
> been later, on the same day. I would have gone walking
> in the city streets, filled with exultation. Let us say
> that I had got into a district of small frame and brick
> houses and of factories. A woman spoke to me from a
> hallway and I went to her. I do know that such an ex-
> perience happened at about that time.
> I went up into a rather small and dirty room and there

laid with a woman of the town. She would have been a
stupid enough woman. As I was about to leave her, having paid her for the service done me, feeling already
rather mean, a child spoke to her from another room.
She had but the two rooms and the second room was divided from the one in which I had lain with her by a thin
curtain. I asked for an explanation and was told, simply,
that her man, a workman, having deserted her, leaving
her with two children, a boy and a girl, and having been
laid off at the factory where she had been employed, she
had taken up this other employment....

   And so I imagine myself, walking again in the street,
still on the same day, and thinking of the theme of the
story "I Want to Know Why." I would simply have been
questioning the two sides of myself, being, in myself,
both the boy who was a horse lover and the trainer who
went off to the whore.

12/28. But how do I know all of this? See "Man and His Imagination," p. 44:

   When you are dealing with the art of writing you are
   dealing primarily with the imagination, and not only your
   own imagination but the imagination of others. Now there
   are two distinct channels in every man's life. We all
   live on two planes. There is what we call the world of
   reality and there is the somewhat unreal world of the
   imagination. These roads do not cross each other but
   the road of the imagination constantly touches the road
   of reality. It comes near and it goes away. All of us
   are sometimes on one road and sometimes on another.
   I think that we are all living more of our lives on the
   road of the imagination, or perhaps I had better say in
   the world of the imagination, than in the real world.

See 43/2-4, where Anderson explicitly says: "the unreal is more
real than the real, that there is no real other than the unreal."

12/30-31. certain cold-storage warehouse, where butter and eggs
were stored. Jeanette Paden, sister of John Emerson, with whom
Anderson boarded in Chicago (see 38/5-6 and its note), confirms
the fact that Anderson rolled barrels in a cold-storage warehouse
and that he "simply despised the work he was doing" (Sutton, Road
to Winesburg, p. 56). Karl Anderson, in "My Brother, Sherwood
Anderson," Saturday Review of Literature, XXXI (September 4,
1948), 6, speaks about Sherwood's following him to Chicago and
the kind of work he did there: "Sherwood spent the next two years
wheeling meat in and out of frigid vaults." When Sherwood himself
speaks of this period of his life in Memoirs, ed. White, he says:

   In the place where I then worked, in a huge cold storage
   warehouse (All day I was handling barrels filled with
   apples and crates of eggs. We piled them high in great

rooms kept at a low temperature. Most of the men who
worked with me were heavy shouldered Swedes and Poles
and Finns), in that place I did not have to work on Saturday afternoons and often on Saturday nights John and I
walked together for hours.   (p. 150.)

Anderson mentions this cold-storage warehouse also at 15/8.

13/25.   waited on [us] others.   The manuscript reads: "waited on
we others." This is one of the few times in this edition of the
"Writer's Book" where a grammatical error is corrected, except
for what the editor considers inadvertent slips of the pen, for example, "had always love" at 24/25.   See the Introduction, "The
Present Edition and Its Procedures."

14/7-8.   this dream world in which we live in this intimacy with
beauty.   With the Sherwood Anderson Papers in the Newberry Library are two lectures called "America: A Storehouse of Vitality."
Clippings from Portland, Oregon, newspapers show that the shorter
of the two lectures was delivered there on July 16, 1931.   In the
longer lecture Anderson says:

> As to the practical value of the imaginative life I think
> we all know that it has a very practical value.   Before
> the thing of beauty can express itself in song, in books,
> in music, in building, in beautiful streets or cities, it
> must of course live as a thing of beauty or meaning in
> the imaginative life of some man.   The dream must so
> pervade his being that it inevitably works down through
> his fingers and becomes expressed in a fact.   The weak-
> er dreams will fade but the stronger dreams will set up
> a kind of fever within.   (p. 18.)

In A Story Teller's Story, ed. White, Anderson says:

> In the world of fancy even the most base man's ac-
> tions sometimes take on the form of beauty.   Dim path-
> ways do sometimes open before the eyes of the man who
> has not killed the possibilities of beauty in himself by
> being too sure.   (p. 60.)

See also 52/17-18, where Anderson warns against getting beautiful
things by doing cheap work, thus destroying "all understanding of
beauty."

14/12-13.   In the Winesburg series of short stories.   Since the
question whether Winesburg, Ohio is a series of short stories or a
novel is still debated by critics, it is well to see what Anderson
himself says about his masterpiece.   In the "Writer's Book" he always speaks of Winesburg as a series of stories, never as a novel.
For example: "In the Winesburg series of stories" (14/12-13);
"all the stories of the book" (25/31); "the Winesburg tales" (27/31);
"your Winesburg stories" (45/27); "Before writing the Winesburg

stories" (54/30-31); and "In my Winesburg series of stories"
(83/2-3). Furthermore, at 48/20 he lists Winesburg as a volume
of short stories, along with The Triumph of the Egg and Horses
and Men, and not as a novel; and at 85/17-25 he uses Winesburg
as an example to substantiate the critical opinion that he is "best
at the short story. "
        In letters that Anderson wrote in the year of the publication
of Winesburg, he speaks of it as a hybrid form. For example,
writing on November 12, 1919, to its publisher, Ben Huebsch, he
speaks about "Mary Cochran, " a work that was never published as
a novel but two of whose stories, "Unlighted Lamps" and "The
Door of the Trap, " were published in The Triumph of the Egg.
Anderson says to Huebsch:

> One of these days I shall be able to give you the Mary
> Cochran book. It has tantalized me a good deal but is
> coming clear now. In its final form it will be like
> Winesburg, a group of tales woven about the life of one
> person but each tale will be longer and more closely re-
> lated to the development of the central character. It can
> be published in fact as a novel if you wish.
>
> It seems to me that in this form I have worked out
> something that is very flexible and that is the right in-
> strument for me. The reason will be plain. I get no
> chances at all for long periods of uninterrupted thought
> or work. I can take my character into my consciousness
> and live with it but have to work in this fragmentary
> way. These individual tales come clear and sharp.
> When I am ready for one of them it comes all at one
> sitting, a distillation, an outbreak [see the note to 80/22].
> No one I know of has used the form as I see it and as I
> hope to develop it in several books. Damn, man, I wish
> I had time to work. (Letters, Newberry Library, 1919.)

To Hart Crane on November 19, 1919, Anderson wrote: "I shall
later have another book of stories grouped into a semi-novel form"
(Letters, Newberry Library, 1919); and to Waldo Frank, sometime
after December 4, 1919, he wrote:

> Out of my necessity I am throwing the Mary Cochran
> book into the Winesburg form, half individual tales, half
> long novel form. It enables me to go at each separately,
> perhaps when I am ready to do it at one long sitting.
> My life now is too broken up for the long sustained thing.
> Every few days I must go wade in mud, and the filth of
> money-making. (Letters, Newberry Library, 1919.)

Writing many years later, in 1931, to Laura Lou Copenhaver, his
wife Eleanor's mother, Anderson spoke of his new book, probably
Beyond Desire, in the following terms:

> The thing on which I am at work seems to get bigger and
> bigger. You will remember I told the story of the boy

[George Willard] in Winesburg by telling the stories of
other people whose lives touched his life. This is going
to be something of the same thing, if it comes off, only
that instead of short stories there will be something perhaps like a series of novels. The first one is about
done. (Letters, ed. Jones and Rideout, p. 246.)

In his Memoirs, ed. White, as in the "Writer's Book, " Anderson consistently calls Winesburg, Ohio a series of short stories:

So I invented a figure I called George Willard and about
his figure I built a series of stories and sketches called
Winesburg, Ohio. (p. 22.)

Later, when I had become a writer and had written and
published books, I wrote and published a book of tales,
called Winesburg, Ohio. (p. 177.)

He [Jacques Copeau] was, at that time, particularly interested in a book of tales I had written and that I had
called Winesburg, Ohio. He said the tales had excited
him. (p. 362.)

I had myself written, in my Winesburg tales, the story
of a woman who seemed to me a rather fine mother.
(p. 409.)

When he [Hemingway] began to write he began with the
short story and I had already published my Winesburg,
Ohio. I had published also my Horses and Men and my
Triumph of the Egg. (p. 462.)

At the time I was being published by Ben Huebsch who
had taken my Winesburg stories after they had been
kicked about in several publishing houses. (p. 490.)

In Rosenfeld's edition of Memoirs there is a section, "Waiting for
Ben Huebsch, " which is omitted from White's edition. When speaking of Winesburg in this section, Anderson says:

The stories belonged together. I felt that, taken together,
they made something like a novel, a complete story. . . .
I have even sometimes thought that the novel form does
not fit an American writer, that it is a form which had
been brought in. What is wanted is a new looseness;
and in Winesburg I had made my own form. There were
individual tales but all about lives in some way connected.
By this method I did succeed, I think, in giving the feeling of the life of a boy growing into young manhood in a
town. Life is a loose, flowing thing. (p. 289.)

14/13-14. written in just such a rooming house. A letter that
Anderson wrote to Waldo Frank on November 20, 1916, gives An-

derson's address at the time he was writing the Winesburg stories.
The letter is written on stationery with the letterhead "Taylor-
Critchfield-Clague Co., Chicago," and at the end of the letter Anderson wrote in his home address: "735 Cass Street, Chicago,
Illinois." Cass Street is now Wabash Avenue, and the rooming
house that stood at 735 no longer exists. A parking lot now covers the site. In the letter to Frank, Anderson wrote:

> Thanks for the check and for liking the story of the
> farm hands [probably "The Untold Lie," published in
> Frank's Seven Arts, I (January, 1917), 215-21, and in
> Winesburg, Ohio.]
>   As a delightful old reprobate in my home town used to
> say, "My life is an open ditch." I wrote the story last
> week.
>   The other day I wrote you a letter [see Letters, ed.
> Jones and Rideout, pp. 4-5] concerning a series of
> stories written last winter. I am sending two for you to
> look at. Personally, I like the Enoch Robinson thing
> ["Loneliness"; see 23/16] better than anything else I have
> ever done. You may not agree with me but I'll be anx-
> ious to see how you react to it. (Letters, Newberry Li-
> brary, 1916.)

In his Notebook Anderson says:

> I myself remember with what a shock I heard people
> say that one of my own books, Winesburg, Ohio, was an
> exact picture of Ohio village life. The book was written
> in a crowded tenement district of Chicago. The hint for
> almost every character was taken from my fellow-lodgers
> in a large rooming house, many of whom had never lived
> in a village. (p. 76.)

Also in Memoirs, ed. White, Anderson speaks about writing Winesburg:

> When I wrote the stories in the book called Winesburg,
> Ohio I was living in a cheap room in a Chicago rooming
> house. I dare say that all of the tales in the book came
> out of some memory or impression got from my boyhood
> in a small town but, as I had lived in several such
> towns, I had no one town in mind.
>   The house in which I had the room was on Chicago's
> North Side and was occupied by a group of people new
> to me. They were all either actively in the arts or they
> aspired to a place in some one of the arts. They were
> young musicians, young writers, painters, actors, and I
> found them delightful. (p. 346.)
>
>   The idea I had was to take them, just as they were,
> as I felt them, and transfer them from the city rooming
> house to an imagined small town, the physical aspects of

> the town having, let us say, been picked up from my
> living in several such towns. (p. 348.)

> I myself think that the real fathers and if you please the
> mothers of the Winesburg stories were the people who
> once lived with me in a Chicago rooming house, the un-
> successful Little Children of the Arts. (p. 350.)

The Winesburg manuscript at the Newberry Library has with it a
note in Anderson's hand. This note probably was written when Anderson found the Winesburg manuscript in a box of old papers in
1938. The note reads:

> At the time these stories were written the author was
> employed as a copy writer in a Chicago advertising agency
> and the paper is no doubt that used for roughing up ad-
> vertisements. It is likely the stories were written two
> or three times, in the writer's room, in a rooming house
> in Cass Street in Chicago, or in hotels as he traveled
> about, visiting clients of his employers.

An excellent investigation into the writing of Winesburg, Ohio is
William L. Phillips, "Sherwood Anderson's Winesburg, Ohio: Its
Origins, Composition, Technique, and Reception" (unpublished Ph.D.
dissertation, University of Chicago, 1949), summarized in "How
Sherwood Anderson Wrote Winesburg, Ohio, " American Literature,
XXIII (March, 1951), 7-30.

14/19-20. the story "Loneliness." The table of contents for
Winesburg lists both "The Tales and the Persons, " and among its
listings is: "Loneliness--concerning Enoch Robinson." In a letter
to Waldo Frank written on December 14, 1916, Anderson speaks
of this story:

> I am glad you liked the story "Mother" and that you
> are going to publish it. Damn it, I wanted you to like
> the story about Enoch Robinson and the woman who came
> into his room and was too big for the room.
> There is a story every critic is bound to dislike. I
> can remember reading it to Floyd Dell, and it made him
> hopping mad. "It's damn rot, " says Floyd. "It does
> not get anywhere. "
> "It gets there, but you are not at the station, " I re-
> plied to Floyd, and I think I was right.
> Why do I try to convince you of this story? Well, I
> want it in print in Seven Arts. A writer knows when a
> story is good, and that story is good. (Letters, ed.
> Jones and Rideout, p. 5.)

Neither Frank's Seven Arts nor Dell's Masses published "Loneli-
ness"; in fact, it never was published in a magazine.
See 26/6-7 and its note for Floyd Dell's reaction to the
Winesburg stories.

14/20-22. a little man in a room and what the imagined figures
his fancy had conjured up had come to mean to him. "Loneliness"
is the story of a twenty-one-year-old aspiring artist who goes
from Winesburg to New York City and at first invites people to
his room and tries to explain his paintings to them. In the course
of time he marries and has two children, but eventually he becomes so absorbed with the people of his fancy that his wife and
children leave him. Then comes another woman who, for a time,
understands him; but, as Enoch relates to George Willard, "I
wanted her to understand but, don't you see, I couldn't let her understand. I felt that then she would know everything, that I would
be submerged, drowned out, you see" (p. 210). So he berates the
woman and she too leaves. Through the door as she leaves go all
of Enoch's imaginary people. Enoch then returns home, "to live
out his life alone and defeated in Winesburg" (p. 208). The story
ends with Enoch Robinson saying to himself, after George Willard
leaves him: " 'I'm alone, all alone here,' said the voice. 'It was
warm and friendly in my room [with his imaginary people] but now
I'm all alone' " (p. 212).

15/3. bleary-eyed. This unusual expression appears in a letter
to Alfred Stieglitz written from New Orleans about August 3, 1924.
In the letter Anderson is describing the sights that give him inspiration as he works on his novel Dark Laughter. Among them
are "bleary-eyed old nigger women with their pipe-stem legs"
(Letters, ed. Jones and Rideout, p. 129).

15/8. cold-storage warehouse. See 12/30-31 and its note.

15/17. white horse. Here the "grey horse" of 15/10 becomes
white. In this line Anderson is probably thinking ahead to the end
of the sentence where he says that the horse is being led "by a
little old man with a white beard" (15/17-18). The horse remains
white in 15/26.
    Interestingly enough, the same, or rather the reverse, in-
consistency appears in the Winesburg story "Paper Pills" (see
83/3 and the note to 10/31-32). Doctor Reefy's "jaded white
horse" (p. 18) turns into a "jaded grey horse" (p. 20).

15/20-21. in the mind of a young man sitting in a window in a
rooming house. See the following notes which comment on Anderson's style: 5/32-6/1 on his sense of rhythm, 9/26-27 on other
examples of sentences made up of a series of prepositional phrases,
55/25-26 on his word repetition patterns, and 85/3-5 on his use
of the passive voice. See also the discussion of Anderson's style
in Earl Hilton, "The Purpose and Method of Sherwood Anderson"
(unpublished Ph.D. dissertation, University of Minnesota, 1950).
Hilton says that Anderson's style is characterized by an unusually
frequent use of prepositional phrases, passive voice, and peri-
phrastic genitives. An example in the "Writer's Book" of the third
is "mind of the story teller's" in 3/5. Hilton continues:

        The greatest distinction of Anderson's style, however,

lies in its rhythm, a rhythm so essential to his communication, according to Rosenfeld [The Sherwood Anderson
Reader, p. xvii] that the reader who is insensible to his
"sonorities and cadences" misses a part of his meaning.
The most characteristic device used in the creation of
this rhythm is the word repetition pattern. (p. 87.)

Finally, see the discussion of Anderson's style in Richard Bridgman's The Colloquial Style in America (New York: Oxford University Press, 1966). After asserting that Anderson "was the first
writer since Mark Twain to take the vernacular as a serious way
of presenting reality," Bridgman goes on to discuss Anderson's
use of the vernacular in Winesburg. He says:

> Winesburg is deliberately primitivistic, stated with a so-
> ber, humorless intensity that moves at a slow pace from
> word to word, object to object. Long series of hardly
> varied declarative sentences are set down, key nouns are
> repeated, qualification is pared, and subordination mini-
> mized. The main resources of the vernacular are used
> by Anderson dead seriously. The result is at once im-
> pressive and irritating. (p. 155.)

15/23. I have spent my life wondering why. In the last decade
of his life Anderson wrote in the chapter "Mr. J. J. Lankes and
His Woodcuts," in No Swank (Philadelphia: The Centaur Press,
1934), p. 25:

> What I am trying to say is that there are always these
> little scenes, presenting themselves for our notice, out
> of the commonplace little incidents of our everyday lives.
> They are ugly. Surely. But let them be truly presented,
> so that we feel them as part of ourselves, and something
> happens.
> Beauty happens. That strange intangible quality of
> looking at life and at things, feeling into life and things,
> making others feel, is in everything this man, Lankes,
> the Virginia woodcut man, is doing.

16/7-9. the restless young men out of the ranks of whom we are
to get the artists of the future. These are the "young American
story tellers" to whom Anderson, "a veteran of the craft" (3/3-4),
is addressing the "Writer's Book."

16/11-12. Such dreams as imaginative young men have, become
at times absurd. See Anderson's novel Many Marriages (New York:
B. W. Huebsch, Inc., 1923), p. 28, where the main character,
John Webster, behaves in much the same fashion:

> There was a dream. One vainly hoped to find, wan-
> dering about somewhere, a woman who by some miracle
> would love with freedom and abandon. Along through the
> streets one went usually in dark badly lighted places

where there were factories and warehouses and poor
little dwellings. One wanted a golden woman to step up
out of the filth of the place in which one walked. It was
insane and silly and one knew these things, but one persisted insanely.

Anderson comments on Many Marriages at 57/9-13 and 59/4-5.

16/16. There may be some accident happen. See the note to
15/20-21 and Hilton's comment that Anderson's style contains an
unusually frequent use of the passive voice.

16/30-31. It is by such absurd dreams, always coming, always
changing, that the imaginative young man lives. See Memoirs, ed.
White, p. 352:

What dreams, hopes, ambitions. Sometimes it has
seemed to me, when, as a young man, I sat at the window of that room, that each person who passed along the
street below, under the light, shouted his secret up to
me.
I was myself and still I fled out of myself. It seemed
to me that I went into the others.
What dreams. What egotism. I had thought then, on
such evenings, that I could tell all of the stories of all
the people of America. I would get them all, understand them, get their stories told.

16/32-17/1. popular short story or novel writer. The use of the
word "popular" is surprising. Throughout the "Writer's Book"
Anderson denigrates the writer who can write salable stories,
plays, and novels that cater to the popular taste.

17/25-26. as the radio announcers cultivate a special tone. Here
the radio announcers are used as an image for all commercial artists who accede to popular demands in art. In a letter written
about November, 1917, to his brother Karl, a successful commercial artist, Anderson says:

I came among artists hoping to find brotherhood there,
but there isn't much of it. As it is in painting, so it
is among writers. Fundamentally most of our American
writing men are graceful and facile fanner[s] [Note:
"that is, unscrupulous men"] and whores altogether. If
one did not laugh at them, he would go mad. The arti-
san and the mechanic talks with fair intelligence of his
tools. The average professional intellectual talks, of
course, like a silly, puzzled child. (Letters, ed. Jones
and Rideout, p. 20.)

18/11. dark. Darkness is a favorite metaphor in the "Writer's
Book, " as it is in many of Anderson's writings. When man is
powerless, through his own fault or the fault of others, to cope

successfully with a situation, Anderson often describes the situation
in terms of darkness. In the "Writer's Book" the prostitute's
"figure was dim, there in the half light" (17/29) when she first
speaks. When the author decides to follow her up the stairs, he
hopes "that the room to which she will take me will be dark"
(18/10-11). His hope is fulfilled: "There was no light in there"
(18/20). "There was light on the ceiling of the room but the floor
of the room was dark. The floor of the room was a dark pit"
(18/23-25). A few pages later Anderson moves back to the story
of the judge--he was called a judge for the first time at 21/19--
and he tells us that the judge met his beloved "in the evening,
when darkness came" (21/32-22/1), "in some dark place" (22/2).
The story of the judge and the story of the prostitute are brought
together by this figure of darkness when Anderson returns to the
man "on the dark stairs, following her up into her two poor rooms,
refusing to look at her, hoping to find her rooms above also dark"
(22/30-32). The passage ends with the man's deliberately deceiv-
ing himself: "In the darkness I can make myself believe she is
Cecelia" (23/1-2). Later in Part I Anderson speaks about his ineffectual father and tells how he would sit in the darkness of their
home and sing "Over the Hill to the Poor-House" (50/29-32).
    See a letter to Waldo Frank, written at the end of 1919 or
the beginning of 1920, in which Anderson describes an unsatisfactory situation in his own life:

> One thing I have found out. I cannot continue to live
> the life I have lived as a businessman. In a sense I have
> been like one living in a damp, dark cellar ever since I
> went back into business after my few months of freedom
> in New York last year. To think straight at all I had to
> get temporarily out of it. In New York I did. (Letters,
> ed. Jones and Rideout, pp. 50-51.)

See also one of Anderson's most highly acclaimed short stories,
"The Man Who Became a Woman," published in Horses and Men
(New York: B. W. Huebsch, Inc., 1923). In this story Herman
Dudley, a young racetrack swipe, learns in a series of adventures
in one night to accept the adult world and his own adult sexuality.
After an encounter with several drunken, brutal men in a saloon,
his own face, seen in the saloon mirror, seems to him to be the
face of a young girl. He then leaves the saloon: "And so there I
was, outside there in the darkness, and it was as cold and wet
and black and God-forsaken a night as any man ever saw" (p. 214).
Later two drunken negro swipes also mistake him for a girl as he
sleeps in the stable loft. He runs out into the night: "It was
black dark and raining hard now and a roaring wind had begun to
blow" (p. 222). Finally, as dawn comes, he falls exhausted into
the whitened skeleton of a horse abandoned in the field near the
slaughter house. He is then cleansed of his mistaken identity and
confirms his male adulthood.

18/11-12. I can imagine her the real Cecelia. See 23/1-2: "In
the darkness I can make myself believe she is Cecelia." Again

Anderson calls attention to the irony of the situation. Cecelia is
unreal and the prostitute is real; but to the author and to the "imaginative young men" (16/11-12) to whom he is writing, Cecelia is
real and the prostitute, the radio announcers, and all artists who
prostitute their art are unreal. Anderson in this passage is expressing by means of the story of the real prostitute and the imaginary Cecelia one of the most frequently repeated themes of his
works, namely, "that the unreal is more real than the real" (43/2-
3). See also 22/21-23, 23/6-8, and 37/10-11 and their notes.

18/30-31. I had not spoken to her. See the note to 10/31-32,
which discusses Anderson's masterful handling of the themes of
loneliness and man's inability to communicate. Even though he
follows her up to her rooms, the author cannot bring himself to
speak to the prostitute: "I did not speak to her, had not as yet
spoken to her" (20/9-10). At the end of the episode neither he
nor the prostitute speaks. Nevertheless, "not having exchanged a
word with her, I knew her story. I knew it as well as though she
had talked to me for hours" (20/22-25). Again irony comes into
play. The author, representing the true artist, does not speak to
the prostitute, who represents both false life and art. She speaks
to him, but, of course, achieves no real communication. She can,
however, communicate with her child--"now her voice was really
soft" (19/28)--and, without words, can communicate to the author
the loneliness and tragedy of her life.

19/29-30. by some subtile impulse, felt me in the place? The
manuscript reads: "by some subtile f̶e̶e̶l̶y̶ impulse, felt me in the
place?" This is another example of a revision made during the
original composition.

21/10-11. a part of the introduction to another tale I have wanted
to write. See 21/16-17: "the story, to which this rambling talk
may serve as a sort of introduction," and 22/13-15: "I had taken
the man, with whom I talked in the field, [and] his story as the
bases for the story I was to write for one of the popular magazines."
Anderson tells the stories of the prostitute and the judge as a kind
of introduction to the real story he is telling in Part I. The important story is the story of Anderson's struggle to maintain his
artistic integrity in the face of the temptation to write a salable
magazine story.

21/12. "He might have spared us that." It is, however, Anderson's decided conviction that he should not spare the reader the
"rather sordid details, happenings, so likely to come into such affairs" (22/18-19). Anderson has "something in mind ... other
than the story of the country boy who later became a judge" (21/17-
19). He has in mind a story that is true to life, that really represents the passions, fears, hopes, and loves of the people he ob-
serves daily in his life. See the notes to 7/10-11 and 7/16-17.
In the "Writer's Book" Anderson is advising young writers to be,
as he was, honest in their portrayal of life.

21/16. this rambling talk. See Cleveland B. Chase, Sherwood
Anderson (New York: Robert M. McBride Company, Inc., 1927),
p. 33. Chase is speaking of the Winesburg stories:

> Anderson tells these stories with a simplicity and a sure-
> ness that show that at last he knows what he is doing and
> how he wants to do it. He has his medium in such com-
> plete control that it is not difficult to be unconscious of
> his mastery of it. His air of simplicity and ingenuousness,
> the apparent rambling, the way in which he appears to be
> haphazardly setting down ideas as they come into his
> mind in an attempt to discover their meaning, his grop-
> ing, his artlessness, his naïveté--these are but tricks of
> the story teller's trade to earn our sympathy for the
> story which he unfolds graphically and without confusion.
> To be sure, that groping naïveté betokens a certain self-
> consciousness on the part of the author, but such self-
> consciousness is an integral part of Anderson, and rarely
> does it become obtrusive.

21/19. a judge. Anderson inadvertently makes the scientist of
6/15-23 into a judge. See the note to 6/15. See also Part III,
"The Writer." In its second sentence Anderson says: "In a certain town a judge told me a story" (67/2-3). Anderson then proceeds to tell the story of an unnamed doctor and Agnes Riley.
See the note to 67/1-70/28 which discusses this story.

22/21-23. it was another case of myself, in my room, a young
laborer, with my dream of my Cecelia and of what I actually found.
See 18/11-12, 23/6-8, 37/10-11, and 43/2-3 and their notes on
Anderson's theory that the unreal is more real than the real. In
this passage, however, the unreal dream of a beautiful Cecelia and
the unrealistic attempt to purge the judge's story of its sordid details and happenings are not real. Both are false and untrue to
life.

23/2-3. It is in the movies, in the theatre, in our magazines, in
our novels. "It" refers to deliberate self-deception, such as the
young laborer's false dream that in the darkness he can make himself believe that the prostitute is the real Cecelia. In his Notebook, pp. 143-44, Anderson also speaks about deliberately false
portrayals of life in popular fiction:

> Where among us live these creatures of the popular mag-
> azine short story, the best-selling novel or the moving
> picture? You read the stories published in these maga-
> zines and they are very skillfully done. There is a
> strange exterior semblance of life in the people who pa-
> rade before us and do for our edification these brave
> clever or humorous stunts.
>
> . . . .
> There is a kind of legerdemain that with practice may

be acquired.   Having tricked your reader by these purely
mechanical details into having faith in the people you are
writing about, you simply make these people do and say
things no human being has ever really been known to do
or say.

In the pages of these magazines no one ever acts as
people do in life or thinks as people do in life and of
course the writers of the stories care nothing for human
life.   To begin caring for human life, thinking of human
life and trying to understand it a little, would so quickly
destroy their technique, stop incomes and jerk the writers down off the pasteboard thrones.

23/6.   Is the dream necessary?   We know from 14/7, 16/11-12,
and 16/30-17/2 that Anderson believed that the dream was necessary.   The dream, but not deliberate self-deception, is necessary
precisely because the unreal is more real than the real, as explained in the following note.

23/6-8.   Is there not something, in the actuality of life, ... that
is better and richer?   The answer to the dilemma is that true art
is the result of the creative blending of the real and the imaginary
--of the "dream" and "the actuality of life, even now, in our own
day, in our own towns and cities."   See a letter written to Alfred
Stieglitz on June 30, 1923.   Anderson is speaking about working
on A Story Teller's Story:

> In the meantime I get along into this semi-autobiographi-
> cal thing on which I am at work.   It is thoughts, notions,
> and tales all thrown together.   The central notion is that
> one's fanciful life is of as much significance as one's
> real flesh-and-blood life and that one cannot tell where
> the one cuts off and the other begins.   This thing I have
> thought has as much physical existence as the stupid phys-
> ical act I yesterday did.   In fact, so strongly has the
> purely fanciful lived in me that I cannot tell after a time
> which of my acts had physical reality and which did not.
> It makes me in one sense a great liar, but, as I said in
> the Testament, "It is only by lying to the limit one can
> come at truth."   (Letters, ed. Jones and Rideout, pp. 99-
> 100.)

See also "A Note on Realism" in Notebook.   (Part of "A Note on
Realism" is reprinted in "Man and His Imagination," pp. 65-71.)

> For some reason--I myself have never exactly understood
> very clearly--the imagination must constantly feed upon
> reality or starve.   Separate yourself too much from life
> and you may at moments be a lyric poet, but you are not
> an artist.   Something within dries up, starves for the
> want of food.   Upon the fact in nature the imagination
> must constantly feed in order that the imaginative life
> remain significant.   The workman who lets his imagina-

tion drift off into some experience altogether disconnected
with reality, the attempt of the American to depict life
in Europe, the New Englander writing of cowboy life--all
that sort of thing--in ninety-nine cases out of a hundred
ends in the work of such a man becoming at once full of
holes and bad spots. The intelligent reader, tricked often
enough by the technical skill displayed in hiding the holes,
never in the end accepts it as good work. The imagination of the workman has become confused. He has had to
depend altogether upon tricks. The whole job is a fake.
(p. 73.)

23/12-13. after twenty-five years of writing, some twenty to
twenty-five books published. It seems safe to assume that the
"writing" mentioned here is Anderson's short story and novel writing. Therefore, disregarding the writing that he published in the
Long-Critchfield agency's house organ Agricultural Advertising and
in the Bobbs-Merrill Reader (see the note to 10/1), we can date
the beginning of his serious publications with the printing of "The
Rabbit Pen" in Harper's in July, 1914 (see the note to 2/4). Sutton, Exit to Elsinore, p. 17, says that Anderson was submitting
manuscripts for publication as early as 1911 and 1912, and that
"The Rabbit Pen, " Windy McPherson's Son, and Marching Men
were probably written before Anderson left Elyria in 1913. Adding
twenty-five years to these dates would give 1936-38 as the date for
the writing of Part I of the "Writer's Book. " We must always remember, however, that Anderson is totally unconcerned about the
accuracy of dates. Nonetheless, by 1938 he had published the following twenty-five books:

Windy McPherson's Son (New York: John Lane, 1916; re-
    vised edition, New York: B. W. Huebsch, Inc., 1921);
Marching Men (London: John Lane, The Bodley Head, Ltd.,
    1917);
Mid-American Chants (London: John Lane, The Bodley
    Head, Ltd., 1918);
Winesburg, Ohio (New York: B. W. Huebsch, Inc., 1919);
Poor White (New York: B. W. Huebsch, Inc., 1920);
The Triumph of the Egg (New York: B. W. Huebsch, Inc.,
    1921);
Horses and Men (New York: B. W. Huebsch, Inc., 1923);
Many Marriages (New York: B. W. Huebsch, Inc., 1923);
A Story Teller's Story (New York: B. W. Huebsch, Inc.,
    1924);
Dark Laughter (New York: Boni and Liveright, 1925);
The Modern Writer (San Francisco: The Lantern Press,
    Gelber, Lilienthal, Inc., 1925);
Sherwood Anderson's Notebook (New York: Boni and
    Liveright, 1926);
Tar: A Midwest Childhood (New York: Boni and Liveright,
    1926);
A New Testament (New York: Boni and Liveright, 1927);
Alice and The Lost Novel (London: Elkin Mathews and

Marrot, 1929);
Hello Towns! (New York: Horace Liveright Publishing Inc.,
    1929);
Nearer the Grass Roots (San Francisco: The Westgate
    Press, 1929);
The American County Fair (New York: Random House,
    1930);
Perhaps Women (New York: Horace Liveright Inc., 1931);
Beyond Desire (New York: Liveright Publishing Corporation,
    1932);
Death in the Woods (New York: Liveright Inc., Publishers,
    1933);
No Swank (Philadelphia: The Centaur Press, 1934);
Puzzled America (New York: Charles Scribner's Sons,
    1935);
Kit Brandon (New York: Charles Scribner's Sons, 1936);
Plays: Winesburg and Others (New York: Charles Scrib-
    ner's Sons, 1937).

The only other book to be published during his lifetime was Home
Town (New York: Alliance Book Corporation, 1940).   After his
sudden death in 1941 his widow, Mrs. Eleanor Anderson, and Paul
Rosenfeld prepared his Memoirs for publication: Sherwood Anderson's Memoirs (New York: Harcourt, Brace and Company, 1942).

23/13-14.   my name up as one of the outstanding American writers of my day.   It would be easy to bring together the names of
critics and writers who during Anderson's own life recognized him
as one of America's outstanding writers.   They would include:
Waldo Frank in "Emerging Greatness," Seven Arts, I (November,
1916), 73-78; Paul Rosenfeld in "Sherwood Anderson," Dial, LXXII
(January, 1922), 29-42; Robert Morss Lovett in "The Promise of
Sherwood Anderson," Dial, LXXII (January, 1922), 78-83; Gertrude
Stein in "Idem the Same--A Valentine to Sherwood Anderson, "
Little Review, IX (Spring, 1923), 5-9; Virginia Woolf in "Ameri-
can Fiction, " Saturday Review of Literature, II (August 1, 1925),
1-3; Thomas K. Whipple in "Sherwood Anderson, " Spokesmen:
Modern Writers and American Life (New York: D. Appleton and
Company, 1928; Berkeley and Los Angeles: University Press,
1962), pp. 115-38; Granville Hicks in "Dreiser, Anderson, Lewis"
in The Great Tradition (rev. ed.; New York: Crowell-Collier and
Macmillan, Inc., 1935), 226-37; Harlan Hatcher in "Freudian Psychology and the Sex Age: Sherwood Anderson, " Creating the
American Novel (New York: Farrar and Rinehart, 1935), pp. 155-
71; and Oscar Cargill in two chapters, "The Primitivists" and
"The Freudians" in Intellectual America (New York: The Macmillan Company, 1941), pp. 322-31 and 676-85.   To quote from a
few of these works, Waldo Frank in 1916 wrote:

> This much is sure, however--and true particularly of the
> novel--that our artists have been of two extremes: those
> who gained an almost unbelievable purity of expression
> by the very violence of their self-isolation, and those who,

plunging into the American maëlstrom, were submerged
in it, lost their vision altogether, and gave forth a gross
chronicle and a blind cult of the American Fact.

The significance of Sherwood Anderson whose first
novel, "Windy McPherson's Son," has recently appeared
(published by The John Lane Company), is simply that he
has escaped these two extremes, that he suggests at last
a presentation of life shot through with the searching
color of truth, which is a signal for a native culture.

Mr. Anderson is no accident. The appearance of his
book is a gesture of logic. Indeed, commentators of to-
morrow might gauge the station at which America has
arrived today by a study of the impulses--conscious and
unconscious--which compose this novel. But it is not a
prophetic work. Its author is simply a man who has felt
the moving passions of his people, yet sustained himself
against them just enough in a crude way to set them
forth. (Reprinted in The Achievement of Sherwood Anderson, ed. by Ray Lewis White [Chapel Hill: The University of North Carolina Press], pp. 20-21.)

Thomas Whipple in 1928, in speaking of Anderson's short stories,
said:

His stories are as devoid of plot as they are of all the
devices taught by correspondence schools for producing
salable fiction. His best stories seem to have no technique at all: each deals with an episode, a crisis in one
or two lives, and Anderson first gives what information
is needed concerning the participants, and then proceeds
with his anecdote. As a writer, his outstanding trait is
his integrity; to maintain such integrity against all the
lures and pressures of Twentieth-century America is a
notable feat which speaks highly for his instinct as a
workman. To possess not only the story-telling knack
but also the critical sense and the severity of taste
necessary for strict self-discipline ... Anderson must
have been endowed with the rigorous conscience of the
true craftsman. He has repeatedly stated that that is
his ideal of writing: to deal with words with the same
honest skill and solid workmanship with which a good
carpenter treats wood or a mason stone. (pp. 120-21.)

Granville Hicks in 1935 wrote:

Incapable of sustained, exact description, Anderson re-
lies upon the lightning flash. Surfaces, deeds, even words
scarcely concern him; everything is bent to the task of
revelation. When he succeeds, there is the character of
Elmer Cowley or Dr. Reefy or Louise Hardy, about
whom we need to be told nothing more. If one were to
judge Anderson only by his best work, one could scarcely
avoid the conclusion that his talent was of the first order.

Here, one would note, was a prose-writer with the courage to create his own idiom and his own rhythms. One
would marvel at the man's penetration, his understanding
of the strangeness and terror that life holds even for the
humblest. And one would find, in such a book as Winesburg, Ohio, an authentic picture of the small town, and,
in Poor White, the record of the small town's transfor-
mation. Except in Poor White, one would find little
about industrialism, and yet one could never be unaware
that the civilization portrayed was in travail. Others
have described more fully how the common people live;
no one has shown so authoritatively what they feel. (pp.
229-30.)

Of course, it is untrue and unfair to cite only the critics who
praise Anderson. For everyone who praised him could be matched
one who condemned him. Suffice it here to quote in part from
one outstanding critic, Lionel Trilling, who in "this notice of
Anderson on the occasion of his death, " wrote a severe critical
article, "Sherwood Anderson, " Kenyon Review, III (Summer, 1942),
293-302, which became the basis for the essay in The Liberal
Imagination (New York: The Viking Press, 1950), pp. 22-23. Although Trilling confesses to "some unconscious residue of admiration" (p. 23) for Anderson and admits that "Winesburg, Ohio has
its touch of greatness" (p. 25), he says:

In their speech his people have not only no wit, but
no idiom. To say that they are not "real" would be to
introduce all sorts of useless quibbles about the art of
character creation; they are simply not there. This is
not a failure of art; rather, it would seem to have been
part of Anderson's intention that they should be not there.
His narrative prose is contrived to that end; it is not
really a colloquial idiom, although it has certain colloquial tricks; it approaches in effect the inadequate use of
a foreign language; old slang persists in it and elegant
archaisms are consciously used, so that people are constantly having the "fantods, " girls are frequently referred to as "maidens, " and things are "like unto" other
things. These mannerisms, although they remind us of
some of Dreiser's, are not the result, as Dreiser's are,
of an effort to be literary and impressive. Anderson's
prose has a purpose to which these mannerisms are es-
sential--it has the intention of making us doubt our familiarity with our own world, and not, we must note, in
order to make things fresher for us but only in order to
make them seem puzzling to us and remote from us....
Anderson liked to catch people with their single human
secret, their essence, but the more he looks for their
essence the more his characters vanish into the vast
limbo of meaningless life, the less they are human beings.... The more Anderson says about people, the less
alive they become--and the less lovable. Is it strange

that, with all Anderson's expressed affection for them, we
ourselves can never love the people he writes about?
But of course we do not love people for their essence or
their souls, but for their having a certain body, or wit,
or idiom, certain specific relationships with things and
other people, and for a dependable continuity of existence:
we love them for being there. (pp. 30-31.)

23/14-15. my books translated into many languages. The standard bibliography for Anderson, Sherwood Anderson: A Bibliogra-
phy, compiled by Eugene P. Sheehy and Kenneth A. Lohf (Los Gatos,
Calif.: The Talisman Press, 1960), as well as Checklist of Sherwood Anderson, compiled by Ray Lewis White (Columbus, Ohio:
Charles E. Merrill Publishing Company, 1969) and the holdings at
Newberry Library, show that Anderson's books have been translated into the following languages: Chinese, Czech, Danish, Dutch,
Finnish, French, German, Greek, Hebrew, Hungarian, Italian,
Japanese, Korean, Norwegian, Polish, Rumanian, Russian, Sloven-
ian, Spanish, and Swedish. This listing does not include translations of individual short stories.

        In 1927 when Anderson's American reputation was perhaps
at its lowest point, he found solace during his second European
trip (see the note to 39/21-22) in the fact that his European reputation seemed secure. He wrote to Paul Rosenfeld from Paris at
the beginning of 1927: "At last A Story Teller, the Note Book,
Winesburg and another book of stories are to be all published in
France this year. 'A Man Who Became a Woman' & 'A Man's
Story' were published here--Bernard Faÿ translation--and they
seem to have opened this door" (Letters, ed. Jones and Rideout,
p. 165). At the end of the same year Anderson wrote to Ralph
Church (see 91/6 and its note) from Marion, Virginia: "My books
keep going big in Germany, and there are to be new Polish, Danish,
Swedish, and Dutch translations this year" (Letters, ed. Jones and
Rideout, p. 181).

23/19-20. For a day, two days, three, a week, I wrote doggedly.
The manuscript reads: "For a w̶e̶e̶k̶/ t̶w̶ day, two days, three, a
week, I w̶r̶o̶t̶e̶ wrote doggedly." The revision at the beginning of
the sentence makes the statement stronger, makes the struggle
appear to be even greater, as if the dogged effort to write the
story for the magazine was such a great effort that it could not
be endured for more than a week. The revision at the end of the
sentence is one of the rather frequent instances of Anderson's
crossing out a word and then deciding to keep the original word.

23/22 and 24. the "don'ts." Edward J. O'Brien, anthologist and
student of the American short story through many years, editor of
the annual volume of The Best Short Stories of ... and the Year
Book of the American Short Story from 1915 and 1941, in his book
on the commercialized short story in America, The Dance of the
Machine (New York: The Macaulay Company, 1929), p. 129, has
this to say about the "don'ts":

There is an undefined, but no less real, censorship in most magazine offices, which determines to a very large extent the ideas and situations which a short story may present. This censorship is based on a curious list of taboos which have no necessary relation to decency or morality. It goes without saying, of course, that the American magazine professes to be highly moral, but in many cases salacious writing is encouraged as a matter of policy, provided that it does not cross a line which is by no means accurately determined.

The real censorship of ideas and situations has little to do with any moral question. The tone of a short story must be optimistic; flirting with sex is desirable, provided that sex is not regarded as real; the story must contain no religious speculation or philosophic ideas which challenge, or even test, currently accepted opinions on any subject; it must present no social or political problems; it must consistently preach what is known as "Americanism"; it must have a happy ending. In other words, the writer must agree with as many average people as possible. Therefore, he is forbidden to present any new ideas. Apparently it is believed that in the mind of the American reader unfamiliarity breeds contempt.

24/21. comfortable positions. Compare with 9/6-8: "The story should be concerned with the lives of people who are in what might be called comfortable circumstances."

24/25-26. I, who had always loved the piles of clean white sheets. A Story Teller's Story, ed. White, pp. 209-10 and 212-14, also tells about Anderson's great love for, and fear of being without, paper, pens, pencils, and ink. On p. 210 he says: "To the writer of prose, who loves his craft, there is nothing in the world so satisfying as being in the presence of great stacks of clean white sheets."

24/29-30. I was always stealing fountain pens and pencils. Anderson wrote to J. J. Lankes from Marion on December 27, 1931, on stationery from Hotel Lanier, Macon, Georgia, with "Macon, Ga." crossed out and "Marion Va" written in: "What do you steal? I always steal paper and fountain pens. Also many lead pencils" (Letters, Newberry Library, 1931).

24/31. as a squirrel stores nuts. See A Story Teller's Story, ed. White, p. 209: "In houses where I live for some time I cache small stores of paper as a squirrel stores nuts."

25/10. sculp. Tennessee Mitchell, Anderson's second wife, was a sculptress as well as a competent musician. When Anderson moved to Chicago from Elyria in 1913 and joined the group which comprised the Chicago Renaissance, Tennessee encouraged him in his writing. At that time she was making her living as a piano tuner and music teacher. She was interested also in the dance, and in the summer of 1916 at Lake Chateaugay, New York, where she had gone to attend a school in rhythmic dancing directed by Alys Bentley, she and Anderson were married. See Schevill, pp. 87-88, and Howe, p. 82. In the winter of 1920, as their marriage was proving less and less successful, Tennessee followed Anderson to Fairhope, Alabama. It was here that Anderson claims to have taught her to sculp. In a letter to Van Wyck Brooks written on May 15, 1920, although he characteristically twists facts by saying that he had "persuaded" her to come--he had actually "run off" without her--he says:

> It has been a wonderful time for me here these three months. In the first place, I persuaded Tennessee to be utterly reckless, chuck her job and income, and run off here with me. That has worked out. She is getting well and is happier than I have ever seen her. What a tremendous thing life is. For several years she has been a tired woman. Here she rested and then suddenly began to play. There are great quantities of red, yellow, and blue clay here, very fine and plastic. Tennessee suddenly began working in it, and already she does really remarkable things. What new joy in life that approach towards beauty coming in a definite form out of herself has given her. (Letters, ed. Jones and Rideout, p. 54.)

The result of Tennessee's sculpturing appeared in Anderson's second volume of short stories, The Triumph of the Egg: A Book of Impressions from American Life in Tales and Poems by Sherwood Anderson, in Clay by Tennessee Mitchell (New York: B. W. Huebsch, 1921). Tennessee's six "Impressions in Clay" appear at the beginning of the book, and three of them are companion pieces for three of the stories: "I Want to Know Why, " "The Egg, " and "Out of Nothing into Nowhere. "

Anderson and Tennessee were divorced in April, 1924. See 72/32 and its note.

25/22. Once I even owned a factory. See the note to 51/7-8 for details on Anderson's manufacturing careers in Cleveland and Elyria. Suffice it here to cite a few quotations. Karl Anderson in his article "My Brother, Sherwood Anderson" says: "From Cleveland Sherwood had gone to Elyria, O., to start a factory making housepaint" (p. 7). While on a trip in 1916 Anderson wrote to Marietta Finley, later Mrs. Vernon Hahn, then a reader for the Bobbs-Merrill Publishing Company. Anderson had changed trains in Elyria: "Just across the track from where I stood was the factory building where I employed myself striving to get rich" (Letters, Newberry Library, Reserved Box 7: Mrs. Hahn's Letters from Anderson; letter of December 8, 1916; reproduced in Sutton's Exit to Elsinore, pp. 41-43, and in his Road to Winesburg, pp. 560-63).

25/23-24. for ten, fifteen years an advertising writer, in a big

Chicago advertising agency. See 4/25-26, 9/15-16, and 34/31-35/1
and their notes. Anderson's statement here is remarkably accurate.
Since he was with the Frank B. White Advertising Agency and its
successor, the Long-Critchfield Company, between 1900 and 1906,
and with Long-Critchfield and its successor, the Taylor-Critchfield-
Clague Company, from 1913 until 1922, it is true that he was with
one Chicago agency for a total of fifteen years.

25/25.   even after I had written and published several books.   The
books Anderson published by 1922 are: Windy McPherson's Son,   .
Marching Men, Mid-American Chants, Winesburg, Ohio, Poor
White, and The Triumph of the Egg.   See the note to 23/12-13.
Since Anderson, however, says "written" as well as "published, "
we should add to this list several unpublished works.   They include "Mary Cochran, " "Immaturity, " "Impotence, " and "Talbot
Whittingham" (Letters, Newberry Library, 1915-1922).   Perhaps
the earliest version of "Talbot Whittingham, " written when Anderson was still in Elyria, is the first book set in his mythical Winesburg, Ohio; and on the back of one of the versions of this unfinished novel he wrote some of his Winesburg stories.   See Phillips, "Sherwood Anderson's Winesburg, Ohio, " pp. 33-34n.
Throughout his life Anderson worked on novels whose protagonist
was named Talbot Whittingham.   An edition of another early fragmentary novel is Gerald Carl Nemanic's "Talbot Whittingham: An
Annotated Edition of the Text Together with a Descriptive and Critical Essay" (unpublished Ph. D. dissertation, University of Arizona,
1969).   See also 54/31-32 and its note.

25/26.   hating the place as I might have hated living in a pest
house.   Anderson reiterates so frequently his aversion to advertising work that no documentation seems necessary.   It is surprising
and interesting, however, to hear him speak in his middle years,
that is, in the middle and late 1920's, of this work as pleasant.
The reason may be that, after the popular and financial success of
Dark Laughter in 1925 (see 26/22), Anderson's reputation declined.
Also in the later 1920's his third marriage was proving unhappy,
and a great feeling of personal and artistic inadequacy often over-
came him (see 65/11-12 and its note).   Therefore, he could write
on May 26, 1926, to Burton Emmett, who had just started to approach him about selling some of his manuscripts: "As a matter
of fact my own experience in an advertising agency was far from
unpleasant.   How many good friends I made there" (Letters, Newberry Library, 1926).   Also in Nearer the Grass Roots, published
in 1929, in the context of describing his buying and publishing the
Marion Democrat and Smyth County News, he says: "One day, on
an impulse, I went to the town and purchased the papers.   I have
been running them now for a month [marginal note: "January,
1928"], and it has been the most normal and happy month I have
had since I threw up my job in the advertising agency in Chicago"
(p. 10).   By the middle and late 1930's, however, when the "Writer's Book" was written, Anderson had achieved a happy marriage,
found a new outlet for his artistic endeavors in writing about the
industrialism that had come to the South, and was fruitfully at

work on a volume of short stories and his Memoirs. Therefore, from the ambience of his immediate happiness he could again look back on his advertising days as ones of drudgery and frustration.

25/27. my books not selling. Anderson had to struggle all of his life to make a living solely by his writing. In 1948 Karl Anderson, in the article "My Brother, Sherwood Anderson, " p. 26, had this to say about the situation: "The royalties of Sherwood's first four books--the fourth of them was 'Winesburg, Ohio'--came to less than $400. (Later he was fond of saying, 'I am the most talked about, most unread, most unbought author in America. ')"

25/27. so-called literary kudos coming. Anderson uses this same expression in a passage in Memoirs, ed. White: "At the time I was being published by Ben Huebsch who had taken my Winesburg stories after they had been kicked about in several publishing houses.... I had been getting a good deal of literary kudos but little or no money on which to live" (p. 490). A sampling of the literary kudos includes, first, Edward J. O'Brien's dedication of The Best Short Stories of 1920 to Anderson in these words:

> It is my wish to dedicate this year the best that I have found in the American magazines as the fruit of my la-bors to Sherwood Anderson, whose stories, "The Door of the Trap, " "I Want to Know Why, " "The Other Woman, " and "The Triumph of the Egg" seem to me to be among the finest imaginative contribution to the short story made by an American artist during the past year. (p. xx.)

In the very next year the dedication to The Best Short Stories of 1921 says:

> In my opinion Sherwood Anderson has made this year once more the most permanent contribution to the Ameri-can Short Story, but as last year's book is associated with his name, I am happy to dedicate this year's offer-ing to a new and distinguished English artist, A. E. Coppard. (p. xvii.)

Secondly, in the same year of 1921, Anderson, young in literary output and in the minds of critics, if not in years, re-ceived the first annual Dial Award, intended to encourage the work of promising young writers. With the Dial Award went a prize of $2000. (The second recipient of the Dial Award was T. S. Eliot after the publication of The Waste Land in 1922.) Thirdly, in 1926 Anderson was given the O. Henry Memorial Award Prize for the story "Death in the Woods" (see 28/16 and the notes to 4/14 and 54/2), which appeared in American Mercury in September, 1926. Apropos of the irony of his receiving this award, on Sep-tember 1, 1925, Anderson wrote to Gilbert Seldes, associate editor of Dial from 1920 to 1925: "Where do you get that stuff about O. Henry awards? Don't you know that I have been making funny cracks about O. Henry as a short story writer for years?" (Letters, Newberry Library, 1925). Anderson accepted the award, nonetheless.

Finally, in 1937 Anderson was elected to membership in The National Institute of Arts and Letters. An article that discusses Anderson's election, after a cautious two-year delay, is Frank Jewett Mather, Jr., "Anderson and the Institute, " Saturday Review of Literature, XXIII (April 5, 1941), 11.

25/29-30. textbook for story writers in schools and colleges. A similar passage in Memoirs, ed. White, anticipates also what Anderson will say in 25/30-26/6 about Winesburg's first two years' sales and its "condemnation":

> That particular book did not sell. It was widely condemned, called "nasty" and "dirty" by most of the critics. The book was more than two years selling the first five thousand.
> . . . .
> The book has become a kind of American classic. It is used as a textbook for story tellers in many schools and colleges. Really the stories might almost be published now in the Ladies Home Journal. (p. 22.)

In a letter to George Freitag of Canton, Ohio, who had written to Anderson about the problems facing the young writer, Anderson, on August 27, 1938, says much the same thing:

> Some of my own stories, for example, that have now become almost American classics, that are put before students in our schools and colleges as examples of good storytelling, were, when first written, when submitted to editors, and when seen by some of the so-called outstanding American critics, declared not stories at all. (Letters, ed. Jones and Rideout, p. 403.)

25/30-31. two years selling the first five thousand. In addition to mentioning this figure in the quotation from Memoirs, ed. White, cited in the previous note, Anderson speaks of it in a letter to N. Bryllion Fagin. This letter was probably written in the fall of 1927 in order to correct some mistakes and omissions in the "Biographical Note" that Fagin appended to his biography The Phenomenon of Sherwood Anderson. Anderson wrote: "Winesburg--as well as Poor White--is in The Modern Library. It may be interesting to you personally that it was 2 years selling 5000. It now sells 5000 to 8000 a year" (Letters, Newberry Library, 1927). See 27/31-28/1, where Anderson also speaks with pride of the fact that Winesburg and Poor White are in Modern Library editions. At 48/22-23 he again speaks of the Modern Library edition of Poor White.

25/31-32. previously published in the smaller literary magazines. The Winesburg stories which had magazine publication prior to their publication in the collected volume are:

"The Book of the Grotesque, " <u>Masses</u>, VIII (February, 1916),
    17;
"Hands, " <u>Masses</u>, VIII (March, 1916), 5, 7;
"The Philosopher, " <u>Little Review</u>, III (June-July, 1916), 7-
    9; (this is the Winesburg story "Paper Pills, " not the
    Winesburg story "The Philosopher"; see Phillips, "How
    Sherwood Anderson Wrote <u>Winesburg, Ohio</u>, " as reprinted
    in <u>The Achievement of Sherwood Anderson</u>, ed. by Ray
    Lewis White, [Chapel Hill: University of North Carolina
    Press, 1966], p. 67);
"The Strength of God, " <u>Masses</u>, VIII (August, 1916), 12-13;
"Queer, " <u>Seven Arts</u>, I (December, 1916), 97-108;
"The Untold Lie, " <u>Seven Arts</u>, I (January, 1917), 215-21;
"Mother, " <u>Seven Arts</u>, I (March, 1917), 452-61;
"The Thinker, " <u>Seven Arts</u>, II (September, 1917), 584-97.

See 48/25-26, where Anderson speaks about publishing in "high-
brow magazines. "

25/32-26/1. had <u>brought</u> me <u>in</u> a total <u>of</u> eighty-five <u>dollars.</u>   In
a passage in Rosenfeld's edition of <u>Memoirs</u>, a passage entitled
"Waiting for Ben Huebsch" and omitted by White in his edition, Anderson says:

> To get the stories published was a harder matter.   In
> New York <u>The Seven Arts</u> and the old <u>Masses</u>, in Chicago
> <u>The Little Review</u> had begun printing them and in one or
> two instances I got as much as ten dollars for one of
> them.   Once later I counted up--it must have been in a
> base moment, when I was thinking of money.   For the
> whole series, printed in this way, I figured I had got
> eighty-five dollars.   I mention the matter because I am
> always getting letters from young writers and they seem,
> most of them, to be up against what I was up against.
> (p. 288.)

One of these young writers was George Freitag, mentioned in the
note to 25/29-30. Anderson tells Freitag: "For the whole series
I got eighty-five dollars" (<u>Letters</u>, ed. Jones and Rideout, p. 404).
Phillips, "Sherwood Anderson's <u>Winesburg, Ohio</u>, " p. 150, says
that only <u>Seven Arts</u> paid; <u>Masses</u> and <u>Little Review</u> did not.

26/2. some <u>literary</u> recognition.   The standard bibliographies of
Sherwood Anderson's works, in particular Sheehy and Lohf's,
White's, and G. Thomas Tanselle, "Additional Reviews of Sherwood
Anderson's Work, " <u>Papers of the Bibliographical Society of Ameri-
ca</u>, LVI (1962), 358-65, give evidence of the critical attention paid
<u>Winesburg</u>, both at the time of its publication and later.   Of course,
some of the reviews were favorable and some were not, but undoubtedly the weight of critical opinion fell on the side of favorable
reviews.   As a sampling, consider the six contemporary reviews
reprinted by John H. Ferres in his critical edition of <u>Winesburg</u>,

Ohio, The Viking Critical Library (New York: The Viking Press, 1966). Of the six, four are favorable:

> M. A. [attributed to Maxwell Anderson by Ferres], "A Country Town," New Republic, June 25, 1919;
> Llewellyn Jones, "The Unroofing of Winesburg: Tales of Life that Seem Overheard Rather than Written," The Chicago Evening Post, June 20, 1919;
> H. L. Mencken, in Smart Set, August, 1919;
> H. W. Boynton, "All Over the Lot," The Bookman, August, 1919.

One is unfavorable: an anonymous article in The Springfield (Mass.) Republican, July 20, 1919. Rebecca West in The New Statesman, July 22, 1922, although she compared Winesburg unfavorably to The Triumph of the Egg, nonetheless praises Winesburg.

There is also a good deal of evidence that Anderson, at the time, acknowledged the favorable recognition that Winesburg received. He wrote to Waldo Frank on May 27, 1919:

> Of course, I knew you would care for the Winesburg book but it is worth a great deal to me to have you say so as you do so beautifully. The book has only been out a few days but already I have had several letters of very deep appreciation of it. (Letters, Newberry Library, 1919.)

To Trigant Burrow on September 15, 1919, he wrote:

> Have you read my new book, Winesburg? The book has been getting rather remarkable recognition even from those who have fought me before. In another year it will no doubt get publication in France and perhaps in other European countries.
>
> . . . .
> It seems to me that I have proven my ability as a writer. I know of no other man in the country who has got such recognition as has come to me. Yet I make no money, and it is evident that the only source of income I might expect to open to me, the magazine field, will not open. The editors of such magazines write me personal letters congratulating me on the fine work I am doing, but laugh at the idea of printing my stuff. It is all very perplexing and disconcerting. (Letters, ed. Jones and Rideout, pp. 48-49.)

Finally, Anderson admits in a letter to Waldo Frank written probably in December, 1919: "I get constant and beautiful reactions from Winesburg" (Letters, Newberry Library, 1919).

The good deal of recognition given to Winesburg is evidenced by the fact that three years after its publication by Huebsch a cheaper Modern Library edition was also published (see 27/32-

28/1 and its note). For this edition Ernest Boyd wrote the Introduction, in which he says:

> The present collection of Winesburg stories gives the
> measure of his genius. In their unpremeditated narrative
> art they have a power of suggestion and revelation which
> we are accustomed to find in the great Russians, in
> Chekhov more than in Dostoyevsky, for there one admires
> the same economy of means, the same rich synthesis of
> life.
> ...The stories are written out of the depths of imagina-
> tion and intuition, out of a prolonged brooding over the
> fascinating spectacle of existence, but they combine that
> quality with a marvelous faculty of precise observation.
> Thus, the impression of surface realism is reinforced by
> that deeper realism which sees beyond and beneath the
> exterior world to the hidden reality which is the essence
> of things. (New York: The Modern Library, 1922,
> p. xv.)

To conclude, even in the late 1920's, when Anderson's reputation was at its lowest point, Winesburg received high praise. N.
Bryllion Fagin in his 1927 biography of Anderson says:

> Winesburg, Ohio, is a thoughtful book.... Winesburg is
> a sad book; a book of drab little stories, a book of the
> tragedy of our life. And yet it is a happy book. Its
> appearance was a happy omen. It is a tribute to the
> sturdiness of the spirit of a people. It is a landmark
> in the evolution of a mature literature.... Winesburg
> is a book of passionate revolt--revolt which is always an
> expression of a deep love of life. (p. 86.)

26/5-6. by most of the literary critics, as a kind of literary
sewer. Although it is not true that most of the literary critics
condemned Winesburg, throughout his life Anderson repeated the
story of the charges of filth and sex-obsession that were leveled
against it. See, for example, Hello Towns!, pp. 244-45; Memoirs, ed. White, pp. 22-25, 349-50; and the letter to George Freitag written on August 27, 1938 (Letters, ed. Jones and Rideout,
pp. 405-406). A concrete example of the kind of criticism against
which Anderson inveighs is Arthur H. Quinn's in American Fiction: An Historical and Critical Survey (New York: D. Appleton-
Century Company, 1936):

> Inspired probably by The Spoon River Anthology of
> Edgar Lee Masters, Anderson has been publishing short
> prose sketches of people in a small town which were col-
> lected in Winesburg, Ohio (1919). The characters are
> lonely, frustrated, futile, and abnormal. Anderson ex-
> plains in the introduction that he intends to draw gro-
> tesques, and it is quite probable that in a small town
> there might be found an insane person with hands which

loved to fondle small boys, another who thinks everyone
is Christ, a woman who takes a pillow to bed with her
instead of a man, a minister who peeps through a hole
in a stained glass window at a woman in her bedroom
across the way, to mention only a few of the eccentrics.
. But why in the name of sanity and maturity, without
which art is sterile, should anyone write about them?
These aberrations occur mostly among adolescents, and
to record them is to place one's self on the level of the
small boy who relieves his mind with a piece of chalk
on a back fence. (pp. 657-58.)

A letter of Anderson to his friend Van Wyck Brooks, written in
August, 1920, a year after the publication of Winesburg, shows the
depth of Anderson's feelings in regard to this kind of criticism:

It did hurt, though, when I found you also rather taking Winesburg, for example, as a sex book. It got under
my hide a bit. I'm usually thick-skinned.
    To me it seems a little as though one were permitted
to talk abstractly of things, to use scientific terms regarding them, in the new dispensation, but when one attempts to dip down into the living stuff, the same old
formula holds. A really beautiful story like "Hands,"
for example, is--well, nasty. God help us! Dozens of
men have told me privately they knew Wing Biddlebaum.
I tried to present him sympathetically--taboo. (Letters,
ed. Jones and Rideout, pp. 59-60.)

26/6-7. critics who, after some ten or fifteen years, began to
praise it highly. Anderson was fond of telling the story of how
Floyd Dell and Henry Mencken first rejected and later praised the
Winesburg stories. The Memoirs pages and the Freitag letter
cited in the previous note tell the same story, and mention Dell
and Mencken by name. Nonetheless, as was mentioned in the note
to 26/2, Mencken wrote a laudatory review of Winesburg in Smart
Set, August, 1919, and he also praised it at the time of its publication in an article in the Chicago American headed "Anderson
Great Novelist, Says Mencken." Mencken, however, did not publish any of the Winesburg stories in Smart Set. Furthermore,
Floyd Dell wrote in "American Fiction," Liberator, II (September,
1919), 47, that Winesburg was "a magnificent collection of tales."
Prior to this praise Dell had thought enough of the Winesburg tales
to print three of them in Masses: "The Book of the Grotesque,"
"Hands," and "The Strength of God." In a letter from Dell to
William Phillips on December 12, 1948, Dell says that there was
"no truth at all" to Anderson's story that Dell rejected the Winesburg tales when he first saw them. He also says that "the origin
of that delusion was the fact that some of the later Winesburg
tales were submitted to vote at an editorial meeting or meetings
and were voted down by the editors. S. A.'s paranoid self-pity
turned this into a conspiracy with me as villain." See Phillips,
"Sherwood Anderson's Winesburg, Ohio," p. 148; pp. 3-6 and 147-

48 give many details of the Dell-Mencken story. Dell also disavows his alleged mistreatment of Anderson in "How Sherwood Anderson Became an Author, " a review of Anderson's Memoirs,
which appeared in New York Herald-Tribune Books, XVIII (April
12, 1942), pp. 1-2, and in "On Being Sherwood Anderson's Literary Father, " Newberry Library Bulletin, V (December, 1961),
315-21. See, however, in the note to 14/19-20, Anderson's letter
to Waldo Frank in 1916, which cites Dell's disapproval of the
Winesburg story "Loneliness. "

26/12-13. we young writers were all looking up to him at the
time. This statement seems to indicate that the "famous literary
critic" of 26/10 is Dell rather than Mencken. As Anderson tells
us in Memoirs, ed. White, p. 336: ."It was through Margery
[Currey] that I met Ben Hecht, Arthur Ficke, her husband Floyd
Dell, who became for a time a kind of literary father to me. "
Nonetheless, in Memoirs, ed. White, pp. 349-350, Anderson also
says:

> I think that later, a good many years later, both men
> [Dell and Mencken] made claims to having been, more or
> less, the fathers of the stories. I think that by the time
> they came to make the claim they had both convinced
> themselves it was true. I think that it is now generally
> recognized that the little book did something of impor-
> tance. It broke the O. Henry grip, de Maupassant grip.
> [See 31/30-31.] It brought the short story in America
> into a new relation with life. I myself think that the real
> fathers and if you please the mothers of the Winesburg
> stories were the people who once lived with me in a Chi-
> cago rooming house, the unsuccessful Little Children of
> the Arts.

Apropos of the paternity of the Winesburg tales, the letter to Waldo
Frank written on May 27, 1919, and cited in the note to 26/2,
goes on to say:

> In regard to writing a review, if you can possibly find
> time to do it [Frank never did], I wish you would do it
> for one of the New York papers or something else. It
> does not need to be done right away but there is a view-
> point on this book that no one can express quite as well
> as you and that ought to be expressed. In a certain
> sense, you are father of the book. (Letters, Newberry
> Library, 1919.)

26/22. a novel that had sold. Anderson is referring to Dark
Laughter, the first of his books published by Horace Liveright. It
will be mentioned by name for the first time at 32/32-33/1. It
netted for Anderson more than $8000 during its first year of pub-
lication. See David D. Anderson, Sherwood Anderson: An Introduction and Interpretation (New York: Holt, Rinehart, and Winston,
Inc., 1967), p. 91.

26/22-24. a publisher who suddenly decided that I was what he
spoke of as "an undeveloped property." See 51/9-11, where Anderson speaks of Horace Liveright's coming to his rescue when he
was down to his last hundred dollars. The passage here referring
to the unnamed publisher is very similar to the passage at 51/9-
52/1, referring to Horace Liveright. In both instances the publisher "plunged on" (26/24) or "exploited" (51/24) Anderson,
bought advertisements in newspapers and on placards on streetcars (26/24-26 and 51/24-26), and made it possible for Anderson
to buy his farm and build his beautiful home (26/27-28 and 51/30).
Documentation for Anderson's relations with Horace Liveright will
be given in the notes to 51/11 and 51/16.

26/27-28. built with it a house in the country. Letters, Newberry Library, 1925, from Anderson to Mrs. Barbara Miller of
Grant, Virginia, and to Mr. William White of the First National
Bank of Troutdale, Virginia, show that Anderson bought Ripshin
Farm from Mrs. Miller for a total of $1450, paying Mrs. Miller
a down payment of $50 on September 15, 1925. From Letters,
Newberry Library, 1926-27, we also know that Anderson had a
cabin built on the property during the winter of 1926, that he and
his wife Elizabeth Prall moved to the farm in the spring of 1926,
and that the large stone house was built from the spring of 1926
until the summer of 1927.

26/28-29. when it was built I couldn't live in it for some five
years. This statement is incorrect, as is the statement in 53/30-
31, where Anderson says: "For two years and while the house
was building." The large stone farmhouse actually was built in
little more than one year's time. Anderson and Elizabeth went to
Ripshin to live on May 1, 1926. By that time the cabin, where
Sherwood was to work, was completed, but work on the house had
only begun. Sherwood and Elizabeth lived in an old barn converted
into a dwelling and called "the green house." It still stands on
the Anderson farm, across the stream from the stone house, and
is now inhabited by tenants of Mrs. Eleanor Anderson. From a
letter written to Ferdinand and Clara Schevill in the late fall of
1926, we know that Sherwood and Elizabeth were living in the main
house by then. Enclosed in the letter is a photograph of the unfinished house with a description of it written on the back. The
description says in part: "This end is finished and we are living
in it." Sherwood and Elizabeth sailed for Europe on December 1,
1926, and on their return to the United States in the spring of
1927 they definitely moved into the house. (Letters, Newberry Library, 1926-27.) By mid-August, 1927, Anderson wrote to Stark
Young: "The house is really pretty well done. One or two
country men dubbing about in the garden" (Letters, ed. Jones and
Rideout, p. 174). Elizabeth Prall Anderson in her memoirs, pp.
144-152, recounts the building of the stone house at Ripshin.
She says: "It was August in 1926 and the house called Ripshin
was finished. Sherwood had good reason to be proud of it. He
had taken joy in every phase of its construction and it had an unusual, unorthodox beauty" (Elizabeth Anderson and Gerald R. Kelly,

Miss Elizabeth: A Memoir [Boston: Little, Brown and Company, 1969], p. 151). If she really means "finished," the year should be 1927.

26/30-31. The next book I sent him was, alas, a book of verse. Nonetheless, the next book that Liveright published for Anderson was not his second "book of verse," A New Testament. The year after Dark Laughter was published in 1925, Liveright published Tar: A Midwest Childhood and Sherwood Anderson's Notebook. A New Testament was not published until 1927.

26/32-27/1. Books, like everything else in America, are sold, not bought. See 51/27-29, where Anderson makes the same statement, and its note, which shows the connection between this statement and the dominant theme and metaphor of the "Writer's Book." See also three letters to Anderson's agent and publishers. Anderson wrote to Otto Liveright on June 13, 1924:

> As to the matter of Horace. You may be sure of this--if I were thinking of a change from Huebsch I'd talk to Horace first of all.
> And I've no doubt more of my books could be sold by vigorous merchandising.
> But on the other hand Ben Huebsch stuck to me when I wasn't worth salt as a property and he'd have to give me a pretty raw deal of some sort before I'd ever quit him. (Letters, Newberry Library, 1924.)

Anderson left Huebsch in the next year, however. Then four years after Horace Liveright "sold" Dark Laughter to the American public, Anderson wrote to him on February 21, 1929:

> I've been reading proofs on Hello Towns.... It's a damn good book--one of the best I ever did. I want you to jig up your sales force. Sell this book.
> It is a real picture of life--fragmentary, as I have been lately, but real. People are going to like it.
> Books sell when you fellows sell them.
> You go and sell this book. It is going to be a go.
> You take my judgment on this, Horace. Shoot the works on this book. I really am right about it. (Letters, Newberry Library, 1929.)

After Horace Liveright's death in 1933, Scribner's sought for and obtained Anderson as one of their authors. Anderson wrote to Maxwell Perkins on August 16, 1940:

> At the same time, Max, I can't live by merely being thought of as a sometime master of my craft.
> It is, Max, my own pretty firm belief that the American people do not buy books. Books are sold to them. Pretty much everything is sold to Americans.
> When I began publishing, I began with Ben Huebsch,

who had a curious reluctance about selling books.   I
stayed with him for a long time, for years.   I was, at
the time, strong enough to work, often at work I hated,
to make a living and support my children and do my
writing at night.   I had finally to quit him or starve.
    I went to Horace Liveright, and while he lived, Horace
did sell my books.   He took a gamble on me, and he
won and I won.   Horace had, as we both know, a lot of
unpleasant things about him, but he did put a roof over
my head and free me from having to sit day after day in
a damn advertising office.
    Which convinced me that my books could be sold.
    (Letters, ed. Jones and Rideout, p. 463.)

27/2-3.   my experimental, half mystic verse.   Anderson here is
speaking of A New Testament, but he could just as well be speaking of his first book of poetry, Mid-American Chants, published by
John Lane in 1918.   See 92/5, where Anderson speaks of the "half
mystic wonder" of "The Man's Story."

27/5.   having what is called literary fame.   When Anderson returned from his European trip in the spring of 1927, he wrote to
Roger Sergel:

            I'm pretty tired of bigness, big feelings, self-induced.
            I went over to Paris, had a success of a sort there.
            You haven't come to that yet.   I mean feeling yourself
            established.   You get what is called fame.
            Sherwood Anderson--
            A man's name.
            You hearing it around.
            Presently a kind of deep sickness.   (Letters, ed. Jones
            and Rideout, p. 168.)

27/6.   I was no longer young.   By September of 1927 Anderson
was fifty-one years old.   When Dark Laughter was published in
1925 he was forty-nine.

27/18.   "Go in for it," my friends said.   Anderson had at least
two opportunities, one in 1905 and the other in 1917, when he "was
a young writer," to turn aside and make money.   Both of the
known opportunities were offered to him by the Curtis Publishing
Company, publishers of the popular magazines Saturday Evening
Post, Ladies' Home Journal, and Country Gentleman.   Anderson in
Memoirs, ed. White, pp. 211-15, tells of his early offer from
Cyrus Curtis himself who had been impressed by the writing Anderson had done praising business in Agricultural Advertising.
Sutton, in his dissertation, "Sherwood Anderson, The Formative
Years," (unpublished Ph.D. dissertation, The Ohio State Univer-
sity, 1943, p. 166), cites two letters from Marco Morrow, the
man who had hired Anderson for the Frank B. White Agency in
1900.   Morrow's letters, written from Topeka, Kansas, on October 11 and November 12, 1941, corroborate Anderson's account that

he wrote a story for George Horace Lorimer which Lorimer rejected because it did not "glorify" business.   Anderson refused to
change the story.   Sutton, however, doubts that Anderson was offered a position as editorial writer.
 The second opportunity that Anderson had to write for the
Curtis Company came in 1917.   From Anderson's letters to Waldo
Frank we learn that the Curtis Company again approached him.
He wrote to Frank from Chicago sometime before October 29,
1917:

> The Curtis people approached me and I proposed to them
> that they send me on a two years' literary pilgrimage to
> the cornfields.   I would like to find some publisher ven-
> turesome enough to send me on a long walk, to last
> about two years, among the farmers and the small town
> people of the Middle West.   I want to pull out of busi-
> ness and go live among the people but don't want to make
> compromises.   I would produce stories, sketches and
> articles.   Don't like the flavor of the Curtis crowd, but
> if I went for them I would work on Country Gentleman,
> not the Post.   That would be better.   Is there any other
> magazine, a little broad in its outlook, that might be in-
> terested in such an idea?   (Letters, Newberry Library,
> 1917.)

Anderson also wrote to Frank sometime before November 7, 1917:

> Here is an odd thing that may interest you.   It may
> prove to you that I am corrupt.   It almost seems to me
> so and keeps me grinning as I go along the street.
> [Barton Wood] Currie of the Curtis crowd wanted me
> to do some country town stories for them.   I dismissed
> the idea, said I couldn't write to order, etc.
> But the damned cuss got an idea into my head.   I
> was a good deal tired and blue and began doing some
> small-town stories in a semi-light vein for my own
> amusement.   They fairly dance along, and I grin all the
> time as I write.   The idea I have is whimsical and tre-
> mendously amusing.   In spite of myself I may do just
> what the cuss wants and make a little money.   (Letters,
> ed. Jones and Rideout, p. 22.)

Here is an instance in 1917 when Anderson resisted the "temptation" to write for money.   See 43/28 and 45/6-7 and 22.

27/18-20.   At that time the movies had just become a gold mine
for writers.   At the time Anderson changed from Huebsch to Liveright, he wrote to his life-long friend John Emerson, Hollywood
producer and actor (see 37/32 and its note), to ask his advice
about movie rights for his books.   In a letter written on April 5,
1925, he tells Emerson about his new contract, and then says:

> The only thing left open in the contract covers play rights

and moving picture rights to my books and stories.
These are perhaps not valuable now, but with the rapid
change of things going on they may be any day. Dreiser
[see 43/12-13 and its note], for example, was recently
offered twenty thousand for movie rights to The Genius.
Liveright wants to handle all such negotiations for me
and there is a question as to what percentage of any
monies got from these rights should go to him. I took
the liberty of asking him to impose on you in my name
to discuss the matter. You and he come to an agreement that seems fair to you both and write it into the
contract. Whatever seems right to you two will be right
with me. (Letters, Newberry Library, 1925.)

Anderson had worked for Emerson's movie company in the fall of
1918 as a publicity man; he calls the job a "sinecure" in Memoirs,
ed. White, p. 407. See also A Story Teller's Story, ed. White,
pp. 22-23. We see from evidence in his letters that throughout
his life he had a desire to get some of his works into the movies.
He never succeeded, however. See 45/18-19, where he says, "I
had even written, two or three times, to agents in New York or
Hollywood." The note to 45/18-19 documents some of this correspondence.

27/24. Then you can write as you want to write. In a letter to
Trigant Burrow on October 12, 1921, Anderson wrote:

The commercial aspect of thing[s] is really more deeply
seated in all of us than we quite dare allow ourselves to
realize. I constantly myself have men come to me, men
who I think love me too, and say: "Now, Anderson, you
could write a novel or a play that would make money.
Why don't you do it and thus make money enough to be
a free man? Afterward you could of course do your real
work." (Letters, ed. Jones and Rideout, p. 75.)

Twice in Memoirs, ed. White, pp. 329-30 and 410, Anderson
speaks in the same vein, and in both instances he is speaking about
the time of his return to Chicago after he left business in Elyria.
The incident on p. 410 is summarized in this way: "I could go into the movies, write the stuff they want, for a time, get myself
some dough. Then I could cut it out." See also 44/20-21, where
Anderson says: "If I go to Hollywood, write drivel there, get
money by it."

27/26-27. when I was writing all of my earlier books, I was very
strong. See the note to 26/32-27/1 and Anderson's letter to Maxwell Perkins which says the same thing.

27/32-28/1. both now to be had at a low price, in The Modern
Library. See the note to 25/30-31. Winesburg, Ohio was published in a Modern Library reprint in 1922 and Poor White in
1926. As to the reprint of Winesburg, from letters between

Huebsch and Anderson we can see Huebsch's reluctance to sell to
Horace Liveright and the Viking Press, publishers of the Modern
Library, the plates of Winesburg. Anderson argues, however,
that a cheaper edition would enhance the book's popularity and not
greatly interfere with the sales of the more expensive edition.
Here and in 48/22-23 Anderson speaks of the Modern Library editions as marks of great distinction.

28/1-2. I was living in a Chicago rooming house. As has been
noted (14 /13-14), Winesburg, Ohio was written in a rooming house
at 735 Cass Street, Chicago, but Poor White was not. Poor White
was begun and nearly completed when Anderson was in New York
in the fall of 1918, working on his "sinecure" in John Emerson's
movie company. He finished Poor White in the winter of 1920 in
Fairhope, Alabama (Schevill, pp. 118-23).

28/4-6. I undressed. It seemed to me that I wanted, ... a great
washing. In Memoirs, ed. White, pp. 249-50, Anderson describes
a similar scene in which he undresses, washes his clothes, his
room, and himself, before he starts his writing. In Memoirs,
however, he puts this scene in his home in Elyria.

28/12-13. I have never been one who can correct, fill in, rework
his stories. This statement is substantially correct, but false if
taken too literally. By temperament Anderson was not inclined to
rework, correct, and fill in details in his stories. The many versions of the same story that fill the vast manuscript collection of
Sherwood Anderson Papers at the Newberry Library attest to the
fact that Anderson, instead of reworking a story, often rewrote it
completely (see 85/2-5). It is possible that Part III, "The Writer," is a concrete example of Anderson's working in this manner.
It seems to the present editor, as is explained in the Introduction
and in the note to 67/1-70/28, that "The Writer" is an early version of the short story "Pastoral."
    On the other hand, Anderson often made specific correc-
tions, deletions, and additions in his manuscripts. The number of
notes in the Textual Apparatus that indicate manuscript changes in
the "Writer's Book" attests to this fact. So does the whole of the
manuscript collection at the Newberry Library. See also William
Phillips' "How Sherwood Anderson Wrote Winesburg, Ohio." When
commenting on Anderson's statement in Memoirs (ed. Rosenfeld,
p. 280; in White's edition the passage is on p. 352), that no word
of "Hands" was changed after its original composition at one sitting,
Phillips says:

> Furthermore, although Anderson insisted that after
> writing the story "Hands," "no word of it ever changed,"
> the manuscript shows that the tale underwent extensive
> revisions of words and phrases after it had been written.
> And in addition to the manuscript revisions, the first
> five paragraphs of the Masses version of "Hands" are a
> re-arrangement of the corresponding first two paragraphs
> of the manuscript version, indicating that Anderson re-

worked the first part of the story before submitting it to
the Masses. (As quoted in The Achievement of Sherwood
Anderson, p. 65.)

Anderson's attitude towards correcting, as well as towards
"clean white sheets" (see 24/25-26), is well expressed in A Story
Teller's Story, ed. White, p. 210:

> To the writer of prose, who loves his craft, there is
> nothing in the world so satisfying as being in the presence
> of great stacks of clean white sheets. The feeling is in-
> describably sweet and cannot be compared with a reaction
> to be got from sheets on which one has already scribbled.
> The written sheets are already covered with one's faults;
> and oh, it is seldom indeed these sentences, scrawled
> across these sheets, can compare with what was intended.

28/13-14. I must try and when I fail must throw away. Evidently Anderson wrote A Story Teller's Story in the manner he describes here and in the quotation from that book given in the previous note. In a letter to Ferdinand and Clara Schevill written in
September, 1923, he speaks about writing A Story Teller's Story:
"As for this present book on which I work now, it has been rewritten several times. The physical labor has been tremendous.
Never did I tear up so much" (Letters, ed. Jones and Rideout,
p. 108). See also 54/2 and 84/16 and their notes for more details on Anderson's practice of writing and throwing away.

28/14-15. Some of my best stories have been written ten or
twelve times. See 85/3-5, where Anderson says: "There are
single short stories of mine that have taken me ten or twelve
years to get written. "

28/16-17. "Death in the Woods, " a magnificent tale, one of the
most penetrating written in our times. This might seem like in-
ordinately high praise from the author himself, but Anderson's
judgment here must be allowed to stand. "Death in the Woods" is
one of the acknowledged masterpieces among Anderson's short
stories (see the notes to 4/14 and 54/2), for which he received
the O. Henry Memorial Award Prize in 1926 (see the note to
25/27). Some of the critics who share Anderson's high opinion
of "Death in the Woods" are:

> Norman Holmes Pearson, "Anderson and the New Puritan-
> ism, " The Newberry Library Bulletin, II (December,
> 1948), 55;
> Horace Gregory, "Editor's Introduction, " The Portable Sher-
> wood Anderson (New York: The Viking Press, 1949,
> pp. 23 and 26-27;
> Irving Howe, Sherwood Anderson (New York: William
> Sloane Associates, 1951), pp. 164-67;
> Jon S. Lawry, " 'Death in the Woods' and the Artist's Self
> in Sherwood Anderson, " PMLA, LXXIV (1959), 306-11;

> Mary Rohrberger, "The Man, the Boy, and the Myth: Sher-
> wood Anderson's 'Death in the Woods,' " Midcontinent
> American Studies Journal, III (Fall, 1962), 48-54;
> Sister Mary Joselyn, O.S.B., "Some Artistic Dimensions of
> Sherwood Anderson's 'Death in the Woods,' " Studies in
> Short Fiction, IV (Spring, 1967), 252-59.

Sister Joselyn, who examines the four interlocking transformations
of the story, concludes her study: "Thus the whole is implicit in
each of the parts, and by these means and others, Anderson succeeds in creating a perfectly integrated work of art" (p. 259).

28/17-18. ten years getting itself written. There is a passage in
"Waiting for Ben Huebsch" in Memoirs, ed. Rosenfeld, which is
very similar to this passage:

> Often I have found that an impression got from a story
> must stay in me for years. It comes into my mind,
> stays for a time. Perhaps I try to write it but it is
> not there. I must throw it aside. [I think for example
> of a story called Death in the Woods. It is a story I
> must have tried to write at least a dozen times over as
> many years. I am not one who can peck away at a
> story. It writes itself, as though it used me merely as
> a medium, or it is n.g.] (p. 286.)

In Memoirs, ed. White, pp. 424-26, Anderson recounts the time in
Palos Park, Illinois, when he, on a snowy, moonlit night, watched
a pack of dogs running in a circle around him as he lay stretched
out on a log in a clearing in the forest. He says:

> It was on that night I got the impulse for one of my best
> stories, the title story for the volume Death in the Woods.
> I did not succeed in writing it at once. It was one of
> the stories I wrote, threw away and rewrote many times.
> (p. 425.)

Actually Anderson did not get the initial impulse for "Death
in the Woods" from the experience with the dogs in the woods
near Palos Park. William Vaughn Miller's dissertation, "The
Technique of Sherwood Anderson's Short Stories" (unpublished Ph.D.
dissertation, University of Illinois, 1969), prints in the appendix
the earliest known version, called "The Death in the Forest,"
pp. 259-68. Miller printed this version from a twenty-two page
holograph in the Sherwood Anderson Papers in the Newberry Library. A note in Mrs. Eleanor Anderson's handwriting attached
to the holograph says: "Early version of short story Death in the
Woods." Miller's dissertation, pp. 245-47, describes the known
manuscript versions of "Death in the Woods": (1), the early "The
Death in the Forest" holograph; (2), a "blue carbon" typescript,
one copy of which is in the "Death in the Woods" folder and the
other copy in the Tar folder at the Newberry Library; (3), a holograph fragment in the Tar folder; (4), a typescript in the Tar

folder which became the printed chapter in Tar; this typescript is
heavily revised in black ink; and (5), a typescript and its carbon
in the "Death in the Woods" folder. This is the version of the
story as it appeared in Death in the Woods (New York: Liveright,
Inc., Publishers, 1933). The version that appeared in 1926 in
American Mercury is identical with the 1933 version except for the
addition of a four-line paragraph about bound children and the de-
letion of three words.

        The published versions of "Death in the Woods" are: (1),
"The Death in the Forest, " Miller's version as reprinted in the
appendix to Ray Lewis White's 1969 critical edition of Tar; (2),
Chapter XII of Tar (Boni and Liveright, 1926, pp. 199-222; ed.
White, pp. 129-41); (3), in American Mercury, IX (September,
1926), 7-13; and (4), the title story in Death in the Woods, pp. 3-
24.

        If Anderson is accurate in saying that "Death in the Woods"
was ten years in getting itself written and since the 1926 version
in American Mercury is virtually the same as the story as it appeared in Death in the Woods, "The Death in the Forest" must
have been written about 1916, the time he was writing the Winesburg tales. It is interesting to hear Schevill speak of "Death in
the Woods" in these terms:

>   It is one of Anderson's great accomplishments and its
>   quality is due to the fact that in writing it he reverted
>   temporarily to his old ideas about style and form.
>   (p. 228.)
>
>   After he had finished this story, he dispatched it to
>   his agent. Perhaps if it had been praised and accepted
>   immediately, his interest in the old form would have re-
>   vived. But Harpers turned it down. The American Mer-
>   cury finally published it in their September, 1926, issue.
>   [See the note to 4/13.] By then it was too late. The
>   momentary urge to return to his old aims had worn off.
>   (p. 230.)

28/22-23. It has not yet come to life, throw it away. See a
letter Anderson wrote to Roger Sergel when he was working on the
revisions of Tar, that is, in the fall of 1925:

>   How many times I have had like that--still have. It
>   means only--I'm sure--that the tale you were telling was
>   not fully alive in you. There are tales I've tried 20
>   times to write and don't get down. Perhaps they do not
>   really belong to me.
>   . . . .
>   Am trying to get the Childhood book done by Oct.
>   12th. It's crowding things a little. (Letters, Newberry
>   Library, 1925.)

29/2. They write me letters. See Part II, "How to Write to a
Writer, " 62/1-66/2, where Anderson discusses the kinds of letters

he receives from aspiring writers.

29/2. "You are our father." The friendship, influence, and later
misunderstanding between Anderson and such younger American
writers as William Faulkner, Ernest Hemingway, F. Scott Fitzgerald, and Thomas Wolfe are too well known to need documentation here. The most explicit statement about Anderson's being
their "father" comes from William Faulkner. In an interview in
New York in 1956 with Jean Stein Vanden Heubel of the Paris Review, Faulkner said: "He was the father of my generation of
American writers and the tradition of American writing which our
successors will carry on. He has never received his proper evaluation. Dreiser is his older brother and Mark Twain the father
of them both" (Writers at Work: The Paris Review Interviews,
edited, and with an Introduction, by Malcolm Cowley [New York:
The Viking Press, 1956, 1958], p. 135).

29/11. And it is so they should begin too. In "Man and His
Imagination," p. 58, Anderson says: "The work of any writer and
for that matter of any artist in any of the seven arts should contain within it the story of his own life." A section of "Man and
His Imagination," including this sentence, was incorporated into "A
Writer's Conception of Realism," an address delivered on January
20, 1939, to aspiring writers at Olivet College, Olivet, Michigan,
published by Olivet College in 1939 and reprinted in The Sherwood
Anderson Reader, pp. 337-47.

29/23-24. but for us, there is, there can be, no success, but
while this belief. The manuscript reads: "but that, for us, there
is, there can be, no success, but that while this belief." The editor has omitted the two "that's." This is one of the few instances
when the editor has omitted Anderson's words. It is the editor's
opinion that the two "that's" obstruct the sense of the sentence and
were inadvertently written by Anderson because he still had in his
mind the "perhaps I am only trying to say that" of 29/18.

29/25. mythical thing called "success." As early as 1917 we
hear Anderson saying to Waldo Frank in two letters, the first
written in March and the second in November:

> Primarily the difficulty with all of us is that, being
> Americans, we in some way got a wrong start in life.
> The notion of success in affairs, in love, in our daily
> life is so ingrained that it is almost impossible to shake
> it off. (Letters, ed. Jones and Rideout, p. 8.)

> I suspect that the thing needed is quite simple--a real
> desire, on the part of a few people to shake off the suc-
> cess disease, to really get over our American mania for
> "getting on." It has got to be pretty deep-seated if it
> gets us anywhere.
> Why is the desire for success so deep-seated? I have
> wondered. Is it because we are neither urban or rural

that we have neither the crude sincerity of the Russians
or the finished gesture at art and life of the Frenchmen?
(Letters, ed. Jones and Rideout, p. 24.)

Ten years later Anderson, in the middle of his career, wrote in
two letters to his son John, then an art student:

> It is ten times as important to be devoted [to the arts]
> as it is to succeed. You will be a fool if you think ever
> that you have succeeded in the arts. (Letters, Newberry
> Library, 1926.)

> It isn't your success I want. There is a possibility
> of your having a decent attitude toward people and work.
> That alone may make a man of you. (Letters, Newberry
> Library, 1927.)

See also 84/15, where Anderson says that the real purpose of
writing "isn't surely to get fame, recognition."

29/30. disease. Anderson wrote to his son John in 1927, "Self
is the grand disease." Later in the same letter he says: "Power,
such as comes with achievement, is something. In the end it becomes a disease. It destroys the man who has it" (Letters, ed.
Jones and Rideout, pp. 167-68). This letter is quoted at some
length in the note to 91/16.

30/8-9. but four hundred dollars, then three, two, one. Anderson speaks about this kind of financial situation in a letter to Burton Emmett, dated by Emmett, not by Anderson, October 21, 1929:

> After the break up of my last marriage I guess I rather
> broke up.
>   I haven't done much decent work for a year.
>   Of course very little money came in.
>   Most of the stuff I wrote I didn't feel like sending any-
> one. I tore most of it up.
> . . . .
>   So I came here [probably Washington, D.C.], almost
> broke. I got down to $50.00, was going to put the novel
> aside, go home and do some articles, etc., when luck
> came. I got in almost $2000.00. That means I can stay
> at the novel and, I hope, see it through this winter.
> (Letters, Newberry Library, 1929.)

30/9-10. on a farm and in the house built by my one successful
book. See 26/22 and its note. In 1925 Anderson wrote to his
brother Karl after Karl sent him greetings for his birthday on
September 13:

> Sent you copy Dark Laughter the other day. Am leav-
> ing here October 8th for long lecture trip. Will be in
> New York late in October sometime. A damn bore but I

> need to rake in the shekels.
> Have bought a small mountain farm in Virginia--Blue
> Ridge Mountains--and will spend next summer there.
> Try not to think too much of birthdays. Slur them
> over all I can.
> The novel seems to have got away from the barrier
> well and is running well up the back stretch. (Letters,
> Newberry Library, 1925.)

See also 54/1-2, where Anderson speaks about "delivering silly
lectures to get more money" for Ripshin.

30/22-23. "Roll Your Own." This is another passage in which
Anderson's irony comes to the fore. As we see in the last of the
letters quoted in the note to 30/24-25, Anderson would permit
Pictorial Review to change the title. He knew, however, that if
the title that fits the story is not acceptable to the magazine, the
magazine's editors will be hard pressed to find a suitable and acceptable title.

30/24-25. never published it. It is possible to verify the truth
of this incident concerning "There She Is, She Is Taking Her Bath"
by letters that Anderson wrote in 1923. In a letter to Jerome and
Lucile Blum written early in the year, Anderson says: "Luck
comes along. A magazine has paid $750 for the story about the
jealous husband" (Letters, ed. Jones and Rideout, p. 91). In a
footnote Jones and Rideout say: "Presumably 'The Man's Story,'
Dial, LXXV, 247-264 (September, 1923). Collected in Horses and
Men." "The Man's Story," however, is not about a jealous husband, and "There She Is, She Is Taking Her Bath," as stated in
31/12, is. Anderson, anxious to get the stories that were to be
published in his third volume of short stories, Horses and Men,
printed in magazines before the fall publication of the book, wrote
to Otto Liveright on April 25:

> Let the Dial have "The Man's Story"--if they want it--
> and will give it publication before October.
> Also, Otto, try to get Pictorial to use the story they
> have before October--as I would like to include it in the
> book. I suppose there is a certain kudos for them in
> being given credit on the book's title page. (Letters,
> Newberry Library, 1923.)

Anderson wrote to Ben Huebsch on May 16:

> Enclosed is the copy for the new book of tales--HORSES
> AND MEN--and I hope you will like it.
> As for these stories I am sure of all of them for the
> book except the story THERE SHE IS--SHE IS TAKING
> HER BATH. Pictorial Review bought magazine rights on
> the story and my agent Otto Liveright says they will
> probably use it in October or November. I suppose we
> would plan publication of this new book for October so

that if they printed the story, even in the November number, it could be included in the book. I would like to
have it in. Would it, therefore, be asking too much to
suggest that you go ahead and set the whole book as we
have it here--with the chance we may have to pull this
story at the last minute? (Letters, Newberry Library,
1923.)

Huebsch wrote back to Anderson on July 10:

Liveright has just called me up to say that there seems
to be almost no chance of the Pictorial Review printing
its story in the immediate future. It appears that there
is a dispute about it between Vance [Arthur Turner
Vance, Pictorial Review's editor-in-chief] and the Circulation Department. That being the case, the story will
have to be killed. (Letters, Newberry Library, Incoming, Ben Huebsch to Anderson, 1923.)

Anderson received more detailed information from Otto Liveright
on July 13:

Mr. Vance is trying to publish THERE SHE IS, SHE IS
TAKING HER BATH in the November number of Pictorial
Review which is released October 15th. He cannot
promise it definitely as there is so much pressure from
the Circulation Department. He will know surely in a
month and I have spoken to Mr. Huebsch about it. He
will be able to hold the book open until Vance answers
definitely. (Letters, Newberry Library, Incoming, Otto
Liveright to Anderson, 1923.)

Anderson answered Liveright on July 24:

About the Pictorial. That is good news. I've a notion
the Circulation objection is the title. If it is tell them
to give the story another title. I won't care. I can't
see what else there is objectionable. (Letters, Newberry
Library, 1923.)

"There She Is, She Is Taking Her Bath" was never given another
title and was never published in Pictorial Review or in any other
magazine. Furthermore, Horses and Men had to go to print without it. Before it appeared in Anderson's last volume of short
stories, Death in the Woods, it appeared in The Second American
Caravan: A Yearbook of American Literature, edited by Alfred
Kreymborg, Lewis Mumford, and Paul Rosenfeld (New York: The
Macaulay Company, 1928), pp. 100-111.

31/6-7. that he personally liked the story. In this phrase for the
second time (see the note to 29/23-24) the present editor omits a
word Anderson has in the manuscript. The manuscript reads:

"that, while he personally liked the story. " It seems to the editor
that retaining "while" obstructs the easy reading of the sentence
because the sentence as a whole does not convey a conditional
meaning.

31/21-22. she was as innocent as a little flower ... if I remember correctly. Anderson does not remember correctly. When the
detective made the report to the jealous husband he said: "She is
as innocent as a little lamb" (Death in the Woods, p. 78).

31/28-30. for a single short story, as much as a thousand, fifteen hundred, even two thousand dollars. Anderson seems rather
conservative in his estimate here. In the last years of the 1920's
the Saturday Evening Post, one of the best-paying magazines, paid
as much as $6,000 for a short story by a well-known author
(Frank Luther Mott, A History of American Magazines, IV [Cam-
bridge, Mass.: Harvard University Press, 1957], 698). Of
course, during the depression years of the 1930's, even the Post
paid less. Nevertheless, $2,000 was not an exceptionally high
figure.

31/30-31. I have had a profound effect upon the art of short story
writing. In Memoirs, ed. White, when speaking of Winesburg,
Anderson says: "it has been said of the Winesburg stories that
they did give story telling among us a new tone" (p. 341), and "I
think that it is now generally recognized that the little book did
something of importance. It broke the O. Henry grip, de Maupas-
sant grip. It brought the short story in America into a new relation with life" (pp. 349-50). Critics agree with Anderson's self-
estimate. In 1927 two biographies of Anderson appeared. Cleveland Chase's, on the whole rather unfavorable, says this about
Winesburg:

> These stories represent the finest combination Anderson
> has yet achieved of imagination, intuition and observation
> welded into a dramatic unity by painstaking craftsmanship.
> They are one of the important products of the American
> literary renascence and have probably influenced writing
> in America more than any book published within the last
> decade. (New York: Robert M. McBride, 1927, pp. 31-
> 32.)

Chapter 4 of N. Bryllion Fagin's biography calls Anderson "The
Liberator of Our Short Story" and says:

> Winesburg, Ohio has become a national classic, and has
> exerted the largest influence [of his three volumes of short
> stories] upon other writers of the short story, as well as
> contributing to the establishment of Sherwood Anderson as
> the leading exponent of our short story. It was Wines-
> burg which made us pause over our unquestioned definition
> of the short story. Perhaps, we began to think, a short
> story is not really something concocted to produce an

effect. Perhaps, we thought, having read Winesburg, a
short story is so called not because it can be read at
one sitting, or because its elements are so arranged as
to produce the maximum effect that can be registered at
one sitting. Perhaps, we thought, a short story has
more to do with life of people than with its own elements.
Perhaps it is so called merely because it contains a
maximum of life in a minimum of space. (pp. 80-81.)

In concluding the chapter Fagin says:

[Anderson] broke away, wouldn't be stopped. He has
fought. He has dared. He has wandered in strange
places, unusual, unfrequented paths. He has created
things for the love of creating. He has said things that
a short story writer, by all the rules of the game and
tradition, should not say. He has spoken of himself and
for himself. And a new short story has emerged. The
American short story, through his efforts, is receiving
a new tradition. Year after year he has gone on writing
in his own way, creating new forms, enlarging and vita-
lizing the substance of a trivial, frivolous genre....
Even if Sherwood Anderson does not himself write a
single other short story of value--if he should stop with
what he has already written--his influence would entitle
him to the gratitude of all serious workers in the short
story, of all lovers of the short story, of all lovers of
American literature. He has brought an age of sincerity,
of honesty, of artistic integrity, into a frail, vulgarized
medium--into the American short story. (pp. 94-95.)

In the Introduction to The Best Short Stories of 1929, Edward J.
O'Brien states:

A comparison of the stories which I published in 1915
with those I am publishing in 1929 reveals an interesting
contrast. Fifteen years ago, it was almost impossible
to find more than one or two stories in a year's file of
all American periodicals which revealed literary gifts of
more than a technical order. In 1915, the best American short stories almost never rose above the standard
of a well-made Scribe play.... To-day such men as
Sherwood Anderson, Ernest Hemingway, Ring Lardner,
and Morley Callaghan, to mention no other names, have
educated a considerable public sufficiently for it to dis-
tinguish between ready-made stories and works of art.
(p. ix.)

In the Introduction to The Best Short Stories of 1933, O'Brien declares:

Sherwood Anderson's explorations of the contemporary
scene attracted no attention at first. No editor was much

interested in his stories and his early work appeared for
the most part in obscure periodicals. Yet these almost
anonymous stories of his, as we now see, marked a departure from the stencilled formalism of the past as profound in its effects as that of Chekhov's stories in Russia.
Almost for the first time, an American artist had attempted in his fiction to present a picture rather than to
write an ephemeral play. The pictorial values of Sherwood Anderson's work were not at first apparent, because
his pictures lacked colour. He was much more concerned to present significant form than to dazzle the eye
with colour. In this his instinct was profoundly right....
He believed in craftsmanship rather than machine production and so ran counter to the spirit of his age.
(p. xvi.)

After Anderson's death critics of the short story continued
to recognize the profound effect that he had on the development of
the genre. In 1945 Herbert E. Bates in The Modern Short Story
(London: Thomas Nelson and Sons) had a chapter entitled "American Renaissance." Its opening sentence is: "To a young English
writer beginning somewhere about 1921 the business of writing
stories, the only possible source of modern American inspiration
would have been the author of Winesburg, Ohio." Bates goes on
to speak of Anderson's life and says that in the years after World
War I, "in the years of immediate bewilderment, he began to write
stories which broke free from all past American tradition and
stereotyped formalism" (p. 163).
      Malcolm Cowley, in the Introduction to the Viking Compass
paperback edition of Winesburg, Ohio (New York, 1960), says:
"He soon became a writer's writer, the only story teller of his
generation who left his mark on the style and vision of the generation that followed. Hemingway, Faulkner, Wolfe, Steinbeck, Cald-
well, Saroyan, Henry Miller ... [Cowley's periods] each of these
owes an unmistakable debt to Anderson, and their names might
stand for dozens of others" (p. 1).
      Frank O'Connor, in The Lonely Voice (Cleveland and New
York: The World Publishing Company, 1962), when speaking of
Winesburg, says: "It is from this remarkable little book that the
modern American short story develops, and the Americans have
handled the short story so wonderfully that one can say that it is
a national art form" (p. 41). O'Connor also remarks: "The year
1919 and Sherwood Anderson signaled the beginnings of a new self-
consciousness; by 1920 Scott Fitzgerald was describing the return
of the troops and the fresh complication this was creating, and
within a couple of years Hemingway and Faulkner were sketching
out the new literature" (p. 39).
      William Peden in The American Short Story (Boston: Hough-
ton Mifflin Company, 1964) asserts:

      The antecedents of the recent or "new" American
      short story have been discussed in such detail in recent
      years that no detailed discussion is needed here. Among

its ancestors are the stories of Gogol, Henry James, Chekhov, Joyce, and Sherwood Anderson. <u>Dubliners</u> (1914), and <u>Winesburg, Ohio,</u> published five years later, are towering landmarks and seminal forces in its development. The new story in America was essentially a post-World War I development, forged in the restless, disillusioned years following Versailles. (p. 11.)

32/6. <u>house is not wired.... we use the old-fashioned coal oil lamps.</u> The editor's visit to Ripshin farm on July 16-17, 1970, was to a house equipped with all possible electrical conveniences, including electric stove and dishwasher in the kitchen (see 32/10-11). Mrs. Eleanor Anderson, however, confirmed Sherwood's statement that as long as he lived in the house there were no electric lights, only coal oil lamps. In an interview with the editor on July 23, 1970, Mr. John Anderson, Sherwood's son, said that his father, looking ahead to a time when he might sell the house, had it wired for electricity when it was built but that he left the wiring unfinished. In the Sherwood Anderson Papers there is a bill from the Johnson Electric Company of Marion, Virginia, dated September 22, 1926. The bill is for $150.00 for "wiring house" (Folder, "Ripshin Farm," Newberry Library). John Anderson's recollection of the house during his father's lifetime is of a house with wires protruding from walls and ceilings but with no light bulbs or electrical appliances. In a letter to Horace Liveright in 1929, at the time his third marriage was breaking up and he was trying to sell the house, Sherwood himself admits:

> When I built the house I wired it throughout for electric lights, building the wiring right into the stone walls, but, as a matter of fact, I have never put in one of the little plants they sell for making electric lights in such places. It would cost but a few hundred dollars to do this. (Letters, Newberry Library, 1929.)

32/8-9. <u>most of our land is covered with trees.</u> In the letter to Horace Liveright cited in the previous note, Anderson also says: "Up in the country where the house is located it is all cut-over timber land with great stretches of second growth timber now growing up" (Letters, Newberry Library, 1929). Ripshin Farm is in the midst of the beautiful forests of the Blue Ridge Mountains of Virginia.

32/9-10. <u>we burn firewood in our cookstove and in our fireplaces.</u> In a letter to Ferdinand and Clara Schevill, written from Ripshin in the late fall of 1926, Anderson says:

> The house is stone--18 inch walls--hot water heating system--9 rooms--2 bathrooms--3 toilets--spring water in the house--all wood in the house oak.
> The farm is about 33 acres. Our own firewood on the place--5 fireplaces.
> Cost of all building, farm, etc., about $10,000.

. . . .
Karl says cost in city would not be under $30,000.
(Letters, Newberry Library, 1926.)

32/13. our Ruby. Ruby Sullivan Barker worked for the Andersons
for different periods of time from 1933 or 1934 until her marriage
in 1940. In a letter she wrote to the editor from Roanoke, Virginia, on August 24, 1970, she verifies many of the facts Sherwood
mentions here in the "Writer's Book." Her letter says in part:

> I did work for the Andersons at Ripshin for a few years.
> There was no electricity during those years. The
> butter was churned by hand, the refrigerators were run
> with kerosene, and the cooking done with wood and coal
> ranges. Also there was a stove that was used for cook-
> ing which burned kerosene. The lamps were kerosene.
> Some of them were the Aladdin type. Also candles were
> used for lighting.
> About 1933 or '34 I worked at Ripshin as a baby sitter
> for some of the Anderson's guests. I do not recall their
> names at this time.
> In the years that followed I helped out with the house-
> keeping and cooking for two or three years....
> Then for about the years of 1937 thru 1939, I worked
> for the Andersons with my younger sister, Charlotte,
> helping me for about one year. She was married at the
> age of 16. Then I was assisted by Miss Faye Price for
> the last years I worked for Mr. and Mrs. Anderson.
> The last year I worked was 1939. I was married in the
> spring of 1940, and was unable to be at the farm that
> year.

32/17. the advantages of an electric washing machine. The protagonist of Many Marriages, John Webster, is a salesman of electric washing machines. Many Marriages (see 57/8-13 and the note
to 16/11-12) is the story of his flight from his job and his family.

32/20-21. has she not lived for years with me? Sherwood was
married to Eleanor Copenhaver for eight years, from 1933 until
his death in 1941. See 53/2-4, where Anderson says: "there is
something grows very close between people who have lived long
together, who have really achieved a marriage."

32/32-33/1. My novel Dark Laughter built it. This is the only
time that Dark Laughter is mentioned by name. It is alluded to in
26/22: "a novel that had sold"; and in 50/19-20: "this beautiful
house a book of yours built." An excellent study of Dark Laughter
is Robert Lenhart Crist's "Sherwood Anderson's Dark Laughter:
Sources, Composition, and Reputation" (unpublished Ph.D. dissertation, The University of Chicago, 1966).

33/2-3. log cabin by a stream in which, on ordinary occasions,
I work. This remark helps to date the composition of the "Writ-

er's Book." The first building that Anderson had constructed on
his newly acquired farm was a cabin on the top of the highest hill
on the property. In a letter to Mrs. John Greear, with whose
family he stayed during the summer of 1925 (see 73/30 and its
note), Anderson gives minute details about the building of:

> ... the log cabin I want to use as a workshop. Mr.
> Greear and I walked up the hill and selected about the
> spot where we decided the cabin should be built. As he
> knows, I want it to face the turn of the road so that it
> looks up the valley of the Laurel [Creek] and towards
> the distant mountains. Also I would make it face that
> way and have the front door on that side.
>   I made a kind of rough plan which I am sending you.
> (Letters, Newberry Library, September 30, 1925.)

The cabin was completed by the spring of 1926.
      In Part IV of the "Writer's Book" Anderson speaks of the
cabin when it was situated on the hilltop. See 71/19 and 72/4.
In 72/13-15, however, he says: "I had to give up the cabin on
the hilltop. I never wrote anything up there that I could bear
printing." Throughout Part I, the cabin is always described as
being by the side of the stream. See 56/20-22, 60/6-8, and 61/6.
Therefore, Part I was written after the cabin was moved from the
top of the hill to its present location, not far from the farmhouse
beside Ripshin Creek. See the note to 72/13-14 for further details
about the moving of the cabin.

33/4. "Can such a place be without electricity? Irony comes into play in this passage as it does in many others. Anderson's
beautiful, large stone house should not be without electricity.
People without electricity must be "anarchists" since it probably
"is against the law" to live in such a primitive way. Furthermore, these people must be "queer" and "foreigners" since "it is
not done." The real Americans have electricity.

33/10. anarchists. Anderson's ironic comments about anarchists
also help to date the composition of the "Writer's Book" towards
the middle or late 1930's when he became disillusioned with the
"radicals," the "economists," and with socialism. See 44/13-14,
83/7-8, and their notes.

33/30. It is synthetic vanilla. A major theme of the "Writer's
Book," the prostitution of art, is expressed in this passage with a
slightly different turn. Here Anderson is speaking of what we
might call the prostitution of business itself, or rather, the prostitution of the young, naive salesman. This passage is immediately
followed by deeply ironic remarks on business:

> "Oh, the world of business!
> "How wonderful!
> "How wonderful!" (33/31-34/1.)

All of page 34 continues the ironic statements about the "very resolute, very courageous" (34/6-7) businessman.

34/5-6. a shrewd and knowing man. In the present context Anderson gives "shrewd" the connotation that he usually attaches to
it. For Anderson "shrewd" is a pejorative term. Therefore it is
surprising to have him, when speaking of the dedication of Winesburg to his mother, misquote it and use the word "shrewd" for
"keen." See 40/15 and its note.

34/14. the first Roosevelt, the Teddy one. Theodore Roosevelt,
the twenty-sixth President of the United States (1901-1909), was
often the object of ironic gibes from Anderson. See Memoirs, ed.
White, pp. 17, 192, and 255. See also A Story Teller's Story,
ed. White, p. 201 and especially p. 158, where Anderson says, in
speaking of his days as a young laborer:

> All about me was the great American world rushing on
> and on to new mechanical and material triumphs. Teddy
> Roosevelt and the strenuous life had not yet come but he
> was implicit in the American mood.

34/19-20. "The trouble with you, " I told myself, "is just the
years you spent in business. " This sentence is quoted by Sutton
in Exit to Elsinore, p. 12, and in his Road to Winesburg, p. 175.
Sutton gives as his source "The Sound of the Stream, " The Sherwood Anderson Reader, p. 365. As the Introduction to this edition
explains, Paul Rosenfeld published first in Memoirs, 1942, and
then in the Reader, 1947, a portion of Part I of the "Writer's
Book" and called it "The Sound of the Stream. "

34/22-23. puzzled as I was puzzled. A letter written at the time
of which Anderson is speaking, written in late February of 1919 to
Waldo Frank, tells of such experiences:

> It is sad that those who have done most for me get the
> least in return. To the men about me in the office
> there I present myself as a strong swimmer. Hardly a
> day passes that some businessman or woman does not
> come to me asking a question.
> "How do you remain so calm and quiet?" they ask.
> I laugh. "It is because I love God, " I say.
> The men and women are baffled. They are angry at
> me. They love me.
> I cannot explain to them that I also am troubled and
> tossed out. I am too much like them.
> I come to the few people who have emerged into self-
> consciousness. It is for that reason you get occasionally
> such letters. (Letters, Newberry Library, 1919.)

See also Anderson's letter to Trigant Burrow, written in September of 1919 (quoted in the note to 26/2) in which Anderson says
that the mixed reception given to his works "is all very perplexing

and disconcerting" (Letters, ed. Jones and Rideout, p. 49).

34/31-35/1. in the fifteen or twenty years during which I was in
business, as advertising writer, as manufacturer. Compare this
statement with 25/23: "for ten, fifteen years as advertising writer." As the note to 25/23-24 shows, Anderson was in the advertising business for a total of fifteen years. He was a manufacturer for six and a half years, from 1906 to 1913. Therefore, he
was in business for nearly twenty-two years, from 1900 to 1922.

35/1-2. five men among my personal acquaintances had killed
themselves. In Memoirs, ed. White, Anderson makes a similar,
though less strong, statement: "I had, during my experience as
business man, known two or three people who afterwards commit-
ted suicide" (p. 416).

35/8. 'What is good for business is good for you.' The irony of
this statement and of the following one--"we are a great brotherhood"--helps to date the composition of Part I in the depression
years of the 1930's. They also connect it with Anderson's views
on capitalism and socialism. See 44/13-14, 44/23, 83/7-8, and
their notes.

35/18-19. a businessman who is by chance shy, sensitive, even
neurotic. Anderson seems still to have in mind the main character of "There She Is, She Is Taking Her Bath." These adjectives
aptly describe John Smith's diffidence and jealousy.

35/19. neurotic. As the Introduction explains, Mrs. Eleanor Anderson wrote in pencil on the manuscript of Part I above words
that were misspelled and/or difficult to decipher. Here, for the
last time, she wrote in a correction; above Anderson's barely legible "neuroctic" she penciled "neurotic." In between pages 80 and
81 of the manuscript there is a 3 by 5 piece of yellow paper on
which Mrs. Anderson wrote: "To p. 81 / 12/15/50." When asked
about going over the manuscript, Mrs. Anderson told the present
editor in an interview on July 17, 1970, that she no longer remembers writing on the manuscript of the "Writer's Book." The
handwriting on the manuscript and on the piece of yellow paper,
however, are undoubtedly hers.

35/24-25. my God, man, a judge! Here Anderson includes the
professional man in his indictment of business. He is implying
that all those who are not in the arts are caught up in the commercialism of American life. On the other hand, in "I Accuse,"
described in the "Writer's Book" 43/10-46/4 and in a manuscript
at the Newberry Library called "J'Accuse" (see the notes to
43/20-21, 43/26-27, and 44/9), Anderson also includes artists in
his indictment of those who succumb to commercialism.

36/10-11. the absurd notion I have that, in the end, I can make
our farm pay. Mrs. Eleanor Anderson in an interview on July 16,
1970, confirmed the truth of the statements in this passage. She

said that only tobacco-growing is profitable on the farms in southwestern Virginia; but since the government strictly regulates the
tobacco crop, it is very difficult today, as it was in Anderson's
time, to make the farms pay for themselves. Sherwood was always spending money on the farm, but he never made it pay.

36/21-22. <u>no man could make claim to aristocracy who destroyed
the land under his feet.</u> There is a manuscript in Box 2 of the
"Memoirs" manuscripts at the Newberry Library called "These
Southern Aristocrats." The manuscript is not included in either of
the published editions of the <u>Memoirs</u>. In it Anderson says that
most of his life after he was forty-five, that is, after 1922, he
lived in the South, first in New Orleans and then in Virginia. He
goes on to say:

> I went north to Virginia and bought a farm there, in
> the hills. In the hills the people were all poor but,
> later, I went down into one of the valley towns. I be-
> gan meeting the people there....
> There was something that constantly annoyed me. It
> was the pretentions of the so-called upper classes. They
> were bitten by the notion of what they called aristocracy,
> a persistent insistence on ancestry, always building it
> up, often enough telling themselves the most monstrous
> lies, which, having told, time and again, they came to
> believe.
> . . . .
> The South, with its slave civilization, having produced
> little or nothing of a cultural nature, having brutalized
> the poor whites, having pretty much destroyed the very
> land for which they fought, by the continual cotton crop-
> ping, having, on the whole, made a failure of living on
> what should have been the most beautiful and richest
> part of the country, had, I presume, to claim something.

There is another manuscript in "Memoirs" Box 2 at the Newberry
Library called "Aristocracy" in which Anderson expresses similar
ideas. In the published <u>Memoirs</u>, ed. White, Anderson speaks at
least twice in the same vein. On pp. 500-501 he tells about his
friendship with a poor woman, decidedly not of the Southern aristocracy, but a person of great pride. He comments:

> [Aristocracy] seemed to me to be always connected with
> the former ownership of slaves, with the ownership of
> rich valley land and money in the bank.
> To tell the truth I had grown a little weary of the talk
> of southern aristocracy and had been asking myself a
> question.
> "But what is an aristocrat?"
> I thought I had found one in the hills. It was my
> little old woman neighbor. (p. 501.)

On p. 555, when speaking of men who do not love and respect the land, Anderson writes:

> In this light what are we to say of the men of our "old
> south, " who cotton cropped all of the fertility out of the
> most beautiful section of our land? We speak of an old
> southern aristocracy. We should think only of their ugli-
> ness, their terrible weakness. Our Stark Youngs and
> Allen Tates are our ultimate vulgarisms.

In an article called "Price of Aristocracy, " published in Today, March 10, 1934, pp. 10-11, 23, Anderson says much the
same thing as he is saying here in the "Writer's Book." For example: "The South is now paying for the sins of an older generation which abused its rich birthright--the land."

37/3. mother, who died of overwork at thirty-five. Anderson
was prone to exaggerate his mother's hard life, and in his writings
he always made her death occur earlier than it did. From Sutton's
research we know that Emma Smith Anderson was born on October
1, 1852, and died "of consumption" on May 10, 1895, when she
was forty-two and Sherwood was eighteen (Sutton, Road to Winesburg, pp. 476 and 507). Anderson speaks of his mother's death
in A Story Teller's Story, ed. White, pp. 21 and 63; in Tar, ed.
White, pp. 175 and 204-12; and in Memoirs, ed. White, pp. 67-68
and 114-15. See also 39/26, where Anderson implies that his
mother died young, and 41/23, where he says "as she died when I
was young. "

37/4. mother of five strong sons and two daughters. In A Story
Teller's Story, ed. White, p. 21, Anderson says: "A family of
five boys and two girls--a mother who is to die, outworn and done
for at thirty--" The seven Anderson children with their birth
dates are as follows: Karl, born January 13, 1874; Stella, born
April 13, 1875; Sherwood, born September 13, 1876; Irwin, born
June 18, 1878; Ray, born May 21, 1883; Earl, born June 18,
1885; and Fern, born December 11, 1890 (Sutton, Road to Winesburg, p. 494). Fern died in infancy, but all the others lived to
maturity. Karl, the eldest, was the last survivor of the family.
He died in 1956.

37/4-6. Her photograph, enlarged from an old daguerreotype and
presented to me by my brother Karl. In a letter to his brother
Karl written from Palos Park, Illinois, in November of 1921, Anderson says: "Many thanks for the picture of Mother. It is a
charming thing" (Letters, Newberry Library, 1921). The editor
saw this photograph in Mrs. Eleanor Anderson's files in her home
in Marion, Virginia, on July 17, 1970.

37/6. hangs above my desk. In Memoirs, ed. White, p. 33, Anderson says: "Mother had been a bound girl and must have been
quite lovely. Her picture, as a young and beautiful woman, is
before me on my desk as I write. " This picture, called "The
Mother, " is the first of eighteen pictures reproduced in Memoirs,

ed. White, between pages 311 and 315. The picture called "The
Memoirist, " with the caption "Anderson in 1941 at 'Ripshin, ' "
shows Anderson writing at his desk with the picture of his mother
on the wall behind him.

37/7-8. photograph must have been taken when she was twenty-
two. See 39/9-11, where Anderson says: "she might have been
eighteen rather than twenty-two when it was taken. " It is impossible from the photograph to tell his mother's exact age. It is,
however, the photograph of a lovely young woman.

37/8-9. in one of the uncomfortable chairs that used to be in all
small-town photographers' studios. In the photograph Anderson's
mother is sitting sideways in a chair with her right elbow resting
on the arm of the chair. Her right hand is held against her right
cheek as she gazes pensively off to her right. It is true, as Anderson says in 39/12, that in the photograph she is very beautiful.

37/10-11. the studio would have been in a small and stuffy room,
upstairs perhaps. The key words in this passage are "would have
been" and "perhaps. " In this passage Anderson is doing the thing
that he continually insists all creative artists must do, namely,
create a mixture of fact and fancy, let the imagination so play on
the factual world that something new is created. Anderson is not
pretending that the circumstances surrounding the taking of his
mother's picture actually were as they are described here. The
literal facts are altered according to his creative imaginings, but
an artistically true portrayal of his mother, his father, and the
photographer is conveyed. See 18/11-12 and 23/6-8, and their
notes, on the relation between the real and the unreal. See also
82/29-30 and 83/17-20, where Anderson speaks about the use of
the imagination, and 84/5-22, where he speaks about the importance of the "flow" of ideas through the imagination.

37/11. above my father's harness shop. Sutton, Road to Winesburg, pp. 496-99, gives information relative to Irwin Anderson's
business ventures. He owned his own harness shop in Camden,
Ohio, from 1875 until at least 1879. Camden is in Preble County,
and the Directory of Preble Co., Ohio, for 1875 lists I. M. Anderson as one dealing in "Harness &c. " It also ran an advertisement which called him a "Manufacturer and Dealer in Harness,
Saddles, Bridles, Collars, Whips, &c. " Sherwood was born in
Camden on September 13, 1876. The Anderson family moved to
Caledonia, Ohio, sometime around 1883. Irwin seems to have
lost his harness shop because, probably in the fall of 1883, he
worked in Mansfield, Ohio, for the Aultman-Taylor Company, at
that time one of the largest farm-machine factories in the country.
Nonetheless, a Caledonia resident remembers him as a harness-
maker who worked hard but "spent his money on drink in saloons"
(p. 499). Several reminiscences of Irwin attest to the fact that he
drank too much.
        The Anderson family moved to Clyde, Ohio, probably in the
summer of 1884. In Clyde Irwin worked for Erwin Brothers, har-

ness manufacturers and dealers.   Thus during the Clyde years he
no longer owned his own shop but worked for others.   See Memoirs,
ed. White, p. 34, where Sherwood speaks about his father's working in his own harness shop before the family moved to Clyde, and
p. 37, where he speaks of him as no longer owning his own shop
but working for another man in Clyde.

37/11-12.   before he lost his shop and became a house painter.
Sutton, Road to Winesburg, p. 513, says that the directory of
Clyde for 1887 describes Irwin as a "House and sign painter."
The directory for 1890-91 describes him only as a "painter." Sutton goes on to say: "Apparently Irwin saw that he could no longer
earn a living at harnessmaking and made during the middle eighties
the change to the trade he was to follow the rest of his life."   In
Memoirs, ed. White, Sherwood speaks of his father's house painting on p. 28 and of his sign painting on p. 38.   Pages 95 and 275
have passages very similar to the passage here in the "Writer's
Book."   Three of Sherwood's highly imaginative accounts of his
father's painting businesses are found in Memoirs, ed. White, pp.
37-38, and in A Story Teller's Story, ed. White, pp. 5 and 72.
        Sutton, Road to Winesburg, pp. 30 and 34-36, says that
Clyde was basically a farm town and was not as deeply affected as
other Ohio towns by the incipient industrialization of the late nineteenth century.   Nonetheless, industrialization was partially responsible for the meager financial resources of the Anderson family.
Irwin had to abandon his harnessmaking craft apparently because,
with the advent of machine-made harnesses, people were no longer
willing to pay more for handmade goods.

37/20-23.   thoughts my mother would never have had.... There
was no Freud.   The best study to date of Anderson's use of Freudian psychology is Frederick J. Hoffman, "Three American Versions of Psychoanalysis," in Freudianism and the Literary Mind
(2nd ed., Baton Rouge: Louisiana State University Press, 1957).
Pages 229-50 discuss Anderson.   Hoffman's opening sentence is:
"At the peak of his career, in the mid-twenties, critics hailed
Sherwood Anderson as the 'American Freudian,' the one American
writer who knew his psychology and possessed a rich fund of
knowledge and experience to which it could be applied."   The remainder of the section on Anderson disproves this erroneous as-
sumption.   On p. 236 Hoffman quotes a letter that he received
from Dr. Trigant Burrow (see 77/27 and its note), written October 2, 1942.   Dr. Burrow says:

> My feeling is that Sherwood Anderson was, like Freud,
> a genius in his own right.   Anderson was a man of
> amazing flashes but again, like Freud, the chief source
> of his material was his own uncanny insight.
>   I can say very definitely that Anderson did not read
> Freud, nor did he draw any material from what he knew
> of Freud through others.   Don't you think that all schools
> like to lay claim to an apt scholar? I think this largely
> accounts for the psychoanalysts' quite unwarrented adop-

tion of Anderson.   Of Anderson I would say that socially
he was one of the healthiest men I have ever known.
His counter-offensive in "Seeds" [a story that grew out
of a conversation between Anderson and Burrow] amply
testifies to this.   Indeed on this score many orthodox
psychoanalysts might very profitably take a leaf from his
book.

The conclusion that Hoffman draws from his investigation of Anderson's knowledge of and dependence on Freud is that: "Anderson
developed his themes quite independently of Freudian influence, but
with such a startling likeness of approach that critics fell into the
most excusable error of their times; it seemed an absolute certainty that Anderson should have been influenced directly by Freud"
(p. 241).
        Occasionally in his works Anderson mentions Freud by name.
As Hoffman points out, he mentions him in Dark Laughter in a line
given to the hero, Bruce Dudley: "If there is anything you do not
understand in human life consult the works of Doctor Freud" (p.
230).   Anderson also mentions Freud in A Story Teller's Story and
in Memoirs.   In A Story Teller's Story, ed. White, pp. 78-90,
Anderson gives the facts of his birth (see 42/25-31) in the context
of the episode of hearing his father tell fanciful tales about his
parentage.   These tales serve as a springboard for Sherwood to
make up a tale about his "fanciful father" and his mother.   In the
midst of this long episode, Sherwood says:

>   And if you have read Freud you will find it of addi-
> tional interest that, in my fanciful birth, I have retained
> the very form and substance of my earthly mother while
> getting an entirely new father, whom I set up--making
> anything but a hero of him--only to sling mud at him.   I
> am giving myself away to the initiated, that is certain.
> (p. 87.)

In Memoirs, ed. White, when speaking of the time when he first
came to know the people associated with the Chicago Renaissance,
he says:

>   At the time Freud had just been discovered and all the
> young intellectuals were busy analyzing each other and
> everyone they met.   Floyd Dell was hot at it.   We had
> gathered in the evening in one of the rooms.   Well, I
> hadn't read Freud, in fact wouldn't read him, and was
> rather ashamed of my ignorance....
>   And now he had begun "psyching" us.   Not Floyd alone
> but others in the group did it.   They psyched us.   They
> psyched men passing in the street.   (p. 339.)

The discussion of the group's penchant for psychoanalysis and
Freudian interpretation of everything goes on until p. 341.   Also
in Memoirs, ed. White, when Anderson speaks about the possibility of a deep love existing between two men or between two women

but not having it based on homosexuality, he writes:

> It is often a love based on natural loneliness, the desire
> for at least one close companion in life.... There is
> among us, in the modern world, with all our new litera-
> ture and sex perversions, the great Sigmund Freud pas-
> sion that swept through the American intellectual world
> in my time, everyone trying to psychoanalyse everyone
> else, too much inclination to suspect all such relation-
> ships as I am speaking of here.
>
> I have myself suffered from all of this. When some
> of my own earlier stories were first published a good
> many critics declared that I had soaked myself in Freud
> but it was not true. I had, at the time, never read
> Freud, had scarcely heard of him. (p. 473.)

37/21-22. Modern knowledge of the queer tangled lines of sex in
all of her had not yet come to America. For several reasons
these are difficult, confusing lines. First of all, there is the difficulty of reading Anderson's handwriting. Did he write "lines of
sex" or "lives of sex"? Secondly, there is the ambiguity regarding the antecedent of "her." Does "her" refer to his mother or to
America? Thirdly, there is the vague reference to Freud, with
blanks written but never filled in. A passage that might throw
some light on these lines is the following from Memoirs, ed.
White. The context of the passage is Anderson's describing his
attempts to write in Elyria and the beginning of his estrangement
from his first wife. His wife was busy with their children and did
not understand him, nor did he understand her.

> Was there ever such a people as the Americans for al-
> ways looking to the children, vaguely hoping they may
> live, may get something out of life we living Americans
> do not quite dare let ourselves take?
>
> Whoa. I may have struck upon something here. Do
> you suppose, dear American readers, if I write this book
> as I should I am quite sure no one but an American will
> ever quite understand it. Do you suppose that we,
> Americans, human beings dropped down as we were in
> such a glorious continent, have always been rather buf-
> faloed by the land itself? That is at least an idea. We
> do all seem to have a dreadful inferiority complex,
> thanks to Mr. Freud, but I swear we do not, as a people,
> feel so damn superior to any other people, even the Eng-
> lish. But do you suppose the land itself has got us that
> way? (p. 245.)

37/29-30. taking away my fear of perhaps ending my days in the
soldiers' home. Anderson's own father died in an old soldiers'
home in Dayton, Ohio, on May 23, 1919, having had little to do
with the children of his first marriage after his second marriage
to Minnie Stevens in 1901 (A Story Teller's Story, ed. White,
p. 63n).

37/32. My lifelong friend John Emerson. John Emerson was born Clifton Paden in Sandusky, Ohio, 1874. He died in Hollywood in 1956 (Who Was Who in America, III, 259). Memoirs, ed. White, speaks several times of "my life long friend Mr. John Emerson" (p. 27).

38/1. we were both boys in the same small town. The Paden family was an important one in Clyde during Anderson's boyhood there. The father of Clifton Paden was mayor of Clyde before his death sometime around 1890 (Sutton, Road to Winesburg, p. 54).

For the third time (see also 29/23-24, 31/6-7, and their notes), the editor has omitted words written by Anderson. The manuscript reads: "My lifelong friend John Emerson, with whom, when we were both boys in the same small town. " It is the editor's opinion that "with whom, when" obstructs the meaning of the sentence. Anderson seems to forget about these words as the sentence unfolds. The editor has substituted for them and for the comma after "town" three periods, a favorite punctuation device of Anderson's.

38/2-3. one of the founders and the first president of The Actors' Equity Society. John Emerson was president of the Actors' Equity Association from 1920 until 1928, and honorary president from 1928 until his death (Who Was Who in America, III, 259).

38/3-4. who married that charming little woman Anita Loos and went to live in Hollywood. John Emerson married Anita Loos in 1919. Anita Loos was born in Sisson, California, in 1893. At the age of five she appeared in her father's stock company. He had become interested in the movie industry at the time of its infancy, and by the time Anita was in her teens she was writing movie scenarios. For five years she wrote scenarios for David W. Griffith. After her marriage to John Emerson she continued her scenario writing, working for Douglas Fairbanks for three years. She and Emerson established their own movie company, the John Emerson-Anita Loos Productions, and later they went to work for Metro-Goldwyn-Mayer. In 1925 Anita Loos wrote her first novel, Gentlemen Prefer Blondes, which sold 40,000 copies. Later she turned her attention to Broadway, writing Happy Birthday for her friend Helen Hayes in 1946. In the fifties the Broadway musical version and the movie version of Gentlemen Prefer Blondes were extremely successful--(Twentieth Century Authors, 1942, pp. 847-48, and First Supplement, 1955, p. 595). Her most recent success is her collaboration with Helen Hayes on Twice Over Lightly: New York Then and Now (New York: Harcourt, Brace and Jovanovich, Inc., 1972). Thus Anita Loos could be considered the epitome of the successful writer of fiction, nonfiction, drama, and movie scenarios. See Anderson's comments on this kind of success in 27/17-20, 43/24-27, and 45/18-22.

38/5-6. were rooming in the same house in Chicago. Sutton, Road to Winesburg, p. 54, tells that Sherwood and his brother Karl lived with Jeanette, Carrie, Alexander, and Clifton Paden in

the Paden home at 708 Washington Boulevard, Chicago, from 1896
to 1898 when Sherwood left Chicago for the Spanish-American War.
Karl, in "My Brother, Sherwood Anderson, " p. 6, says:

> During my eighteenth year I left home to study at the
> Art Institute in Chicago.... I had been boarding with a
> family on the West Side of Chicago for about two years
> when Sherwood followed me there to share my room.
> He was nineteen then, a callow youth of medium height.
> At once he captured the hearts of the family with whom
> we were staying by his good natured assurance.

Memoirs, ed. White, pp. 145-56, gives a lengthy description of the days when Sherwood and John Emerson were rooming
together in Chicago. Sherwood starts the description by saying,
"His sister kept a rooming house there, on a street over in Chicago's vast West Side. We had known each other as boys and I
had for him a rather intense boyish admiration. " He then begins,
however, to speak of John's "quick shrewd mind. " When John
wanted to advance in a job, "he would set about accomplishing his
advancement with a cold, shrewd, patient determination that filled
me with admiration. " But this admiration soon wore off, and the
passage as a whole gives a rather uncomplimentary picture of
Emerson and his desire for money and success. See the comments
on Anderson's use of the word "shrewd" in 34/5 and 40/15.
    Emerson is presented in a much better light in Memoirs,
ed. White, p. 16, when Sherwood speaks of a time he was in bed
for a month with an injured hip:

> There was a boy from my own Ohio town who had
> come to the city. It was John Emerson, who years
> later became a well known figure in the American
> theatre and the first president of the actors' equity so-
> ciety. He was a clerk there in a Chicago warehouse
> and, during my illness, he came every week end and di-
> vided his weekly wages with me.

38/7. I went off to the Spanish-American War. Anderson enlisted in Company I, Sixteenth Infantry Regiment, Ohio National
Guards, known in Clyde as the McPherson Guards, on March 28,
1895, at the age of eighteen. Probably in 1896 he went to Chica-
go, and at the outbreak of the war in 1898 he had been working in
the cold-storage warehouse for a little over a year. The United
States declared war on Spain on April 21, 1898, and on April 25
Company I of the Ohio National Guards was called into service.
Anderson and his company arrived in Cuba on January 3, 1899,
six months after the armistice was declared on August 13, 1898.
On April 21, 1899, Anderson left Cuba and arrived in Savannah,
Georgia, on May 2, where Company I was discharged from fede-
ral service by May 24. Anderson was back home in Clyde on
May 26, 1899 (Sutton, Road to Winesburg, pp. 37 and 65-79;
Memoirs, ed. White, pp. 166n, 191n, and 198n).
    In a publicity essay written in 1918 and printed in A Story

Teller's Story, ed. White, as Appendix I, where it is called "Sherwood Anderson's Earliest Autobiography," Anderson says:

> The Spanish War saved me from this [working as a common laborer in Chicago]. I enlisted, frankly not through patriotism--but in order to get out of my situation. To my amazement, when I returned to my home town to become a soldier, I was greeted as a hero--one who had given up a lucrative position in the city in order to fight for his country. My natural shrewdness led me to take advantage of this situation, and I enjoyed it thoroughly. (p. 346.)

Karl Anderson, in "My Brother, Sherwood Anderson," p. 7, says that Sherwood wrote to him as he was going off to war: "I prefer yellow fever in Cuba to living in cold storage in Chicago."

38/8-9. he called me Swatty. There are three letters in the Newberry Library, for the years 1918 and 1920, written to Anita Loos and signed "Swat." A picture of Anita Loos at Ripshin Farm is inscribed in her hand "To dearest Swatty." Elizabeth Prall Anderson in her memoirs, Miss Elizabeth, mentions on pp. 47 and 109 that Anita Loos, but not John Emerson, called Sherwood "Swatty." In Memoirs, ed. White, pp. 26-27, Sherwood says:

> As a lad and in the small Ohio town where I spent most of my boyhood I was known by the nickname of "Jobby" and later my friend John Emerson gave me another nickname. He called me "Swatty." A swatty is an old soldier. He sits in an easy chair, in the sun, before the door of an old soldiers' home. I think the two names describe very well two sides of my nature. I want to sit and dream. I want to move restlessly about, see everything, hear everything, feel everything.

38/11. You have no sense of money. Part of the "Anderson myth," self-perpetuated, is that Anderson had no business sense, no money sense. The truth is that in fact he had a rather "shrewd" business sense, and towards the end of his life, in his Memoirs, he admits it. Pages 12-14 of White's edition tell of a secretary whom Anderson employed to help him with his writing when he was still working in the advertising office in Chicago. He says that he rented a small office on a side street in the business district where he could go to write, in the afternoons and evenings, while working at his other job. He would dictate his stories and letters to his secretary. (Whether or not all of these facts are true is, for Anderson, unimportant.)

The secretary left Anderson's employ to get married, and when she came to say good-bye there was "a wicked twinkle in her very nice eyes. She spoke with a certain hesitance" (p. 13). The gist of the conversation between Anderson and her is that she recognized his business acumen. She tells him:

"You see, since I have been with you ... you know
how many letters I have taken for you ... to your clients,
to your friends. I wanted to say, before I left you....
You see, you have continually been saying to these men
with whom you do business ... you say, 'I am no business man.' You are always playing the innocent. You
put on an act of innocence. You make yourself appear
naive.
"Good God, man, don't keep it up until you believe it
yourself." (p. 14.)

See also Memoirs, ed. White, p. 410.
    Many letters of Anderson's give evidence of business sense,
for example, the following letter to Horace Liveright from New
Orleans on August 28, 1925:

I am going lecturing about October 15th. If Mr. Leigh
of the Leigh Lecture Bureau has not given you my dates,
have somebody in the office get in touch with him so the
new novel [Dark Laughter] can be pushed in the towns
where I appear. (Letters, ed. Jones and Rideout, p.
146.)

38/19-20. fear of coming poverty and old age was strong. This
fear of old age and poverty is a recurring theme in the "Writer's
Book." It is also mentioned in:

50/14-15: "And what was this fear that had come upon me,
    the fear of old age, an old age of poverty?"
52/19-20: "And so, why all this silly struggle? Why this
    absurd fear?"
54/18-21: "She [his wife] knew nothing of the absurd fear
    of old age, trembling feet going down stairways, trembling
    hands trying to hold the pen, through which I was pass-
    ing."

See the note to 50/26-27, where a passage from Memoirs, ed.
White, explains in part Anderson's fear of poverty.

38/21. she never knew anything else but poverty. See 9/17-18
and its note, which disproves the extreme poverty of the Anderson
family.

38/24. A Story Teller's Story. This book, with the subtitle The
tale of an American writer's journey through his own imaginative
world and through the world of facts, with many of his experiences
and impressions among other writers--told in many notes--in four
books--and an Epilogue, was published by Huebsch in 1924. Ray
Lewis White brought out a critical edition in 1968. It is the first
of Anderson's autobiographies, followed by Tar in 1926 and the
posthumous Memoirs in 1942. As 72/32 and 73/11 tell us, Anderson wrote A Story Teller's Story while he was in residence in
Reno, Nevada, waiting for his divorce from his second wife, Ten-

nessee Mitchell.

38/25. a really gorgeous book, one of the best.   This statement
gives a clear idea of Anderson's opinion of the book.   For contemporary critical opinion, on the whole favorable, see the reviews
that appeared at the time of its publication, for example:

> William Rose Benét, in Saturday Review of Literature, I
> (October 18, 1924), 200.
> Louis Bromfield, in Bookman (New York), LX (December,
> 1924), 492-93.
> C. Cestre, in Revue Anglo-Américaine, III (December,
> 1925), 175-78.
> Herbert S. Gorman, in Literary Digest International Book
> Review, II (December, 1924), 15-16.
> Harry Hansen, in Nation, CXIX (December 10, 1924), 640-
> 41.
> Ernest Hemingway, in Ex Libris (American Library, Paris),
> II (March, 1925), 176-77.
> Arthur Kellog, in Survey, LIII (December 1, 1924), 288-89.
> Sinclair Lewis, in New York Herald Tribune Books, Novem-
> ber 9, 1924, pp. 1-2.
> Robert Morss Lovett, in New Republic, XL (November 5,
> 1924), 255-56.
> Lloyd Morris, in New York Times Book Review, October
> 12, 1924, pp. 6 and 22.
> Gertrude Stein, in Ex Libris (American Library, Paris), II
> (March, 1925), 177.
> Walter Yust, in New York Evening Post Literary Review,
> November 1, 1924, p. 4.

38/26. a book that flowed.   "Flow" is a favorite word of Anderson's.   See 56/25, where he confesses that, as he was trying to
force himself to write a salable short story, the words refused to
flow.   See also 84/8-22, where he speaks at length about the importance of not stopping the flow of ideas, and 86/29-30, where he
says: "How the words and sentences flow, how they march."
"March" is another of Anderson's favorite words.

38/26-27. flowed out of my fingers as the water in the mountain
stream.   See 57/9, where he says he wrote A Story Teller's
Story "as in some delicious dream."   There is, however, proof
from letters written at the time of the composition of the book
that A Story Teller's Story was not written with great facility.   A
good deal of material flowed from Anderson's pen, but, as he
wrote to Otto Liveright from Reno in September of 1923, he had
to "revise it rigidly" (Letters, Newberry Library, 1923).   Six
months earlier, in the spring of 1923, he wrote to Gertrude Stein
and Paul Rosenfeld about the actual composition of the book.   To
Gertrude Stein he says:

> You see, in this book on which I am at work I am try-
> ing to make a kind of picture of the artist's life in the

midst of present-day American life. It has been a job.
So much to discard. Have never thrown away so much
stuff. I want to make it a sort of tale, you see, not a
preachment. (Letters, ed. Jones and Rideout, p. 95.)

To Paul Rosenfeld he says:

> In the meantime I work--rather intensely. As for the
> actual work that creeps out from under my pen--I can't
> be sure of it yet.
>   But a process is going on--a sort of process of inter-
> nal adjustment perhaps. On these days, sometimes I
> feel as though it were a kind of inner distillation with
> the hope perhaps of finding some new primary colors on
> my palette when it is all over.
>   . . . .
>   As a matter of fact I've written a good deal--have
> plowed straight on thinking to go back and balance and
> weigh what I have done a little later. (Letters, New-
> berry Library, 1923.)

38/29-30. book that every young writer should read. In the late
summer or early fall of 1923, as work on A Story Teller's Story
was nearing completion, Anderson wrote to Ferdinand and Clara
Schevill:

> As for work--I have tried to do this book--big (physi-
> cally) on the position of the literary artist in American
> life. It is outside my field but I did want to have a
> kind of say. There is a chance I may say something
> that will mean something to some younger Sherwood An-
> derson some day.
>   . . . .
>   As for this present book--on which I work now--it
> has been rewritten several times. The physical labor
> has been tremendous. Never did I tear up so much.
> (Letters, Newberry Library, 1923.)

38/30-31. book that has never had the audience it deserved.
Shortly after the book's publication Anderson wrote to Paul Rosenfeld, describing the difficulty he foresaw in gaining an audience
for A Story Teller's Story:

> As a matter of fact, I have no cause for complaint about
> the book. I believe sales are not much yet and may
> never be great, but such an outpouring of fine letters
> from fine people. At first I sometimes got several in
> one mail. What is my great handicap is really the
> dealers. I am known as a dangerous man, and dealers
> will not stock me. I think Many Marriages did it. The
> whole mood is one out of which I have quite passed now,
> but the public does not know that. (Letters, ed. Jones
> and Rideout, pp. 133-34.)

See 57/10, where Anderson says that A Story Teller's Story and
Many Marriages are "terribly misunderstood" books.
    The critics, however, were generally favorable in their
opinion of A Story Teller's Story.   See the note to 38/25.   Robert
Morss Lovett shows that he understands what Anderson is speaking
about in the "Writer's Book, " as well as what he attempted in A
Story Teller's Story, when he writes in New Republic:

> Mr. Anderson's story of himself is not a conventional
> autobiography, plodding from weary day to weary day
> with chronological precision and completeness.... The
> record gains in vividness and reality, as do many of Mr.
> Anderson's stories, by the fact that he does not impose
> a pattern, even a simple chronological order, on his ma-
> terial, but lets that material possess him in retrospect
> and tell itself in a form which is inherent in its sub-
> stance and grows with its unfolding.   (p. 255.)

Lloyd Morris in New York Times Book Review compares A Story
Teller's Story favorably with The Education of Henry Adams and
calls it "a book probably unequaled in our recent literature for
austerity of moral courage and sincerity of conviction" (p. 6).
William Rose Benét's review in Saturday Review of Literature is a
mixture of adverse criticism and praise.   In censuring the book
Benét uses two of the figures--the pen and the river--used by Anderson himself in the "Writer's Book. " Benét writes: " 'A Story
Teller's Story' runs forth from the itching pen of a predestined
romancer in a bright and rapid river of memorialized experience,
but the river wanders into a marsh at the end and disappears
among quaking quicksands of half-hearted speculation. " This sentence, however, is immediately followed by high praise: "Nevertheless, two-thirds of the book is unusually rich narrative and
several true stories in the narrative course are, in my own esti-
mation, among the very best stories Anderson has ever told. "
The episode about the young man and woman in the field and the
marriage that ensued, an episode which Benét entitles "The Dark
Field, " is "one of the great short stories of our generation" (p.
200).

38/31.   but that will have.   In 1969 a Viking Compass paperback
edition of A Story Teller's Story was published, with a preface by
Walter Rideout.   He opens his preface with these words:

> Although A Story Teller's Story is one of Sherwood
> Anderson's best books, misunderstanding as to its nature
> and purpose may well have contributed to the decline of
> his literary reputation during the years just before and
> after his death.   When this autobiography of an imagina-
> tion was originally published on October 15, 1924, it re-
> ceived generally favorable reviews, including an enthusi-
> astic endorsement from Sinclair Lewis, and sold mode-
> rately well.   But in the thirties and forties critics fre-
> quently complained that the autobiographical "facts" were

unreliable and that the book was disorganized in structure and thought. Now, forty-five years after A Story
Teller's Story was published, we can see that this first
objection is irrelevant, the second mistaken.

Another recent evaluation of A Story Teller's Story is in Rex Burbank's biography Sherwood Anderson (New York: Twayne Publishers,
Inc., 1964), pp. 118-19:

> A Story Teller's Story may best be defined as a romance-
> confession made up of familiar essays that are held to-
> gether--like the tales in Winesburg--by a common theme
> and by a mythical rather than a chronological structural
> sequence.... A Story Teller's Story contains some of
> Anderson's finest writing. While it hardly deserves to
> be classed with Walden or with Leaves of Grass, it does
> share two qualities with those masterpieces. First, it
> has an intangible but pervasive quality which suggests the
> presence of an authentic person and of a vital, sensitive
> inner life.... Second, it shares with these two books a
> structural cohesion and movement which have unfortunate-
> ly gone unappreciated by most critics but which make the
> book a significant expression of the "American myth."
> Admittedly--almost defiantly--an imaginative biography,
> it deliberately scorns the primacy of the world of fact
> and compels an imaginative, mythical interpretation.

39/2. to celebrate Halloween. A Story Teller's Story, ed. White,
pp. 40-43, recounts the tale that on Halloween farm boys would
pull cabbages up by their roots, bring them into town, and, grasping them by the long roots and stalks, hurl them against the doors
of darkened houses. If the thundering of the cabbages against the
door did not disturb the inhabitants, the boys would go on to
another house. If the cabbage assault did call forth a scolding and
a pursuit, the boys would return time and time again to the house.
Anderson's mother, according to the account, would wait behind
the door of their darkened house and pursue each of the boys who
threw a cabbage. After all the cabbage-throwing was at an end, the
Anderson children would gather up the "spoils." "Often as many as
two or three hundred cabbages came our way and these were all
carefully gathered in" (p. 42). They were then planted, head down,
in the back yard. They thus provided the main ingredient for the
cabbage soup that was the mainstay of the Anderson diet throughout
the winter months.
        A Story Teller's Story, ed. White, p. 43, has a footnote
which says that the same story is told in Appendix I, "Sherwood
Anderson's Earliest Autobiography," pp. 342-43; in Tar (1926 edition), p. 288; and in " 'Writer's Book,' Newberry Library Manuscript, p. 87." The footnote quotes the "Writer's Book," 38/24-
39/1.

39/3. My mother was a bound girl. Throughout his life Anderson

told the erroneous story that his mother from an early age was
"bound out" to work for farm families. See A Story Teller's
Story, ed. White, p. 33; Memoirs, ed. White, p. 33; and a letter
written on October 7, 1925, to John Taylor of the Encyclopaedia
Britannica in response to a request for some facts about his life.
The letter to Taylor is ample proof that to Anderson "the unreal
is more real than the real. " He says:

> I was born at Camden, Ohio, September 13, 1876.
> My father, Irwin Anderson, was, I have heard him say,
> a North Carolina man--the son of a planter. Have never
> looked up his people. My mother's maiden name was
> Emma Smith. She was Italian on her mother's side,
> Scotch-Irish on her father's side. Her father was a
> laborer, a lumberman, and was killed by a falling tree
> when she was a child and she became a bound girl. It
> was peasant stock. (Letters, Newberry Library, 1925.)

Sutton gives us the facts that are more real than Anderson's
imaginative ones. He tells us that Sherwood's grandmother, Margaret Austry Smith, who had been born in Germany with no Italian
blood in her veins, was deserted by her first husband, William H.
Smith, and probably supported herself and her two girls--Emma
was the elder--by going into a family with her two children and
doing the housework for room, board, and perhaps a little pay.
Subsequently Margaret Smith married for a second time, had
another daughter, and was left a widow when her second husband,
Lewis Maer, died in 1861. Sutton thinks that Emma probably left
her mother at the time of her stepfather's death when she was nine.
It is known that she went into the home of Mr. and Mrs. James
I. Faris, near Morning Sun, Ohio, "as soon as she was able to
work. " The arrangement with the Faris family seems to have
been rather loose, probably very friendly and charitable.   Therefore, Emma was never strictly speaking a "bound girl" (Sutton,
Road to Winesburg, pp. 476-77 and 481-82).
      In regard to his mother's life as a "bound girl, " see also
39/16-17, 39/28-29, and their notes. In regard to his mental
picture of his grandmother, see 41/29-42/3.

39/9-10. she might have been eighteen rather than twenty-two.
See the note to 37/7-8. If, as Anderson says in 37/11, the
daguerreotype was taken in a studio above his father's harness
shop, her age would be twenty-two or twenty-three rather than
eighteen.

39/13-14. a few months each winter at a country school. Appendix I of Tar, ed. White, prints William A. Sutton's "The Diaries of Sherwood Anderson's Parents, " pp. 219-30. A fuller
description of the diaries and of Sutton's analysis of them is given
in the note to 42/24-25. Emma's diary for the year 1872, the
year she was 18-19, shows her rather routine existence with the
Faris family. It records a round of household duties and church
and school activities. Evidently she attended school regularly be-

cause she mentions it frequently in the diary.   Once she lists the
other pupils in her grade, and once she refers to grades "at the
close of school term of winter" (p. 220).

39/15-16. When she was eighteen ... or could it have been at
sixteen?   Emma Smith did not leave the Faris household until her
marriage to Irwin Anderson in 1873.   She was twenty-one at the
time.

39/16-17.   a hundred dollars with which to make her start in life.
Emma earned her board and room with the Faris family by helping
with the housework.   In her diary for the year 1872, under the
heading "Receivable," she made fifteen notations of money received
from "J. Faris."   These payments were in sums from twenty-five
cents to five dollars.   Her recorded duties include washing, iron-
ing, cleaning, and baking (Sutton, "Diaries," in Tar, ed. White,
p. 220).
        Emma did not have to make her start in life independently
of all help.   Although there is no evidence that she was given a
gift of a hundred dollars, this may have been true.   Nevertheless,
she was married at the Faris farmhouse on March 11, 1873, by a
minister of the Hopewell Church of Morning Sun, Ohio, and the
Faris family gave a reception for her after the ceremony (Sutton,
Road to Winesburg, pp. 483 and 494).

39/19-20.   rather than the characters in the absurd story I was
trying to force myself to write.   This whole phrase is inserted
down the right hand margin of the page and thus gives evidence of
one instance when Anderson might not have made his revisions
during the original composition of the "Writer's Book."

39/21-22.   so much of the world seen.   Anderson was an inveter-
ate wanderer.   During his life he traveled to many sections of the
United States and lived for a time in small towns in Ohio, in Chicago, Cleveland, New York, Mobile and Fairhope, Alabama, New
Orleans, Reno, Kansas City, San Francisco, and Marion, Virginia.
He also took trips to Europe: for the first time in 1921 with
Tennessee Mitchell Anderson and Paul Rosenfeld, for the second
time in 1926-27 with Elizabeth Prall Anderson and his son John
and his daughter Marion, and for the third time to Amsterdam in
1932 as a member of the American delegation to the left-wing
World's Congress Against War.   He died in 1941 in Colon, Pana-
ma, four days after he embarked on a goodwill tour to South
America.

39/22.   men and women of distinction met.   During the last decade
of his life, at the time he was working on his Memoirs and the
"Writer's Book," Anderson projected plans for a work to be called
"Rudolph's Book of Days."   It was to be an autobiographical work
but in the third person, like Tar, and was to discuss Anderson's
friends of "distinction."   The Introduction to Memoirs, ed. White,
pp. xviii-xxii, reproduces a list of friends originally jotted down
on twenty-four separate sheets of paper, one sheet for each initial

of the alphabet. Those among the nearly fifty names listed on the
alphabetized sheets mentioned by name in the "Writer's Book" are:
Karl Anderson, Ralph Church, Theodore Dreiser, John Emerson,
Horace Liveright, Maurice Long, Anita Loos, Frederick O'Brien,
Carl Sandburg, Gertrude Stein, and Stark Young.

39/23-24. who in all America had been so rich in friends as myself? See the "Foreword" to Memoirs, ed. White, pp. 28-29:

> It happens that I have met, in the course of the life,
> briefly outlined here, a good many so-called "notable"
> men and women, famous writers, painters, singers, ac-
> tors, publishers. Whom have I not met? I have re-
> mained a restless man, always moving about. It hap-
> pens that, as writer, I came into writing at a fortunate
> time. New paths were being made. Often nowdays my
> name is coupled with that of Theodore Dreiser, Sinclair
> Lewis, Masters, Sandburg, Eugene O'Neill and others,
> as, shall I say, a "pioneer." Naturally I am interested
> in these men met, women met, so-called "notable" men
> and women with many of whom I found friendship, but
> (and this fact may disappoint you who have happened to
> pick up this book) these notable ones are not and have
> not been my central interest. Some of them may or may
> not appear in the pages of my book and if they do appear
> will appear but incidentally for, in my writing, I have al-
> ways written of, shall I say, "obscure" people and it is
> these who have given me life.

39/26. In actuality I knew so little of her. I had always been
making up stories about her. See 41/22-24, where Anderson says
substantially the same thing. See also the note to 37/3, which
shows that Anderson was eighteen when his mother died. Surely
it is no mere coincidence that in Anderson's masterpiece, Winesburg, Ohio, Elizabeth Willard dies when she is forty-two and
George is eighteen.

39/28-29. to the house of the farmer where she was to serve,
half a slave, half free. As the notes to 39/3 and 39/16-17 show,
Emma Smith's life with the Faris family was probably characterized by hard work and simple joy on Emma's part and by kindness
and charity on the Faris' part. Emma certainly was not "half a
slave, half free," but rather, as her wedding and reception show,
treated like a member of the family.

39/32-40/1. so much that would make it seem sad, a tragedy.
See 9/9, where Anderson also says that salable short stories cannot be sad or "gloomy."

40/4-5. seeing the failure in life of the man she married. Let
us hear first what Anderson has to say about his father in his
autobiographies. In A Story Teller's Story, ed. White, p. 5, he
writes: "My father, a ruined dandy from the South, had been re-

duced to keeping a small harness repair shop and, when that failed,
he became ostensibly a house painter." In Tar, ed. White, p.
173, he says: "Men like Tar's father take life as it comes.   Life
rolls off them like water off a duck's back.   What's the use hanging around where there is sadness in the air, trouble you can't
remedy, being what you are?" In Memoirs, ed. White, p. 274,
he states: "Life had run out early for her and her man, my
father, hadn't made good.   To tell the truth he must have been to
many people rather a joke." Again in Memoirs, ed. White, this
time on p. 81, he remarks:

> We had gone broke, down and out, and do you think
> he ever brought anything home? Not he. If there wasn't
> anything to eat in the house, off visiting he'd go. He'd
> go visiting around at farm houses near our town. They
> all wanted him. Sometimes he'd stay away for weeks,
> mother working to keep us fed, and then home he'd come
> bringing, let's say, a ham. He'd got it from some
> farmer friend. He'd slap it on the table in the kitchen.

Now let us hear what Sutton found out about Sherwood Anderson's father, Irwin McLain Anderson, 1845-1919.   He was born
in West Union, Ohio, on August 7, 1845, the son of James Anderson and Isabella Bryan Huggins Anderson.   The family lived on a
farm just outside West Union.   During the Civil War he saw a
good deal of action as a private, first with the infantry (June,
1863, to March, 1864) and then with the cavalry (August, 1864, to
July, 1865).   He remained active in the G. A. R. throughout his
life.   Sutton corroborates Sherwood's statements that during his
adult years his father was no great success financially (see 37/11
and its note).   Certainly he drank too much.   Nonetheless, he was
well-liked in Clyde and his family was thought of as one of the
"respectable" families in the town (Sutton, Road to Winesburg, pp.
470, 485-88, and 512-20).

Furthermore, Sutton's analysis of the diaries kept by Emma
and Irwin Anderson gives a quite different picture of Irwin, at
least at the age of twenty-six and twenty-seven, than that perpetu-
ated by his writer-son, Sherwood.   At the beginning of the diary
Irwin wrote the Latin motto Praestare Fidem Morti--to do one's
duty faithfully till death (Sutton's translation)--and almost every
entry, except for Sundays, speaks about his work, about receipts
and disbursements, and often gives a list of harnesses and saddles
made, sold, ordered, or received.   Nonetheless, Sutton also points
out that his father's will mentioned a note for $150 loaned to Irwin
on September 17, 1870.   The note was still unpaid when his father
died in 1886, "which fact may be the most eloquent over-all comment on Irwin's business career" (Tar, ed. White, pp. 222-24).

The final word about his father, however, still belongs to
Sherwood.   In Memoirs, ed. White, pp. 76-85, there is a section
called "Unforgotten." This is the essay that Anderson published in
Reader's Digest, XXXV (November, 1939), 21-25, under the title
of "Discovery of a Father"; Rosenfeld prints it under the same
title in his edition of Memoirs, pp. 45-49, and in The Sherwood

Anderson Reader, pp. 698-703.   See also Memoirs, ed. White,
p. 44, where Sherwood says:

> I do know that it was only after I had become a mature
> man, long after our mother's death, that I began to a
> little appreciate our father and to understand a little his
> eternal boyishness, his lack of feeling of responsibility
> to others, his passion for always playing with life, quali-
> ties that I have no doubt our mother saw in him and that
> enabled her in spite of the long hardship of her life with
> him to remain always a faithful and, for anything I ever
> heard her say, a devoted wife.

40/7-8.   washing other people's dirty clothes to feed and clothe the
boys and girls.   This passage is very -similar to passages in A
Story Teller's Story and Memoirs where, as in the "Writer's
Book, " Sherwood gives his own version of his mother's and father's
place in the home.   In A Story Teller's Story, ed. White, p. 12,
he says:

> If her husband, the father of the boys, is a no-account
> and cannot bring money home--the money that would feed
> and clothe her children in comfort--one feels it does not
> matter too much.   If she herself, the proud quiet one,
> must humiliate herself, washing--for the sake of the few
> dimes it may bring in--the soiled clothes of her neigh-
> bors, one knows it does not matter too much.

In Memoirs, ed. White, pp. 28, 38, and 67-68, Sherwood says
much the same thing.   See especially p. 156:

> Mother dead now, killed by poverty.   All the later
> years of her life, when we children were all small, had
> been spent being a wash woman, washing other people's
> dirty clothes to keep her little family alive.
> Father, although oddly lovable, never having any sense
> of responsibility for the children he had helped bring into
> the world.

Sutton verifies Sherwood's statement that his mother worked
hard to maintain the family, although her life was not one of un-
mitigated hardship.   Sutton also attests to the fact that she was
more highly respected than her husband (Road to Winesburg,
pp. 505 and 514-15).
Sherwood himself recognized the qualities that he inherited
from his father.   In A Story Teller's Story, ed. White, p. 21,
after describing his mother in terms quoted in the note to 37/4,
he goes on to describe his father:

> A father, whose blood and whose temperament I am to
> carry to the end of my days.   How futile he was--in his
> physical life as a man--in America--in his time--what
> dreams he must have had!

40/15. "Whose shrewd observations etc." Anderson is quoting
from memory. The dedication to Winesburg, Ohio reads:

TO THE MEMORY OF MY MOTHER
EMMA SMITH ANDERSON

Whose keen observations on the life about her
first awoke in me the hunger to see beneath the
surface of lives, this book is dedicated.

As the note to 34/5-6 mentions, Anderson's substitution of the word
"shrewd" for "keen" is surprising. Almost always in his writings
"shrewd" is a derogatory term, usually connected with the making
of money. See, for example, Memoirs, ed. White: "There were
all sorts of scheming shrewd men who understood what you did not
understand. In New York Jim Fisk, Jay Gould, that queer figure
of the Erie Railroad, Daniel Drew" (p. 118); "Already he had a
chain, four restaurants, all alike, in four Ohio towns. I had asked
my banker and he had told me. 'A good shrewd fellow,' the banker had said" (p. 267); and "There was a rich man who had made
money and what a strange thing money. The man had been shrewd.
He had, no doubt, a certain talent, the talent of acquisitiveness"
(p. 509).. See also a letter Anderson wrote to his son John in
April of 1926: "There is a kind of shrewdness many men have
that enables them to get money. A low order o[f] mentality often
goes with it" (Letters, ed. Jones and Rideout, p. 153).

40/16-17. Did she make such observations? See A Story Teller's
Story, ed. White, p. 9: "When she spoke her words were filled
with strange wisdom (how sharply yet I remember certain comments of hers--on life--on your neighbors)--but often she com-
manded all of us by the strength of her silences." Anderson habit-
ually speaks of his mother as a patient, silent woman.

40/21. It is a lie and not a lie. This is another way of Anderson's saying that "the unreal is more real than the real" (see
43/2-3). See also A Story Teller's Story, ed. White, p. 190,
where he says, "the fancy is a great liar"; and Memoirs, ed.
White, p. 21, where he says: "Facts elude me. I cannot remember dates. When I try to deal in facts at once I begin to lie. I
can't help it."

40/21-22. in an introduction to another book. In the "Foreword"
to Tar, ed. White, Anderson says:

I have a confession to make. I am a story teller
starting to tell a story and cannot be expected to tell the
truth. Truth is impossible to me. It is like goodness,
something aimed at but never hit. (p. 5.)

"Where is Truth?" What an unsatisfactory question to
be compelled to keep asking, if you are a teller of tales.
Let me explain--if I can.

> The teller of tales, as you must all know, lives in a
> world of his own. He is one thing, as you see him walk-
> ing in the street, going to church, into a friend's house,
> [or] into a restaurant, and quite another fellow when he
> sits down to write. While he is a writer nothing happens
> but that it is changed by his fancy and his fancy is al-
> ways at work. Really, you should never trust such a
> man. Do not put him on the witness stand during a trial
> for your life--or for money--and be very careful never
> to believe what he says under any circumstances. (p. 7.)

> All tale telling is, in a strict sense, nothing but lying.
> That is what people cannot understand. To tell the truth
> is too difficult. I long since gave up the effort. (p. 8.)

40/28-29. My imagination goes to work on them. See "Man and
His Imagination," p. 49:

> This whole matter of what we think of as realism is
> probably pretty tricky. I have often told myself that,
> having met some persons for the first time, some other
> human being, man or woman, and having had my first
> look, I cannot ever even see him or her again.
> If this is true, why is it true? It is true because
> the moment I meet you and if we begin to talk, my
> imagination begins to play. Perhaps I begin to make up
> stories about you.

41/7-8. a good many years ago, I painted. At the time when Anderson moved back to Chicago from Elyria and became associated
with the Chicago Renaissance, his latent interest in painting was
aroused. His brother Karl was an aspiring painter in Chicago and
introduced Sherwood to the Margery Currey-Floyd Dell studios in
the Fifty-Seventh Street colony in 1913. Sherwood's paintings were
given a one-man show at the Radical Book Shop in Chicago in 1920.
Anderson speaks about this show in Memoirs, ed. White, p. 366.
One year later, through the efforts of Paul Rosenfeld, he also had
a show at The Sunwise Turn book store in New York (Schevill,
pp. 83-84, 133-34). When he was in Reno in 1922 and 1923 his
letters often speak about the painting he is doing. The present
editor saw several of Anderson's pictures in Marion, Virginia:
two water colors, one a landscape and one an abstract design; two
chalk sketches, a front view and a profile of a black man's face;
and one pencil drawing of the hills and the road of the approach
to Ripshin Farm.

41/20. There may be beautiful paintings here. Throughout his
life Anderson was interested in painting and seems to have been a
creditable amateur critic. One of his deepest and longest-lasting
friendships was with Alfred Stieglitz and his wife, Georgia O'Keeffe.
John Anderson and Charles Bockler were constantly assisted in
their artistic aspirations by Anderson's words of encouragement
and advice and by his efforts to interest his wealthy friends in

their work. Of the masters, those who seem to have been his
favorites, judging by the frequency of his references to them in
letters, were the late nineteenth-century and early twentieth-century
Impressionists and Post-Impressionists: Cézanne, Gaugin, Picasso,
Renoir, and Van Gogh. He often mentions Whistler in his letters
but only to depreciate his work.

41/23.   she died when I was young.   See 37/3, 39/26, and their
notes.

41/25-26.   something of my mother in every woman I have loved
and in every woman of whom I have written.   The influence that
Anderson's mother had on his life needs no further documentation
than the numerous quotations from his three autobiographies, A
Story Teller's Story, Tar, and Memoirs, that have already been
given. It is also true that many of the attributes of Emma Anderson can be seen in the characterization of Elizabeth Willard in
Winesburg, especially in the stories "Mother" and "Death," and of
Ma Grimes in "Death in the Woods," the "bound girl" who spent
her life patiently, silently, and laboriously "feeding animal life."
Nonetheless, it is rare in Anderson's writings that he, as here,
explicitly says that the women of whom he writes are projections
of his mother.

41/29-31.   some of my brothers have often told me it is false but
to me it is a true picture.   See Tar, ed. White, p. 6, and "Man
and His Imagination," p. 49, where Anderson also speaks about
his brothers' protestations that he is not telling the "truth" about
their grandmother. In a typescript in Box 2 of "Memoirs" manuscripts at the Newberry Library, Anderson confesses that he deliberately made his grandmother Italian rather than pure-blooded
German. The typescript is entitled, in Mrs. Eleanor Anderson's
hand, "My Sister." Also penciled in at the top of the manuscript
are the words "Unfinished. See other version." A note accom-
panying the typescript, also in Mrs. Eleanor Anderson's hand,
states: "Story of a Christian Life Made from this." "Story of a
Christian Life" is a section in Memoirs which speaks of Sherwood's
sister Stella. The typescript, when speaking of his grandmother,
says:

> Later, when I became a writer and, as all writers do,
> plunged back into my boyhood and my young manhood,
> often re-creating it, she, the old woman with the one
> eye, with the great breasts and the wide hips of the
> peasant she was, was to become one of the favorite fig-
> ures of my imaginative life. Later I was to re-create
> and re-create her. My brothers always swore that she
> was German but I made her Italian. It may have been
> because I fancied the notion of having, in my own veins,
> to mix with my northern blood, some of the warm blood
> of the South.
>   "But she was German," said my older brother Karl
> ... this after I had written of her in one of my books,

A Story Teller's Story.
"And so she may be to you, " I replied. I am sure that
in the argument concerning the old woman, had later, it
was difficult for my brothers to understand my position.
"If I choose to have an Italian, rather than a German,
grandmother, what is it to you? If you prefer that your
own grandmother be an old German, all right.
"Shall a man who has spent all of his life creating
people not have the privilege of creating a grandmother?"
(pp. 81-82.)

See the notes to 39/3, 42/12, and 42/12-13, which give some
"truth" about Anderson's grandmother.

42/1-3. My own mother and my grandmother is my own mother
and grandmother. See Memoirs, ed. White, p. 21:

When, for example, I wrote of my own father and
mother I depicted people my brothers and my sister could
not recognize.
"Anyway, " I said to myself, "I have made a picture of
my father and mother. " They were my father and mother
as I felt them.

42/4-6. I have created for myself, out of my own thoughts, my
own feelings, also my brothers, all of my friends. See "Man and
His Imagination, " p. 65:

May it not be that all the people we know are only
what we imagine them to be?... To be sure I do not
want to discount the difficulty. It is very hard to understand any other human being. It is difficult to tell truly
the story of another, but it is, I think, rather a grand
challenge.

42/6. my wife, my sons and daughters. Anderson's wife at the
time of the writing of the "Writer's Book" was Eleanor Copenhaver,
whom he married in 1933. He had also been married to Cornelia
Lane, from 1904 until their divorce in 1915. They had three
children. Robert Lane Anderson was born August 16, 1907. He
succeeded his father as editor of the Smyth County News and
Marion Democrat and died in Marion in 1951. John Sherwood Anderson was born December 31, 1908. He now lives in Chicago
and is on the art faculty at Kennedy-King College in Chicago.
Marion Anderson, Sherwood's only daughter, was born October 29,
1911. She is now Mrs. Russell Spear and lives in Madison,
North Carolina, where she and her husband edit the Madison Mes-
senger. Cornelia Lane Anderson died in 1967. (Interviews with
Mrs. Eleanor Anderson, July 17, 1970, and with John Anderson,
July 23, 1970.) Anderson was married to Tennessee Mitchell from
1916 until their divorce in 1924 (she died in 1929), and to Eliza-
beth Prall, from 1924 until their divorce in 1932. Elizabeth Prall
Anderson recently published her memoirs: Miss Elizabeth: A

Memoir, by Elizabeth Anderson and Gerald R. Kelly (Boston:
Little, Brown and Company, 1969).

42/12. who wants to get rid of her. Sutton, Road to Winesburg,
p. 482, shows that this statement is not true. Sutton thinks
that Emma Anderson's mother kept all three of her daughters with
her until the death of her second husband, Lewis Maer, in 1861.
See the note to 39/3.

42/12-13. my grandmother was married four times. Although
Anderson makes this statement in A Story Teller's Story, ed.
White, p. 9, and in Memoirs, ed. White, p. 44, Sutton in Road to
Winesburg, pp. 476-79, proves that this statement is untrue. Mar-
garet Austry, also spelled "Oystry" and "Ostracy," was born in
Germany on September 10, 1830. She came to the United States
when she was three or four years old. She was married twice,
the first time to William H. Smith in Butler County, Ohio, on
December 22, 1851. She had two daughters by him and was
granted a divorce on the grounds of desertion on December 4,
1857. Her second husband was Lewis Maer, also spelled "Myers."
She married him on March 29, 1858, in Butler County, Ohio.
Maer died of cholera in Oxford, Ohio, in September of 1861. Margaret Maer lived until June 30, 1915, and never married again.

42/13-14. Let us say that my mother's father is dead. William
Smith deserted Margaret in March, 1854, when Emma was seventeen months old and two months before Margaret's second daughter,
Mary Ann, was born. So "let us say that my mother's father is
dead" certainly was true as far as Margaret and her children were
concerned.

42/15. The girl child will be a handicap to her. Margaret Aus-
try Smith took her two daughters, Emma, aged five, and Mary
Ann, aged three, to live with her when she married Lewis Maer
in 1858, a year and three months after her divorce from Smith.
Another daughter, Margaret, was born on March 1, 1859 (Sutton,
Road to Winesburg, p. 476).

42/19 and 22. Loneliness. As was pointed out in the notes to
10/31-32 and 14/19-20, the idea of loneliness preoccupied Anderson throughout his life. See, for example, the letter he wrote to
Ralph Church on December 30, 1934, where he speaks about "a
curious loneliness, separateness, that dominates lives" (Letters,
ed. Jones and Rideout, p. 308).

42/24-25. the courtship of the man who became my father. As
was mentioned in the note to 39/13-14, Appendix I of Tar, ed.
White, pp. 219-230, gives William A. Sutton's analysis of the
diaries kept by Emma and Irwin Anderson, along with excerpts
from these diaries. The diaries themselves are with the Anderson Papers at the Newberry Library. Both diaries were kept in
diary booklets, Irwin's being slightly larger than Emma's, and
both are for the year 1872. Emma's lacks entries for ninety-nine

days but Irwin's lacks entries for only two days. In Emma's diary
the first mention of "Irvin, " as she consistently spells his name,
is on January 9, when she notes that "Anderson was Chairman" at
a prayer meeting. Not until Thursday, September 19, does she
note that "Anderson was to come to play croquoa [sic], but called
on me. " From Irwin's diary we know that on September 12 he
went to a croquet party at the James Faris home, and that on
September 19 he "called on Miss Smith. "
      Since Irwin was more regular in his entries than was Emma,
we can follow their courtship through his entries. He records
visits to Emma on October 1, 8, 22, 27, and 31, as well as a
party at the Faris home on October 17. He visited her on November 12, 15, 19, and 28, and on December 10, 15, and 19. On
Christmas Eve he "went to own Christmas Tree with Emma. " In
her diary Emma also notes that Irwin called on her on November
19; she mentions too that he fixed a harness on November 22. It
would seem that neither kept a diary for 1873 (pp. 225-29).

42/26. could, if challenged, describe vividly my own birth. Anderson did just this in A Story Teller's Story, ed. White, pp. 78-
90. In this long passage which speaks about his "real birth" and
his "fanciful birth, " he says in part:

> Such a birth in an Ohio village--the neighbor women
> coming in to help--rather fat women in aprons.
> . . . .
> And then the doctor coming hurriedly, father having
> run for him. He would be a large man with side whis-
> kers and large red hands. (p. 80.)

> The story I had set myself down to tell was that of
> my own birth into the world of fancy--as opposed to the
> rather too realistic birth already depicted, and that, as
> I have explained, took place in Camden, Ohio.
> Very well then, a year has passed [since his "fanciful
> father" married his mother] and I am being born a
> second time, as it were, but this second birth is quite
> different from the one in the Ohio town. There is more
> punch to it. Reading of it will lift you, who have been
> patient enough to follow me so far, out of your common
> everyday humdrum existences. (pp. 86-87.)

> And now I am being born. It is late in the afternoon
> of a still hot day and I, having just been ushered into
> the world by the aid of a fisherman's wife, who also does
> duty as a mid-wife in that isolated place and who has now
> left to return again late at night--I having been so born
> am lying on the bed beside mother and thinking my first
> thoughts. In my own fancy I was, from the very first, a
> remarkable child and did not cry out as most newly born
> infants do but lay buried in deep thought. (p. 88.)

42/28-29. my father running along a street in an Ohio village to

fetch the doctor. As was quoted in the previous note, Anderson's
vivid description of his "real" birth in A Story Teller's Story included a description of his father's running to get the doctor.   So
does the description in Tar, ed. White, pp. 78-83, of the birth of
the Mooreheads' youngest son, who, in the fictionalized account, is
named Will.   In neither A Story Teller's Story nor Tar, however,
is there mention of a horse and buggy.   In both accounts the doctor
comes on foot.

43/2-3.   the unreal is more real than the real.   Anderson expresses this theory frequently.   See the quotations from his other
works cited in the notes to 12/28 and 23/6-8, as well as Anderson's remark in the "Writer's Book" that he "can imagine her
[the prostitute] the real Cecelia" (18/11-12).   Anderson's essays
on Margaret Anderson and Gertrude Stein in No Swank (Philadelphia:
The Centaur Press, 1934) also comment on the relationship between the real and the unreal.   In "Margaret Anderson: Real--
Unreal" he reviews her autobiography, My Thirty Years' War, and
speaks of the joy it brought him to reminisce about the days of
the Little Review and the Chicago Renaissance.   He says that then
for a short time: "I saw men of my own real-unreal world all
drawn together" (p. 112).   In "Gertrude Stein" he remarks:

> The world of art, of any art, is never the real world.
> The world of the novel or the story is not the world of
> reality.   There is a world outside of reality being cre-
> ated.   The object is not to be true to the world of re-
> ality but to the world outside reality.   (p. 84.)

43/3-4.   there is no real other than the unreal.   About the time
he was writing the "Writer's Book," Anderson, the veteran story
teller (see 3/3-4 and 43/6-7), speaks in Memoirs, ed. White, p.
348, of writing the Winesburg stories in the Chicago rooming
house:

> And so the stories came, in this rather strange way,
> into existence.   I had, in relation to them, a somewhat
> new feeling.   It was as though I had little or nothing to
> do with the writing.   It was as though the people of that
> house, all of them wanting so much, none of them really
> equipped to wrestle with life as it was, had, in this odd
> way, used me as an instrument.   They had got, I felt,
> through me, their stories told, and not in their own per-
> sons but, in a much more real and satisfactory way,
> through the lives of these queer small town people of the
> book.

43/10.   some five or ten years ago ... I was living in New Orleans at the time.   Since Anderson lived in New Orleans from the
time of his marriage to Elizabeth Prall in 1924 until the building
of Ripshin in 1926, as well as during the winter of 1922, we can
tentatively date the composition of Part I, "Prelude To A Story,"
at 1936, adding the "ten years" mentioned in the text to the last

year of his residency in New Orleans. We must always remember, however, Anderson's complete disregard for the accuracy of dates.

43/12-13. a picture, written by a man of talent who had once been my friend. The note to 43/20-21 describes a holograph in the Anderson Papers at the Newberry Library called "J'Accuse," in which Anderson, in his indictment of American artists, scholars, scientists, and teachers who "surrender to the money standard of life" (p. 78), explicitly mentions Theodore Dreiser and the 1931 film version of An American Tragedy.

If Anderson has Dreiser in mind in this passage, it is strange that he uses the word "once." In an interview with the present editor on June 5, 1969, Mrs. Eleanor Anderson said that Sherwood's and Dreiser's friendship extended over a period of thirty years and that he and Dreiser remained friends until Sherwood's death. The greatest strain on Sherwood's and Dreiser's friendship came in 1926 when Dreiser published a poem he called "The Beautiful" in the October issue of Vanity Fair. Franklin P. Adams printed in parallel columns in the New York Herald Tribune Dreiser's "The Beautiful" and Sherwood's Winesburg story "Tandy," proving beyond doubt that Dreiser had stolen the poem from Anderson (see William A. Swanberg, Dreiser, New York: Charles Scribner's Sons, 1965, pp. 313-14). Mrs. Eleanor Anderson remembers that Sherwood's response, when the plagiarism was pointed out to him, was, "Dreiser is too great a writer to have to copy from me or anyone else." Sherwood speaks about this incident in Memoirs, ed. White, p. 459.

43/14-15. shocked by what seemed to me a terrible selling out. In the second letter written to George Freitag on August 27, 1938, Anderson says: "Formerly I used to grow indignant because so many writers seemed to be selling out. Now I think it doesn't matter. I think every man writes as well as he can. Ordinary people need to be amused, taken away from thought" (Letters, ed. Jones and Rideout, p. 408).

43/19. what I wrote was a kind of American "I ACCUSE." Mrs. Eleanor Anderson in an interview on July 16, 1970, told the present editor that during his life Sherwood wrote several versions of "I Accuse" or "J'Accuse." Sherwood himself says the same thing in a typewritten fragment in Box 2 of the "Memoirs" manuscripts at the Newberry Library. At the back of Box 2 there are many sheets of fragmentary material not included in Rosenfeld's or White's editions. See, for example, the comments on "My Sister" in the note to 41/29-31. The fragment in question here, with "this needs a beginning" penciled in Roger Sergel's hand, starts with page 8 and then repeats pages 8 and 9. On the second page 9 Sherwood writes:

> It seems I am a little off the track. I started to write of the experiences of a book writer in trying to write a play, but never mind. There is a lot involved in this matter. Let me go on. Several times in my

life I have begun the writing of a kind of manifesto, addressed to American writers, and after all, the man who
writes for the theatre is a writer; makers of plays, of
novels, writers of short stories for popular magazines,
journalists, we are all in the same boat. How many
times have I begun the writing of this manifesto, putting
at the top of the page the words "I Accuse." I have
never been able to go on because I have been unable to
convince myself that my own hands were clean.

43/20-21. "I ACCUSE" at the head of the first of a great pile of
sheets. From San Francisco, sometime after April 8, 1932, Anderson wrote to Laura Lou Copenhaver. He spoke of a novel that
he was finishing and of another work: "another book to be called
I Accuse--this already nearly done since I have been out here--an
indictment of all our crowd--writers, painters, educators, scientists, intellectuals in general" (Letters, ed. Jones and Rideout,
p. 258). The "I Accuse" mentioned in this letter seems to be the
manuscript in the Newberry Library called "J'Accuse" (see the note
to 43/12-13). The manuscript is written on stationery from many
different hotels, but mainly from "The Clift" in San Francisco. It
is an indictment of "the mob of us, in America, educators, thinkers, painters, tale-tellers, professional men, scholars, scientists,
all of us always hedging. We are presumed to be men of brains,
of talent. We want to lead" (p. 26).
    The "J'Accuse" manuscript differs from "I Accuse" as
described in the "Writer's Book" in two important respects. In
"J'Accuse" Anderson includes himself in his accusations: "wanting
to whiplash myself a bit" (p. 18); "not only the others, myself too,
God knows" (p. 28). Secondly, Anderson speaks out against "young
scientists, doctors, social workers, schoolteachers, college professors, all the world of us here in America who are always pretending to ourselves we are leaders" (p. 19). There are, however,
many interesting similarities between "J'Accuse" and "I Accuse,"
as subsequent notes will show.

43/22. I called the roll. The writers and works which Anderson
mentions by name in "J'Accuse" are Theodore Dreiser and his An
American Tragedy and Eugene O'Neill and his Strange Interlude.
He rather haughtily dismisses Sinclair Lewis because he is "not as
important as Dreiser or O'Neill ... in spite of Nobel Prize" (p.
39). See 79/30-31, where Anderson also speaks about Lewis and
the Nobel Prize. He also mentions Faulkner by name but he
praises rather than condemns him. See also 44/12, where Anderson says that many of the men he names in "I Accuse" were his
personal friends.

43/26-27. rushed off to Hollywood. Anderson's attitude towards
Hollywood in "J'Accuse" is shown by the following quotation:

In the average American, I grant you, there seems to be
little or no resentment that always, in American movies,
life is mirrored forth as something sentimental, second-

rate--cheap to be exact--all always over sentimentalized,
over dramatized in the cheapest possible way.

A side of life always being reflected forth that has no
reality ... love not love ... death not death ... drama
never, never drama.

They know it on the movie lots, don't think they don't
know it. (pp. 41-42.)

Anderson's ambivalent attitude towards Hollywood, however, is
shown in a letter to Frederick O'Brien (see 82/4-5 and its note),
written in New Orleans on April 20, 1926:

> I hear fine reports of the sale of Dreiser's book [An
> American Tragedy was published in 1925]. Someone told
> me the other day they had seen an article in the New
> York World saying it had sold 30,000 and that Dreiser
> had had an offer for $90,000 for movie rights. That
> seems unbelievable but it may be true and I hope it is.
>
> After all Dreiser is a genuine story teller and even
> though he is a difficult and heavy writer he gets some-
> where and has something to say. (Letters, Newberry
> Library, 1926.)

In 1926 Paramount Studios, then called Famous Players,
bought the rights for a silent film of An American Tragedy. The
studio must have had second thoughts, however, and it was not
until 1930 that it finally decided to produce a sound version. On
January 2, 1931, Dreiser signed a contract with Paramount for
$55,000. When the film was completed Dreiser was not pleased
with it and sued Paramount for what he considered a distortion of
the novel (W. A. Swanberg, Dreiser, pp. 369-78). This is the
context out of which Anderson speaks in the "Writer's Book."

44/9. an acceptance of whoredom? The passage in "J'Accuse"
where Anderson speaks about the folly of selling a daughter into a
house of prostitution and then getting out an injunction against the
keeper of the house is very similar to 43/32-44/9. In "J'Accuse"
Anderson says:

> Like Mr Dreiser going to court, after selling his boy
> Clyde of An American Tragedy into the talkies--trying by
> a court action to make the keepers of a house--(from
> whom he had taken $100,000--$50,000--how much was
> it? It doesn't matter)--to say, by a court action--you've
> got to keep the truth of the boy intact.
>
> A second and greater American Tragedy because Mr
> Dreiser is a true man.
>
> Is it lack of sophistication--American confusion? I
> think so. I'm not saying that, given the same chance to
> sell out people, whose lives have been lived in books of
> my own--men and women brought to birth by me in mo-
> ments of love--
>
> My dream children--as real surely as any living chil-

dren.
I'm not saying I wouldn't have done what Mr Dreiser
did. (pp. 127-28.)
Writers, play-makers, you cannot--having written an
honest book--afterward sell it to the talkies for your
$25,000--$30,000--$100,000 without the dirt of the whole
transaction hanging forever over the book and you.
(p. 136.)

"Writer's Book" 43/32-44/9 is the most explicit statement of a
major theme of the work, namely, the selling out of the imagination by cheap work. See also 12/14-15, 17/25-26, 35/24-25,
44/28-29, 50/2, and their notes.

44/10-11. on a certain night in New Orleans. It would seem that
in the "Writer's Book" Anderson is fusing in his memory two
events and possibly two of his attempts to write the manifesto "I
Accuse." He is probably telescoping a night in New Orleans in
1926 when he heard that Dreiser had been offered a large sum of
money for the movie rights to An American Tragedy and a night
in San Francisco in 1932 when, after Dreiser's law suit, he might
have seen the movie version of An American Tragedy. We know
from "You Be the American Zola" in Memoirs, ed. White, pp.
542-45, that he visited San Quentin Prison in 1932 and that he was
annoyed when he was told by "Tom Mooney," alias for Thomas J.
Zechariah, convicted of murder in 1917 and pardoned in 1939,
"I'm the American Dreyfus. You be the American Zola" (p. 545).
Thus the movie version of An American Tragedy, the visit to Tom
Mooney in San Quentin, and the remembrance of news received in
New Orleans about Dreiser and movie rights might all have coa-
lesced to form the passage in the "Writer's Book" about "I Ac-
cuse." Since the New Orleans incident occurred in 1926 and the
San Francisco incidents in 1932, the "some five or ten years ago"
of 43/10 would place the composition of Part I about 1936 or 1937.

44/13-14. They wanted, or thought they wanted, a new world.
Phillips, "Sherwood Anderson's Winesburg, Ohio," pp. 100-101n,
says that Anderson in the early thirties "advocated more direct
social criticism for the writer, an attitude which soon gave way
again in the late thirties to his earlier one of the writer as an
artist responsible to his own imagination." The quotations cited
from "J'Accuse," written in 1932, and the quotation in the letter
to Laura Lou Copenhaver cited in the note to 43/20-21, suggest
that in the early thirties Anderson was sympathetic toward the
thought of social revolution. In the middle and late thirties, however, after the policies of Franklin Roosevelt and the New Deal
had won his support, Anderson took a dim view, and here in the
"Writer's Book" an ironic tone, towards the "radicals" and their
"causes" (44/13 and 21-22). See also 83/10-11: "I am not trying, when I tell stories, to represent, to speak for the proletariat."

44/15-16. whole world was, seemingly, dominated by the economists. See 57/10-13, where Anderson longs for the day "when the world has again passed out of our dark age of belief that life can be remade on a sounder and happier basis by economic professors." In such a day his Many Marriages will be understood.

44/18-19. writing of so-called proletariat stories. See 83/9, where Anderson speaks disparagingly of his agent who says that his book has "a good proletariat angle."

44/22. "But, please, what cause?" See "The Writer's Trade" in Hello Towns!, pp. 327-28:

> Why do I not fully, wholeheartedly, accept my position as writer? Why do I not say to myself, "I am a worker. Why not accept my trade?" Well, I do sometimes and when I do I have the most fun.
> If I set myself up--if I have opinions of my own, if I make myself stand for certain principles in life, as sure as I am alive I will do something tomorrow that will do the cause, for which I am trying to stand, a thousand times more harm than it will ever do good. And besides, what have I to do with causes? How am I to know a good cause from a bad one? Who am I, a scribbler, a teller of tales, to be fooling with causes? I should have the dignity of my own trade.

44/23. the overthrowing of capitalism. See 83/7-8, where Anderson also says derisively: "We are to be saved by communism, or socialism, or fascism." Documentation of the evolution of Anderson's social thought will be given in the note to 83/7-8.

44/28-29. the continual selling out of the imaginative lives of people. One of the most frequently repeated tenets of Anderson's critical creed is his insistence upon the obligation that the writer has to the world of the imagination. One of his clearest statements of this tenet is in "Man and His Imagination":

> It seems to me that the obligation of the writer to the imagination is pretty obvious. I am, to be sure, speaking of the writer as a story teller. There is the obligation to himself, to his own imagination, its growth, what he does to it, the obligation to the imaginations of other people, and there is the third and perhaps most important obligation. The writer in his creative mood is creating figures of people, to be true imaginary figures, and there is the writer's tremendous obligation to these imaginary figures. I think this is the most important of all the obligations. It is the obligation least understood. It is, I think the thing to talk about. It is the obligation too often forgotten by our professional writers. (p. 45.)

In the "Writer's Book" Anderson comments on all three as-

pects of this obligation.   First, the artist's obligation to his own
imagination is the main theme of the whole of Part VI, "Note--On Saving Ideas. " Anderson's constant inveighing against what he calls
the prostitution of art (see the note to 44/9) is but another way of
expressing the "selling out" of his own imagination by the artist.
Secondly, the writer's obligation to the imaginations of other people
is touched upon in the passage here in Part I where Anderson
says: "The suffering of the world, the most bitter suffering, does
not come primarily from physical suffering.   It is by the continual
selling out of the imaginative lives of people that the great suffering comes. " Thirdly, what Anderson calls "the most important"
of these obligations, the obligation to the characters of one's imagination, is discussed in 54/21-23 and 55/27-32. See the note to 55/29-
30 for excerpts from Anderson's other writings which speak about the
importance of fidelity to the characters of one's imaginative world.

45/5.   I tore up what I had written.   See 46/2-4, where Anderson
says: "I was compelled to tear up, to throw in the wastebasket
the thousand of words of my American 'I Accuse.' "   It is likely
that the "I Accuse" described in the "Writer's Book" was destroyed
by Anderson.   There is no manuscript that completely fits its
description in the Sherwood Anderson Papers as they exist now.

45/8-9.   gone to Hollywood, being in California, to see a friend
working in one of the great studios.   Anderson was in Hollywood in
April, 1932, and the friend referred to here might be John Emer-
son.   John Emerson was at that time working for Metro-Goldwyn-
Mayer (see the note to 38/3-4), and Anderson on April 8 described the
M-G-M studios in the diary he was writing for Eleanor:

> Here thrown upon a great open field were fragments
> of Russian villages, a college campus--the street of a
> small middle-western town, the entrance to a large hotel,
> the prow of a ship, half a street car, a jungle village, a
> mine, a street in the suburb of a city, an armory--
> These but a fragment of what I saw--all artificial, all
> paper maché.
> Here in this place you get again the envious thing
> about American life. I talked to a writer.... What
> about the people? The nice people, he said, are the
> mechanics ... in other words the workers. (As quoted
> in Schevill, p. 282.)

45/11-12.   like the offices we used to sit in, in the advertising
agency.   In Memoirs, ed. White, pp. 407-408, Anderson speaks
about the time he worked for John Emerson's movie company in
New York in 1918.   In the Memoirs passage he compares, as he
does here, movie studios to advertising offices, even to factories,
and talks about creative writing's subservience to business:

> Why how very like the factories to which I had been
> going as advertising writer. There was immediately
> something sensed. "It is not the actors or the makers

of plays, those who write for the theatre, who are in
command here, " I told myself.   There was immediate
disillusionment.   As it was in the factories, the workers
every year less and less having anything at all to say
about the work they did (this discovered earlier when I
was a young factory hand), as it was in politics (this
made clear to me by friends among Chicago newspaper
men), so here also, in this new art of the theatre, the
movies, there was a force, certain men, up above all
writers, all actors.
"Business is business. "
"It's money makes the mare go. "

45/18-19.   I had even written, two or three times, to agents in
New York or Hollywood.   An example of such a letter is one writ-
ten to Mr. Harry Dimand, Belmont Hotel, 3rd at Hill Street, Los
Angeles, California, dated January 31, 1928:

From time to time someone has talked about picture
possibilities of my books, but I always run up against
this attitude of theirs, that they have no picture possibilities.
Someday, of course, someone will get at it and make
some picture showing more of the drama of the insides
of people.   It can be done, surely.   I am certain that
all it requires is a little more intelligent approach.   You
had better get hold of someone and put this through for
me.   (Letters, Newberry Library, 1928.)

45/22.   There had been no offers.   Some offers, it would seem,
had been made.   Letters in the Newberry Library for 1925 show
that Gilbert Seldes, associate editor of Dial, which had awarded
Anderson its first annual award for his story "I'm a Fool" (see
the note to 25/27), approached Anderson about getting "I'm a Fool"
into the movies and that Anderson turned the matter over to Otto
Liveright.   "I'm a Fool" was published in Anderson's third volume
of short stories, Horses and Men, and Otto Liveright wrote to him
on July 23, 1926:

Cecil B. DeMille's office has just telephoned from the
coast for the price of the motion picture rights of your
book of short stories, HORSES AND MEN.   I do not
know whether they want an individual story or several
of them, but I think it would be a good idea to put a
price on the entire book.   A minimum of five thousand
dollars is what I suggest.   If you will leave it in my
hands I will use my best judgment.   Please wire to me
immediately what you would like to do in the matter.
(Letters, Newberry Library, Incoming, Otto Liveright to
Sherwood Anderson, 1926.)

Also with the Sherwood Anderson Papers there is a sixteen-page
manuscript entitled "I'm a Fool, Use for a Movie. "   It begins:

> It seems to me that a fine picture, for some youngster
> of the movies, could be made from the story
> I'm a Fool.

Nevertheless, "I'm a Fool" never became a movie. The closest it
came to production by the mass media was a radio broadcast. On
August 1, 1938, Anderson wrote to Anita Loos:

> There was a little play, made from my story "I'm a
> Fool, " on the radio the other evening, done by Orson
> Welles, and they tell me it was quite charming. I didn't
> hear it. Did you? (Letters, ed. Jones and Rideout,
> p. 402.)

Another offer from the movies occurred in 1933. Anderson
wrote to Laura Lou Copenhaver early in May: "Went to lunch with
a nice man from Paramount pictures, and they want a story. That
can wait" (Letters, ed. Jones and Rideout, p. 285). We know
from letters between Anderson and Paul Muni that there was talk
about their collaborating on a film. For example, Anderson wrote
to Muni on May 8, 1933:

> Now, what I think about the story is this: you are
> going to have a busy summer and so am I. I suggest
> that you sit down and dictate an outline of the story just
> as it lies in your mind and send it on to me. If in the
> fall you still feel that I am the man to work with you, I
> would make this other suggestion. I think that before
> tackling a mining story with you, I should go back again
> for a month or six weeks into the mining country and
> perhaps to the same country you visited. I should spend
> a time there going about in the mines and among the men
> to get myself full of the atmosphere of the place and the
> life. Then I should come to you wherever you are and
> spend another month or six weeks in actual work on the
> story. If you are making a movie, I could come to that
> place, or if you are back on the stage, I could come to
> where you are. I believe we could work together. I
> think we should spend an hour or so a day talking about
> the story as it progresses. I believe there is a chance
> of getting over a real story and yet having in it a possi-
> bility for the movies as they are now. (Letters, ed.
> Jones and Rideout, pp. 288-89.)

As all the bibliographies of Anderson attest and as Mrs.
Eleanor Anderson confirmed in an interview with the present editor
on July 17, 1970, the fact remains that none of Anderson's works
was ever made into a movie.

45/26-27. let us say twenty-five thousand. In the letter to Paul
Muni quoted in the previous note Anderson goes on to say:

> However, if when the time comes you still feel you

want to work with me, I would suggest that you try to
get for me $10,000 for my work.   I should think the
company might also undertake to pay my expenses while
I am in the mining town and also the expenses of coming
to you wherever you are to do the story.   Of the $10,000
I should think $2,000 might be paid to me as an advance
and the other when the story is completed to your satisfaction.   (Letters, ed. Jones and Rideout, p. 289.)

Thus we see one instance in which Anderson was "tempted" (45/22)
by the possibility of making a large sum of money in the movies.

45/27.   your Winesburg stories.   Although Winesburg was never
made into a movie, it has been made into a play.   In fact, there
are three dramatic versions of Winesburg: one by Anderson himself, one by Christopher Sergel, and one by Gerry Morrison (Sherwood Anderson Papers, Newberry Library).   Anderson is remarkably accurate in "An Explanation," the preface to the published
version, Plays: Winesburg and Others (New York: Charles Scribner's Sons, 1937):

> The author tried, with several collaborators, to make a
> play of the Winesburg tales but without much success.
> There were several versions made that all rather sharply
> violated the spirit of the book.   Finally all of these ef-
> forts had to be thrown aside and an entirely new play
> made by the author.   In this work he was however as-
> sisted, rather tremendously, by Jasper Deeter, Roger
> Sergel, and others.   The play was produced at the Hedge-
> row Theatre, Moylan-Rose Valley, Pennsylvania, and has
> been in the repertoire there for three years.   In the play
> the author has not tried to follow the exact pattern of the
> stories in the book but has tried rather to retain only
> the spirit of the stories.

The Hedgerow Theatre production had its premiere June 30, 1934.
The other plays printed in Plays: Winesburg and Others are "The
Triumph of the Egg," "Mother," and "They Married Later."
    In an interview with the present editor on June 5, 1969,
Mrs. Eleanor Anderson said that Sherwood knew that he was not a
dramatist, just as he knew that he was not a poet.   She said that
he always throught of himself as a story teller but that he wrote
poetry and drama because he was always striving for "the hidden
poetry in prose" and for "the hidden drama in lives."

46/3.   thousand of words of my American "I ACCUSE."   The
"J'Accuse" manuscript in the Newberry Library is 145 pages and
approximately 14,500 words long.   Whatever version of "I Accuse"
Anderson is speaking about, more probably it was not "the thousand
words" of manuscript that he destroyed but, rather, the "thousands
of words."

46/9.   sentimentalize one of your stories.   The "J'Accuse" manuscript in the Newberry Library concludes with the following words:

> Suppose the chance had come to me. It might have.
> The book [Winesburg] afterward sold, over the world, in
> reprints, translations, etc., hundreds of thousands of
> copies.
> Suppose I had sold my people to the movies.
> They sentimentalizing them, jazzing them up--
> Making these poor little figures of American people,
> so like myself, so like everyone I have ever known in
> America--making them cheap, trashy, flashy.
> Myself not dirtying my own work thus but, for money,
> letting someone else do it.
> For money.
> For money.
>
>   x   x   x
>
> It's what is done here, is always being done here in
> America--not only to writing but to painting, sculpture,
> music--
> Learning.
> It's the American Tragedy O. K.
> Money. Money.
> It's the real American Tragedy.   (pp. 143-45.)

46/9-10. twist the characters of the stories about. One example
of how closely Anderson watched over the artistic integrity of his
works and their characters can be found in a letter written on
October 10, 1932, to The Dramatic Publishing Company of Chicago.
In New York on February 10, 1925, the Provincetown Playhouse
had produced Anderson's one-act play "The Triumph of the Egg"
as a "curtain-raiser" for Eugene O'Neill's two-act Different. The
dramatization of "The Triumph of the Egg" was made by Raymond
O'Neil and was published by The Dramatic Publishing Company in
1932, as well as in Plays: Winesburg and Others in 1937. The
foreword to The Dramatic Publishing Company's edition is the
letter of October 10, 1932, in which Anderson says in part:

> At the last, by my friend Mr. Raymond O'Neil's ver-
> sion of the story, you see the two people, the unsuccess-
> ful little restaurant keeper and his wife, they having
> thrown themselves sobbing on the bed. This ending did
> a little violate my own conception when I wrote the story.
> To me the whole point of the play should be that the
> audience stays balanced between laughter and tears. In
> the Provincetown Players' version and after the outburst
> of ineffectual anger on the part of the father--his throw-
> ing the eggs about the room, etc.--he goes behind the
> restaurant counter. For a moment he stands there,
> looking about, perplexed, his anger dying, hurt. He sits
> down on a stool, and his head falls into his hands. His
> elbows are on the counter.

. . . .
The father is sitting with his head in his hands, half
raises his head.   Curtain.   I do not really know how
much of this is from the Provincetown Players' version
and how much my own imagination has built up since,
but of this I am quite sure: to do the little play in this
way will gain tremendous effectualness and will leave the
audience, as it should be left, balanced between laughter
and tears.   (Letters, ed. Jones and Rideout, pp. 263-
64.)

46/19.   far west in Virginia, in a sweet land of stars, softly
rounded mountains and swift running mountain streams.   Ripshin
Farm in Grayson County, Virginia, is twenty-two miles outside
Marion and is in the southwest corner of the beautiful Blue Ridge
Mountains of Virginia.   At the point where Laurel Creek and Rip-
shin Creek meet, the motorist turns off the county road onto the
Anderson farm.   The house at Ripshin is approached over a bridge
that crosses Ripshin Creek.

46/31-47/1.   an old, old struggle and my life had been filled with
compromises.   In a letter from an earlier period than that of the
composition of Part I of the "Writer's Book, " a period when his
marriage with Elizabeth Prall was breaking up, we see this "old,
old struggle" and perhaps what Anderson calls his "compromises. "
He wrote to Ferdinand and Clara Schevill on June 2, 1929:

To tell the truth, I have been this year more dispiri-
ted than I ever remember to have been.   That made me
determined to fight it out with myself, if I could.
. . . .
There was a great temptation to throw everything up
and try something new, as I had done so often before--a
new place, a new woman, a new book to write, etc.
I have not done it this time, but have hung on here,
having my son [Robert, who was editing the Smyth County
News and the Marion Democrat] with me, fighting constantly the impulse to flee, to be near someone, like
your two selves, for example, who, thank God, have
never given up loving me and always seemed glad to
have me about.
I have, however, stayed, in such depression much of
the time as I never knew before.
Now I begin to be a little cured, partly by nature, the
lovely hills and streams here--it now getting richer than
I have ever seen it before--and partly by getting weaned
away from myself to again begin thinking of other lives
and loving and enjoying people again.   (Letters, ed.
Jones and Rideout, p. 194.)

47/3.   paying little attention to criticism.   Anderson would have
liked to pay little attention to criticism, but in actual fact he was
extremely sensitive to adverse criticism, probably because of his

awareness of his lack of formal education. See 85/11-15, where
he says that he asks his wife to go over all criticism of his work
and show him only the more favorable. Another place where he
admits to his sensitivity is in his first autobiography. In A Story
Teller's Story, ed. White, pp. 227-28, he says:

> All during the last years of my life as a manufacturer
> and later as a Chicago advertising man I had secretly
> been writing tales and now they were beginning to be
> published. In some places they had been praised, in
> others blamed. I had loved the praise. It had made me
> feel very much as I had felt, as a manufacturer, when I
> had made a little money and had begun to dream of build-
> ing a great factory and being father to workmen--that is
> to say, rather grand and noble. When my tales dis-
> pleased people and when some critic wrote condemning
> me and calling me a dull or an unclean man, I got furi-
> ously angry but always tried quickly to conceal my anger.
> I was really so angry that I did not want, on any account,
> to let the other fellow know how angry and hurt I was.
> Often the critic seemed merely to want to hurt.

Nevertheless, in two letters written after his reputation began to wane, he tries to argue for the helpful influence of adverse
criticism. These letters were called forth by Lawrence S. Morris'
review of A New Testament, "Sherwood Anderson: Sick of Words, "
New Republic, LI (August 3, 1927), 277-79, in which Morris says
that the Anderson of Winesburg and the other early excellent short
stories is dead. Anderson wrote to Stark Young, probably in mid-
August of 1927:

> About the New Republic matter. There is a sense in
> which the man is right. I mean about the dying condition
> of the Winesburg S[herwood] A[nderson].
> There is too much talk anyway of the sweet, naive
> S. A. --adolescence, etc.
> In general I think this kind of body-punching criticism
> is a good thing. There is too much softness.
> Of course, it made me sick for a day. What hurts,
> however, is the ugliness--bad workmanship, etc., evident
> revengeful feeling, so much unconcealed joy in the death.
> It was so damned funereal.
> You know what would have happened to me had I gone
> on being the S. A. of Winesburg.
> However, it isn't this man's business whether or not
> there is a new and worth-while S. A. coming along. That
> is up to me.
> Anyway, dear man, I'm working at it. (Letters, ed.
> Jones and Rideout, p. 174.)

In a letter to Alfred Stieglitz written on August 18, 1927, Anderson speaks about "Marin. " The artist John Marin was a friend of
Anderson's and Stieglitz's, but the context of the letter indicates

that Anderson means "Morris" rather than "Marin." He says:

> About the Marin's [read Morris'] thing. The man has
> some right on his side. He was rather revengeful and I
> thought ugly.
>   So much joy over funerals. I think you have been
> checked out from time to time.
>   Just the same I like thumping criticism. I'm some-
> thing of a champion--know a little about handling the
> gloves.
>   The champion who doesn't get a mauling now and then
> isn't any good. He goes soft. It's like a horse who
> never goes to the races--just does an occasional exhibi-
> tion ride. (Letters, Newberry Library, 1927.)

47/4-5. the long years--some ten, twelve, even fifteen of them.
Here starts a passage in which Anderson repeats many of the
things he has said earlier in Part I. For example, the passage
between 25/23 and 26/3 also speaks about working in an advertising agency for ten or fifteen years even after he had published
Winesburg and had got "some literary recognition" (26/2).

47/6-7. my books translated into many languages. See 23/14-15,
where Anderson uses these exact words.

47/8-9. brought new life into American story telling. See 31/30-
31, where Anderson says: "I have had a profound effect upon the
art of short story writing." See the note there for documentation
of Anderson's influence on the development of the American short
story.

47/9-10. to go on writing advertisements to get clothes, food, the
right to space. Anderson is here aptly describing his life during
the early years of his writing career. He also describes it in a
letter to Trigant Burrow written from Chicago at the very beginning of 1919, after he had written all of the Winesburg stories but
before Winesburg, Ohio was published:

> I may be wrong, you know, Brother, but it seems to
> me that I am now ripe to do something, and I hate to
> see the years and the days go by in the writing of ad-
> vertisements for somebody's canned tomatoes or in long
> days of consulting with some fellow as to how he can
> sell his make of ready-made clothes instead of the other
> fellow. I want to go up and down the great valley here
> seeing the towns and the people and writing of the[m] as
> I do not believe they have been written of.
>   Well, you see how it is. The modern system will
> pay me five thousand a year for writing the canned to-
> mato advertisements. It doesn't want the other, or
> rather it thinks it doesn't want them. (Letters, ed.
> Jones and Rideout, p. 45.)

47/20. <u>advertisements</u> <u>for</u> a <u>certain</u> <u>medicine</u>. This line intro-
duces a passage, 47/20-48/8, in which Anderson uses a new meta-
phor for "selling out" artistic integrity. His first metaphor was
prostitution. His new metaphor is writing advertisements for laxa-
tives. See <u>Memoirs</u>, ed. White, p. 414, where he combines these
two metaphors:

> I had been given an assignment. I was to write that day
> a series of advertisements for the daily newspapers, a
> new cathartic.
>   And so, I was to spend the day delving in people's
> bowels. I had come in through the wet streets, some
> of the others already there. "Hello girls." We, in the
> so-called "copy department," were making a struggle.
> Sometimes, at lunch, in some little saloon, we talked it
> over among ourselves. "For God's sake let us keep
> trying. It may be we can hold on." There would have been
> two or three of us who dreamed of someday becoming
> real writers. This fellow was, in secret, working on a
> play, that fellow on a novel.
>   "We are little male whores. We lie with these busi-
> ness men. Let us at least try to keep our minds a little
> clean. Let us not fall for this dope that we are doing
> something worth doing."
>   "Hello girls."

47/31-32. <u>writing</u> <u>words</u> <u>about</u> <u>men</u> <u>and</u> <u>women</u> <u>in</u> <u>privies</u>. See
<u>Memoirs</u>, ed. White, pp. 122-23, where Anderson speaks about
writing "I'm a Fool" in his Chicago advertising office when there
was "before me an assignment to write certain advertisements of
pills to cure people's bound up bowels" (p. 122). In the "Writer's
Book" also he speaks about writing "I'm a Fool" in his Chicago
advertising office (88/19-89/19).

48/11-12. <u>it</u> <u>is</u> <u>easy</u> <u>to</u> <u>cheat</u>. Several times in <u>Memoirs</u>, ed.
White, Anderson speaks about the fakery in the advertising office.
For example, on p. 331 he speaks about "stealing" accounts, and
on p. 395 about "staging" copywriters. See also a letter that he
wrote to Waldo Frank probably at the end of August, 1919, shortly
after the publication of <u>Winesburg, Ohio</u>:

> All the time in the back of my mind I am working
> and working trying to devise some plan by which I may
> live and get out of business. It is going to be harder
> than ever for me to face the thing this year. Every-
> thing in me that is worth a damn draws away.
>
> . . . .
>   Always there has been a kind of cunning in me. I
> have been able to sabotage very successfully but I grow
> very weary of it and I am losing my cunning. Often I
> feel that I should rather starve than stay another day at
> any occupation other than the occupation of the writer.
> (Letters, Newberry Library, 1919.)

48/15. I wrote them all on the train. A similar incident is re-
counted at the beginning of "I Court a Rich Girl" in Memoirs, ed.
White, pp. 201-202. In the Memoirs version also Anderson cheats
the manufacturer because he writes the advertisements on the train
on the way to the town, and thus "precious days and nights [are]
gained" (see 49/1). In the Memoirs account, however, Anderson
goes to a town in Kentucky and his assignment is to write advertisements for machines to be used in digging ditches on hillside
land.

48/19-20. having already written and published. Anderson's facts
are remarkably accurate here. He makes only one mistake, namely, the inclusion of Horses and Men, which was not published until
1923. By the time he left advertising in 1922, Anderson had
written and published Winesburg, Ohio, 1919, The Triumph of the
Egg, 1921, and three novels: Windy McPherson's Son, 1916,
Marching Men, 1917, and Poor White, 1920.

48/22-23. Poor White, a novel that had been put into the Modern
Library. Anderson's self criticism here is also accurate. He
lists first among his books his masterpiece Winesburg, Ohio, and
then he lists his other volumes of short stories. He places the
novels he had written by 1922 after the volumes of stories, and
the only novel that he mentions by name is undoubtedly his best,
Poor White. Anderson again mentions with pride that Poor White
has been published by the Modern Library (see 27/32-28/1). In
fact, Anderson wrote the Introduction to the 1926 Modern Library
edition. In this Introduction he says in part:

> There is this book, "Poor White"--now to be pub-
> lished in the Modern Library, tricked out in a new dress,
> going to call on new people. The Modern Library is
> something magnificent. Long rows of names--illustrious
> names. My book, "Poor White, " feels a little like a
> countryman going to live in a great modern sophisticated
> city. (p. vi.)
>
> As on that day when I first saw "Poor White" as a
> book, I shall see it new and fresh again. There will be
> for me a new time of excitement when I see it in this
> new, strong house--in this new, strange, great city of
> books.
> Will you, the reader, be excited as I am? Will you
> see and feel the town and the people of my book as I
> once felt them?
> That of course I cannot know. I wish "Poor White"
> were better done. The book is, however, far from me.
> It is no longer mine.
> And when it comes to that, I wish all books were
> better done.
> They will never be too well done--at least not by me.
> (p. viii.)

When Poor White was first published by Huebsch in November of 1920, Anderson wrote to his friends about its reception. For example, to Hart Crane he wrote:

> I have your fine letter about Poor White, and naturally I am pleased to hear from you that it hit you. When a man publishes a book, there are so many stupid things said that he declares he'll never do it again. The praise is almost worse than the criticism, but you know how to take a story naturally and simply and how to react naturally and simply. It does one good. (Letters, ed. Jones and Rideout, p. 63.)

To Jerome and Lucile Blum on January 7, 1921, he wrote:

> I've been getting a good deal of spread-eagle talk--notices, etc.--on my new book but don't fancy it sells much. My books never do. (Letters, Newberry Library, 1921.)

Contemporary reviews of Poor White were, in fact, favorable. For example, see:

> Robert C. Benchley, in Bookman (New York), LII (February, 1921), 559-60;
> Francis Hackett, in New Republic, XXIV (November 24, 1920), 330;
> Robert Morss Lovett, in Dial, LXX (January, 1921), 77-79;
> C. Kay Scott, in Freeman, II (January 5, 1921), 403.

Anderson's biographers also single out Poor White as his best novel. See, for example, Schevill, p. 127; Howe, p. 123; David Anderson, p. 60; and Brom Weber, Sherwood Anderson (Minneapolis: University of Minnesota Press, 1964), p. 32. Current critics who praise Poor White include Horace Gregory who, by selecting it as the only novel in The Portable Sherwood Anderson (New York: The Viking Press, 1949), calls attention to its importance. Walter Rideout in his Introduction to the Viking Compass paperback edition of 1966 contends that Poor White speaks powerfully to contemporary man and is the most structurally unified of Anderson's novels. William Phillips in "Sherwood Anderson's Two Prize Pupils," The University of Chicago Magazine, XLVII (January, 1955), 9-12, and Frederick J. Hoffman in "The Voices of Sherwood Anderson," Shenandoah, XIII (Spring, 1962), 5-19, both cite Poor White as the best of Anderson's novels. Hoffman praises Poor White in these words: "The novel is a creative work of mythic history that deserves more attention than it has received" (p. 16). Others who recognize the mythical and historical importance of Poor White are Horace Gregory in his Introduction to The Portable Sherwood Anderson and Anderson himself in Memoirs, ed. White, p. 354:

> It was the novel Poor White, later put into the Modern

Library series of books. I wanted to tell the story of a
town, what happened to it when the factories came, how
life in the town changed, old patterns of life broken up,
how the lives of people of the town were all affected by
the coming of the factories. The book has since become
a sort of historical document of that change. It is used
nowdays by a good many historians to give present day
students a sense of the so-called "industrial revolution, "
brought down into a single American town.

48/25-26. my stories were published in high-brow magazines.
By "high-brow magazines" Anderson probably means the "little
magazines" that in the 1910's, 1920's and 1930's could afford to
publish experimental writers but could.not afford to pay them.
See 25/32, where Anderson says that his Winesburg stories were
"published in the smaller literary magazines. " From the time of
his first published story, "The Rabbit Pen, " in Harper's in 1914,
until the publication of "I'm a Fool, " for which he won the Dial
prize and the $2000 which was partly responsible for his being
able to leave advertising in 1922, Anderson published twenty-eight
stories in ten magazines. Of these ten, six would be considered
little magazines: Little Review, Smart Set, Masses, Seven Arts,
Dial, and Broom; four would be considered commercial magazines:
Harper's Magazine, Forum, Vanity Fair, and The Bookman. See
the note to 5/6-7.

48/25-26. a certain awe of me I could take advantage of. A
Story Teller's Story, ed. White, p. 242, speaks of a business con-
ference with six or eight men for the promotion of the sale of
plows in Oklahoma and Texas:

> I tried to appear attentive. There was a trick I had cul-
> tivated for such occasions. I leaned a little forward and
> put my head in my hands, as though lost in deep thought.
> Some of the men in the room had heard that I wrote
> stories and had therefore concluded that I had a good
> brain. Americans have always a kind of tenderness for
> such cheats as I was being at the moment. Now they
> gave me credit for thinking deeply on the subject of
> plows, which was what I wanted.

48/32. "It is my way of courting sin. " The thought would seem
to indicate that this sentence should not be in quotation marks, that
Anderson did not say this sentence to the manufacturer but to himself. The editor has let it stand, however, as Anderson wrote it.

49/16. once in two years, take a few months off. Anderson says
the same thing in Memoirs, ed. White, p. 393, when recounting
the days he worked in the Chicago advertising agency:

> I was there working in that place. I got a little
> money ahead and then quit. I went away, often to the
> south, to Mobile or New Orleans. I got a room in a

cheap rooming house in one of these cities.

There is evidence of at least four such escapes from advertising.
During the winter months of 1913-14 he took a long vacation in the
Ozarks with Cornelia.   Harry Hansen in Midwest Portraits (New
York: Harcourt, Brace and Company, 1923), p. 122, says that
Anderson claims to have written a novel there, a novel that he
soon realized was not good and that he threw out of the train win-
dow on the way back to Chicago.   In 1918 he left Chicago for New
York, worked on his "sinecure" in John Emerson's movie company,
and started Poor White.   In January of 1920 he temporarily left
both Tennessee and his advertising job and went south, first to
Mobile and then to Fairhope, Alabama (see the note to 25/10).   At
this time he finished Poor White and started Many Marriages.
Lastly, in January of 1922, with the $2000 from the Dial prize,
he again went south, this time to New Orleans.   He lived in the
French Quarter and continued work on Many Marriages.   His fi-
nances, however, compelled him to return to Chicago in March.
See Schevill, pp. 122-23, and Howe, pp. 54-55 and 140-41.

49/17.   There had been a legend created about me.   Anderson has
become the subject of several self-perpetuated legends, for example, the legend that he had no sense of money (see the note to
38/11), the legend of the young businessman who forsook his career for the sake of his art (see the note to 51/19), and the legend
of the unschooled artist who scorned reason and the intellect and
relied only on intuition and emotion (see the note to 7/16-17).   The
legend referred to here, that Anderson was an unusually good advertising copywriter, most probably is true.   The fact that he always got his advertising job back after his "months off" gives it
credence.   Anderson also speaks about this legend in Memoirs, ed.
White, p. 394.   After his "quittings" he would go back to the advertising
agency and ask for his job back.   The employers would make him
wait until an "emergency" occurred:

> What an uproar now arises.   Men are running up and
> down.   Conferences are being held.
> "Where is Smith?   Where is Jones?   Where is Al-
> bright?"
> "We must have something absolutely original now."
> "Where is that Anderson?   Where is he?"

49/20.   "staged."   As was mentioned in the note to 48/11-12, Anderson mentions the "staging" of copywriters in Memoirs, ed.
White, p. 395.   In A Story Teller's Story, ed. White, p. 190, he
also comments:

> Among advertising men, with whom I later associated,
> we managed things better.   We took turns doing what we
> called "staging" each other.   I was to speak highly of
> Smith who in turn did the same of me.   The trick is not
> unknown to literary men, but it is difficult to manage in
> autobiography.

49/23-24. Let me remain small, as obscure a figure as possible.
Perhaps another legend that Anderson created about himself, or, a
better way to express the same thing, another of Anderson's am-
bivalences, was his insistence that he always wanted to remain obscure. In Memoirs, ed. White, p. 410, he remarks: "There was
a place for me but not in the theatre or in the movies, I told myself. I had got this notion fixed in my head. 'You can make it
all right if you will only be satisfied to remain small,' I told myself." In the next sentence, however, he admits that he "had to
keep saying it over and over to myself. 'Be little. Don't try to
be big.'" In A Story Teller's Story, ed. White, too, when speaking of the time he started to write in Elyria, he says: "Utter obscurity, the joy of obscurity. Why could not one cling to that?"
(p. 230); "Utter obscurity, the joy of obscurity. Why had I not
been content with it?" (p. 231). In a letter to N. Bryllion Fagin
written in July, 1927, Anderson states: "To tell the truth I would
be a happier man if I lived in entire obscurity" (Letters, Newberry
Library, 1927). A letter written at the time Anderson is describing here in the "Writer's Book," that is, written when he is making his break with the advertising business, throws light on Anderson's simultaneous desire for recognition and desire for obscurity.
He wrote to Paul Rosenfeld on July 8, 1922:

> As to the matter of my going to pieces. I hardly
> know whether your analysis of what is wrong is the cor-
> rect one for Sherwoodio or whether as usual it is all my
> own fault. What I think is that I have allowed people to
> make me a bit too conscious of myself. A certain
> humbleness toward life in general, that has always been
> my best asset, was perhaps getting away from me. One
> begins to be taken up by people of little or no intelli-
> gence and soon cannot discriminate. I have thought the
> remedy to be a long period of being unknown--even if
> necessary losing my name.
> Well enough I know, Paul, that we have done little
> enough, and I have seen what seemed to be the effect of
> the sort of thing of which I am speaking on Sandburg and
> Masters. In both these cases I am of course speaking
> from reports only.
> At any rate I suddenly find myself in a somewhat new
> position in life--the prize, the Literary Digest writing
> me up, Vanity Fair, etc. The thing penetrated down into
> channels of life it had not reached before. I want, you
> see, a period of living a pretty obscure life, although
> God knows I need my real friends. (Letters, Newberry
> Library, 1922.)

49/25-26. It had been my thought all along that, if ... These
words are the beginning of a long complicated sentence. "If" in
49/26 makes the whole sentence conditional, but the condition introduced by "if" is never completed. Replacing "if" with "perhaps"
would retain some of the conditional connotation of the sentence
and, at the same time, prevent the sentence from dangling unfin-

ished at the end. Therefore, a suggested reading is: "It had
been my thought all along that perhaps I could keep what I called
'an honest mind,' helping others in the making of money by the
creating of often false notions of values but all the time knowing
just what I was doing, not continually lying to myself as most of
the others about me ... and these often quite lovable men ...
some of whom I liked intensely, even loved ... were constantly
doing, some of them even occasionally begging of me ... this
would happen when we were in our cups and I had broken forth,
saying that we were all whores ... not to talk so."

49/26-27. what I called "an honest mind." This is another expression of the main theme of the work, maintaining artistic integrity. Even if Anderson helps in the creating of "often false
notions of values" (49/28), if he knows what he is doing and does
not lie to himself (49/29), he will retain his integrity.

50/1-2. when we were in our cups. See the letter written to
George Freitag on August 27, 1938, in which Anderson speaks
about his years in advertising in these terms:

> The men employed with me, the businessmen, many of
> them successful and even rich, were like the laborers,
> gamblers, soldiers, race track swipes I had formerly
> known. Their guards down, often over drinks, they told
> me the same stories of tangled, thwarted lives. (Letters,
> ed. Jones and Rideout, p. 406.)

50/2. saying that we were all whores. Anderson was fond of using this metaphor to depict an artist's, or even a businessman's,
selling out to the money principle. See, for example, the passage
from "J'Accuse" quoted in the note to 44/9, the passage from
Memoirs, ed. White, quoted in the note to 47/20, and the letter
to his brother Karl quoted in the note to 17/25-26. See also the
letter written on September 21, 1925, to David Karsner: "It is
rather a wrong notion--this waiting for money in order to do good
work. As well tell a girl to go on the street to get money to afford living with a man she loves" (Letters, Newberry Library,
1925).

50/12. as my mother had done. The sentence from 50/10 to 13
provides another example where the editor has not attempted to
"improve" Anderson's style. The obvious redundancy of "like my
mother" and "as my mother had done" is allowed to stand.

50/15. fear of old age, an old age of poverty? See the notes to
38/19-20 and 50/26-27.

50/19-20. this beautiful house a book of yours built. At 26/22
Anderson speaks about, but does not name, "a novel that had sold."
At 32/32-34/1 he mentions the novel by name: "My novel Dark
Laughter built it for me."

50/26-27. from a long line of men and women. Although we know
from Sutton, Road to Winesburg, that Anderson exaggerated the
poverty of his early years, the following passage from Memoirs,
ed. White, pp. 27-28, gives some insight into his obsessive fear
of poverty:

>   I understand rich men, the hunger in them, fear in them,
>   that makes them rich, that sharpens the accumulative
>   faculty. The whole thing, while it lasted in me, may
>   have been due to early poverty. I can't be sure.
>   There is this fact, interesting, at least to me, that I
>   live now, for most of the year, in the country, in a very
>   beautiful hill country and, in my country, the wooded
>   hills, in the fall, are very beautiful but sometimes, in
>   the early fall and when the leaves begin to turn, I do not
>   see the beauty.
>   There is a dread, a fear that settles down upon me.
>   I go blindly along, often filled with a nameless misery.
>   Is it because of the physical poverty of early youth?
>   In my boyhood and in our house the fall was a time of
>   fear. There would be no butter to spread on bread.
>   Father, when he worked, was a house painter. There
>   were no houses to paint. Sometimes there was lack,
>   not only of butter, but of the bread itself.

50/28-29. most of the time, rather a gay dog. See Memoirs, ed.
White, p. 78, where Anderson says:

>   I know that, as a small boy, I wanted my father to be a
>   certain thing he was not, could not be. I wanted him to
>   be a proud silent dignified one. When I was with other
>   small boys and he passed along the street, I wanted to
>   feel in my breast the glow of pride.
>   "There he is. That is my father."
>   But he wasn't such a one. He couldn't be. It seemed
>   to me then that he was always showing off.

See also the analysis of Anderson's father in the note to 40/4-5,
especially the final paragraph.

50/29. darkness. See the discussion of Anderson's use of darkness as a metaphor for ineffectiveness, frustration, and self-deception in the note to 18/11.

50/30. our house in a street of workingmen's houses. Is Anderson confusing here "a house in a street in a factory town" (9/26-
27) which he remembers from his days as a laborer and the houses
in which the Anderson family lived when he was a boy? A "house
in a street of workingmen's houses" seems to fit better Anderson's
Chicago warehouse days than the days that the Anderson family
lived in the small Ohio towns of Camden, Caledonia, and Clyde.
Sutton, Road to Winesburg, tells us that Clyde, when Sherwood
lived there from the age of eight until perhaps twenty, was pri-

marily a farming, not a factory, town.   Sutton, p. 18, quotes Anderson's description of Clyde in Memoirs, ed. Rosenfeld: "There
were many little white frame houses.   All the residence streets
were lined with maples. " It is known that while in Clyde the Anderson family lived in the Piety Hill district on Race Street, and
also on Spring Avenue, Vine Street, Mechanic Street, and Duane
Street (Sutton, Road to Winesburg, p. 20).   Memoirs, ed. White,
shows a picture of one of these houses, which may well be "in a
street of workingmen's houses, " perhaps on Mechanic Street, but
which indeed looks very pleasant.

50/32.   "Over the Hill to the Poor-House. " In 1874 David Braham
wrote the music for George L. Catlin's lyrics, and this song became one of the more popular songs of the late nineteenth century
(Sigmund Spaeth, A History of Popular Music in America [New
York: Random House, 1948], p. 182.)

51/2.   his father and his father's father.   Irwin's father was James
Anderson, who died May 11, 1886.   His father's father was Robert
Anderson, who died February 9, 1841.   There is no evidence that
these Anderson men lived "precariously" (51/3-4).   When Robert
Anderson died he left 226 acres of land in Adams County, Ohio,
which were sold for $1, 638.   When James Anderson died he also
left a substantial estate but did not will anything to his son Irwin;
in fact, he did not even cancel a note showing that Irwin owed him
$150 (see the note to 40/4-5).   James made only one of his five
surviving children his heir, presumably because he, Benjamin, was
the one who stayed on the family farm and made a home for his
mother and father in their last years (Sutton, Road to Winesburg,
pp. 469-73).

51/5.   And, if it had not happened that, ...   These words introduce another long complicated sentence (see the note to 49/25-26).
It seems to the present editor that the conditional meaning introduced by the words "if" and "not" is not sustained in the remainder
of the sentence.   Furthermore, the "when" in line 11 is clearly
redundant.   "And" is supplied later in line 11 to facilitate easy
reading.   Nonetheless, with all these suggested changes the sentence ends with a sense of incompleteness.   Anderson's punctuation of three periods at the end indicates that Anderson intends to
keep the reader wondering about the character of Horace Liveright.
A suggested reading for the sentence is: "And, it had happened
that, twice in my life, I was comparatively rich so that I could
indulge a passion for luxurious living, once for a few years when
for a time I left advertising and became a manufacturer, and
again when, on the streets of New Orleans, I was down to my last
hundred dollars and I had met that strange figure among American
publishers, Horace Liveright, the man among American publishers
to whom justice has never been done, a strange figure of a man,
physically very handsome, often toward certain people to whom he
took a fancy ... I was one of them ... very tender, toward others
a sadist, loving to hurt or humiliate them, a bold gambler, a Don
Juan, who, like all Don Juans, could not love any one woman and

must therefore have many women ... "

51/7-8.   when for a time I left advertising and became a manufacturer.   See 25/22, where Anderson says: "Once I even owned
a factory. "   See also "J'Accuse, " p. 47:

> I had, by accident, got into business as an advertising
> writer and found myself rather slick at that.   I grew
> ambitious and became, first, the figurehead president of
> a mail-order house at Cleveland and then a manufacturer.
> I won't go into the story of how I cheated everyone with
> whom I dealt.

Sutton, Road to Winesburg, pp. 151-55, tells us that on
Labor Day, 1906, Anderson went to Cleveland to become titular
president of the United Factories Company.   Mr. George A. Bottger was the secretary-treasurer and, in actuality, Anderson shared
the control of the company with him.   The United Factories Company wanted to handle the mail-order business for several factories,
and Anderson was invited to join the company because of his experience with Long-Critchfield as a successful solicitor of mail
orders.   Bottger told Sutton: "Anderson had some very big ideas
for a factory combine.   The scheme failed for lack of a head.
Each factory wanted to be boss" (p. 152).   Another obstacle to Anderson's success with his new company was the deception perpe-
trated by an incubator manufacturer in Illinois who sold him, for
him to resell, defective incubators.   Bottger said: "We lost thousands of dollars and wound up in a law suit" (p. 154).   Anderson
left the United Factories Company at the end of the year for which
he was hired, that is, in the late summer of 1907.   Sutton thinks
that Anderson had to borrow money, or to pretend that he had it,
in order to go into a mail-order business selling roof paint in Elyria in 1907.
   The first years of his mail-order business in Elyria were
prosperous.   Some men, probably John Emerson and Walter E.
Brooks, from whom Anderson rented his factory, lent him money
to start the Anderson Manufacturing Company, which sold a paint
called "Roof-Fix, " a name coined by Anderson.   The cost of manufacturing "Roof-Fix" was about one-fifth the sale price, and Sutton
thinks that Anderson made a good deal of money around 1908 and
1909.   In 1908 the Purcell Company of Lorain, Ohio, another
paint manufacturing company, was absorbed by the Anderson Manufacturing Company.   At this time Anderson inaugurated his plan of
selling stock in the company to his dealers.   The plan was called
"Commercial Democracy, " and it was in connection with this enter-
prise that Anderson wrote the magazine Commercial Democracy
and probably the work he called "Why I Am a Socialist. "   See the
note to 10/1.   In November of 1911 a new company was formed,
the American Merchants Company.   This company was to serve as
merchandising outlet for the Anderson Manufacturing Company.
Anderson put up no money for the new company when it was incorporated, although he became one of its directors.   When Anderson
left Elyria in 1913 the Anderson Manufacturing Company ceased to

exist and the American Merchants Company was reorganized by
Waldo Purcell (Sutton, Road to Winesburg, pp. 164-74). A statement by a Doctor Saunders, one of the stock-holders of the American Merchants Company, well summarizes the results of Anderson's business venture in Elyria:

> As a consequence of Anderson's leaving, his investors
> were faced with the problem of clearing up the business.
> The company was heavily in debt. Available funds were
> used to pay debts. Then the assets were liquidated to
> take care of debts then unpaid. (Sutton, Road to Wines-
> burg, p. 147.)

Therefore, neither the Cleveland nor the Elyria manufacturing career was financially successful. The years when Anderson
"left advertising and became a manufacturer" were not one of the
two periods in his life when he was "comparatively rich" (51/6),
although he remembers them as such. Once again Anderson is
perpetuating his well-entrenched legend that Anderson the businessman was rich and Anderson the artist was poor.

51/11. Horace Liveright. Anderson's publisher from 1925 to
1933 was Horace Liveright (1886-1933). In Memoirs, ed. White,
the section called "Meeting Horace Liveright," pp. 490-504, opens
with these words:

> It was a time when Horace Liveright was the out-
> standing figure in the American publishing world. He
> was tall and very handsome. Having come to New York
> from Philadelphia he had got a job on the stock exchange
> and once, when I was lunching with him, he told me of
> how he had, by a quick succession of speculations, run
> a few hundred dollars into a hundred thousand dollars.

Anderson, however, goes on to speak of other things, among them
Ben Huebsch, and in the last analysis the section is more about
building his Virginia farm than about Horace Liveright. The section entitled "More about Publishers," pp. 517-19, gives a better
picture of the unorthodox ways of Horace Liveright, mixing stock
speculation, show business, and chorus girls with book publishing.
This section also gives a good picture of Liveright's generosity:
"And there was his check book, always at hand, often with a bottle
of whisky on the desk beside it" (p. 517). See also Walker Gilmer, Horace Liveright: Publisher of the Twenties (New York:
David Lewis, 1970). Gilmer devotes one chapter, pp. 106-19, to
Liveright's relations with Anderson.

We know from letters in the Newberry Library for 1925
to 1927 that Anderson signed a contract with Liveright on April
11, 1925. The terms of the contract included the stipulation that
Anderson give Liveright one book a year and that Liveright pay
Anderson $100 a week for five years, giving Anderson an assured
income of a little over $5000 a year. Anderson's royalty was
fifteen percent on all books sold, ten percent on Modern Library

editons. By 1927, however, Anderson was finding it difficult to
produce a book-length work each year, and the weekly advances
from Liveright had turned into a source of embarrassment, then
annoyance, and finally debt. Anderson had to ask Liveright to
stop payments. Nevertheless, in 1925 and 1926, because of the
advances from Liveright and the good sales of Dark Laughter, Anderson truly could say that he was "comparatively rich" (51/6).

51/16. a bold gambler. In "More about Publishers" in Memoirs,
ed. White, p. 518, Anderson says:

> Horace was a gambler and, if he believed in you, would
> gamble on you and I have always thought, since the
> man's death, that too much emphasis has been put on
> the reckless splendor of the man rather than his never
> failing generosity and his real belief in men of talent.

Anderson goes on to recount the financial failure of the Boni and
Liveright firm in 1933. According to Anderson, the failure was
brought on, not by Liveright's generosity to writers, but by his
speculation on the stock market. Anderson visited him when, at
the age of forty-nine, he was ill and near death. The section
ends: "I took the elevator down out of that apartment building and
walked in the street below with tears blinding my eyes" (p. 519).

51/16. a Don Juan. See Memoirs, ed. White, p. 491:

> So one day I was walking in one of the streets of New
> Orleans and there was Horace Liveright. He had come
> down there. He was striding along with a beautiful wo-
> man clinging to his arm. Horace was famous for his
> women, that I knew. I had already, on many occasions,
> seen him with many women and they were always beauti-
> ful.
>   He stopped and introduced me to the woman he had
> brought with him to New Orleans.
>   "Meet Mrs. Liveright, " he said and I laughed.
>   "But why does he need to do this to me?" I thought.
>   "I'll not let him get away with it, " I thought.
>   "Mrs. Liveright, oh yeah?" I said.
>   Well, it was Mrs. Liveright and I was sunk and so
> was Horace. There was an uncomfortable moment.
>   "It may have been an uncomfortable moment for you
> but it was a lot more than that for me, " Horace later
> told me.

51/19. courage to walk away from my factory. "Courage" is an
important word here. Again Anderson is perpetuating the impres-
sion--and who can say that it is wrong?--that he consciously and
with a good deal of courage changed the course of his life in 1913,
when he was thirty-six years old. On November 28, 1912, he
suffered a mental collapse, walked out of his office in Elyria,
wandered about in a state of amnesia for four days, and finally

was hospitalized in Cleveland on December 1.   Realizing that his
illness and subsequent repudiation of business were crucial in his
life as an artist, Anderson told and retold the story.   It is re-
counted in A Story Teller's Story, ed. White, pp. 215-36 and in
Memoirs, ed. White, pp. 20 and 238-53.   In A Story Teller's
Story he contends that, while dictating a letter to his secretary he
suddenly stopped in the middle of a sentence and said to her: "I
have been wading in a long river, and my feet are wet."   He goes
on:

> Again I laughed as I walked lightly toward the door and
> out of a long and tangled phase of my life, out of the
> door of buying and selling, out of the door of affairs....
> "My feet are cold wet and heavy from long wading in a
> river.   Now I shall go walk on dry land," I said and as
> I passed out at the door a delicious thought came.   "Oh,
> you little tricky words, you are my brothers.   It is you,
> not myself, have lifted me over this threshold.   It is
> you who have dared give me a hand.   For the rest of
> my life I will be a servant to you," I whispered to my-
> self, as I went along a spur of railroad track, over a
> bridge, out of a town and out of that phase of my life.
> (p. 226.)

The best factual inquiry into the details of Anderson's illness and subsequent departure from Elyria is recorded in William
Sutton's Exit to Elsinore and his Road to Winesburg.   They tell of
the amnesia attack, the hospitalization in Cleveland, the return to
Elyria until February, 1913, and the final departure for Chicago.
Included in the Appendix of both is what Sutton calls "The Amnesia Letter," seven pages of notepaper-jottings that Anderson
made during his wanderings and mailed to his wife Cornelia from
Cleveland at 5:00 p.m. on November 30.   The original of his letter
is in the Sherwood Anderson Papers at the Newberry Library.
The title of Sutton's monograph is taken from this letter, for the
phrases "Elsinore," "get to Elsinore," "went to Elsinore," "near
Elsinore," and "go to Elsinore" all appear in the jottings.   Also
included in the Appendixes are the statement dictated by Anderson
while in the Cleveland hospital and a letter that Anderson wrote to
Marietta Finley on December 8, 1916.   In commenting on the re-
currence of the word "Elsinore," almost as a refrain, in the Amnesia Letter, Sutton says:

> The first impulse might be to think that Anderson had
> thus thought of himself as Hamlet on the torture rack
> identified symbolically as Elsinore (Elyria).   Further
> examination reveals, however, that he is not wanting to
> leave Elsinore but is rather pointed toward it....
> The letter, as will be seen, is full of fearsome and
> unsatisfactory ugliness, and Elsinore represents the es-
> cape hatch.   As Anderson said in many ways, his basic
> approach to literature was therapeutic, to give him re-

> lease from consciousness of his world, to work out
> through the manipulation of imagined life the problems
> of his own, to find understanding for himself through
> probing the lives of his imagined characters. This is a
> veritable refrain, as many biographical passages show.
> The fantasy world of the fictional Elsinore, so closely
> identified with his kindred sufferer, Hamlet, is the door-
> way to escape, to the pleasant land where the head no
> longer hurts. (Road to Winesburg, pp. 191-92.)

The two sentences which immediately follow this quotation are cited
in the note to 7/14.

51/21-22. through with all idea of moneymaking forever. Although
the words "all" and "forever" make it impossible to say that Anderson was completely accurate in this statement, it does present one
aspect of his attitude towards money in the years after Elyria.
The other aspect, of course, is his shrewdness about money, an
attitude which he knew never completely left him (see the note to
38/11). Nonetheless, Anderson's repudiation of money and business after Elyria was authentic, and it often motivated him during
the remaining years of his life. See, for example, a letter to
Trigant Burrow written on October 12, 1921:

> As you know, my own books do not sell much, but I
> suppose a smart publisher could sell twice as many; at
> least several have come to me with the proposition that
> they would undertake to do something like that if I would
> only come to them. I've stuck to Ben because my years
> as a businessman cured me so effectually of any desire
> to make money that there is almost a satisfaction in
> some of Ben's inefficiencies as a publisher. (Letters,
> ed. Jones and Rideout, p. 74.)

51/22-23. after a few years had walked into the arms of Horace.
Here, as always, dates are of little importance to Anderson. The
"few years" actually were twelve, from 1913 when Anderson left
Elyria until 1925 when he accepted Liveright's offer in New Orleans.

51/24. he had exploited me. See the note to 26/22-24, which
discusses the similarity between the passages in 26/22-26 and
51/24-29. What actually does Anderson mean by "exploited"?
The meaning is certainly related to the idea that Liveright "plunged"
on him (26/24) and to the idea that "people in America do not buy
books. They do not buy anything. Everything is sold to them"
(51/27-29). See also 26/32-27/1, where Anderson says: "Books,
like everything else in America, are sold, not bought."

51/29. Everything is sold to them. See the note to 26/32-27/1.
See also Memoirs, ed. White, pp. 291-92, where the buying and
selling of books by publishers is linked to writing advertising copy
as well as to prostitution. In this Memoirs passage Anderson is

speaking of the days when he and other aspiring artists were
forced to write advertisements in a Chicago advertising agency:

> "Hello girls, " I said, coming in of a morning, trying
> to put as brave a front on it as I could, as were all the
> others. I guess they all knew what I meant. I wonder
> sometimes what girls in a parlor house talk about when
> there are no customers about. Afterwards, as I found
> out, it is not so different in publishing houses. The
> racket going on there too. People do not buy books.
> Books are sold to people. When things are sold to people
> there will always be a racket.

This quotation provides a good example of the fusion of the principal theme of Part I (the integrity of the artist), its principal metaphor (prostitution), and two concrete examples of selling out this
integrity (advertising writing and book selling).

51/31-32. paintings ... beautiful beds ... beautiful chairs. Here
an ambivalence is discernible even in Anderson's attitude towards
artistic integrity. If Horace Liveright "exploited" him, the exploitation resulted in the fact that Anderson had a beautiful mountain home, beautiful paintings, beautiful furniture for his home.
In recognizing this ambivalence Anderson also recognizes the contradiction that is in the life of all artists.

52/3. this terrible contradiction. According to what has preceded
this statement, the artist is enabled to purchase the beauty and
luxury that he needs and loves because he himself is exploited by
businessmen. According to what follows, the artist is a sensualist
and a lustful man because he loves and needs this beauty and
luxury. A partial resolution of the contradiction lies in the disci-
pline--"the intensity of concentration" (52/6-7)--that the artist
must impose upon himself in order to do good work. In regard to
this artistic discipline, see 71/11-17 and the notes to 71/12-13
and 71/16-17.

52/4. he is a sensualist. See a letter from Anderson to Ettie
Stettheimer written in June of 1926: "It is a shabby affair--living
by writing. I am really a sensualist, wanting always lovely people,
lovely things about" (Letters, Newberry Library, 1926). See also
74/27 and its note.

52/9-12. We want passionately ... luxuries. This sentence provides another instance in which Anderson revised his manuscript,
apparently at the time of composition, in order to give a more
precise meaning to the text. The manuscript reads:

> We want passionately the luxuries of life, the things we
>   , our books,
> duce ~~are really all~~ paintings, statues, the songs we make,
> the music we make, these are all luxuries.

It would seem that Anderson originally intended to write:

> We want passionately the luxuries of life,
> the things we produce are really all [luxuries.]

Anderson revised the sentence so that it became:

> We want passionately the luxuries of life,
> the things we produce, our books,
>   our paintings,
>   statues,
>   the songs we make,
>   the music we make,
>   these are all luxuries.

52/13. who but his fellow artists. See "The Education of an Artist" in Hello Towns!, p. 308:

> The world is ruled by the paradox. Who loves luxury
> as does the artist? If he is a good artist he is a sen-
> sualist. He is as unmoral as a dog. A fine dog has the
> sense of smell highly developed. The artist would have
> all of his senses developed like that.
> There the man is, trying to train himself all the time.
> Color, the feel of fabrics, the seductive lines of the hu-
> man form.
> The lines formed by hills falling away into valleys.
> Horses pulling loads up hills.
> Voices heard in silent streets at night.
> Every impulse of the artist is toward luxury. Nothing
> destroys like luxury.

52/16-17. getting them by cheapening our own work. See The Modern Writer, pp. 39-40:

> If you handle your materials in a cheap way you become
> cheap. The need of making a living may serve as an
> excuse but it will not save you as a craftsman. Nothing
> really will save you if you go cheap with tools and ma-
> terials. Do cheap work and you are yourself cheap.
> That is the truth.

52/29-30. comfortable circumstances in life. See 9/7-8 and its note. The people in "comfortable circumstances" are also the "approved people" of 52/25, and it is "a publisher's need" (52/28), not art, that insists they be the subject of Anderson's salable short stories.

52/32. a struggle going on between them and me. See a letter that Anderson wrote to his brother Karl in September of 1926. Anderson is speaking about the difficulty he is having with a novel he alternatively called "Another Man's House" and "Other People's Houses, " a novel which he never completed. He admits to Karl:

"The people of the novel want to emerge as individuals aside from
myself and what I think they should be, and I have difficulty letting
them.   It is only when I can do it I get something pure" (Letters,
ed. Jones and Rideout, p. 161.)

53/3-4.   people who have lived long together, who have really
achieved a marriage.   Sherwood and Eleanor Copenhaver were
married for eight years.   See 32/20-21 and its note.   With Eleanor, Sherwood finally achieved a marriage that was lasting and
happy.

53/10-11.   persistently buying me expensive shirts, ... overcoats.
Mrs. Eleanor Anderson in an interview with the present editor on
July 17, 1970, admitted that she bought Sherwood expensive gifts.
Even after her marriage, she continued to work as National Secre-
tary for the Y.W.C.A.

53/13-14.   ties that have cost at least three dollars each.   Mrs.
Eleanor Anderson in an interview on July 17, 1970, verified the
fact that in rural Virginia in the 1930's ties costing three dollars
were indeed expensive.

53/16-17.   the orchard back of my house.   See Memoirs, ed.
White, p. 493:

> I had determined to have a house of stone to stand at the
> recess where Ripshin joined Laurel Creek.   There was
> a fine old apple orchard at that spot and my house, when
> built, would be protected from the storms by the surround-
> ing hills.

Several letters written during the year when Anderson was building
his house also speak of the apple orchard.   For example, on the
back of a picture of Ripshin sent to Ferdinand and Clara Schevill
in the late fall of 1926, Anderson says:

> This is a side view of the house.   This end is finished
> and we are now living in it.   The two wings at the back
> are of logs.   They look into an apple orchard....   Rip-
> shin Creek is at the foot of the orchard.   My work
> cabin is on a hill--about the place marked X.   Looks
> over Iron Mountain.   In front of the house we will have
> our flower garden.   (Letters, Newberry Library, 1926.)

53/18.   hill where I could see the front of the house.   The editor's visit to Ripshin Farm, July 16-17, 1970, confirmed the accuracy of Anderson's description of his house and grounds.   The
apple orchard is behind and a little to the side of the house, that
is, south and a little to the west.   The front of the house faces
north and overlooks a walled flower garden with a low hill behind
it.   The view of the house from the top of this hill is most impressive.   One's eye can easily follow "the line of the wall rising
out of the ground and then following along the roof" (53/23-24).

53/29. an architect who had made the drawings for me. A friend
from New Orleans days, William Spratling, at that time a professor of architecture at Tulane University, made the drawings for
Ripshin. See a letter written to Charles and Mabel Connick from
New Orleans in early March of 1926. After extending an invitation
to come to Virginia, Anderson continues: "We will get at the house
as soon as we get there. An architect friend is making drawings.
He makes some and brings them to the house--a patient man. We
make changes every time" (Letters, Newberry Library, 1926). In
1926 Spratling and William Faulkner collaborated on a satire:
Sherwood Anderson and Other Famous Creoles: A Gallery of Contemporary New Orleans (published by the Pelican Bookshop Press
in Royal Street New Orleans, 1926). The book is made up of
Spratling's pen and ink sketches of the artists, writers, and journalists of the French Quarter during the 1920's. The first sketch
is of "Mister Sherwood Anderson"; the last one, untitled, is of
Spratling and Faulkner. Preceding the first sketch is a two-page
foreword by "W. F." in a style intended to parody Anderson's.
Hemingway's parody of Anderson's style in The Torrents of Spring
catches the idiosyncrasies of Anderson's style better than does
Faulkner's foreword. Hemingway's satire is probably cleverer;
it is certainly lengthier and crueler. Spratling has also published
his autobiography: File on Spratling: An Autobiography (Boston:
Little, Brown, and Company, 1967). Its primary purpose seems
to be to debunk the reputation of Spratling's friends, Faulkner and
Anderson both included.

53/30. I had not followed the drawings. This statement is not
entirely true. See a letter to Mark Anthony, another friend of
New Orleans days, written on May 28, 1926: "Tell Bill that our
carpenter has studied his plans until they are almost worn out"
(Letters, Newberry Library, 1926). Nonetheless, it may have
some truth to it. See also Memoirs, ed. White, p. 493:

> I had got an old man named Ball to be my builder and
> he was full of confidence. Bill Spratling, who was then
> teaching architecture at Tulane University, in New Or-
> leans (He went afterward to Taxco in Mexico and set up
> as a silversmith. He prospered there.) drew some
> plans for me.
>   However, we could not use the plans much as neither
> the builder Ball or myself could understand the blue-
> prints.
>   "But never mind, " Ball said. "We'll get along. "

53/30-31. For two years and while the house was building. See
the note to 26/28-29, which shows that the house was built in little
over one year's time. Nonetheless, from the time Anderson made
his first payment on September 15, 1925, to Mrs. Barbara Miller
for her farm until the withdrawal of the last workmen from the
stone house in August, 1927, "two years" had elapsed.

53/31-32. all the money made for me by Horace Liveright going

into it.   To Ferdinand and Clara Schevill in the late fall of 1926
Anderson wrote: "Cost of all building, farm, etc., about $10,000"
(Letters, Newberry Library, 1926).   To Roger Sergel in late August, 1926, Anderson wrote: "We have about got a house.   Our
debt on it, all told, may be $4,000, a stone house with barn & a
tenant house, also a cabin for me" (Letters, ed. Jones and Rideout, p. 160).   We know that during 1926 Anderson made more than
$8000 on Dark Laughter (see the note to 26/22); and in 1926 Live-
right published two books for Anderson--Sherwood Anderson's Notebook and Tar--neither of which was commercially successful.   In
the following year, the year in which the house was completed,
Liveright published A New Testament, Anderson's second book of
poetry, a book which Liveright could hardly "plunge on" (see
26/31).   Therefore, Anderson had to supplement the money made
for him by Liveright by money made on lecture tours (see the
following note).

     Here in the "Writer's Book," however, Anderson does not
mention that the sales of Dark Laughter and the lecture tours also
financed a trip to Europe.   He sailed for Europe on December 1,
1926, with Elizabeth, his son John, and his daughter Marion.   In
his letters to Karl throughout the winter and spring of 1926-27,
Sherwood repeatedly tells him that he cannot afford the trip, but
he goes anyway.   Another source of expense for both Sherwood
and Karl at this time was the illness of their youngest brother,
Earl, who had suffered a paralytic stroke.   Karl was carrying the
brunt of the medical expenses, although Sherwood constantly wrote
that he would soon send his share of the money.   Earl died shortly
after Sherwood returned from Europe in March, 1927.   Sherwood
then embarked on a spring lecture tour (Letters, Newberry Library,
1926 and 1927).

53/32-54/2.   once having to stop building for four months while I
went delivering silly lectures.   The lecture tour Anderson refers
to here is probably the one he made between March and June of
1927 when, after his return from Europe, he had to lecture in
order to raise the money that was still needed for the completion
of Ripshin.   During the fall and winter of 1925-26, however, he
had also gone on a lecture tour, to get the money he owed Mrs.
Barbara Miller for the farm and to pay for the beginning of the
work on his cabin and stone house.   Furthermore, as early as
1924 Anderson had started to lecture; in a letter to Ferdinand
Schevill written in the summer of that year he tells him that lecturing "will be better than being an ad man and stealing spoons"
(Letters, Newberry Library, 1924).   As late as 1931 he was still
lecturing; he wrote to Paul Rosenfeld on April 7, 1931:   "I am
doing some lecturing again this year, but this time I am not lecturing about writing or the arts and so do not mind doing it.   My
talks will be largely about newspapers and industry" (Letters, Newberry Library, 1931).   Therefore, the implication that only once
he stopped his total absorption in the building of Ripshin to deliver
lectures is false.

     Anderson's general attitude towards lecturing, however, is
reflected in this passage in the "Writer's Book."   We see this

attitude reflected also in a letter written to Montgomery Wright of
The Kansas City Star on March 15, 1926, that is, at the end of the
tour in the fall and winter of 1925-26 referred to above:

> In regard to lecturing, all I can say is that I find it
> hard enough to keep my relations to other men and wo-
> men in the world somewhat balanced without attempting
> to get people in the mass. In spite of what everyone
> says about people that come to lectures, I think they do
> come in a pretty good spirit, really wanting something,
> but what can a man give them by standing up in front of
> them gabbing at them? Everyone, I presume, really
> wants a little decent affection and understanding, and I
> know now that they are never going to get them from a
> lecturer. (Letters, Newberry Library, 1926.)

54/2. I had done no writing. It is not true that from September,
1925, until August, 1927 (see the note to 53/30-31), Anderson had
done no writing, although it is true that these years represent a
low ebb in Anderson's creative energy. He went on trying to
write, nonetheless. He did what he advises writers to do in Part
VI: "A man should write and throw away. Write and throw away
again" (84/15-16). He was trying to write, among other things,
the novel he called "Another Man's House" or "Other People's
Houses, " a novel with Talbot Whittingham once again as the protagonist (see the note to 25/25). Early in the summer he is optimistic about this writing. He wrote to Mary Reynolds on May 27,
1926: "I have got a farm here I have had my mind on for a year
or two, and we are living on it. It is in the lower part of southwest Virginia, a lovely spot. Just at present I am up to my eyes
in two things: building a stone farmhouse, and writing a novel";
and the next day he wrote to Alfred Stieglitz: "This is a heavenly
place and I have been working hard and steadily" (Letters, Newberry Library, 1926). By the end of the summer, however, he is
terribly depressed. See, for example, the letter to Karl quoted
in the note to 52/32, as well as the following letter to Roger Sergel written in late August. He tries to console Sergel about Sergel's own difficulties with a book, and says:

> Dear man. How many times have I gone through that
> story and must yet go. Only last week my creeping to
> Elizabeth, tears in my eyes, saying [all] I had ever
> written was nothing, declaring I would never write any-
> thing really decent.
>   A man plows on and then dies. God knows about it
> all. This summer I have destroyed 30[, 000] to 40, 000
> words of a novel twice.
>   Rubbish piled up. The real flaw always eluding a man.
> Then when it is almost hopeless, a bit comes.
>   This year I undertook too much, a house & a novel
> too. I want the house there and paid for if it can be
> managed. It will cut my living cost down, down. (Let-
> ters, ed. Jones and Rideout, p. 160.)

Just as it is true that Anderson had done some writing, but
not writing that pleased him, it is also true that not all the writing
he did at this time was poor. It seems that he was able to write
short things but not a novel. For example, it was at this time
that he wrote the final version of his excellent story "Death in the
Woods" (see 28/16-17 and its note).

54/2-3. It didn't matter. The implication is that Anderson's artistic energies were absorbed and fulfilled by the building of Ripshin. This implication is strengthened a few lines later (54/7-12)
when he recounts that a friend once told him that his house was
as beautiful as a poem and as beautiful as several of his best
short stories. In other words, the building of his house was an
artistic undertaking and an artistic achievement.

In Memoirs, ed. White, pp. 494-95, Anderson also draws
a comparison between building a house and writing creatively. The
Memoirs passage, however, does not imply that the building of the
house fully satisfied Anderson's artistic impulses.

54/4. cement tank. In a letter to Karl written on July 16, 1926,
Sherwood says: "The water supply is from a spring--feeding a
tank--on the hill above the house" (Letters, Newberry Library,
1926). The cement tank still stands on the top of the small hill
that overlooks the north, or front, side of the house. It is no
longer used for water storage, however.

54/8. "Live all the rest of your days in it." Anderson lived in
the house from 1927 until the fall of 1928. By January, 1929,
however, Elizabeth had left him and gone back to her family in
Berkeley, California, and Sherwood had moved out of Ripshin. At
this time he was traveling a good deal in the South, gathering information for his articles on the new industrialization of the South.
Whenever he returned to Marion he lived with his son Robert, who
by this time had assumed the editorship of the Smyth County News
and the Marion Democrat. He wrote to Roger Sergel in the fall
of 1929 that he was "staying with Bob in a tiny apartment above
the print shop in Marion" (Letters, Newberry Library, 1929). He
was then trying to sell Ripshin. His plan was to interest five
other men in buying partial interest in the house and farm and to
establish a lodge to which the men could go for vacations. He
wrote to several of his friends, for example, Horace Liveright,
Burton Emmett, Maurice Long, and Ferdinand Schevill, telling
them about the advantages that Ripshin offered as a resort: trout
fishing in the spring and summer, pheasant and quail hunting in
the fall, beautiful scenery at any season (Letters, Newberry Library, 1929, 1930). Anderson was never able to carry out this
plan, nor to sell Ripshin. Then, in 1933, shortly before his marriage to Eleanor, he started writing to his friends that he had decided not to sell the house and farm. For example, he wrote to
J. J. Lankes from Kansas City on February 4, 1933: "You know,
Lankes, I've been trying to sell that Ripshin for three or four
years, and now I think I'll go back there to live, perhaps this
spring" (Letters, ed. Jones and Rideout, p. 277). Sherwood and

Eleanor lived at Ripshin until his death in 1941.

54/10.   "Brother Death. " This story is the last one in the volume
Death in the Woods.   It was written specifically for this volume in
a hotel in Kansas City in 1933.   See 75/6, where Anderson speaks
about writing well in a cheap hotel in Kansas City.   For the circumstances surrounding the writing of "Brother Death, " as well as
Anderson's opinion of it, see the letter he wrote to Ferdinand Schevill on March 2, 1933:

> I got the proofs for the new short story book, and they
> have been returned.
>   The truth is that when I got the book before me, I
> was not satisfied with it--two or three very fine stories
> and several just fair.   I threw out two or three.
>   Then I wrote a new story--the last one in the book,
> when you see it--called "Brother Death" that I think will
> make the book.   It is, I'm pretty sure, one of the finest
> stories I've done, and I even dare say one of the finest
> and most significant anyone has ever done.
>   Sounds cocky, doesn't it?   (Letters, ed. Jones and
> Rideout, pp. 277-78.)

See also a letter to Paul Rosenfeld written on July 14, 1933.   After
telling Rosenfeld that he is not hurt by his adverse criticism of
Beyond Desire in "The Authors and Politics, " Scribner's, XCIII
(May, 1933), 318-20, Anderson speaks about "Brother Death":

> As for the new book of short stories, that you say you
> have not read, most of them are four or five years old,
> but at the end of the book there is a story called "Broth-
> er Death, " written last winter after the rest of the book
> was in press, that I think does thoroughly refute all you
> say of me.   (Letters, ed. Jones and Rideout, p. 292.)

See also a letter to Gerturde Stein written in early September,
1933:

> I wrote one good story last winter, in a book called
> Death in the Woods.   I'd send the book on to you, only
> the publisher went smash and I haven't any copies.   The
> one story I liked best was called "Brother Death. "
> (Letters, ed. Jones and Rideout, p. 295.)

Anderson's criticism of his work in this instance is just.
"Brother Death" is considered one of Anderson's best stories.   See,
for example:

Walter Havighurst, Masters of the Modern Short Story (New
     York: Harcourt, Brace and World, 1955), pp. xii-xiii.
Earl Raymond Hilton, "The Evolution of Sherwood Ander-
     son's 'Brother Death, ' " Northwest Ohio Quarterly, XXIV
     (Summer, 1952), 125-30.

Schevill, pp. 300-301.

"Brother Death" is the only story mentioned here in the "Writer's Book" that is included in Maxwell Geismar's Sherwood Anderson: Short Stories (New York: Hill and Wang, 1962).

54/10-11. "The Untold Lie." Of the four stories mentioned here by Anderson, this is the only Winesburg story. It was first published in Seven Arts, I (January, 1917), 215-21. After its publication in Winesburg it was reprinted in The Sherwood Anderson Reader and in Selected Short Stories of Sherwood Anderson (Edition for the Armed Services, Inc., 1945). "The Untold Lie," as well as "Brother Death," is often singled out as one of Anderson's best stories. For example, Malcolm Cowley in the Introduction to the Viking Compass paperback edition of Winesburg, Ohio affirms that Anderson started a new trend in American short story writing by concentrating on single significant moments. Cowley goes on to say: "The best of the moments in Winesburg, Ohio is called 'The Untold Lie' " (p. 6). See also:

> Herbert Gold, "The Purity and Cunning of Sherwood Anderson," Hudson Review, X (Winter, 1957-58), 551; reprinted in Charles Shapiro, ed., Twelve Original Essays on Great American Novels (Detroit: Wayne State University Press, 1958), p. 201.
> Jarvis Thurston, "Anderson and 'Winesburg': Mysticism and Craft," Accent, XVI (Spring, 1956), 119-20.

54/11. "The New Englander." This story was first published in the Dial, LXX (February, 1921), 143-58, and then in Anderson's second volume of short stories, The Triumph of the Egg. It is also included in The Sherwood Anderson Reader and Selected Short Stories of Sherwood Anderson, Edition for the Armed Services. Brom Weber in "Anderson and 'The Essence of Things,' " Sewanee Review, LIX (Autumn, 1951), 687, says of "The New Englander": "This story will remain one of the finest embodiments of the merits potentially contained in Anderson's lyrical-symbolic method." Frederick Hoffman in Freudianism and the Literary Mind, pp. 244-45, also discusses its symbols, which graphically express the sexual repression of Elsie Leander, the New Englander. Anderson in A Story Teller's Story, ed. White, p. 155, speaks about writing a section of Poor White and "The New Englander." He says: "I remember ... how at a railroad station at Detroit I sat writing the tale of Elsie Leander's westward journey, in The Triumph of the Egg, and missed my own train--these remain as rich and fine spots in a precarious existence." See 86/2-88/14, where Anderson speaks about writing a story, which he does not name, at a railroad station in Harrodsburg, Kentucky. See also the note to 86/2.

54/11. "The Man's Story." This story was first published in the Dial, LXXV (September, 1923), 247-64, and then in Anderson's third volume of short stories, Horses and Men. It has also been printed in The Sherwood Anderson Reader and Selected Short Stories of Sherwood Anderson, Edition for the Armed Services. Anderson seems to have had a special fondness for this story. See 57/3-7, where the circumstances surrounding the writing of "The Man's Story" are alluded to, and 89/30-92/6, where the writing is described in detail. In an interview with the present editor on June 5, 1969, Mrs. Eleanor Anderson said that it was true that Sherwood usually answered the question as to which was his favorite story with his oft-repeated quip, "Ask a mother which is her favorite child" (see 63/9-10). Nevertheless, she confessed that Sherwood always (and she emphasized "always") maintained that "The Man's Story" was his favorite.

See Memoirs, ed. White, p. 278, where Anderson heaps high praise on "The Man's Story." He is recalling the image of his father kneeling by the fire and pretending to burn a deed for some property in Cincinnati. He declares:

> When years later the scene gave me the idea for one of the finest short stories I or any other man ever wrote, "The Man's Story, " in the book Horses and Men, the woman in the room with the absorbed man, the poet (and if father was not a poet, at that moment, what was he?), the flare of light from a fireplace filled with papers, the woman shot by a rejected lover, not wanting to disturb the poet, lighting the papers in the room and walking across the room to fall dead at his feet, it is a story that will someday be counted one of the very great and beautiful short stories of the world and father gave me the key for it.

In the case of "The Man's Story" Anderson's favoritism in regard to this one imaginative child seems to have clouded his critical judgment. Critics in general do not agree that it is "one of the very great and beautiful short stories of the world, " nor even one of Anderson's greatest.

54/18-19. She knew nothing of the absurd fear of old age. See 50/24-26, where Anderson says: "the fear in me that night, of which my wife knew nothing ... it would have shocked her profoundly to be told of it." See also 38/19 and 52/19-20, where Anderson also speaks about the fear of poverty and old age.

54/21-22. to force the people of my imaginative world into a world dictated by others. See the notes to 44/28-29 and 55/29-30.

54/25-26. between me and a certain man of God. The "What Say" column of the Smyth County News for July 7, 1932 (Archives, Virginia State Library, Richmond), prints a letter to Anderson written on June 1, 1932, by the Reverend Arthur H. Smith, Pastor of the Wicker Park Methodist Church, 2016 Evergreen Avenue, Chicago, and Anderson's reply, written June 6, 1932. The letter from the Reverend Mr. Smith was written, not from Winesburg,

as 54/28-29 says, from Chicago.   After the initial exchange of
letters Smith wrote at least two other letters to Anderson, one on
March 2, 1936, the other on July 23, 1940 (Letters, Newberry Library, Incoming, the Reverend Arthur H. Smith to Sherwood Anderson).   In his letter of July 23, 1940, Smith invited Anderson to a
Winesburg Reunion to be held August 15-17, 1940:   "Let me assure
you we will show you every possible courtesy if you can come."
Anderson answered Smith's letter on August 1, 1940:

> It sounds delightful; but, alas, engagements already
> made will I am afraid, prevent my being there.
> Do, however, take my greetings to the people of the
> real Winesburg.
> As you know mine was a purely imagined town and I
> would be much hurt if anyone there should think of it and
> its people as having lived in any place but my imagina-
> tion.
> I wish I might know better the real Winesburgers.
> (Letters, Newberry Library, 1940.)

54/27-28.   whether Methodist, Baptist or Lutheran I had forgotten.
Anderson probably had forgotten this detail and did not refer to his
correspondence with the Reverend Arthur H. Smith.   The "What
Say" column of the Smyth County News clearly identifies the Reverend Mr. Smith as Pastor of the Wicker Park Methodist Church.
The other two letters from Smith to Anderson are on stationery
with his name and church's address stamped at the top.   The
March 2, 1936, letter is from Brighton Park Methodist Church,
2115 West 36th Street, Chicago, and the July 23, 1940, letter is
from the Mandell Methodist Church, 4724 Gladys Avenue, Chicago.
Anderson probably had received the 1936 letter by the time he
wrote "Prelude To A Story, " but probably not the 1940 letter.

54/30.   There was then really such a town.   Winesburg, Ohio, is
only seventy-five miles from Clyde and fifty miles from Elyria.
It is probably true, however, that Anderson did not know of its
existence when, first in Elyria and later in Chicago, he wrote
stories and novels about people in his "mythical" Winesburg.   Only
three months after the publication of Winesburg, Ohio in March of
1919, however, he became aware of its existence.   He wrote to
Ben Huebsch on June 14, 1919:   "Here is an interesting development.   There is a Weinsburg [sic], Ohio.   I'll stay out of that
town" (Letters, Newberry Library, 1919).

54/31-32.   I had attempted two or three novels, set in a mythical
Winesburg, Ohio.   It is impossible to determine exactly how many
novels Anderson is referring to here.   Phillips in "How Sherwood
Anderson Wrote Winesburg, Ohio" describes the discarded novel
whose main character is called Talbot Whittingham and whose setting is Winesburg.   The manuscript version of eighteen of the
twenty-five Winesburg tales is written on the back of this discarded
novel, called alternatively "The Golden Circle, " "Talbot the Actor, "
and "Talbot Whittingham."   Another attempt at a novel called "Tal-

bot Whittingham, " the one edited by Gerald Nemanic in his dissertation (see the note to 25/25), is set in Mirage, Ohio. We will
just have to take Anderson at his word of "two or three."

55/4. the little book listed only towns on railroads. For a similar account of the "real" and "mythical" Winesburg, see Memoirs,
ed. White, p. 22. See also a holograph in Box 2 of the "Memoirs"
manuscripts at the Newberry Library called "More About Publishers. " This holograph is not printed in either Rosenfeld's or White's
edition of Memoirs. It probably is an alternate version of part 3
of what became "Pick the Right War, " Memoirs, ed. White, pp.
182-87. In this holograph Anderson speaks about his early published works, Windy McPherson's Son, Marching Men, and Mid-
American Chants. He then goes on to say:

> I had begun to write of the little lives I knew, people
> with whom I had lived, had walked with and talked with,
> had perhaps even slept with, and the result was Wines-
> burg, Ohio.
> It was no particular town. It was people. I had got
> the characters of the book everywhere about me, in
> towns in which I had lived, in the army, in factories and
> offices in which I had worked.
> So there they were, these people of my book, of my
> purely mythical Ohio town.
> For it was a mythical town. When I gave the book
> its title I had no idea there really was an Ohio town by
> that name. I even consulted a list but it must have been
> a list giving only towns that were situated on railroads,
> and later the people of the actual Winesburg protested.
> They declared the book immoral and that the actual in-
> habitants of the real Winesburg were a highly moral
> people. (pp. 10-11.)

55/6-7. The preacher in the real Winesburg had written a history
of the town. The Reverend Arthur H. Smith, a native of Winesburg, wrote a book called An Authentic History of Winesburg,
Holmes County, Ohio, Including a Winesburg "Who's Who" (Chicago:
n. p. , 1930). The Reverend Mr. Smith mentions Anderson's Winesburg on p. 70, under the heading "A Few Side Notes":

> If you have been disturbed because of Sherwood An-
> derson's book, "WINESBURG, OHIO" (a burlesque) and
> resented it as an insult and a slander on our home town,
> it will put your mind to rest in perfect peace if you will
> remember that Mr. Anderson did not know that there
> was such a town as Winesburg, Ohio, when he wrote his
> book, which, by the way, is well worth reading. The
> imaginary town he writes about is a much larger town
> and has a railroad. Where he got the name is not known.
> But "we (of our actual beloved Winesburg) should worry!"

Smith explains his use of the word "burlesque" in his March 2,

1936, letter to Anderson:

> Perhaps you remember that about June 1--1932 I sent
> you a copy of my book "An Authentic History of Wines-
> burg, Ohio"--On June 6--1932 you wrote me relative to
> your book "Winesburg, Ohio."
> I greatly appreciate your explanation. My son is a
> Senior in "Northwestern University," Evanston, Ill. One
> of the books in his required reading is your "Winesburg,
> Ohio."
> He showed his Professor your letter to me and the
> Prof. copied it.
> Now, Mr. Anderson, I used the name "burlesque" in
> my History, P. 70, as I had only skimmed your book
> hastily before writing mine in 1930 so I ask your pardon.
> But you will note even there I exonerated you fully of
> any wrong intent in your book as a "slur" upon our real
> Winesburg--
> I wanted the Winesburgers to get that straight, as a
> few of them were quite "agitated" about it--I never was
> I assure you.
> In the hurry--and stress of my pastoral and home
> duties I used the word loosely--"burlesque"--for which I
> am sorry. I take your explanation gladly. (Letters,
> Newberry Library, Incoming, Reverend Arthur H. Smith
> to Sherwood Anderson, 1936.)

55/7-8. as I gathered a small German community. The Reverend
Mr. Smith's history tells us that Winesburg was founded by "The
Four Bachelors": John Michael Smith, born in Wuertemberg, Germany; the Reverend William Smith, a young minister who had just
graduated from a theological seminary in Germany; Frederick Hap-
pold, also born in Germany; and Dr. August Scheurer, born and
educated in Germany (pp. 15-16 and 20-22). Many of the other
early settlers were also of German extraction, and even in 1930
German names abound.

55/8. devoted I hoped to the raising of the grape. The Reverend
Mr. Smith's Authentic History does not lead the reader to conclude
that the raising of the grape or the enjoying of its produce were
central concerns of Winesburg's inhabitants. They are presented
as God-fearing, church-going, music-loving, hard-working citizens.
Smith also explains how the town got its name:

> The town having been laid out, a town meeting was
> called for the purpose of giving it a suitable name. At
> this meeting Dr. August Scheurer suggested the name of
> Weinsburg in honor of Weinsburg, Wuertemberg, Ger-
> many, noted for its heroic and faithful women. These
> women, when once their native village was besieged,
> begged of the besieging general only one request, that
> is, to be allowed to take with them their most costly
> treasure, which on being granted, they immediately

carried their husbands safely out of the town of Weinsburg, ever after known in history because of its "Wei-
bertreu. " The seplling was changed to Winesburg by the
United States postal authorities in 1833, when a Post
Office was established. (p. 18.)

55/11-12. He wrote me a letter. Anderson's words here are an
accurate description of the letter printed in "What Say" in the
Smyth County News for July 7, 1932.

55/13-14. wrote him a hot letter. Anderson's letter as printed
in the Smyth County News is not a "hot" one. It is, as are most
of Anderson's letters, a kind, gentle one but one that makes his
true feelings clear. It objects to Smith's using the term "burlesque, " and it says many of the things about Winesburg that Anderson says throughout the "Writer's Book, " for instance, that it
was first condemned, called "filth, " later praised, even translated
into almost all of the European languages. As is clear from the
passage in Smith's history that mentions Winesburg (see the note
to 55/6-7), Smith did not suggest that if Anderson had ever been
to Winesburg and had written of the inhabitants as he wrote of the
people of his mythical town, he would have brought shame to them
(see 55/14-17).

55/17-19. "If the people of your real Winesburg are a third as
decent as the people of my Winesburg, you should be happy and
proud. " In his letter Anderson defends the people of his mythical
Winesburg in these words: "Do not be offended if I say that I
hope that the real people of the real Winesburg, Ohio, are at
bottom as decent and have as much inner worth" ("What Say, "
Smyth County News, July 7, 1932).
        In the "Memoirs" holograph quoted in the note to 55/4, An-
derson also remarks:

> For certainly the people of my book, who had lived their
> little fragments of lives in my imagination, were not
> specially immoral. They were just people, and when I
> answered the preacher's letter I told him that if the
> people of his real Winesburg were as all around decent
> as those of my imagined town then the real Winesburg
> might--must--be indeed a very decent town to live in.
> (pp. 11-12.)

55/21-22. I had not minded when some of the critics had condemned me for my stories. See 47/2-3, where Anderson also
protests that he is not bothered by adverse criticism. On the
other hand, see 65/1-2, where he says he is "inclined to think"
that the critics who do not praise him are "fools, " and 85/14-15,
where he says he asks his wife to show him only the favorable
criticisms. The latter two statements are probably the truer statements of Anderson's real attitude towards critics. A good summing
up of his attitude is found in a letter to his mother-in-law, Laura
Lou Copenhaver, written in early October of 1936: "Criticism is

as usual--generous, mean, personal, smart-alecky, often penetrating. We have few big critics, Mother, but, on the other hand,
criticism in America is never venal, as in Europe" (Letters, ed.
Jones and Rideout, p. 364).

The year that Anderson wrote this letter he published Kit
Brandon, and in the same letter to Laura Lou Copenhaver he also
remarks: "It is impossible to tell how Kit will go" (p. 363). Kit
Brandon was reviewed by:

> Hamilton Basso, in New Republic, LXXXVIII (October 21,
> 1936), 318;
>
> Howard Mumford Jones, in Saturday Review of Literature,
> XIV (October 10, 1936), 13;
>
> Alfred Kazin, in New York Herald Tribune Books, October
> 11, 1936, pp. 1-2;
>
> Mark Van Doren, in Nation, CXLIII (October 17, 1936),
> 452-53;
>
> Stanley Young, in New York Times Book Review, October
> 11, 1936, p. 3.

An example of criticism "as usual" is Kazin's review, headed
"Sherwood Anderson, Still Shuffling Along: Grasping and Shy and
Awkward and Strangely Moving." Kazin affirms that, although the
subject matter of Southern factory towns and rum-running and the
quicker tempo of the prose seem to make Kit Brandon appear different from Anderson's other novels, the difference is only on the
surface. When Kazin compares Anderson with the other novelists
of the 1930's, he says: "Though the others tower above him, he
alone has kept the spiritual log of what it has meant to be an
American in our time. It is important to recall today, when so
many in his generation gaze at their laurels, that he has never
lost his curiosity or his faith" (p. 2).

55/23-24. there had been a great outcry about filthiness in me.
See 26/4-6, where Anderson speaks about Winesburg's being condemned as "filth" and a "literary sewer."

55/25-26. any condemnation of any of the people in any of my
stories. Anderson's repetition of the word "any" may seem awkward and even redundant, but it is deliberate. One of Anderson's
most characteristic stylistic devices in his repetition of words.
See, for example, the repetition of the pronoun "she" seven times
in the first paragraph of "Death in the Woods." In the first paragraph Anderson is calling the reader's attention both to the old
woman, the central character of the story who "feeds" the narra-
tor's artistic life, and to her seeming insignificance. Here in the
"Writer's Book" Anderson is calling to the reader's mind his oft-
repeated theme that "any" condemnation of his characters is, for
him, a travesty of art and of life. See the notes to 5/32-6/1 and
15/20-21, which comment on Anderson's use of rhythm and word
repetition patterns.

55/26. I had always deeply resented. See A Story Teller's Story,

ed. White, pp. 93-94. The words enclosed in brackets and preceded by asterisks are material that Anderson added in the galleys:

> A public speaker, in speaking of my Winesburg tales,
> praised me as a writer but spoke slightingly of the fig-
> ures that lived in the tales. "They weren't worth telling
> about, " he said, and I remember that I sat at the back
> of the room, filled with people, hearing him speak, and
> remember sharply also just the sense of horror that
> crept over me at the moment. [*"It is a lie. He has
> missed the point, " I cried to myself.] Could the man
> not understand that he was doing a quite unpermissible
> thing? As well go into the bedroom of a woman during
> her lying-in and say to her--"You are no doubt a very
> nice woman but the child to which you have just given
> birth is a little monster and will be hanged. " ...As I
> sat listening certain figures, Wing Biddlebaum, [*Hugh
> McVey,] Elizabeth Willard, Kate Swift, Jesse Bentley,
> marched across the field of my fancy. They had lived
> within me, and I had given a kind of life to them. [*They
> had lived, for a passing moment anyway, in the conscious-
> ness of others beside myself.] Surely I myself might
> well be blamed--condemned--for not having the strength
> or skill in myself to give them a more vital and a truer
> life--but that they should be called people not fit to be
> written about filled me with horror.

In a letter that Anderson wrote in August of 1938 to Mary Helen
Dinsmoor and that is quoted in her thesis ("An Inquiry into the Life
of Sherwood Anderson as Reflected in His Literary Works, " unpublished M. A. thesis, Ohio University, 1939, p. 70), Anderson
says:

> I was like a woman when her child is attacked. I swear
> I could not understand for, to me, the people of my
> tales were very much like all people I have ever known.
> They were no more normal or abnormal. It seemed to
> me that I had found some spot of beauty in each of them.

55/29-30. To sell them out, as is always being done, in the
imaginative world. See the note to 44/28-29, which explains Anderson's theory of the threefold obligation that a writer has to the
imagination. Here Anderson is once again speaking of the third
and, to his mind, the most important obligation, the writer's obligation to the characters of his imagination. This obligation is a
favorite theme throughout Anderson's writings. See, for example,
Anderson's letter to Carrow De Vries quoted in the note to 8/25
and his letter to Norman Holmes Pearson quoted in the note to
81/16. See also "A Note on Realism" in the Notebook (also
printed in "Man and His Imagination"):

> The writer who sets himself down to write a tale has
> undertaken something. He has undertaken to conduct his

reader on a trip through the world of his fancy. If he is
a novelist his imaginative world is filled with people and
events. If he have any sense of decency as a workman
he can no more tell lies about his imagined people, fake
them, than he can sell out real people in real life. The
thing is constantly done but no man I have ever met, having done such a trick, has felt very clean about the matter afterwards. (p. 74.)

See also a section of "Man and His Imagination" that is not part of
"A Note on Realism":

People are always being violated. What is not generally
understood is that to do violence, to sell out a character
in the imaginative world, is as much a crime as to sell
people out in the real world. As I have already tried to
say, this imaginative world of ours, the imaginative lives
we live, are as important to us as are real lives. They
may be more important. (p. 58.)

Finally, see The Modern Writer:

Consider for a moment the materials of the prose
writer, the teller of tales. His materials are human
lives. To him these figures of his fancy, these people
who live in his fancy should be as real as living people.
He should be no more ready to sell them out than he
would sell out his men friends or the woman he loves.
To take the lives of these people and bend or twist them
to suit the needs of some cleverly thought out plot to
give your reader a false emotion is as mean and ignoble
as to sell out living men or women. (p. 39.)

56/7. "But I have a right now to put money first. " In the left
hand margin in pencil in Paul Rosenfeld's hand is written, "Reader
371. " Close examination shows that "Memoirs" was written first,
then erased, and "Reader" written over the erasure. Three more
times in the manuscript of "Prelude To A Story, " Rosenfeld penciled in "Memoirs, " then erased it, and penciled in "Reader" and
a page number. See the notes to 59/17, 59/32, and 61/22. The
page numbers correspond to the pages in The Sherwood Anderson
Reader where the passages from "The Sound of the Stream" are
found.

56/9-10. Maugham's Of Human Bondage. Its first edition was
published in New York by George H. Doran, August 12, 1915. The
first English edition came out the next day, published in London by
William Heinemann. Since 1915 it has remained Maugham's most
popular novel, and probably his best.

56/12. Put in Maugham's paragraph. It is now impossible to determine what paragraph Anderson had in mind. The present editor
made a thorough search among the books of Anderson that still re-

main in the stone house at Ripshin and at the Copenhaver home in
Marion.   Anderson's work cabin by the stream at Ripshin no longer has any books in it.   The copy of Of Human Bondage that Anderson had in his hands on the afternoon he wrote this passage in
"Prelude to a Story" can no longer be identified.   In an interview
on July 23, 1970, Anderson's son John told the editor that he
thought it very likely that his father wrote "put in Maugham's
paragraph" because he was not sure where he could find the passage that his memory told him was somewhere in Maugham's novel.

56/14-15.   by his writing and by his plays, after his Of Human
Bondage, had got rich.   Maugham, who had grown up in relative
poverty, "got rich" for the first time, not in 1915, but in 1911
when four of his plays, Lady Frederick, Mrs. Dot, Jack Straw,
and The Explorer, enjoyed successful runs in London (Karl G.
Pfeiffer, W. Somerset Maugham: A Candid Portrait [New York:
W. W. Norton and Company, Inc., 1959], pp. 49-50).   From 1911
on, Maugham continued to write novels, stories, and plays that
sold very well.   This is not to say that they were not also good
literature.

56/20-22.   my cabin, across the road from my house and hidden
away under trees by a little creek.   This is a very accurate description of the present location of Anderson's work cabin.   Ripshin Creek runs along the east side of the house.   Farther to the
east is the road.   Down the road to the south is the confluence
of Ripshin Creek and Laurel Creek.   The cabin stands on the bank
of Ripshin Creek, a little to the east of the confluence.
      See the notes to 33/2-3 and 72/13-14 for details about the
moving of the cabin down from the top of the highest hill on Anderson's farm to its present location by the side of the stream.

56/25.   the words refusing to flow.   "Flow" is one of Anderson's
favorite words.   See 38/26, 84/8-9, 86/29-30, and their notes.

56/30.   now they shall serve me.   See the letter, written to Roger
and Ruth Sergel in January of 1930, which reflects the struggle
that Anderson is speaking about here:

> In all my early writing and until my last [third] mar-
> riage I wrote pretty much what I damn pleased when I
> pleased.
>   Then I became, I think now, very decidedly middle-
> class.   I do not mean by doing what you are, but do
> mean by writing for money.
>   It is perhaps only when we try to bend the arts to
> serve our damn middle-class purposes that we become
> unclean.
>   So I tore my novel up and severed my connection with
> Vanity Fair.   (Letters, ed. Jones and Rideout, p. 206.)

The novel that Anderson tore up was called "No God, " then "No
Love, " and then "Beyond Desire. "   It should not be confused with

Beyond Desire, published in 1932.

57/3. Once I had written for ten hours. The circumstances given
here (57/3-7) are a brief description of the writing of "The Man's
Story" as told in greater detail in 89/30-92/6.

57/8-9. day after day passing as in some delicious dream. See
38/26-27, where Anderson also speaks about the ease with which
he wrote A Story Teller's Story. The note to those lines gives
documentation to show that Anderson labored over this book as he
did over all of his others.

57/10. another. This word shows that Anderson thought that A
Story Teller's Story was also misunderstood. See 38/30-31, where
Anderson says that it is "a book that has never had the audience it
deserved but that will have."

57/10. terribly misunderstood book. One example of contemporary
misunderstanding of Many Marriages is in Cleveland Chase's biography: "Anderson has stretched out the material for a mediocre
short story into a full length novel and has made the material itself worthless in the process" (p. 54). Since Many Marriages ran
serially in the Dial from October, 1922, until March, 1923, and
was published as a book by Huebsch in February of 1923, Chase is
assuming, as many other critics have done, that Many Marriages
was first written as a short story and then unwisely expanded to
the dimensions of a full length novel. Janice Ellen Cole in her
dissertation, "Many Marriages: Sherwood Anderson's Controversial
Novel" (unpublished Ph. D. dissertation, University of Michigan,
1965), after a thorough investigation of the two extant manuscripts
of Many Marriages and the letters that Anderson wrote at the time,
argues that Many Marriages was first written as a novel and then
shortened for its serialization in the Dial, although she concedes
that her theory cannot, no more than the commonly held one, be
proved with certitude. Cole says:

> Nowhere in the letters quoted in this chapter, or in
> any letters of the period in the Anderson Collection, is
> there any mention of material being added to the Dial
> version of Many Marriages. As has been said, there
> are, however, a number of letters in which shortening
> the novel for the Dial is discussed. (p. 63.)

On the other hand, we have Anderson's own words to refute this
argument. Anderson prefaced his book-length edition with "An Explanation":

> I wish to make an explanation--that should perhaps be
> also an apology--to the readers of the Dial.
>   To the magazine I make due acknowledgement for the
> permission to print in this book form.
>   To the Dial reader I must explain that the story has
> been greatly expanded since it appeared serially in the

magazine. The temptation to amplify my treatment of
the theme was irresistible. If I have succeeded in thus
indulging myself without detriment to my story I shall
be glad.

The editor, however, after her own study of Anderson's letters
and the two manuscripts of Many Marriages, accepts the thesis put
forward in Cole's dissertation, in spite of Anderson's "Explanation. "

Two more important aspects of what Anderson would call
the "misunderstanding" of Many Marriages are the charges of immorality and lack of artistry leveled against it. To quote Chase
again: "The book rambles; repeats words, thoughts, symbols;
were it not so thoroughly confused and meaningless, it would come
very close to being immoral" (p. 54). Most of the critics who reviewed Many Marriages when it was published found more to blame
than to praise. See, for example:

H. W. Boynton, in Independent, CX (March 31, 1923), 232;
Heywood Broun, in New York World, February 25, 1923,
    Section E, p. 6;
Henry Seidel Canby, in New York Evening Post Literary Re-
    view, February 24, 1923, p. 483;
Gerald Gould, in Saturday Review of Literature, CXXXVI
    (September 8, 1923), 281;
Ludwig Lewisohn, in Nation, CXVI (March 28, 1923), 368;
Robert Littell, in New Republic, XXXVII (April 11, 1923),
    6-8;
Burton Rascoe, in New York Tribune Book News and Re-
    views, February 25, 1923, p. 17;
Percy N. Stone, in Bookman (New York), LVII (April, 1923),
    210-11;
New York Times Book Review, February 25, 1923, p. 10.

F. Scott Fitzgerald, however, in an article entitled "Sherwood Anderson on the Marriage Question" in the New York Herald, March
4, 1923, Section 9, p. 5, (see Cole, pp. 17-18), praised the book,
giving special attention to Anderson's style. Other friends of Anderson also praised the book, but in private letters to him. For
example, Gertrude Stein and Theodore Dreiser both wrote laudatory appreciations of Many Marriages shortly after its publication
(Letters, Newberry Library, 1923). Years later, on December 6,
1935, Dreiser again wrote: "You say I think the novel is not your
field. I don't know that I ever emphasized that. It may be yet
your greatest field. I loved Many Marriages at a time when many
quarreled with it" (Letters, Newberry Library, 1935; also quoted
in Cole, p. 14).

In Memoirs, ed. White, p. 152, Anderson says that Many
Marriages was "not understood, " and in a letter to Georgia
O'Keeffe written in December of 1935 he says, as he does in the
"Writer's Book, " that it was "terribly misunderstood" (Letters, ed.
Jones and Rideout, p. 338). A clear indication of Anderson's at-
titude towards Many Marriages, as well as an example of his crit-

ical judgment on his works, is given in a letter to Ulrico Hoepli
of the Casa Editrice Libraria Ulrico Hoepli in Milan, Italy. Anderson wrote on June 5, 1937:

> It is a little difficult for any writer who has written
> many books to pick out one of them and to say, "This is
> the most important of my efforts." It is too much like
> asking a mother who has many children to say which of
> her children is her favorite.
>
> A novel of mine called Dark Laughter has had the
> largest immediate sale of any of my work. A book of
> short stories called Winesburg, Ohio is, I believe, the
> book of mine most often selected by American critics.
> It was written some twenty years ago and has become
> more or less an American classic.
>
> I think that I myself am fondest perhaps of another
> called Many Marriages, but this may be only true be-
> cause the book, when published, was very generally
> abused by the critics.
>
> You will see how difficult it is for a writer to make
> a selection. When I was a boy in an American country
> town, there was in the town an old horse-trader who had
> a favorite saying: "The best horse I ever owned I own
> now." I think most any writer would be inclined to say
> that his best work is the one not yet done. (Letters, ed.
> Jones and Rideout, p. 380.)

See the note to 16/11-12, where a passage from Many Marriages is quoted.

57/11-13. Our dark age of belief ... by economic professors.
See the passages 44/12-32 and 83/7-11, where Anderson speaks
against the idea of what we might call "propaganda literature, "
literature with "a good proletariat angle" (83/9) or "so-called proletariat stories" (44/19). Such propaganda literature arises in a
world "dominated by the economists" (44/16). See also a letter
written from Ripshin on June 14, 1937, to Dorothy Norman, editor
of Twice a Year:

> I have been thinking for several years that we would
> presently grow tired of the rather hard-boiled, pessimis-
> tic, wisecracking attitude toward life. In fact I have
> sometimes said to myself that we are again in a dark
> age that clings to the belief that a good life may be at-
> tained through economic readjustment alone. It is pretty
> hopeless. (Letters, ed. Jones and Rideout, p. 383.)

See also Memoirs, ed. White, p. 554:

> The time will come when men will look back upon my
> times, speaking of it as another dark age. Any civiliza-
> tion absorbed in economics, the economic interpretation
> of history, etc., etc. is but a savage and brutal civiliza-

tion.
There will be a renaissance and then my own work
and my own life will be appreciated.   For in a muddled
time I have lived fully and very richly.

57/13.   will come into its own.   Recent critics still quarrel with
the greatness of Many Marriages.   See, for example, Rex Burbank's 1964 biography of Anderson.   In the Preface Burbank says
that the general reader and the critic usually agree upon Anderson's successes and failures.   They both rank Many Marriages
among the failures.   In the body of the biography Burbank explains
why:

> The chief weakness of Many Marriages is that the
> symbols--of which the picture of the Virgin is one of the
> most important--are made to carry a greater rhetorical
> burden than they can bear, being used in lieu of action
> to convey the themes.   Anderson's thesis is not imagi-
> natively realized through either symbols or action, and
> the novel lapses therefore into mere rhetoric....
> Many Marriages is a thoroughly irresponsible work,
> both artistically and intellectually; but we need not ques-
> tion Anderson's integrity of purpose.   The irresponsibility
> consists in his failure to condense his material, to tight-
> en the structure of the book, and to examine the nature
> and consequences of his themes and the assumptions be-
> hind them.   Above all, it is irresponsible because his
> mouthpiece, Webster, wins his argument too easily; he
> has no articulate antagonist to challenge his assumptions.
> In the absence of any discernible dialectic or narrative
> conflict, Webster's supposedly sophisticated ideas about
> life and sex become the maunderings of a terribly ig-
> norant man, and his symbolic act of psychic and physi-
> cal rebirth is reduced to absurdity.   (pp. 111-12.)

57/14.   joy.   The word that the editor has emended to read "joy"
looks a bit like "jole."   The sentence on 60/10--"The burning took
a long time but it was a joy"--also has the word that looks like
"jole"; but in this case the "le" could be construed as a "y."
Therefore, the editor reads what looks like "le" in 57/14 also as
"y. "

57/17-18.   the self, for the time, completely gone.   Anderson
started Many Marriages in the late winter or early spring of 1921
when he was in Fairhope, Alabama, with Tennessee (see the note
to 25/10).   He finished it in New Orleans when he returned there
in January, 1922.   By March, 1922, he wrote to Gilbert Seldes of
the Dial about serial publication (Letters, Newberry Library, 1921-
22).   See 74/32-75/5, where Anderson may be reminiscing about
finishing Many Marriages in New Orleans.

57/28-29.   already mentioned that my house stands by a mountain
stream.   See 56/5-6.

58/3.   the sounds coming in.   Ripshin Creek, running over the
many rocks in its bed (see 86/4) is very audible from the master
bedroom on the first floor of the east side of the house.

58/5.   somewhere I have written.   See Memoirs, ed. White, p.
505: "The creek, near the house, that murmured and talked to
you at night as you lay awake in bed was another matter.   It was
fed by other mountain springs and was cold and clear."

58/13.   a city park.   In a letter to Roger Sergel written on March
26, 1928, Anderson comments on the Sergel's move into an apartment at 6016 Stony Island Avenue in Chicago, "almost exactly an
address at which I once lived."   Anderson lived on the South Side
near Jackson Park shortly after his return to Chicago from Elyria.
Floyd Dell, Margery Currey, and other artists and writers of the
Chicago Renaissance lived in apartments which had originally been
erected for the Columbian Exhibition in Chicago in 1893 (see 58/19-
20).   In the letter to Sergel, Anderson mentions the fact that
"there used to be a lot of low, one-story buildings on Stony Island
near 57th Street," and goes on to say:

> I think Jackson Park is one of the loveliest parks in
> America.   How many adventures I have had in that park!
> How many hours have I spent wandering about in it at
> night and dreaming!
> . . . .
> I went to Chicago when I was quite a young man.   All
> sorts of love adventures in Jackson Park, a good many
> of which I have written about.   (Letters, ed. Jones and
> Rideout, pp. 182-83.)

58/25.   her father was a streetcar conductor.   In A Story Teller's
Story, ed. White, pp. 171-74, Anderson tells of having an affair
with the wife of a streetcar conductor, whom he used to meet in
the park, when he was a young laborer and living in an ugly apartment building where many streetcar employees lived.

58/28-29.   of Fred, of Mary, of Tom, of Ester.   It is impossible
to determine exatly whom Anderson is speaking about in this passage.   Fred could possibly be Fred O'Brien (see 82/4-5 and its
note) or Fred Booth, an unsuccessful novelist and short story writer, friend of Anderson, Waldo Frank, and Paul Rosenfeld in the
late 1910's (Letters, Newberry Library, 1918-1919).   Mary could
be several people who were close to Anderson in his lifetime:
Mrs. Burton Emmett, Mary Chryst Anderson, his son Bob's wife,
Mary Vernon Greear, one of his secretaries, or "Old Mary,"
whose sister's house he rented in Palos Park, Illinois, between
1920 and 1922 and who brought him his dinner and regaled him
with stories of her youthful days in vaudeville (see Memoirs, ed.
White, pp. 420-24).   Tom very likely is Tom Smith, one of Horace Liveright's editors.   Ester might possibly be the Virginia
mountain woman whose trial for cursing a certain Carl was covered
in the Smyth County News and Marion Democrat (see Welford Dun-

away Taylor, "Sherwood Anderson, " Virginia Cavalcade, XIX
[Spring, 1970], 46).

59/1. Hugh McVey. He is the main character in Anderson's
novel Poor White (see 48/22). See also the quotation from A
Story Teller's Story cited in the note to 55/26, where he is incor-
rectly listed among the Winesburg characters. In both the Introduction to the Modern Library edition of Poor White and in Memoirs, ed. White, p. 354, Anderson says that Poor White is more
the story of the town of Bidwell, Ohio, than it is the story of Hugh.

59/2. Carl Sandburg. Sandburg (1878-1967) was an editorial writer on the Chicago Daily News and an aspiring poet befriended by
Harriet Monroe and Poetry magazine when Anderson first knew
him. Anderson never had a close friendship with Sandburg nor a
high opinion of his literary worth. See "The Sandburg, " Memoirs,
ed. White, pp. 466-69, where Anderson reminisces about the Chicago Renaissance, about Dreiser, Sinclair Lewis, Eugene O'Neill,
and Ben Hecht, and in regard to Sandburg says, among other
things: "Here, in the poet Sandburg, was, I thought, a man who
had collected more, in respect and admiration, while giving less
than any poet of my time.... He was a man who had never made
a fight for any other first rate poet of his time" (p. 467).

59/2-3. Ben Hecht. Hecht (1893-1964) wrote for the Chicago
Daily News from 1914 until 1923, when he founded, assisted by
Sandburg and Maxwell Bodenheim, his literary burlesque, Chicago
Literary Times. Hecht went from Chicago to New York to Hollywood becoming, with his collaborator Charles MacArthur, the kind
of successful playwright and movie producer whom Anderson casti-
gates through most of the "Writer's Book. " See, however, a letter
of Anderson to his mother-in-law, Laura Lou Copenhaver, written
on October 13, 1936:

> Had a long talk yesterday with Ben Hecht, who has
> gone sour on the movies. You know we were once great
> friends in Chicago. His old mother was killed in an
> automobile accident in Los Angeles, and the last thing
> she said to him before dying was that he should have
> stuck to me and gone with me on my road. (Letters,
> ed. Jones and Rideout, p. 365.)

In a letter to Waldo Frank written in the spring of 1917
Anderson speaks of both Sandburg and Hecht:

> I saw Sandburg the other night, and we had a long
> evening together. He liked my songs [Anderson was
> working on his Mid-American Chants] very much, and I
> liked him. There is something Scandinavian about him,
> a suggestion of closed-in icy places. Most of his verses
> do not sing, but he does. Ben Hecht called him a true
> poet who could not write poetry. (Letters, ed. Jones
> and Rideout, p. 12.)

59/3. John Emerson. The manuscript reads "Jane Emerison."
Since the editor found no mention in any of Anderson's writings,
published or unpublished, to a Jane Emerison, the editor assumes
that this is one of Anderson's "slips of the pen" (see the Introduction) and changes the name to John Emerson. John Emerson (see
37/32-38/7 and notes) was a close friend of Anderson from their
youth together in Clyde until Anderson's death.

59/3. Maurice Long. Anderson knew Maurice Long, the owner
of a large laundry in Washinton, D.C., for less than two years,
from March of 1930 until Long's death in December, 1931; but
during that short time he became one of Anderson's closest friends
(Letters, Newberry Library, 1930-31). In Memoirs, ed. White,
pp. 520-24, there is a moving account of Anderson and Long's
friendship and of the real love that existed between them. In the
Preface to the Memoirs, p. 4, Long is listed with other close
friends of Anderson:

> To myself, and wanting a better, I use often the word
> "sweet" in describing these men. There is a kind of
> warmth, a going out to others in them. I think of the
> critic Mr. Burton Rascoe, that perfect gentleman and on-
> ly real sophisticate I have known, Lewis Galantière, of a
> certain Irish owner of a huge laundry in the city of Wash-
> ington, a flame of a man, Maurice Long, of Lewis Gan-
> nett, George Daugherty and Marco Morrow, of Tommy
> Smith and Heywood Broun.

59/4. Doctor Parcival. "The Philosopher--concerning Doctor
Parcival" is the fifth of the Winesburg stories. Parcival is an unsuccessful doctor who one afternoon refuses to go to the aid of a
young girl fatally hurt in an accident. No one in the town notices
Doctor Parcival's absence, but he becomes convinced that the
town's people will hate him for his refusal, that he will be "crucified" by them. He tells George Willard: "Everyone in the world
is Christ and they are all crucified" (New York: B. W. Huebsch,
1919, p. 48).
    In a letter to Jasper Deeter of the Hedgerow Theatre,
written on July 9, 1934, Anderson speaks about his dramatic version of Winesburg, mentioning most particularly the characterization of Doctor Parcival. He tells Deeter how he would like the
actor to play the part:

> Let him try thinking of Parcival as a man who wants
> above everything else closeness to others, human brother-
> hood. The man is wiser than all the others about him,
> sees life more clearly than the others, and this is what
> stands in the way of the closeness he wants. He is in
> an American small town of the Middle West. He is a
> doctor, but medicine doesn't interest him much. Jap, I
> have thought for a long time that one of the most charac-
> teristic things about American life is our isolation from
> one another.... The crucifixion of Christ is real to him.

He feels it going on and on in people. There is the
same identification. "We are all Christs, and we will
all be crucified. " (Letters, ed. Jones and Rideout, pp.
305-306.)

59/4-5. The naked man in the room with his daughter. In Many
Marriages John Webster, after undressing and walking up and down
before a statue of the Virgin Mary, tries to explain to his daughter
Jane what he considers the true meaning of love and sex. See the
quotation from Rex Burbank's biography of Anderson cited in the
note to 57/13; see also Anderson's comment in Memoirs, ed.
White, p. 152:

> I called my book Many Marriages, meaning to convey
> the feeling of contacts among people, of the flesh and
> not of the flesh--something deeply of the spirit that
> nevertheless has the flesh in it.
> The book was not understood. When it was published
> I was widely cursed for it. There was a scene between
> a father and daughter that was taken for incest.
> What stupidity. It hurt me deeply when it happened.

59/17. There were no more voices, only laughter. In the left
hand margin of the manuscript Rosenfeld wrote "Memoirs, " then
erased it, and wrote "Reader p. 371. " See the notes to 56/7,
59/32, and 61/22.

59/23-24. I had come out of my house wearing bedroom slippers.
Here is one more example of a slight inconsistency in Anderson's
text. In 53/7 he had said: "After all of this I went barefooted
out of my house. "

59/32. cigarettes, does not run far. For the third time, this
time in the right hand margin of the manuscript, Rosenfeld wrote
"Memoirs, " erased it, and wrote "Reader 372. " See the notes to
56/7, 59/17, and 61/22.

60/9. I burned it page by page. This is the culmination of Anderson's struggle to maintain his artistic integrity which has been
the central concern of the whole of Part I, "Prelude To A Story. "

60/11-12. an absurd performance ... a child. Anderson often
uses the word "absurd" to characterize his struggle to write a salable short story and the circumstances surrounding this struggle.
He also links the struggle to childishness. Nonetheless, both the
absurdity, to a slight degree, and the childishness, to a far greater degree, are presented as integral to the experience. Artists
are men who engage in absurd dreams: "Such dreams as imaginative young men have, become at times absurd" (16/11-12). When
Anderson contemplates the beauty of his house he forgets "entirely
the absurd struggle that had been going on" (53/21-22). He sums
up the purpose of Part I by saying: "I am trying to set down here
the story of a real if absurd experience" (107/26-27), and he

thinks it will be "a joy to other writers, other artists, to know
that I also, a veteran among them, am also as they are, an eternal child" (60/15-17). Finally he says: "I dare say that all men,
artists and others, are, as I am, children at bottom" (60/28-29).
Therefore, the "absurd and silly experience" in the "absurd and
childish form" (61/10-11 and 19-20) related throughout Part I is
an experience that is likely to happen to all artists, "no doubt in
all time" (61/22).

61/1-3. I thought that the voices in the stream ... whispered to
me. These words are quoted by Schevill in his criticism of
Memoirs. Since Schevill's biography appeared in 1951, he is
speaking of Rosenfeld's edition, and he cites "The Sound of the
Stream" as the source of the quotation. Schevill believes that the
final result of Memoirs, as of Winesburg, is "the creation of
myth. " He then says:

> If the Memoirs is less complete and integrated than
> Winesburg, it gains by its greater exploration of the na-
> ture of myth. All of these diverse mythological elements
> reach their climax in the chapter called "The Sound of
> the Stream. " Lying in bed at night Anderson hears, in
> the rush of the stream that runs past his house, the
> voices of the many characters he has created in the
> special integrity of their imaginary presences. He is in
> need of money and has received an offer from a big com-
> mercial magazine. All he has to do is to write their
> kind of story. In desperation he tries, but the words
> will not come. The world of imagination is being be-
> trayed. With a feeling of joy, Anderson finally burns
> up his attempt at a popular story, and the release is
> immediate: "I thought that the voices in the stream by
> my house had stopped laughing at me and that again they
> talked and whispered to me. " The necessity of myth,
> the demand for illuminating images which will generate
> meaning, continues. The book ends on the note of
> search, "Life, not death, is the great adventure, " for
> the nature of myth is eternal rebirth. (pp. 349-50.)

61/22. no doubt in all time. Here, at the very end of Part I,
Rosenfeld for the last time, again in the right hand margin of the
manuscript, penciled in "Memoirs, " erased it, and wrote "Reader
373. " See the notes to 56/7, 59/17, and 59/32. For the last
time also Rosenfeld changes "Prelude To A Story. " His version
ends: "no doubt throughout time" (Memoirs, p. 445).

62/1. How to Write to a Writer. In a folder at the front of Box
2 of "Memoirs" manuscripts in the Newberry Library there is a
list of "Omissions" (see the note to 3/1). Under the heading
"Previous Cuttings" is listed: "How to Write a Writer (End). "
Evidently "How to Write a Writer" was cut from Memoirs and put
into the "Writer's Book, " possibly because Anderson thought it
was incomplete.

As the note to 1/2 explains, the present editor found only four typed pages of the manuscript of the "Writer's Book" among the Sherwood Anderson Papers. The first of the typed pages is entitled "How to Write to a Writer." It has no typed number because it is a title page, but "7a" is written in by hand at the top. The second page has a "2" typed at the center of the top; it is then crossed out and "7b" is written in. The next page has "5" typed and then "12" written in. The last page has "6" typed and then "13" written in. At first glance it might look as if pages 3 and 4 of the typescript were missing, but many more than two pages have been lost. Typescript pages 2 and 3 are separated from 5 and 6 by 45 pages in Anderson's manuscript and 15 pages in the present edition. Typescript pages 2 and 3 are the same as the first four-and-a-half pages of Part II (62/1-64/18); the last two typescript pages are the same as the last four pages of Part V, "Notes on the Novel" (79/32-81/32). The loss of approximately thirteen pages of typescript, if all of the intervening pages were typed, remains a mystery.

One of the "Works" housed with the Anderson Papers is his "Journal," two boxes of holographs, typescripts, and galley sheets of work done between 1928 and 1940. In the folder for 1933 the present editor found the first two typescript pages; in the folder for 1937 she found the last two pages. Since Mrs. Eleanor Anderson and Paul Rosenfeld shortly after Anderson's death organized the material in the "Journal" boxes, it is likely that "How to Write to a Writer" was written about 1933 and "Notes on the Novel" about 1937.

62/2. I am sure my own experience. The opening lines of "How to Write to a Writer," as well as its title and the words "by Sherwood Anderson," are canceled in pencil in the typescript described in the previous note. The cancellation continues through 62/30.

62/4. letters from younger writers. See 29/1-8, where Anderson speaks about young writers who come to him, who write him letters, and who say that because of his novels a great door has swung open to them. See also in Memoirs, ed. White, the section called "Letters, Autographs, and First Editions," the section that White, p. xxxv, says may originally have been written for the "Writer's Book." It begins: "I presume that every author of any standing must get a good many letters" (p. 545).

62/8-9. a frank honest opinion. In a reply to one of the many letters he must have received, Anderson wrote to Mr. E. Gonklin of Hanover, New Hampshire, on April 28, 1925:

> I am in receipt of your charming letter of April 29 [sic], together with the manuscript of the story "The Cathedral," which I have read with much interest.
> Inasmuch as you asked me to be perfectly frank with you I would suggest that it would be better not to try to get publication for this manuscript yet. It shows un-

doubted ability as a writer but is rather melodramatic
and for that reason does not ring very true. I think it
would be much better for you to keep on writing without
trying to get publication for a time. I, myself, wrote
for eight or ten years before trying for publication and I
think that is a common experience with writers.

Try as hard as you can to see things as they are and
find the drama in things as they are, without trying to
force your situations in order to make a story. In other
words, try to let the story grow naturally out of the materials at hand. (Letters, Newberry Library, 1925.)

62/13. However, she hadn't much time. From the mention of the
young woman's "passionate desire to be a writer" (62/12) until the
disclosure of her unwillingness to risk losing her young admirer
"for the sake of going on with my art" (62/19-20), Anderson deftly
employs his skill in ironic understatement. Irony is also employed
in the passage about the schoolteacher (62/21-30), and especially
in the supposed letter from a young writer given at 63/20-26.

63/1-2. 'The Lost Millionaire.' The same hand which made the
long deletions (62/1-62/30 and 63/27-64/18) and crossed out the
typed numbers and wrote in new numbers on the four pages of
typescript also made three changes in the text. The first change
occurs when "The Lost Millionaire" is canceled and "Windy Mc-
Pherson's Son" is written in. Mrs. Eleanor Anderson told the
editor during her visit to Ripshin Farm on July 17, 1970, that the
handwriting is undoubtedly Paul Rosenfeld's. Nonetheless, Rosenfeld never published any of Part II of the "Writer's Book."

63/10-11. You do not tell her which is your favorite. In an interview on June 5, 1969, Mrs. Eleanor Anderson told the present
editor that Sherwood was always annoyed when a person asked him
which was his favorite story. She said he always answered as he
does here in the "Writer's Book." See the note to 54/11, the
letter to Ulrico Hoepli quoted in the note to 57/10, and Memoirs,
ed. White, pp. 9 and 297. See also Sherwood's letter of October
2, 1925, to Jay L. Bradley, a fifteen-year-old boy who wrote asking for advice on how to become a writer. Sherwood very kindly
answers all of Jay's questions and then says: "Your third ques-
tion--what is my personal favorite among my own books?--is too
much like asking a mother which is her favorite child. They are
to me somewhat different from what they are to the public, and I
simply can't answer the question" (Letters, ed. Jones and Rideout,
p. 149).

63/12. Often. In the typed copy of Part II in the "Journal" boxes
at the Newberry Library, the typist changed this word to "after
all."

63/15-16. must write of a new book every day. Anderson wrote
to his mother-in-law Laura Lou Copenhaver early in October,
1936: "You have to remember that many of these poor wretches,

newspaper critics, try to cover a new book every day.   Ye gods!"
(Letters, ed. Jones and Rideout, p. 364).

63/21.   'Stung by a Bee.'   Rosenfeld makes his third handwritten
change in the typed copy here.   He cancels "Stung by a Bee" and
substitutes "The Triumph of the Egg."   Then he cancels this title
and writes in its place, "I'm a Fool."

63/27-64/18.   It seems to me ... insulted.   This passage is deleted by Rosenfeld in the typed copy of Part II.   See the note to
63/1-2.   The second page of the typescript fragment ends with the
word "She."

63/29-30.   They have a great desire to be writers.   See "So You
Want to Be a Writer?" in Saturday Review of Literature, XXI
(December 9, 1939), 13-14, later condensed in Reader's Digest,
XXXVI (January, 1940), 109-11.   The article makes the same dis-
tinction between the desire to be a writer and real interest in
good writing:

> In any group of young writers you will inevitably find
> those who want to write and those who merely want to
> be writers.   They want, it seems, what they think of as
> a kind of distinction that they believe comes with being a
> writer.   It's an odd thing.   I daresay a kind of distinc-
> tion, always I fear a bit synthetic, does come to a few,
> but really there are so many writers nowadays.   (Satur-
> day Review, p. 13.)

See also a passage in Hello Towns!:

> If you are to have any individuality as a workman you
> have to go alone through the struggle to find expression
> for what you feel.   You have of course to train your
> hand and your eye.   Just because you ache to do some-
> thing is no sign you can do it.   Talent is given you.
> You have it or you haven't.   A real writer shows him-
> self a writer in every sentence he writes.
>   The training is another matter.   It is a question of
> how keen is the desire, how much patience and perse-
> verance there is.   Sometimes I think it largely a matter
> of physical strength.   How much disappointment can you
> stand before you throw up the sponge?   (p. 232.)

63/32.   ring a time clock.   Three times in Memoirs, ed. White,
on pp. 355, 393, and 419, Anderson speaks about ringing a time
clock while working as an advertising writer in Chicago.   The time
clocks that Anderson would have used in the first quarter of the
twentieth century had a bell that rang when the time was recorded.
In Memoirs, ringing a time clock becomes almost a symbol of op-
pression, money-making, and frustration of artistic talent.   For
example, Anderson says on p. 355:   "The feeling of tenseness
still in me, the rushing, pushing Chicago streets still in me, Illi-

nois Central train to be caught, to be at the office at just a certain hour, a time clock to be rung. "

63/32-64/1. Nowadays employment is hard to get. If "How to Write to a Writer" was written in 1933 as the typescript found with the "Journal" manuscripts indicates, Anderson is writing these words during the worst years of the Great Depression.

64/3-4. yearning a great many women seem to have. In the article "So You Want to Be a Writer, " cited in the note to 63/29-30, Anderson also says: "It may be a new novel by Miss Ethel Longshoreman. It seems women are nowadays writing our novels more and more. I guess they do it instead of getting married. It may be because of unemployment among the men. I don't know. Anyway it's a fact" (p. 13).

64/5. She was the wife of a friend. See Memoirs, ed. White, "Letters, Autographs, and First Editions, " pp. 545-46, where Anderson tells a similar, though shorter, story about "the daughter of an old friend. "

64/10-11. gave her down the river. This is another of Anderson's unusual expressions. The reader expects "sold her down the river. " The expression "to sell down the river" originated in slave days when a slave would be punished by being sold to a plantation on the lower Mississippi where conditions were generally at their worst (Mitford M. Mathews, ed., A Dictionary of Americanisms on Historical Principles [Chicago: University of Chicago Press, 1951], II, 1403).

64/20. write about people she knew something about. See A Story Teller's Story, ed. White, p. 287, where Anderson also speaks about the necessity of an artist's staying at home for his materials:

> One had first of all to face one's materials, accept fully the life about, quit running off in fancy to India, to England, to the South Seas. We Americans had to begin to stay, in spirit at least, at home. We had to accept our materials, face our materials.

65/2. fools. See A Story Teller's Story, ed. White, p. 228, where, as here, Anderson admits that he is deeply hurt by adverse criticism. Externally he might be able to seem unperturbed, but interiorly he is "furious": " 'They may be right, ' I said aloud, generously, when inside myself I thought the critics often enough only dogs and fools. " See also the notes to 47/3 and 55/21-22.

65/5. hit the mark at which he aimed. In a letter written on March 8, 1929, to Dwight Macdonald, then on the staff of Time and later one of the editors of Partisan Review, Anderson says: "I long since gave up the notion that the thing aimed at would be likely to be understood by the average reviewer" (Letters, New-

Commentary   247

berry Library, 1929). See also A Story Teller's Story, ed. White,
p. 241, where Anderson says:

> How many times I have sat writing, hoping I had got at
> the heart of the tale I was trying to put down on the pa-
> per when inside myself I knew I had not. I have tried to
> bluff myself. Often I have gone to others, hoping they
> would say words that would quiet the voices within. "You
> have not got it and you know you have not got it. Tear
> all up. Well, then, be a fool and go on trying to bluff
> yourself. Perhaps you can get some critic to say you
> have got what you know well enough you have not got,
> the very heart, the very music of your tale."

65/11-12. Writers are often terribly depressed. See the letter
written in 1926 to Roger Sergel and quoted in the note to 54/2.
See also the following two letters, the first written in 1929 and the
second in 1933. Anderson wrote to Ferdinand and Clara Schevill
on December 28, 1929, the day before Tennessee Mitchell Anderson was found dead in her Chicago apartment:

> My whole mood has been very silly for a long time.
> I think I might define it as just plain damn unspeakable
> gloom. The black dog was on my back all the time I
> was in Chicago and came right down here [St. Petersburg,
> Florida], still comfortably perched on my back. The
> beast was so heavy on the way down that I remember
> little of the trip. I did have, I'm afraid, a feeling al-
> most of satisfaction in getting away from Chicago.
> . . . .
> In this mood, as you may guess, my work does not
> progress much. I write every day and tear up at night.
> That is the way I have been going for a long time.
> However, no more of this. My kind of men, I guess,
> just have to go through these times. When they can no
> longer go through them, they die, I fancy. I won't do
> that just yet. (Letters, ed. Jones and Rideout, p. 201.)

From Marion on May 8, 1933, Anderson wrote to Burton Emmett:

> There is nothing I can do or will do--put down, say or
> sing--that will not be forgotten, a little sound floating
> down the wind. However, Burt, it stays in my mind
> that we also are a part of something, of some incompre-
> hensible thing. If we could understand, we would be
> gods. We aren't.
> . . . .
> You must understand, Burt, that I myself have passed
> time and again through this dark valley, when I felt my-
> self shut out from others and from life, as I have a
> hunch you now feel yourself shut out. (Letters, ed.
> Jones and Rideout, p. 286.)

See also 74/23-26, where Anderson says: "As a writer I have
had endless miserable days. Black gloom, having settled upon me,
has often stayed for days, weeks and months, and these black
times have always been connected with my work." See also 85/16,
where Anderson speaks of "days of misery, of black gloom."

65/31-32. impossible to answer his gracious letter. See "Letters,
Autographs, and First Editions," in Memoirs, ed. White, p. 546:
"People do many nice things to you in letters. Someone has read
a book of yours. It gave him pleasure and he sat down and wrote
to you, expressing thanks for the pleasure given. Often such a
one sends no return address."

67/1-70/28. The Writer. This whole section is very different
from the rest of the "Writer's Book." First, it is written on very
different paper. Whereas the rest of the "Writer's Book" is written on single sheets of unlined white paper, 8 1/2 by 11 inches,
"The Writer" is written on a tablet of lined, very coarse white
paper, now turning yellow, 8 by 12 1/4 inches. The pages are
not numbered, and some of them are still stuck together at the
top by the glue of the tablet.
     Secondly, the whole character of the section is different
from the other sections. The "Writer's Book" as a whole is an
autobiographical essay. "The Writer," on the other hand, is a
story, a third-person fictional narrative. Even though the "I" of
the story, as throughout the "Writer's Book," is Anderson, the "I"
does not actually tell the story. In fact, he is present only twice,
at the beginning and the end, thus framing the story and giving it
that particular characteristic of all of Anderson's stories, the
quality of first-hand observation of the drama of life, but of the
drama being played out in the lives of others. In the second
sentence the reader is told that "in a certain town a judge told
me a story" (67/1-2). In the next to the last sentence "I" asks
a question: "And what did you feel?" (70/26). The story is thus
the judge's and the doctor's; it is a story about the similarity of
their reactions to repressed love, about the universality of isolation, and about the inability to communicate love. For a discussion of points of similarity between "The Writer" and the early
portion of "Prelude To A Story," see the notes to 10/2-4 and 21/19.
     "The Writer" is characteristic of Anderson in its manner
of telling and in its subject matter, but it is not a finished or artistically polished story. The similarity between this attempt to
tell the judge's and the doctor's stories and a story that Anderson
published in Redbook in 1940 suggests to the present editor that it
could be an early attempt to tell the story that became "Pastoral,"
Redbook, LXXIV (January, 1940), 38-39, 59. Another version of
"Pastoral" was published in Memoirs, ed. White, pp. 222-30. In
Memoirs we have a dramatic and highly effective story that, the
present editor suggests, was just taking form in Anderson's mind
when he wrote the version that found its way into the manuscript
of the "Writer's Book."
     One of the biggest differences between "Pastoral" and "The
Writer" is the fact that "Pastoral" is told by a first-person nar-

rator. The "I" of "Pastoral" is a personal, although not close, friend of the doctor, and he tells the doctor's story without the intermediary, the judge. The "I" of the story is also the man, with the lawyer, who reads the doctor's letters after his death. Thus the story "Pastoral" gains in immediacy while, at the same time, retaining Anderson's characteristic "looking on" attitude. Another improvement that Anderson makes in the story is in the depth of characterization. The doctor is more sharply delineated, and the drugstore clerk whom he loves, although given no name, is more fully depicted and individualized than is Agnes Riley in "The Writer."

Therefore, it seems to the editor, the inclusion of "The Writer" with the "Writer's Book" manuscript provides a concrete example of a story by Anderson that was rewritten several times. See 28/14-15: "Some of my best stories have been written ten or twelve times"; and 85/2-3: "I have seldom written a story, long or short, that I did not have to write and rewrite."

71/1-2. The Workman, His Moods. As with "A Sermon" and "How to Write to a Writer" (3/1 and 62/1), the listing of "Previous Cuttings" under "Omissions" in the folder at the front of Box 2 of the "Memoirs" manuscripts contains the heading "The Workman, His Moods," but there is no manuscript with this title in the "Memoirs" materials. Here we have another case of something taken from "Memoirs" material and put into the "Writer's Book."

71/5. lived in rooming houses or in the cheaper kind of hotels. For Anderson's life in rooming houses, see 9/23-24, 14/13-14, and 38/5-6, and their notes. One "cheap" hotel in which Anderson stayed is the Puritan Hotel in Kansas City. See 75/6 and its note.

71/12-13. in bed your imaginative life is beyond your control. See A Story Teller's Story, ed. White, p. 92:

> And what a world that fanciful one--how grotesque, how strange, how teeming with strange life! Could one ever bring order into that world? In my own actual work as a tale teller I have been able to organize and tell but a few of the fancies that have come to me. There is a world into which no one but myself has ever entered and I would like to take you there, but how often when I go, filled with confidence, to the very door leading into that strange world, I find it locked. Now, in the morning, I myself cannot enter the land into which all last night, as I lay awake in my bed, I went alone at will.

71/16-17. demand some control. Just as Anderson speaks here about the free-roaming fancy (71/13) and about the free flow of imagination in 84/8-22, he also speaks about the control that must be exercised in the production of all good art. The freedom and control of the imagination is another aspect of the "contradiction"

(see 52/3 and 9) that the artist must resolve.   Anderson also
speaks about this control and freedom in a letter to the poet and
short story writer Carrow De Vries, written on August 9, 1939:

> The free flow wanted comes, I've a notion, from uncon-
> sciousness of the act of writing.
> It is true that as a man walks along a street or sits,
> often with friends, he hears bits of conversation or the
> sounds of the street, while at the same time his thoughts
> go wandering, doing many strange things.
> A certain amount of control is, of course, possible,
> or there would be no work done at all.
> . . . .
> No one ha[s] ever been able to entirely control this
> flow.   It is undoubtedly controlled at times, even for
> long periods, in the consummation of some work of art.
> (Letters, ed. Jones and Rideout, pp. 445-46.)

71/18.   I went to the country and having a little money.   Portions
of three sections of the "Writer's Book," Parts I, IV, and VII,
are printed in Paul Rosenfeld's 1942 edition of Memoirs.   Part I
is entitled by Rosenfeld "The Sound of the Stream"; Part IV is entitled "The Fortunate One"; and Part VII is entitled "Writing
Stories."   "The Fortunate One" is the last section of his edition
(pp. 503-507) and is made up of parts of "The Workman, His
Moods" and parts of the last section of "Memoirs" manuscripts.
71/18 to 72/31, with numerous changes, is printed in the middle
of "The Fortunate One" (pp. 505-506).   The opening passage of
"The Fortunate One" (pp. 503-504) is taken from 73/29-74/20.

71/18-19.   built a cabin on a high hill.   The first building that
Anderson had erected on his Virginia farm was his work cabin on
the top of the highest hill on the property.   See the notes to 33/2-
3 and 72/13-14.

71/20.   what a magnificent view.   The site where Anderson's cabin
stood on the top of the hill commands a view looking south across
the Blue Ridge Mountains into North Carolina.

72/1.   Nature, so on parade, was too much for me.   In Memoirs,
ed. White, pp. 494-95, Anderson speaks also about the beautiful
location of his hilltop cabin and of the difficulty he had writing
amid such beauty.   In the Memoirs passage it is also implied that
he could not work because his creative impulses were engaged in
the building of his house.   See the note to 54/2-3.   The Memoirs
passage reads in part: "It was all too grand.   I sat in the cabin
and there were the blank sheets on the desk before me and down
below, on Ripshin Creek, the materials for my house were being
brought in" (p. 494).

72/6-7.   reading it aloud in a cornfield.   Very early in his writing career Anderson wrote to Waldo Frank, in November of 1917:

> I have always thought of myself as peculiarly wind-blown, a man approaching the bucolic in my nature. You know how I have had the notion that nothing from my pen should be published that could not be read aloud in the presence of a cornfield.
> And many people have written me of what they call the "morbidity" of my work. It has been puzzling and confusing. (Letters, ed. Jones and Rideout, p. 21.)

72/11-12. never tried the experiment. See the note to 74/12, which quotes Anderson in Memoirs and Elizabeth Prall Anderson in Miss Elizabeth as saying that Sherwood read portions of Tar aloud in the cornfield. The admission here that Sherwood never actually read his prose aloud to the growing corn is probably nearer to the literal truth than the embroidered accounts of both Sherwood and Elizabeth, although it would not be unlike Sherwood to do such a thing.

72/13-14. I had to give up the cabin on the hilltop. See the note to 33/2-3. In an interview with the editor at Ripshin on July 16, 1970, Mrs. Eleanor Anderson said that Sherwood, after he realized that he was not writing well in his hilltop cabin, had each log numbered and the cabin moved, log by log, down the hill to its present location by the shores of Ripshin Creek. Mr. Worth Price, Mrs. Anderson's present caretaker at Ripshin, confirmed this information. As a young workman on the farm, Mr. Price helped move the cabin. Neither he, Mrs. Anderson, nor John Anderson could remember the exact date of the move. They all agreed, however, that it was moved after 1933. In Memoirs, ed. White, p. 495, Sherwood says:

> I went again into my hilltop cabin. What really happened was that I never did write a word in that cabin. Even after I got clear of Horace's weekly payments I could not work up there. It may be that the view from the hilltop was too magnificent. It made everything I wrote seem too trivial. I had, in the end, and after my house was built, to move the cabin down the hill, tuck it in away under trees by the creek.

72/14-15. I never wrote anything up there that I could bear printing. Since the testimony of Mrs. Eleanor Anderson, John Anderson, and Worth Price agree that Sherwood did not move his cabin down to the side of Ripshin Creek until after 1933, it is not true that he published nothing that was written in the cabin when it was on the top of the hill. See the note to 54/2 and the Bibliography. It is probably true, however, that Sherwood was dissatisfied with most of the writing he did when the cabin was there.

72/16. times of being very pagan. Throughout his life Anderson speaks of himself as being "pagan," but, in point of fact, he reveals himself to be a deeply religious man. He concludes a letter to Marietta Finley Hahn on May 25, 1917, with these words:

"Yours for the gods of the grass and the cornfields and the rhythms
that may lead to them" (Letters, Newberry Library, Reserved Box
7: Mrs. Hahn's letters from Anderson). Also in a letter to Waldo
Frank written from the Adirondacks in 1917, he speaks about a
new book. Since he mentions the character Joseph Bentley he may
be referring to the four-part sequence in Winesburg called "Godli-
ness, " one of whose main characters is Jesse Bentley. He may
also be referring to a book called "Immaturity, " which he never
finished, or to another attempted novel, "Ohio Pagan, " which he
never published as a novel but two of whose stories, "An Ohio Pagan" and "Unused, " were published in Horses and Men. He tells
Frank:

> As I have loafed and danced and waited in the sun up
> here this summer, a peculiar thing has taken place in
> me. My mind has run back and back to the time when
> men tended sheep and lived a noma[d]ic life on hillsides
> and by little talking streams. I have become less and
> less the thinker and more the thing of earth and the
> winds. When I awake at night and the wind is howling,
> my first thought is that the gods are at play in the hills
> here. My new book, starting with life on a big farm in
> Ohio, will have something of that flavor in its earlier
> chapters. There is a delightful old man, Joseph Bentley
> by name, who is full of old Bible thoughts and impulses.
> (Letters, ed. Jones and Rideout, p. 15.)

In 1929 we have two more statements in much the same
vein. Anderson wrote from Dykemans, New York, to the Baroness
von Kaskull in the summer of 1929, telling her of the difficulty he
had with his writing until:

> One day I went off into the hills alone--as low a man
> as you ever saw.
> Something happened. Perhaps I saw God's face on the
> surface of the rocks.
> Anyway I came home and began to write. I am a man
> you would not be ashamed to know. If I sell the house
> in the country, all right. If not, I shall give it to the
> Baptist church.
> It is not money that makes a man write. He does it
> by God's grace.
> Or by knowing people like you. (Letters, Newberry
> Library, 1929.)

In "Virginia Falls" in Hello Towns! Anderson describes a Saturday
in October, a beautiful day with clear sunlight bringing out the
vivid fall colors:

> I imagined Christ walking with his disciples. Did God
> often let such a light fall on him? Did he think of trees,
> fields of grass, cattle on hills, flowering weeds, as well
> as men? I myself get well fed-up on men and women

and their everlasting souls, their problems, not so important after all.
     Some of the pagan people see God in trees, cattle,
weeds, fields of grain. I am more than a little a pagan
myself. (p. 331.)

72/17-18. in wood gods, rain gods, in fairies. This passage is
quoted in an essay by Cyrus J. Harvey called "Winesburg, Ohio:
A Reinterpretation, by George Willard, Undergraduate," which appears at the beginning of his B.A. honors thesis, "Sherwood Anderson's Natural History of Winesburg, Ohio" (unpublished B.A.
thesis, Harvard University, 1948). Harvey gives as his source
for the quotation Memoirs, ed. Rosenfeld, p. 505. Since he quotes
from Rosenfeld's version, his quotation is slightly different from
the manuscript version. When making the point that most of the
significant action in Winesburg takes place at night, Harvey says:
" 'It has seemed to me,' Anderson writes, 'that formerly, when
man believed in wood gods, in fairies dancing in the grass, in giants living in castles hidden in mountains, life must have been
richer.' "

72/22. I have lighted candles. Even when Anderson was living in
the city and many years before he wrote the "Writer's Book," he
acted in much the same way. He wrote to Waldo Frank from Chicago in late December of 1917:

>   I find myself compelled to turn to little playful things.
>   The night is cold and bleak. Unlovely people hurry along
>   unlovely streets. I creep into my room and pull the
>   blinds. I light my candle. The flame dances and throws
>   grotesque shapes on the wall. In the midst of my roar-
>   ing, ugly city there is a hush, imagined. I am an old
>   priest in an old place. I am a firm believer in the gods.
>   (Letters, ed. Jones and Rideout, p. 29.)

72/32. I was getting a divorce. Anderson was in Reno from the
spring of 1923 until he obtained his divorce from Tennessee Mitchell in April of 1924. Sherwood and Tennessee were married
with the understanding that they would both retain their independence. It is not true, however, as Sherwood says in 73/3, that
she wanted the divorce, nor is there evidence that she loved
another man. She never remarried after she and Sherwood were
divorced. Sherwood, on the other hand, was in love with Elizabeth Prall, and he was the one who left Tennessee and went to
Reno to establish residency in order to obtain a divorce there.
He repeatedly wrote back to Tennessee, as well as to his
many friends, asking that Tennessee be reasonable and not oppose the divorce. A good indication of his true feelings at the
time is given in a letter to Otto Liveright written from Reno in
July of 1923:

>   Of course T. knows the whole situation, as I have
>   been perfectly frank with her from the start. Have even

been in direct communication with her to ask her to let
someone out here act as her attorney to receive service
and expedite the whole matter as much as possible.
She has refused--first on the ground that something concerning a matter in Chicago with which I had never anything to do and that involved, she claimed, the liability
of her being involved with another man's suit for divorce,
etc., etc.--Well anyway, that fell through. Now she
takes the ground that I must wait until such time as a
divorce will not hurt her economically--which means, of
course, to be at the mercy of her whim.
   Naturally I am going right ahead--as I have told her,
and if she, after a lifetime of scolding and storming at
such people, wants to put herself in the position of hanging on to a marriage that has no reality but the technique
of law, I'm going to give her the opportunity.
   That is my program now and I'm going through with it.
The silence of which you speak she has maintained, I believe, with everyone. God knows what kind of thinking
is back of it--none, I fancy.

. . . .
   I am working, I think well, and have much work
mapped out ahead. I'll float. With T. I think it is just
a kind of dogged determination not to face simple facts
and an unwillingness to make the gesture that would be
most generous and fine. I shall certainly ask nothing
more of her. (Letters, Newberry Library, 1923.)

Anderson received the divorce on April 4, 1924, after Tennessee
consented to give a Reno attorney, L. D. Summerfield, power of
attorney in her case. Clarence Darrow was Sherwood's Chicago
lawyer.
   Anderson discusses his marriage to Tennessee, the divorce,
and his stay in Reno in Memoirs, ed. White, pp. 441-45.

73/1. I rented a little house. We know from letters written from
Reno in 1923 and 1924 to Ben Huebsch, Alfred Stieglitz, and Otto
Liveright that Anderson's address in Reno, at least for part of
the time, was 33 E. Liberty Street (Letters, Newberry Library,
1923 and 1924).

73/7. I began to write joyously. See a letter Anderson wrote to
Gertrude Stein on May 9, 1923:

   For one thing I'm doing a quite frankly autobiographical book. That may take something of the tendency to
   be too much interested in self out of me, unload it, as
   it were.
   Then I am getting a book of tales, call it Horses and
   Men, ready for book publication this fall. There are, I
   fancy, some good things in it. (Letters, ed. Jones and
   Rideout, p. 96.)

73/11-12. A Story Teller's Story, a very gorgeous book. In Memoirs, ed. White, p. 442, Anderson says: "It was at Reno that I wrote one of my best books, A Story Teller's Story." See also 38/24-29, where he says that A Story Teller's Story is "a really gorgeous book" and also implies that it was written with great ease. The note to 38/26-27 shows that, in point of fact, a great deal of labor was expended on A Story Teller's Story.

73/12. a gay book, a laughing book. In Memoirs, ed. White, p. 238, Anderson describes A Story Teller's Story as "a book more or less, if not entirely, authentic. It has I think the true authenticity of a thing felt. What fun it was writing it."

73/14. getting a divorce under our absurd American laws. See the note to 72/32.

73/30. a certain family. Sherwood and Elizabeth lived with the John F. Greear family on a farm outside Troutdale, Virginia, during their first summer in southwestern Virginia, that is, during the summer of 1925. The editor visited the Greear farm during her stay in Marion, July 16-17, 1970.

73/31-32. young boys in the family. In Memoirs, ed. White, p. 486, Anderson gives their names: "in the Greear family a troop of boys. They all bore biblical names, John, Joshua, David, Philip, Solomon."

74/2. housed pigs. David Greear, one of the sons of John F. Greear, who died in 1973, told the editor in an interview on July 17, 1970, that the house in which Sherwood wrote Tar (see 74/12) was a former tenant house, not a hog house. He said that it had not been used for years and that it stood on the edge of the cornfield. He confirmed Sherwood's statement in 74/4-6 that he and his brothers cleaned it out so that Sherwood could use it for writing. This tenant house no longer exists.
    In 1925 Sherwood was not calling his working place a hog house. He wrote to Alfred Stieglitz on August 14: "The cabin where I go to write (it costs me nothing) is a deserted one in a big cornfield on top of a mountain" (Letters, ed. Jones and Rideout, p. 145). In his Memoirs, also, Sherwood refers to it as "a small one room cabin that had not been occupied for years" (ed. White, p. 486).

74/8. a madness of writing. If this expression means that Anderson wrote Tar with great ease, the expression is inaccurate. If, on the other hand, it means that he worked hard and long over Tar, the expression is apt. A series of letters written when he was working on Tar recounts his labors. Towards the end of July, 1925, he wrote to Gertrude B. Lane, one of the editors of Woman's Home Companion:

> I think it is time that I wrote you something about the progress of the Childhood book. As I undertook to write

> it and you undertook to publish it, if you found it satis-
> factory, it worried me a great deal. I have worked on
> it all summer and thrown away all I have written. About
> two weeks ago I came up to this little place in the moun-
> tains of Virginia, and am living here where there is a
> large family of children.
>
> The change gave me just the start I wanted, and now
> the book is going fine. I believe it is going to be some-
> thing very real, and I hope you will like it. If it goes
> as well as it started, the next two months should see me
> through it. (Letters, Newberry Library, 1925.)

At the same time he wrote to W. Colston Leigh of the Leigh Lecture Bureau:

> As I wrote you before, I am an erratic cuss about my
> writing. The book on which I have been at work all sum-
> mer has been a failure until just now. At last it is
> going well. I am at a little town in the mountains of
> Virginia with my wife, and I'm working hard every day.
> If the gods are good I may finish the book while I am
> here. (Letters, Newberry Library, 1925.)

Nevertheless, the book did not get finished during Anderson's stay
with the Greears. Anderson wrote to Otto Liveright on September
1, 1925:

> During the month up in the country I wrote about
> 50,000 words on the Childhood book but threw away about
> half of it when I came home as not quite up to what I
> wanted. It keeps going along. (Letters, Newberry Li-
> brary, 1925.)

The articles for Woman's Home Companion were finished only in
time to be published from June, 1926, until January, 1927. Tar
was published as a book by Liveright also in 1926.

74/9. the corn about me grew tall. See Memoirs, ed. White,
p. 487, where Anderson discusses what the corn growing all
around meant to him as he was writing Tar. Calling himself "a
kind of corn field mystic," he waxes poetic about the corn: "The
corn, the corn, how significant in all American life." The significance of corn to Anderson is clearly seen in the first of his
Mid-American Chants. The prose poem is called "The Cornfields," and in it Anderson says in part:

> Into the ground I went and my body died. I emerged in
> the corn, in the long cornfield. My head arose and was
> touched by the west wind. The light of old things, of
> beautiful old things, awoke in me. In the cornfield the
> sacred vessel is set up.
>
> . . . .
>
> I awoke and the bands that bind me were broken. I was

determined to bring love into the heart of my people.
The sacred vessel was put into my hands and I ran with
it into the fields.   In the long cornfields the sacred
vessel is set up.   (pp. 11-12.)

74/10.   through the open windows, through the low doorway.   Here
we have another of Anderson's inconsistencies.   At 74/2 he says
that the hog house in which he wrote had no windows or doors.   In
Memoirs, ed. White, p. 486, the inconsistency is straightened out.
The tenant house originally had windows, but evidently when it was
no longer occupied the windows were boarded up: "The cabin stood
in the tall corn.   It had no windows.   For years the dust had
blown in through the openings where the windows had been and
through the open door. "

74/12.   I wrote a book of childhood, an American childhood.   See
Memoirs, ed. White, pp. 486-87:

> I was in the corn field at work.   I wrote a book there,
> a book of childhood I called Tar.   Often enough I had
> said to myself that a book should be so written that it
> could be read aloud in a corn field.
>
> . . . .
>   I even tried what I had often thought of trying.   When
> I had written a chapter of my book I went outside my
> cabin and read it aloud to the corn.   It was all a little
> ridiculous but I thought, "No one knows. "
>   And the corn did seem to talk back to me.
>   "Sure, you are all right.   Go ahead, " it seemed to
> say.

See also Elizabeth Prall Anderson's Miss Elizabeth, pp. 133-34:

> We spent the summer of 1925 in Troutdale, Virginia,
> in the farmhouse of the John Greear family, while Sher-
> wood worked on his next book, Tar--A Midwest Child-
> hood.   It cost only two dollars a day for board, room,
> laundry and mending.   The Greears were amiable, hos-
> pitable people with five sons: David, Philip, Solomon,
> John and Joshua, all of whom adored Sherwood....
>   When Sherwood, in his exploratory wanderings, came
> upon a small cabin in the middle of a cornfield, the
> Greear boys obligingly swept out the accumulated dust
> and built him a crude table on which to write.   Sherwood
> had become obsessed with the corn and the living things
> that surrounded him.   He confessed to me that at times
> he would run outside the cabin and read chapters of Tar
> aloud to the cornfield.   It may have saved his life.
> Some time later, after we became known around the
> countryside, one of the mountain men said they had sent
> someone crawling through the cornfield toward the little
> cabin to spy on Sherwood, because they thought he was
> a revenuer.   When they heard him orating to the corn-

stalks, they concluded that, instead, he was merely crazy.

See also 72/11-12 and its note.

74/18-19. wished only to live in the Now. See 86/26-28, where Anderson says: "Once I wrote a poem about a strange land few of us ever enter. I called it the land of the Now." See the note to 86/27-28, which tries to identify this poem. See also 91/22-23, where Anderson speaks about glorious moments, "of these moments, of these visits a writer sometimes takes into the land of the Now."
    In an essay on D. H. Lawrence called "Lawrence Again" in No Swank, Anderson praises Lawrence as a man who lived in the land of the Now. In comparing Lawrence to other men, Anderson states:

> Let them tackle the problem of the Now, as Lawrence did, try to penetrate that, go into the immediacy of the living Now. If there is darkness, let them try to penetrate and understand darkness, the strange terrible darkness of the Now. Lawrence did. Lawrence was always willing to shoot the works, to plunge. (p. 96.)

Anderson also has something to say about the relation between the "usable past" and the Now. The Partisan Review in 1939 sent a questionnaire to many prominent American writers. Question 1 was: "Are you conscious, in your own writing, of the existence of a 'usable past'? Is this mostly American? What figures would you designate as elements in it? Would you say, for example, that Henry James's work is more relevant to the present and future of American writing than Walt Whitman's?" Anderson's answer to this question is:

> I am afraid I do not know what you mean by "usable past." It seems to me that for the story teller everything is usable. I am afraid that my difficulty in trying to answer these questions is that I spend little time thinking of either the past or the future. It is my passionate desire to live in the NOW. Mine is not a very critical mind. No, I do not believe that Henry James's work is more relevant to American writing than Walt Whitman's. There is more of the earth in Whitman's. No matter what fool things man does the earth remains. ("The Situation in American Writing: Seven Questions (Part II)," Partisan Review, VI [Fall, 1939], 104.)

74/20. "Life Not Death Is The Adventure." Karl Anderson in his article "My Brother, Sherwood Anderson," p. 27, writes: "Life, not death, was the essence of his being. Life was for him the great experience." The last words of Sherwood Anderson's Memoirs are: "When I die I would like this inscription put on my grave: LIFE NOT DEATH IS THE GREAT ADVENTURE" (ed. White, p. 560).

74/22. over my grave. Sherwood Anderson is buried in the older
of the two cemeteries in Marion, Virginia. His beautifully simple
tombstone was designed by his friend, the sculptor Wharton Eshe-
rick. Its base is a V-shaped slab of granite. Resting on this
base is a tall semi-circular granite stone containing the following
inscription:

1876-1941

SHERWOOD ANDERSON

"LIFE, NOT DEATH, IS THE GREAT ADVENTURE"

74/23. I have had endless miserable days. See the note to 65/11-
12.

74/27. I have been too lustful. See 52/2-8, where Anderson
speaks about the contradiction that exists in all artists between the
life of the senses and the life of artistic discipline. Here at
74/27-28 Anderson also implies that the artist cannot be too "lustful." The artist must impose upon himself, or submit himself to,
the restraints of artistic discipline. The periods of "black gloom"
mentioned at 74/24 are perhaps involuntary periods of restraint,
depression, and artistic sterility. See also 77/32-78/10, where
Anderson says that perhaps all artists are lustful men, men "highly sexed." Nevertheless, when they are engaged in the work of
their art, their creative energies are absorbed by the demands of
that art.

74/29. these rich glad times. In Part IV, "The Workman, His
Moods," Anderson has already spoken of two of these times: the
time he wrote A Story Teller's Story in Reno and the time he
wrote Tar in the cabin on the Greear farm. Now he turns his attention to two other times when he wrote well: in a "tall old
house" in New Orleans (75/1) and in a "cheap hotel" in Kansas
City (75/6). In the concluding section of the "Writer's Book,"
called simply "Note," Anderson goes into greater detail about these
times of intense creativity. From 85/30-31, where he starts
speaking about "these glorious moments, these pregnant hours,"
until the end of the "Writer's Book," Anderson speaks about the
circumstances surrounding the writing of three short stories, thus
proving by three concrete examples that it is "impossible to create
the conditions, the place, the associations under the influence of
which he will work best" (74/30-32). See, in particular, the letter
that Anderson wrote to Waldo Frank, quoted in the note to 88/25.

75/1-2. a tall old house in the old quarter of New Orleans. In
this passage Anderson is probably referring to a house at 708 Royal Street, New Orleans, where he lived during the winter of 1922,
when he completed Many Marriages (see the note to 57/17-18).
He wrote to Karl Anderson from this address on February 1:

I am living in an old house in the old Creole section

of New Orleans, surely the most civilized spot in America. . . .

. . . .

As to the new book--if it comes off--as pray God it
may--it may have to be printed in a special limited sub-
scription edition--as already much harder and, I believe,
more penetrating stuff has gone into it than into anything
else I have printed.

At any rate I am very much the workman these days,
trying as I never have to make every day count.

And surely few men have been so blessed of the gods.
Now, for a time I have money enough on which to live
and a strong body that does not tire too easily.   I have
already had more recognition than I expected to get in a
lifetime.   Naturally I'm trying hard to make the time
count.   (Letters, Newberry Library, 1922.)

Anderson may also be referring to a house at 540-B St.
Peter Street in New Orleans where he lived when he wrote Dark
Laughter during the fall and winter of 1924.   His letters at that
time, however, do not reflect the joy with which he wrote Many
Marriages.   He wrote to Ferdinand Schevill, probably in the fall
of 1924:   "In the novel I am trying to get and give just the slow
aftereffect of war-hatred on the emotions of people.   You can see
how elusive such a theme.   I have had to create a style for it"
(Letters, Newberry Library, 1924).   To Paul Rosenfeld in December of 1924 he wrote: "I am gloomy about the finished novel.   It
is on a shelf in my workshop.   I started another and another and
put them both aside" (Letters, ed. Jones and Rideout, p. 133).

75/6. a cheap hotel, in Kansas City.   From January to March,
1933, Anderson stayed at the Hotel Puritan in Kansas City, Missouri.   His letters from this hotel comment on the ironic character of its name.   He describes it in a letter to Charles Bockler
on January 20 in these terms:

I am writing from Kansas City, from a little, rather
tough hotel, full of little actors, prize fighters, auto
salesmen out of work, and whores, also out of work.   I
stumbled into the place and, to my amazement, got a
grand room, clean, with a bath and an outlook over the
city, for $5.50 a week.   It's gaudy, and I really love
these loose, non-respectable people about, drunk or so-
ber.   (Letters, ed. Jones and Rideout, p. 275.)

See the note to 54/10 for details about his writing "Brother Death"
in this hotel room.

75/25-26. He could not bear my knowing what he himself knew.
In regard to Anderson's theory that an artist cannot work in rich
surroundings, see a letter to Laura Lou Copenhaver written on
May 23, 1931.   Anderson is speaking about a lecture he delivered
at Purdue University:

I told them little stories of common people in towns
and in factories, and I guess they liked it. What interested me was this. They seemed most touched by a
story of something John once said to me. John had re-
marked, regarding Ripshin, that it was very nice, but
that neither he [n]or I could ever work there. "It sets
us too far above all the people around us, " John said.

I told them that story and also the story of the old
farmwoman who said: "I guess it's nice you being here.
I don't think you are an uppity man, but, well, before
you came, we were all poor together here. " They got
the significance of those two stories. It was interesting
to see a queer hush come over the room when I told
them. (Letters, ed. Jones and Rideout, pp. 246-47.)

76/1. Notes on the Novel. This heading is also listed in the
folder at the front of Box 2 of "Memoirs" manuscripts under the
headings "Omissions" and "Previous Cuttings. " Therefore, Part
V of the "Writer's Book" was also cut from "Memoirs" material.

76/2. A novel may be thin or fat but fatness, richness. Note
the similarity between the opening words of Part V, "Notes on the
Novel, " and Part VI, "Note--On Saving Ideas. " Part VI commences: "What strikes you about many writers is a certain thinness, poverty" (82/2-3). Furthermore, the themes running through
Parts V and VI are similar in two respects. They both deal with
an important aspect of the creative process, the development of
the imagination in order to free thoughts and ideas so that they
will "flow" (84/8-22) and produce rich work. They both also
speak against "a tendency to be economical, to save" (76/7-8).
See, for example, in Part VI: "this saving of ideas, of so-called
material, has always struck me as curiously niggardly" (82/23-25);
"the way to learn to use the imagination is to use it" (82/29-30);
and "I think that we dull our own imaginations by trying to save
our thoughts, our ideas" (84/5-6).

Part V, "Notes on the Novel, " however, goes into two additional aspects of the work of the writer that are not treated in
Part VI. Part V also talks about the place of sex in literature
and about the relation between the novel and the short story. For
further reflections of Anderson on the relation between the novel
and the short story, see also Part VII, "Note, " 85/26-30 and
89/21-29.

76/13-14. begins writing at the age of thirty. If Anderson began
his serious writing as soon as he went to Elyria in 1907, he began
writing no earlier than at the age of thirty-one. In any event, he
published his first story, "The Rabbit Pen, " in 1914 when he was
thirty-eight, and he published his first novel, Windy McPherson's
Son, in 1916 when he was forty. Even though here in the "Writer's Book" he says that the age of thirty "is young enough"
(76/14), he wrote to Roger Sergel in 1923: "What I have felt all
the time is that every new workman is something added and that
every new man will help also to make it possible for future artists

here to begin working at 25 instead of 35 or 40" (Letters, ed.
Jones and Rideout, p. 119.)

76/15.   many never do.   See a letter written to Alfred Stieglitz
on September 6, 1922:   "Now, Man, do not speak of being old
Stieglitz, even in fun.   About everyone in America is either old at
25 or they never get beyond 18.   You are and have been such a
glorious exception that I dislike even jokes about your being old
Stieglitz" (Letters, Newberry Library, 1922).

76/17.   live in a new land.   See a letter to Van Wyck Brooks
written on May 31, 1918:

> It is probably true that the reason our men who are
> of importance--Lincoln, Whitman, Twain, Dreiser, etc.--
> all begin when they are almost old men is that they have
> to spend so much of their lives putting down roots.   The
> strength goes into that.   We have, you see, Lincoln pro-
> ducing a few notable utterances, Whitman some clean
> stuff out of much windiness, Twain Huck Finn, Dreiser
> Sister Carrie, etc.   (Letters, ed. Jones and Rideout,
> p. 38.)

76/19-20.   spent the vigor that expresses itself in physical ac-
complishment.   In July, 1931, Anderson delivered a lecture in
Portland, Oregon, called "America: A Storehouse of Vitality."
With the Sherwood Anderson Papers there are two typed lectures
with this title (see the note to 14/7-8).   In the longer of the two,
Anderson speaks at length about physical accomplishments in
America and the maturing of the imaginative life:

> The mere physical task of settling America, of bind-
> ing it together as one nation, of making it possible for
> men of the Pacific coast to communicate quickly with the
> Atlantic coast, of moving vast quantities of goods from
> place to place, called for the development here of a
> heroic kind of man of action.
> The American man then became a man of action.   In
> our day it is becoming harder and harder to realize just
> what he did, just what he suffered.   He has been so ro-
> manticized by our sentimentalists, made so altogether
> one thing, has been so spoiled for us, if I may say so,
> by our bad writers, that it is hard to comprehend what
> he did and the speed with which he did it.
>   . . . .
> When the day of the need for great physical action
> has passed we shall have to find some new kind of action.
> It will come, I believe, with a greater and greater
> development of our emotional and imaginative lives.
> Perhaps the change has already begun.
> It has surely begun among our prose writers and after
> all I presume you will grant that prose writing--if it be
> an art at all--is the art likely to lie closest [to] the

everyday lives of people. People's lives are, you see,
the prose writers' materials. (pp. 10-11.)

And it likely only when a nation is settled, when it
begins to seem to people settled, when the physical drive
necessary for the physical making of the nation has spent
itself that the time comes for the flowering of this imaginative man.

I myself believe that the time for a fuller and fuller
growth of the imaginative life has come or is rapidly
coming.   There is a slackening of the older impulses.
(p. 14.)

76/20-21.   prose poem to Mr Theodore Dreiser.   In 1923 Anderson dedicated Horses and Men to Dreiser with the words: "To
Theodore Dreiser In whose presence I have sometimes had the
same refreshed feeling as when in the presence of a thoroughbred
horse. " Following the Foreword there is a two-page prose poem
entitled "Dreiser, " pp. xi-xii, which reads:

Heavy, heavy, hangs over thy head,
Fine, or superfine?

Theodore Dreiser is old--he is very, very old.   I do
not know how many years he has lived, perhaps forty,
perhaps fifty, but he is very old.   Something grey and
bleak and hurtful, that has been in the world perhaps
forever, is personified in him.

When Dreiser is gone men shall write books, many of
them, and in the books they shall write there will be so
many of the qualities Dreiser lacks.   The new, the
younger men shall have a sense of humor, and everyone
knows Dreiser has no sense of humor.   More than that,
American prose writers shall have grace, lightness of
touch, a dream of beauty breaking through the husks of
life.

O, those who follow him shall have many things that
Dreiser does not have.   That is a part of the wonder and
beauty of Theodore Dreiser, the things that others shall
have, because of him.

Long ago, when he was editor of the Delineator, Dreiser went one day, with a woman friend, to visit an or-
phan asylum.   The woman once told me the story of that
afternoon in the big, ugly grey building, with Dreiser,
looking heavy and lumpy and old, sitting on a platform,
folding and refolding his pocket-handkerchief and watching
the children--all in their little uniforms, trooping in.

"The tears ran down his cheeks and he shook his
head, " the woman said, and that is a real picture of
Theodore Dreiser.   He is old in spirit and he does not
know what to do with life, so he tells about it as he sees
it, simply and honestly.   The tears run down his cheeks
and he folds and refolds the pocket-handkerchief and
shakes his head.

Heavy, heavy, the feet of Theodore. How easy to
pick some of his books to pieces, to laugh at him for so
much of his heavy prose.

The feet of Theodore are making a path, the heavy
brutal feet. They are tramping through the wilderness
of lies, making a path. Presently the path will be a
street, with great arches overhead and delicately carved
spires piercing the sky. Along the street will run children, shouting, "Look at me. See what I and my fellows of the new day have done"--forgetting the heavy
feet of Dreiser.

The fellows of the ink-pots, the prose writers in
America who follow Dreiser, will have much to do that
he has never done. Their road is long but, because of
him, those who follow will never have to face the road
through the wilderness of Puritan denial, the road that
Dreiser faced alone.

Heavy, heavy, hangs over thy head,
Fine, or superfine?

This prose poem to Dreiser was originally published in Little Review, III (April, 1916), 5.

76/27-28. Mr Dreiser, when he began writing his novels. Theodore Dreiser (1871-1945) wrote his first novel, Sister Carrie, in
the fall, winter, and spring of 1899-1900. He was twenty-nine
years old when Sister Carrie was finished. Anderson first became
acquainted with Dreiser through letters in 1915 when Floyd Dell
interested him in the publication of Windy McPherson's Son. It
was largely through Dreiser's efforts that the John Lane Company
published Anderson's first novel in 1916. Anderson did not become a personal friend of Dreiser until Anderson's visit to New
York in the winter of 1922-23 (Letters, Newberry Library, 1915-
17; Memoirs, ed. White, pp. 23, 451-55; Swanberg, Dreiser,
pp. 82-85 and 187-88).

See 43/10-31 and notes for Anderson's views on Dreiser
and the movie version of An American Tragedy. See also 79/20-
80/7 for Anderson's views on Dreiser as a pioneer among the
American writers who treat sex honestly in their work.

76/30-77/1. the fate of his Sister Carrie. Dreiser's own account
of the "suppression" of Sister Carrie is given in "The Early Adventures of Sister Carrie, " Colophon, I, Part 5 (1931). Writing
thirty years after the event, Dreiser says in part:

I took it first to Henry Mills Alden, editor of Harper's
Magazine, who read the manuscript and, while expressing approval, at the same time doubted whether any publisher would take it. The American mass mind of that
day, as he knew, was highly suspicious of any truthful
interpretation of life. However, he turned it over to
Harper & Brothers, who kept it three weeks and then in-

informed me that they could not publish it.

I next submitted it to Doubleday Page, where Frank
Norris occupied the position of reader. He recommended
it most enthusiastically to his employers, and it seemed
that my book was really to be published, for a few weeks
later I signed a contract with Doubleday Page and the
book was printed.

In the meantime (as I was told by Frank Norris himself, and later by William Heinemann, the publisher, of
London), Mrs. Frank Doubleday read the manuscript and
was horrified by its frankness. She was a social worker
and active in moral reform, and because of her strong
dislike for the book and insistence that it be withdrawn
from publication, Doubleday Page decided not to put it in
circulation. However, Frank Norris remained firm in
his belief that the book should come before the American
public, and persuaded me to insist on the publishers
[sic] carrying out the contract. Their legal adviser--one
Thomas McKee, who afterwards personally narrated to
me his share in all this--was called in, and he advised
the firm that it was legally obliged to go on with the
publication, it having signed a contract to do so, but that
this did not necessarily include selling; in short, the
books, after publication, might be thrown into the cellar!
I believe this advice was followed to the letter, because
no copies were ever sold. But Frank Norris, as he himself told me, did manage to send out some copies to book
reviewers, probably a hundred of them. (n. p.)

In general Dreiser's account is true, except for the glaring exaggeration that "no copies were ever sold. " Vrest Orton in Dreiserana (New York: The Chocorua Bibliographies, 1929), p. 17, quotes
a letter from one of Doubleday's secretaries:

These are the actual facts about SISTER CARRIE, as revealed by the analysis card.
The first edition consisted of 1, 008 copies of which 129
were sent out for review, 465 [sic] were sold, and the
balance, 423 copies, were turned over to J. F. Taylor &
Company.

Simple addition shows that the secretary's figure of copies sold
should be 456 not 465. Swanberg's biography of Dreiser, pp. 92
and 97, tells us that from these 456 copies Dreiser received royalties of $68.40; from the British edition brought out by William
Heinemann in London in 1901 he received only $100 more. The
reviews of Sister Carrie after the American edition were generally
unfavorable, those in England slightly better. Swanberg explains:

Not a critic in the nation realized that this was a novel
so transcendent in its realism and its humanity that it
stood alone, that its imperfections deserved forgiveness,
that it called for a new standard in criticism and a fight

for recognition. No such enthusiasm was possible in
1900 over a heroine who not only sinned but spoke un-
grammatically. (p. 92.)

In 1907 the B. W. Dodge Company of New York reprinted
Sister Carrie, and in this edition it sold well. Orton says: "The
Dodge edition of Sister Carrie sold extremely well. It went through
several different printings, and helped establish the B. W. Dodge
Company as up and coming publishers" (p. 23). Swanberg says
that in the Dodge edition "Sister Carrie was almost if not quite a
best seller" (p. 120). Other early editions were by Grosset and
Dunlop in 1908, by Harpers in 1911, and by Boni and Liveright in
1917. Especially after Boni and Liveright's promotion of the book,
Dreiser had little reason to complain about the reception given to
Sister Carrie.

77/7. of which I have already spoken. See 26/1-6, where Anderson speaks about the condemnation of Winesburg, Ohio and 53/24-
55/19, where he tells about his correspondence with the Reverend
Arthur H. Smith on the subject of Winesburg.

77/8. when I was called sex-obsessed. See a letter written to
Paul Rosenfeld in the fall of 1921:

> Brooks, I believe, once called me "the phallic Chekhov."
> I really do not believe I have a sex-obsession, as has so
> often been said. I do not want to have, surely. When I
> want to flatter myself, at least, I tell myself that I want
> only not to lose the sense of life as it is, here, now, in
> the land and among the people among whom I live. (Let-
> ters, ed. Jones and Rideout, p. 78.)

This letter to Rosenfeld is interesting in the light of a sentence
that Rosenfeld wrote in "Sherwood Anderson," Dial, LXXII (January,
1922), 35:

> Anderson has to face himself where Freud and Lawrence,
> Stieglitz and Picasso, and every other great artist of the
> time, have faced themselves: has had to add a "phallic
> Chekhov" to the group of men who have been forced by
> something in an age to remind an age that it is in the
> nucleus of sex that all the lights and the confusions have
> their center, and that to the nucleus of sex they all re-
> turn to further illuminate or further tangle.

In later years most critics, and Anderson himself, attributed the
coinage of the term "the phallic Chekhov" to Rosenfeld. See Memoirs, ed. White, p. 451: "I remember that Paul Rosenfeld soon
called me 'The Phallic Chekhov.' " See also Cleveland Chase's
biography of Anderson, pp. 38-39. Chase is an example of a
critic contemporaneous with Anderson who, although generally unfavorable, nevertheless recognizes Anderson's purpose in using
sex as a symbol and indicator for all the drives in man:

Anderson has been widely criticized for the sordidness
of Winesburg; he has been called ignorant, perverted,
immoral; even his friend, Paul Rosenfeld, termed him
"the Phallic Chekhov." And there can be no question
that he has chosen unpleasant subjects and that he is
greatly preoccupied with sex. More than two-thirds of
the stories have definitely sexual themes. This is partly
due to the influence upon him of D. H. Lawrence and of
the psychoanalysts, but even more it is because, using
sex as a point of departure, he is able to depict emotions
and reactions that are true not only of sex, but of almost
all other human relations. It is for this reason that we
close a book dealing so largely with sexual problems, not
conscious so much of its sexual nature as of the way in
which it has exposed the difficulty which the individual experiences in orienting himself in regard to his environ-
ment and to the people around him.

Just as the emotions these characters have are more
significant than the characters themselves, so these "sexual crises" have implications much wider than those of
mere sex. In most of the stories the climax throws
light not so much upon the sexual nature of the characters
concerned as upon their general emotional make-up. A
similar thing might have happened in a realm quite disas-
sociated from sex. Whatever his reason for so doing, Anderson has used sexual examples. To do this constantly
is, to my mind, a decided weakness in craftsmanship; it
in no important way invalidates the integrity of the conception of the stories. We may question Anderson's taste
in concentrating so much upon sex; we cannot question his
right to do so. Creative writing cannot be limited by the
fickle demands of "good taste."

77/11-12. half a dozen in one morning's mail. See a letter written to Van Wyck Brooks on August 22, 1920:

There came, and still come, odd, hurtful reaction[s]
from some things I write. A woman I have once know[n],
strange men and women I have never seen write me
queer, abusive letters. "Why do you wallow in ugly lies
about life?" they ask. I have got a dozen such letters
in a week. (Letters, ed. Jones and Rideout, p. 62.)

77/18-19. after the publication of my Triumph of the Egg and I
was living in a Chicago rooming house. Anderson was not living
in a rooming house in November of 1921 when The Triumph of the
Egg was published. He was dividing his time between his residence at 12 East Division Street, Chicago, and the house he rented
in Palos Park, Illinois. He wrote to his brother Karl from Palos
Park in November, and in speaking of one of Karl's paintings,
says: "When you have time will you have your man there box up
the painting and send it to 12 East Division Street--Chicago? Is
there any chance you will be out here this winter? The new book

The Triumph of the Egg will be published this week" (Letters, Newberry Library, 1921). See 27/31-28/2, where Anderson says that
Winesburg, Ohio and Poor White were written in a Chicago rooming house. The truth of the matter is that only Winesburg was
written in the rooming house at 735 Cass Street, Chicago.

77/26. were from women. See a similar passage in Memoirs,
ed. White, p. 177:

> Later, when I had become a writer and had written
> and published books, I wrote and published a book of
> tales, called Winesburg, Ohio, and when it was published
> there was an outbreak of bitter denunciation. Letters
> kept coming to me, many letters, and they were all from
> women.
> "You are unclean. You are one who has a filthy
> mind," they said and, for a time, there was so much of
> it that I began to distrust myself. I went about with
> head hanging in shame.
> "It must be true. So many say it that it must be
> true."

77/27. Mr Trigant Burrow. Anderson first met Trigant Burrow
(1875-1950), a physician and psychoanalyst, when he and Tennessee
were together in the Adirondacks in the summer of 1916. At first
Burrow made a favorable impression on Anderson; in fact, Anderson probably got the inspiration for his short story "Seeds" from
conversations with Burrow during that summer. Looking forward
to his next summer's vacation in the Adirondacks, Anderson wrote
to Waldo Frank sometime in March, 1917:

> You must definitely plan to be with me the second
> week in June. After that a Johns Hopkins man will be
> on the same side of the lake. That week we can have to
> loaf and think and talk. (Letters, ed. Jones and Rideout,
> p. 10.)

By the end of the summer, he wrote again to Frank, this time on
August 27:

> Burrow has been a sharp disappointment to me. Put
> to the test he proved to have no gift of companionship.
> The man wanted to reform, to remake me; his attitude
> was like Dell's. Tell me why men constantly get the im-
> pression that I am a thing to be molded. (Letters, ed.
> Jones and Rideout, p. 15.)

Anderson speaks of Burrow in Memoirs, ed White, p. 284:

> I never went to a psychoanalyst but I have often thought
> of what must have happened, at least at the first, some
> other man attempting to thrust in and in, to search out
> your very soul, resentment, all kind of resistance.

"Whatever I am you let me alone. " The psychologist
Trigant Burrow will remember an experience once had
with me, at Lake Chateaugay, in northern New York, he
trying to get at me, my resistance, the half comic situation that developed between us.

See the letter from Burrow to Frederick Hoffman apropos of Anderson's understanding of Freud, quoted in the note to 37/20-23.

77/31-32. it was something I did not want. The Memoirs passage
quoted in the note to 77/26 continues:

But did I want what they were thinking about? I was
puzzled and hurt.
"I do not, " I cried to.myself. Perhaps, after all, I
wanted only someone to whom I could address myself.
There was something warm in many women and I wanted
warmth and, too often, men, seeing the adoration I had
for many women, thought of me as the women of the
letters had thought.
However it was not so with women known, and seen.
That was a comfort to me. (ed. White, p. 177.)

78/3. lustful man. See 74/27 and its note.

78/8-9. he begins to enter women in a new way. In a letter
written on August 27, 1938, to George Freitag, Anderson says:

I knew a painter once who said to me, "I want to make
love to a thousand, a hundred thousand women. " I understand him. He didn't really want to bed the women. He
wanted to go into them, penetrate into the mystery of
women. It was because of something he wanted in his
art. (Letters, ed. Jones and Rideout, pp. 408-409.)

78/9. Balzac. Balzac was one of Anderson's favorite authors.
According to A Story Teller's Story, ed. White, Anderson started
to read Balzac when he was still young, when he was reading such
other authors as Laura Jean Libbey, Walter Scott, Harriet Beecher
Stowe, Jules Verne, Stephen Crane, Fielding, Shakespeare, Cooper,
Stevenson, Howells, and Mark Twain (p. 117). On p. 261 he compares Balzac to Leonardo da Vinci and other great painters and
says: "Balzac had made his readers feel the universality and wonder of his mind. " The epilogue to A Story Teller's Story, which
was published as the story "Caught, " American Mercury, I (February, 1924), 165-76, is the story of a writer of some promise who
sells out his artistic ability by producing, year after year, football stories for high-paying magazines. One of the chief symbols
in the story is a fine leather-bound edition of Tales from Balzac,
which Anderson had been reading before the writer came into his
room and which the writer, in his frustration over his wasted talent, keeps fingering and tearing. Finally the short story writer
leaves Anderson, and the epilogue ends: "From the floor of my

room the name Balzac is grinning ironically up into my own American face" (p. 341).

78/11-12. No woman ever entirely absorbs the artist. In a letter
to his artist son John, probably written in 1926, Anderson speaks
about the relation between an artist's love for his work and the
artist's love for a woman:

> The very capacity you have for feeling will inevitably
> make it burst into a flame occasionally about some
> woman. My own experience will, I am afraid, be of
> little help. In the end art is the essential thing, I think.
> . . . .
> In the end you may prove a great disappointment to wo-
> men, as I have and as most artists have.
> Suddenly you go off. What was all-absorbing is no longer
> so. It is more terrible for the woman than going to
> another woman. You go into something indefinite, into a
> place where they cannot follow. (Letters, Newberry Li-
> brary, 1926.)

78/20-21. dust under your feet. See "A Dedication and an Explanation" in Memoirs, ed. White, pp. 7-9, which also speaks about
the difficulty a woman has in living with a man who is an artist.
Anderson remarks:

> It is dreadful to live with such a man. It is only
> possible ... only a saint could do it.
> Why, there are months and months when you are mere-
> ly dust under his feet. For him you have no existence.
> As well, during such times, be married to one of the
> dummies in a store window. (p. 8.)

78/24-25. Let us say that the woman and I. In the passage in
Part V from 78/24 to 79/17 Anderson once again discusses the
creative process, speaking about the flights of fancy that an artist
takes while seemingly engaged in the ordinary occurrences of life.
These flights of fancy are the "seeds" of stories, to use one of
Anderson's favorite expressions. One of his most explicit statements about the working of the imagination in the creative process
is in A Story Teller's Story, ed. White, pp. 255-58. The section
begins:

> I was walking in the street or sitting in a train and
> overhead [the manuscript reading] a remark dropped from
> the lips of some man or woman. Out of a thousand such
> remarks heard almost every day one stayed in my head.
> I could not shake it out....
> A few such sentences in the midst of a conversation
> overhead or dropped into a tale someone told. These
> were the seeds of stories. How could one make them
> grow?

79/12. write, in imagination, ten, a hundred novels. Anderson
gives concrete form to this theory in one of his short stories,
"The Lost Novel, " originally published in Scribner's Magazine,
LXXXIV (September, 1928), 255-58, and reprinted in Alice and The
Lost Novel and in Death in the Woods.

79/21. the pioneer. See the passage from Memoirs, ed. White,
quoted in the note to 39/23-24, where Anderson includes himself
along with Dreiser, Lewis, Masters, Sandburg, and O'Neill as
"pioneers" in twentieth-century American literature. In the Introduction to Dreiser's Free and Other Stories which Anderson wrote
for the 1918 Boni and Liveright Modern Library edition, Anderson
singles out Dreiser above all the others:

> If there is a modern movement in American prose writ-
> ing, a movement toward greater courage and fidelity to
> life in writing, then Theodore Dreiser is the pioneer and
> the hero of the movement. Of that I think there can be
> no question. I think it is true that no American prose
> writer need hesitate before the task of putting his hands
> upon his materials. Puritanism, as a choking, smother-
> ing force, is dead or dying. We are rapidly approaching
> the old French standard wherein the only immorality for
> the artist is in bad art and I think that Theodore Dreiser,
> the man, has done more than any living American to
> bring this about. (pp. vi-vii.)

79/27-28. sex a normal place. In the light of this remark it is
interesting to read a letter that Anderson sent to his son John and
Charles Bockler in the fall of 1929:

> As a prose writer, and that is to say, "as a man who
> pretends to depict human life, " I have gone as far, I
> suppose, as a man can go on the road of feeling. I have
> wrecked myself time and again.
> It is all involved in sex. I think my generation went
> a little nuts on that, myself with them. We rather cen-
> tered all feeling in sex.
> We got results, did a kind of work, I dare say. I
> know I have done a few beautiful tales.
> . . . .
> Just because they had power, they were overplayed,
> given a position of too much importance.
> Their power over the minds of men is really gone, I
> think.
> We have got new people growing up who will never
> know the inhibitions against which we fought. (Letters,
> ed. Jones and Rideout, p. 195.)

79/30-31. Mr Sinclair Lewis ... the Nobel Prize. The first
American to be given the Nobel Prize for Literature was Sinclair
Lewis (1885-1951), who received this award in 1930. In an ad-
dress before the Swedish Academy on December 10, 1930, Erik

Axel Karlfeldt, Secretary of the Academy, explained why the award
went to Lewis. He cited among Lewis' works Main Street, Babbitt,
Arrowsmith, Elmer Gantry, and Dodsworth. His concluding words
were:

> Yes, Sinclair Lewis is an American. He writes the
> new language--American--as one of the representatives
> of the 120, 000, 000 souls. He asks us to consider that
> this nation is not yet finished or melted down; that it is
> still in the turbulent years of adolescence.
> The new great American Literature has started with
> national self-criticism. It is a sign of health. Sinclair
> Lewis has the blessed gift of wielding his land-clearing
> implement, not only with a firm hand, but with a smile
> on his lips and youth in his heart. He has the manners
> of a pioneer. He is a new builder. (Why Sinclair Lewis
> Got the Nobel Prize, New York: Harcourt, Brace and
> Company [n. d.], p. 8.)

In his acceptance speech Lewis spoke about his contemporaries in
American literature whom he considered great. They included An-
derson, Dreiser, Mencken, O'Neill, Sandburg, Masters, Cather,
Cabell, Hemingway, and Faulkner.

79/32. this recognition. These words are at the beginning of the
last two of the four typewritten pages of the "Writer's Book" that
the present editor found with the "Journal" manuscripts at the Newberry Library. See the note to 62/1 for a description of these
pages. The passage from "this recognition" to "of his work"
(80/20), however, is all canceled by Rosenfeld. After this cancellation the typescript continues to the end of Part V.

80/1. tender about life. In Memoirs, ed. White, Anderson also
calls Dreiser tender:

> How wide my acquaintance has been but I have met
> few enough really tender men, men not seeking to justify
> their own existences. I think of men like Theodore
> Dreiser and Eugene O'Neill. (p. 3.)

> On the one hand Dreiser can be the most gentle of
> men. He is, of all American writers I have known, the
> most essentially tender toward others. If you are hurt
> Dreiser is hurt with you.
> On the other hand Dreiser can become suddenly vio-
> lent. (p. 535.)

80/2-3. Mr Lewis is very seldom tender. In "Man and His Imagination, " p. 42, Anderson also contrasts Lewis and Dreiser:

> Now to take two outstanding men among our more fa-
> mous American story tellers, Mr. Sinclair Lewis and
> Mr. Theodore Dreiser, what a difference is immediately

noted. As we read, we feel that the one man, no doubt
in some secret inner part of himself, has been at some
time in his life, deeply hurt by his contact with life and
wants to get even. He seems to want to pay life back,
get even with it by showing people up, throwing up in
his work constantly the ridiculous, the absurd and pre-
tentious, while in the work of the other man, as we
read, we feel constantly a great tenderness for all life.

80/5. Main Street. Lewis' novel was published by Harcourt,
Brace and Howe in 1920, the same year that Huebsch brought out
Poor White for Anderson. Poor White did not sell, but Main
Street was an immediate success and throughout the years has sold
more than 500,000 copies. Perhaps it always rankled Anderson
that Main Street was a best seller while Poor White was not. He
wrote to Hart Crane on March 4, 1921: "There seems to be a
good deal of talk of Poor White, but it doesn't really sell much.
I suppose Main Street, for example, has sold more in one week
than Poor White altogether (Letters, ed. Jones and Rideout, p. 70).
      Main Street and Winesburg, Ohio have often been coupled
together as landmarks in the "revolt from the village," to use
Carl Van Doren's phrase, which many American writers chroni-
cled in the early decades of the twentieth century. One example
of the coupling of Main Street and Winesburg is found in N. Bryllion Fagin's biography:

> In Winesburg we have a group of short stories which,
> united by a common setting and a universality of experi-
> ence, render vividly the life of a Mid-Western commu-
> nity. It is the subjective, the anthropological counter-
> part of Main Street. We receive practically no definite
> outline of Winesburg. We have no picture of its exterior,
> as we have in Main Street. We have a deeper, a finer
> study of character, of inner brooding, of thwarted desires,
> of obscure yearnings. Main Street represents the revolt
> against provincialism, against the narrowness and ugli-
> ness of our citified small towns. In Gopher Prairie
> there is no comprehension of beauty. There is no vision
> beyond that of commercial success. There is no appre-
> ciation of art beyond that of the ladies of the Thanatopsis
> Club. In Main Street we have men practicing their occu-
> pations--a doctor, a hardware dealer, a banker, a school-
> teacher, a druggist, a tailor. In Main Street we have a
> list of ugly externals. In Winesburg, we have a group of
> men and women studied for their inner, subconscious
> life--their individual life. The complexion of the soul,
> rather than the complexion of the face, comes to the sur-
> face. Winesburg is an expression of the triumph of the
> spirit--even the spirit of Main Street yokels--over mat-
> ter. (pp. 81-82.)

80/7. Sauk Centre. Since Anderson is speaking about Main Street,
the text would be more consistent if Gopher Prairie, the town

Lewis created for the setting of Main Street, were substituted for
Lewis' birthplace, Sauk Centre, Minnesota. Although Lewis always
denied it, most critics consider Sauk Centre to be the prototype of
Gopher Prairie.

80/8. boys never went swimming. In "Four American Impressions," originally printed in New Republic, XXXII (October 11,
1922), 171-73, and reprinted in Sherwood Anderson's Notebook,
pp. 47-55, the four writers whom Anderson considers are Gertrude
Stein, Paul Rosenfeld, Ring Lardner, and Sinclair Lewis. Of
Lewis he says:

> The texture of the prose written by Mr. Lewis gives
> me but faint joy and I cannot escape the conviction that
> for some reason Lewis has himself found but little joy,
> either in life among us or in his own effort to channel
> his reactions to our life into prose. ...
> For after all, even in Gopher Prairie or in Indianapo-
> lis, Indiana, boys go swimming in the creeks on summer
> afternoons, shadows play at evening on factory walls, old
> men dig angleworms and go fishing together, love comes
> to at least a few men and women, and everything else
> failing, the baseball club comes from a neighboring town
> and Tom Robinson gets a home run. (pp. 53-54.)

Among the fragments in Box 2 of the "Memoirs" manuscripts
in the Newberry Library we find this comment written in longhand
on the back of p. 12 of an untitled typescript:

> Why was it that, in that town of the American Northwest
> where Mr. Sinclair Lewis spent his boyhood there were
> no such evenings spent with other young men and boys.
> What a different book his Main Street might have been
> had a circus ever come to his town, had the baseball
> team of that town ever whipped a team from a neighbor-
> ing town.

80/10-11. Lewis' doctor shaking the ashes out of his furnace.
This scene is towards the beginning of Chapter XV of Main Street.
Dr. Will Kennicott has just been called out in the middle of a December night to perform an appendectomy, and his wife Carol, for
whom Gopher Prairie is still tolerable, hears him return home
early in the morning. Anderson is inaccurate in saying that there
was no fire:

> At six, when the light faltered in as through ground
> glass and bleakly identified the chairs as gray rectangles,
> she heard his step on the porch; heard him at the fur-
> nace; the rattle of shaking the grate, the slow grinding
> removal of ashes, the shovel thrust into the coal-bin,
> the abrupt clatter of the coal as it flew into the fire-box,
> the fussy regulation of drafts--the daily sounds of a
> Gopher Prairie life, now first appealing to her as some-

thing brave and enduring, many-colored and free. She
visioned the fire-box: flames turned to lemon and metal-
lic gold as the coal-dust sifted over them; thin twisty
flutters of purple, ghost flames which gave no light,
slipping up between the dark banked coals. (New York:
Harcourt, Brace and Howe, 1920, pp. 177-78.)

80/15-16. American life through Mr Lewis' eyes. See Memoirs,
ed. White, p. 536:

I have always thought that he [Dreiser], and not Lewis,
among our American writers, should have been given the
first Nobel Prize given to an American writer. I have
thought that it was given to Lewis because Europe wanted
to see Americans as a race of Babbitts.

80/19. Babbitt. See "Four American Impressions, " p. 55 in
Sherwood Anderson's Notebook:

In my own feeling for the man from whose pen has come
all of this prose over which there are so few lights and
shades, I have come at last to sense, most of all, the
man fighting terrifically and ineffectually for a thing
about which he really does care. There is a kind of
fighter living inside Mr. Sinclair Lewis and there is,
even in this dull, unlighted prose of his, a kind of dawn
coming. In the dreary ocean of this prose, islands begin
to appear. In Babbitt there are moments when the people
of whom he writes, with such amazing attention to the
outer details of lives, begin to think and feel a little,
and with the coming of life into his people a kind of nervous, hurried beauty and life flits, like a lantern carried
by a night watchman past the window of a factory as one
stands waiting and watching in a grim street on a night
of December.

80/19-20. general tone of his work. A good summary of Anderson's attitude towards Sinclair Lewis can be found in an article on
Lewis that he wrote in 1930. A strike in the cotton mills of Marion, North Carolina, a strike in which six persons were killed, occasioned a pamphlet by Lewis in which he championed the cause of
the strikers. The pamphlet, called Cheap and Contented Labor:
The Picture of a Southern Mill Town in 1929 (New York: United
Feature Syndicate, Inc., 1929), occasioned an attack on Lewis by
Anderson. Anderson tentatively entitled his article "Labor and
Sinclair Lewis. " In a postscript to a letter written on February
20, 1930, to Nelson Antrim Crawford, editor of Household Magazine, in Topeka, Kansas, Anderson explains why he wrote the article against Lewis:

I've been laying for that bird ever since he wrote Main
Street. Now he is on the labor lay, and I wanted to skin
him alive. He'll do to the factories what he did to the

small towns, the doctors, preachers, etc. (Letters, ed.
Jones and Rideout, p. 208.)

Subsequent letters from Anderson to Crawford give more information on the motives behind his writing of the article. On March
13, he states:

In the same mail which brought your letter, there
came a note from my agent O. K. Liveright in New
York. He said that the Labor and Lewis article had
been over at the Saturday Evening Post, that they liked
it enormously, but were unwilling to give Sinclair Lewis
as much publicity as this article gave him. I think they
have missed the whole point, as it is not Lewis I am
hitting, but rather a whole school of thought. (Letters,
Newberry Library, 1930.)

On March 18 he says:

I think you will find in it what I think is a true criticism, not only of Lewis, but of the whole modern Mencken, hard-boiled attitude. It takes strength to be tender,
and these men haven't strength. It is too easy to attack
individuals. (Letters, ed. Jones and Rideout, p. 216.)

The "Labor and Sinclair Lewis" article eventually was published
in a greatly shortened version in Scribner's as "Cotton Mill." Before it was published, however, Anderson entered into correspondence with John Hall Wheelock, one of Scribner's editors. Anderson wrote on March 24, 1930:

I had heard something of how you felt about the Labor-
Lewis article, through my agent, Mr. Liveright.
After some searching of my own soul in this matter,
I have about concluded that, whereas I was taking Mr.
Lewis' hide off for his attitude toward the lady in Baltimore, the small town, etc., I was myself doing something of the same sort of thing to him. Of course, I
have no personal feeling about Mr. Lewis, but I suppose
there is a natural tendency in all of us to occasionally
flay some fellow citizen.
I have decided to drop it, and I think you will agree
with me. It is much better to do the constructive thing
you suggest and let the parallel be drawn by other people.
I therefore think that it would be better to make this
whole article entirely constructive by dropping the whole
Lewis thing. This will shorten the article a good deal,
but will leave in it all the constructive part and what I
believe is its real beauty. (Letters, ed. Jones and
Rideout, pp. 216-17.)

"Cotton Mill," with all the part on Sinclair Lewis cut, was published in Scribner's, LXXXVIII (July, 1930), 1-11.

The original "Labor and Sinclair Lewis" is with the Sherwood Anderson Papers at the Newberry Library. Much of what
Anderson says about Lewis and Main Street in the "Writer's Book"
is also said in "Labor and Sinclair Lewis." For example:

> There is no doubt the book is done with a certain
> skill. As I read people passed before me in the pages
> of the book and when I lifted my eyes from its pages
> certain living people, seen through a window, passed be-
> fore me along the streets of the town I was in. In the
> pages of the book held in my hand that day people, Mr
> Sinclair Lewis' people, were living their lives. I re-
> member yet the peculiar feeling of hatred the book gave
> me. I had myself always been a small town man.... I
> like to hang about the courthouses of small towns, go to
> ball games there, go fishing with small town men in the
> spring and hunting with them in the fall....
> But let us return to Mr Sinclair Lewis' town. I
> haven't a copy of the book with me as I sit writing of it
> but I remember a man back of an ugly little house on a
> side street, shaking ashes through an ash sifter. I re-
> member hot and dusty places. The air is filled with
> heavy rank smells. I remember pretentious people,
> mentally dishonest people. (p. 17.)

> Mr Lewis has made, in American literature, this pic-
> ture of the American small town. I am not saying that
> he has worked with any such intentions. I am but telling
> what happened. He made for us a town in which no
> grass ever grew. Grapes and apples never ripened
> there. There were no spring rains. It was a town to
> which no ball team ever came, no circus parades. I
> am convinced that, to a large extent, the great success
> of the book was due to just that quality in it which
> aroused people's contempt. There is that streak in all
> of us. We all adore hating something, having contempt
> for something. Mr Lewis gave us a small town we could
> thoroughly dislike; he has given us a preacher we can
> dislike, a businessman, a doctor. (p. 18.)

80/22. The writing of the short story is a kind of explosion.
This is the first of two instances in the "Writer's Book" where
Anderson defines the short story. The other is at 85/26-28:
"The short story is the result of a sudden passionate interest. It
is an idea grasped whole as one would pick an apple in an orchard. "
Anderson speaks of the short story as "a distillation, an
outbreak" in the letter to Ben Huebsch quoted in the note to 14/12-
13, and as "the short stop" in a letter to Paul Rosenfeld written
from Reno in late 1923 or early 1924. The letter to Rosenfeld
also speaks of the difficulty he experiences in forcing himself to
work on some things that he knows are fragmentary. Both of the
stories mentioned in this letter were published in Anderson's third
volume of short stories, Horses and Men:

Your comments--[on] "[An] Ohio Pagan" and "The Sad
Horn Blowers"--they are both true criticisms--something
fragmentary there. I felt it and had to ask myself,
"Shall I try to go back and carry them through?" The
old Chinese used to write a thing called "the short stop."
The notion was to touch something off and then let it
complete itself in the reader.

Is this an excuse? I don't know. I have destroyed many fragments. These I decided not to destroy
and I could not work on them as my mind was reaching
toward something else. I refer you to a song of Mid-
American Chants.

"I'm the broken end of a song myself."
It's true. Perhaps I shall never quite complete,
round out, anything. Often enough I have to give just
the broken ends. (Letters, Newberry Library, 1934.)

Certainly Anderson did not always give "just the broken ends." In
the best among his stories, such as "The Untold Lie," "Death in
the Woods," "Brother Death," "The Man Who Became a Woman,"
"I Want to Know Why," and many others, he produced completed
works of art.

80/23. Mr H. G. Wells who once described the writing of the
short story. The present editor has not been able to find the
metaphors used by Wells for the writing of the short story and the
novel referred to by Anderson in this passage. One of H. G.
Wells' rare pieces of short story criticism is his Introduction to
The Country of the Blind and Other Stories (London: Thomas Nelson and Sons [1911]). In this Introduction Wells says in part:

Some things are more easily done as short stories than
others and more abundantly done, but one of the many
pleasures of short-story writing is to achieve the impossible.

At any rate, that is the present writer's conception of
the art of the short story, as the jolly art of making
something very bright and moving; it may be horrible or
pathetic or funny or beautiful or profoundly illuminating,
having only this essential, that it should take from fifteen
to fifty minutes to read aloud. All the rest is just what-
ver invention and imagination and the mood can give--a
vision of buttered slides on a busy day or of unprece-
dented worlds. (p. viii.)

During the years when Anderson first began to write, H. G.
Wells was one of his favorite authors. In Memoirs, ed. White,
p. 451, Anderson writes: "I had been for some time under the
spell of H. G. Wells and Arnold Bennett." He goes into more detail in "Waiting for Ben Huebsch" in Memoirs, ed. Rosenfeld,
p. 289:

I considered then, as I now consider, that my earlier

stories, both Windy McPherson and at least in the writing, Marching Men, had been the result not so much of
my own feeling about life as of reading the novels of
others.   There had been too much of H. G. Wells, that
sort of thing.   I was being too heroic.

80/29-30.   The actual physical feat of writing either a long or a
short novel.   Anderson is no doubt reflecting his own experience
in the writing of novels, a form in which he never excelled as he
did in the short story.   At the very beginning of his writing career
he wrote to Waldo Frank to thank him for the article "Emerging
Greatness" in Seven Arts, I (November, 1916), 73-78, which
praised his first novel, Windy McPherson's Son.   He then goes on
to say:

> I like particularly your slap at my ending of the novel.
> What you say is no doubt true.   In secret I do not mind
> telling you that I never knew how to end a novel and am
> afraid I never will.   Always feel as though I were just
> at the beginning when the thing has to be wound up and
> put aside.   (Letters, ed. Jones and Rideout, p. 3.)

In the middle of his career, shortly after he moved to Ripshin in
the spring of 1926, he wrote to Karl Anderson:

> I have worked myself here.   The organization of a
> new novel is such a racking process.   All the life of the
> book has to [be] organized.   I have just been going
> through that process.
>   Yesterday I worked until--when night came I had to
> go to bed.
>   I fancy you know that feeling of exhaustion--something
> however gained--put down.   (Letters, Newberry Library,
> 1926.)

80/30.   is another matter.   See 89/25-26, where Anderson says:
"writing of the long story, the novel, is another matter."   The
note to 89/26-27 discusses Anderson's inability to articulate a
complete theory of short story writing.

81/1-2.   must carry the theme within himself in all the changing
circumstances.   As Anderson was working in the spring of 1926 on
the novel he called either "Another Man's House" or "Other
People's Houses, " he wrote to Horace Liveright:

> In the meantime I got right into the new novel.   As
> often happens with me, I had to make three or four starts
> with it.   I had the whole theme in my mind, but it is a
> delicate thing to handle, and I had to get the characters
> fitted into the theme.   Twice after writing several thou-
> sand words I had to throw it all away.   My people got
> off the track.   I did not understand them well enough.
> They were not what I wanted.   I went off to the country

or walked around the streets and waited.   At last I think
I have a start that will do fine.

The man's name is Talbot Whittingham.   The central
figures of the novel are this man Whittingham and his
wife Katherine--their relations to each other and of
Whittingham's relationship with other women.   (Letters,
ed. Jones and Rideout, p. 154.)

Evidently Anderson was not able to carry through his theme.   He
never completed this novel.

81/10-12.   Some minor character in his novel begins suddenly to
run away with his book.   See a letter to his son John written in
1931 shortly after he sent Perhaps Women to the publisher:

I get a long story started and sometimes it breaks in
two.   Some minor character comes in, as though a
stranger had suddenly walked into a house.   That changes
everything.   The new person may be absorbingly interesting.

You try to bend the new one into whatever you are doing and pretty often it spoils all.

Just the same it is something.   There is the new one
also wanting his, or her, story really told.   (Letters,
Newberry Library, 1931.)

81/16.   He must orchestrate his work.   See a letter written to
Horace Liveright from New Orleans on April 18, 1925, in which
Anderson speaks of Dark Laughter:

You see what I am trying to give you now, Horace, is
something of the orchestration of the book.   The neuroti-
cism, the hurry and self-consciousness of modern life,
and back of it the easy, strange laughter of the blacks.
There is your dark, earthy laughter--the Negro, the
earth, and the river--that suggests the title.   (Letters,
ed. Jones and Rideout, p. 142.)

81/16.   give it what is called "form. "   In 1926 Anderson wrote to
Jerome Blum about the difficulty he has achieving form in his
novels.   Speaking about the same book, called either "Another
Man's House" or "Other People's Houses, " about which he wrote
to his brother Karl and to Horace Liveright (see the notes to
80/29-30 and 81/1-2), Anderson remarks to Blum:

I got started on a new novel--a rather delicate busi-
ness--then checked my start, started again--checked
again, etc.   It will come off eventually and it may be
that this present start will get somewhere.

Anyway am working on it every day and that is fun.
It's the old business of trying to get too much into one
book and getting it messed up.   The simple direct form
of the thing only seems to emerge for me after a lot of

sweating. I put doodads all over the house and then
have to go around and knock them off. (Letters, Newberry Library, 1926.)

In other letters and in published works Anderson tries to
explain what form means to him. In 1929 he wrote to Dwight Macdonald, telling him that he has read the book by Irving Babbitt that
Macdonald suggested and that he found its prose heavy and its insistence on the observance of "laws" incorrect:

Why, indeed there are laws. There are laws all such
men as Babbitt will never in this life comprehend. There
are laws within the laws, laws that ride over the laws.
. . . .
The law of which you are so sure may be breaking to
bits before your very eyes. You may not know it.
This thing called form in art. It exists, of course.
It is the force that hold[s] the thing of loveliness together.
Often I walk about knowing there is form existent
everywhere, in lives, things, in nature too.
It does not become form to me until I comprehend
form in it.
There is a little reaching, a straining after the thing,
the form. In comprehending it I create it too.
It happens I am an artist, and so this process of
creation goes on constantly in me. (Letters, ed. Jones
and Rideout, p. 191.)

In 1930 Anderson wrote to Charles Bockler about form in painting
as well as in prose:

I think it would be a great mistake to waste any time
at all thinking of "form" as form. It is one of the
things artists, and most of all half-artists, babble of
when their minds are most vacant.
Form is, of course, content. It is nothing else, can
be nothing else. A tree has bark, fiber, sap, leaves,
limbs, twigs.
It can grow and exist and not grow in the soil of your
own being. It is so with women too.
The great thing is to let yourself be the tree, the sky,
the earth. Enter into your inheritance. It is difficult
and can only happen rarely, as between a man and woman.
My meaning is that life is not so separated from art.
How often I go away from the presence of talking artists
into the street, the field.
What I want is there. If I go in and come out clean,
even now and then, in the end these same people who
say I have no form will be prattling of the "form" in my
work. (Letters, ed. Jones and Rideout, p. 202.)

In "A Note on Realism" in his Notebook Anderson explains what he means by saying "form is content":

> The life of reality is confused, disorderly, almost al-
> ways without apparent purpose, whereas in the artist's
> imaginative life there is purpose. There is determina-
> tion to give the tale, the song, the painting Form--to
> make it true and real to the theme, not to life. (pp. 75-
> 76.)

In A Story Teller's Story, in the context of speaking against the
"formula" story with its "Poison Plot, " Anderson says:

> What was wanted I thought was form, not plot, an alto-
> gether more elusive and difficult thing to come at.   (ed.
> White, p. 255.)

> In certain moods one became impregnated with the seeds
> of a hundred new tales in one day. The telling of the
> tales, to get them into form, to clothe them, find just
> the words and the arrangement of words that would
> clothe them--that was a quite different matter. (ed.
> White, p. 257.)

> The words used by the tale teller were as the colors
> used by the painter. Form was another matter. It grew
> out of the materials of the tale and the teller's reaction
> to them. It was the tale trying to take form that kicked
> about inside the tale teller at night when he wanted to
> sleep. (ed. White, p. 261.)

These quotations from A Story Teller's Story remind the reader of
the first story in Winesburg, "The Book of the Grotesque, " the
story that helps to give form to the whole book. This story describes an old writer who feels as if a "young thing" is inside him
driving figures of grotesques before his eyes. The writer must
get out of bed in the night and write down the stories of the grotesques. Their stories are, of course, Winesburg, Ohio.
       One of Anderson's most explicit statements about form in
art is a letter written to Norman Holmes Pearson in the fall of
1937. In this letter Anderson tells Pearson that the Winesburg
story "Hands" was "the first one I ever wrote that did grow into
form. " He also links form and morality in art (see the note to
8/25) and speaks against betraying imaginary lives (see the notes
to 44/28-29 and 55/29-30). Although the whole letter is well
worth studying for Anderson's attitude toward form, only excerpts
will be quoted here:

> I presume that we all who begin the practice of an
> art begin out of a great hunger for order. We want
> brought into consciousness something that is always there
> but that gets so terribly lost. I am walking on a country
> road, and there is a man on a hillside plowing. There
> is something nice, even beautiful, in the man striding at

the plow handles, in the breasts of the horse pulling, in
the earth rolling back from the plow, in the newly turned
earth below and the sky above.

We want not only to know that beauty but to have him,
at the plow handles, know.

You see, Pearson, I have the belief that in this matter
of form it is largely a matter of depth of feeling. How
deeply do you feel it? Feel it deeply enough, and you
will be torn inside and driven on until form comes.

. . . .

I think this whole thing must be in some way tied up
with something I can find no other word to describe aside
from the word "morality." I suppose I think that the
artist who doesn't struggle all his life to achieve this
form, let it be form, betrays this morality. It is terribly important because, to my way of thinking, this
morality may be the only true morality there is in the
world.

. . . .

And what is so little understood is that, in distorting
the lives of these others--often imagined figures, to be
sure--to achieve some tricky effect, you are betraying
not only this indefinable thing we call form, but that you
are betraying all of life--in short, that it is as dirty
and unworthy a thing to betray these imagined figures as
it would be to betray or sell out so-called real people in
real life.

And so this whole matter of form involves, for the
story writer, also this morality. (Letters, ed. Jones
and Rideout, pp. 387-88.)

To conclude the discussion of Anderson and form, let us
listen to one of his critic-biographers. Howe says:

A great deal of cant has been written to the effect
that Anderson's stories are "moving" but "formless"--
as if a work of art could be moving unless it were
formed or form could have any end other than to move.
Those who make such remarks are taking form to signi-
fy merely the executive plan or technical devices that go
into the making of a work of art.... Actually, however,
form can be properly apprehended only by relating tech-
niques and strategies to their organic context of emotion
and theme, and it is consequently difficult to imagine a
work of art with acknowledged authenticity of emotion to
be simultaneously lacking in form. Valuable and finely
formed fictions, such as some of Anderson's stories and
Lawrence's novels, result not merely from the contriv-
ance of skilled intention but also from the flow of released unconscious materials--which is to be taken not as
a plea against the use of the blue pencil but as a statement of what it is used on. (pp. 151-52.)

81/18. The novel is the real test of the man. It is disappointing
to hear Anderson, one of the acknowledged masters of the short
story, succumb to the popular notion that the novel is superior to
the short story. Undoubtedly, as he is at pains to show here, the
physical feat of writing the longer work is greater than that of
writing the shorter work, but the test of artistic worth is not
judged by length or physical exertion expended. Here in the "Writer's Book" and in some of the letters quoted, especially in the
notes to 80/29-30 and 81/1-2, Anderson confuses external criteria--
quantity and effort expended--with intrinsic worth. At other times,
however, he is conscious of the intrinsic worth of his stories. He
recognizes that "Death in the Woods" is "a magnificent tale, one
of the most penetrating written in our times" (28/16-17), that "I'm
a Fool" is "a very beautiful story" (89/4), and that "I will be best
and with the most affection remembered, [for] my Winesburg, Ohio"
(40/12-13). His biographer Brom Weber gives one explanation
why he persisted, until the end of his life, in his attempts to write
novels:

> It was not merely the pressure of publishers, as well
> as readers and critics, which pushed Anderson toward
> the novel against his natural inclination to work in short-
> er forms. Anderson shared the erroneous cultural be-
> lief that a novel is qualitatively as well as quantitatively
> more valuable than a short work. Had he been a young-
> er man in the late 1910's and early 1920's, it is possible
> that he might have been able to develop the lyrical novel,
> a delicate form that would have best utilized his talents
> as it did those of Virginia Woolf, his admirer. But he
> had insufficient time in which to work slowly and perfect
> his art in every form. (p. 34.)

For further analysis of Anderson's position in regard to the
novel and the short story, see the note to 89/26-27.

81/23-24. when the novel does not quite come off, if it have but
few alive spots in it. See Bryllion Fagin's remarks on Poor White
in his biography of Anderson:

> The true novelist needs great patience to weave all his
> threads into a unified design. Anderson is too hasty,
> too intense to command such patience. Poor White is
> more like a collection of short stories. There is the
> story of Hugh McVey and the story of Clara Butterworth;
> of Henry Shepard and Sarah Shepard; of Allie Mulberry;
> of--There are twenty-nine distinct stories. Sometimes
> they merge into the novel and sometimes they don't. But
> all of them merge into the life which gave them birth--
> the inner life of a changed and changing America.
> (pp. 40-41.)

81/28-31. often enough the failure ... is worth more than all of
the great successes. At the end of the letter to Dwight Macdonald,

quoted in the note to 81/16, Anderson speaks about failure and
success.   The original of this letter is not with the Sherwood Anderson Papers in the Newberry Library.   Jones and Rideout print
the letter from an imperfect copy and indicate blanks in the copy
by means of dashes:

> I would have you understand all this.   I would like it
> if all young men began to understand.   My own errors,
> my looseness, my constant experiment--and failure is
> the only decent thing about me, man.   I would like you
> to understand that, man.
> I would like you to comprehend fully that what is to be got
> at to make the air sweet, the ground good under the feet,
> can only be got at by failure, trial, again and again and
> again failure.   (Letters, ed. Jones and Rideout, p. 193.)

81/31-32.   the slick books that slide so easily over all of the reality of lives.   See "An Apology for Crudity" in Notebook, p. 197:

> Consider the smooth slickness of the average magazine
> story.   There is often great subtlety of plot and phrase
> but there is no reality.   Can such work be important?
> The answer is that the most popular magazine story or
> novel does not live in our minds for a month.

82/1.   Note--On Saving Ideas.   The heading "On Saving Ideas" is
listed under "Omissions" and "Previous Cuttings" in the folder at
the front of Box 2 of "Memoirs" manuscripts in the Newberry Library.   Therefore, Part VI, as well as Parts II, IV, and V,
seems to have been cut from "Memoirs" material.

82/2-3.   a certain thinness, poverty.   See the note to 76/2, which
discusses the similarity between Part VI, "Note--On Saving Ideas, "
and Part V, "Notes on the Novel. "

82/4-5.   Fred O'Brien, wrote a book called White Shadows on the
South Seas.   The list of friends whom Anderson intended to include
in his autobiographical "Rudolph's Book of Days" (see the note to
39/22) includes Frederick O'Brien, along with the notion that Anderson knew him in New York and San Francisco (Memoirs, ed.
White, p. xxi).   On the book shelves in Mrs. Eleanor Anderson's
home in Marion, Virginia, there is a copy of O'Brien's White
Shadows on the South Seas (New York: The Century Company,
1920).   Anderson is correct in saying that O'Brien wrote two more
books about the islands of the South Seas; in fact, he wrote even a
third.   They are: Mystic Isles of the South Seas (New York:
The Century Company, 1921), Atolls of the Sun (New York: The
Century Company, 1922), and Mysteries of the South Seas (New
York: Garden City Publishing Company, 1932).

82/10.   He was a grand story teller.   In a section called "Two
Irishmen" in No Swank, Anderson speaks about Fred O'Brien and
Maurice Long: "They were the two best story-tellers I ever knew.

Never losing the balance of a tale; catching, in talk, the pathos of
lives; understanding, tender, imaginative men" (p. 33). See 58/28,
where Anderson speaks about a certain Fred, and 59/3, where he
speaks about Maurice Long.

In the winter of 1925 Fred O'Brien was living on the Medi-
terranean coast at Alassio, Italy, and Anderson wrote to him on
February 15 apropos of a new book. The letter encourages O'Bri-
en to write as if he were talking but gives no hint that Anderson
thinks he is exhausting his theme:

> Your life out there sounds pretty healthy and happy
> and I only hope you are at work on that book of yours.
> You may have to drive yourself at it for a while, but if
> you can only put yourself freely into it, as you talk, you
> will be caught up by it and be carried along and have a
> corking book. I only hope you do it. (Letters, New-
> berry Library, 1925.)

On May 20 Anderson wrote from New Orleans to Otto Liveright:

> Frederick O'Brien, the man who wrote "White Stars
> in the South Seas" was here last week and is going to
> New York to live. I talked to him about you. If you
> would like to have him on your list you can get him I
> am sure. He told me he would get in touch with you.
> (Letters, Newberry Library, 1925.)

Either Anderson meant to write White Shadows on the South Seas
in this letter or "White Stars in the South Seas" never found a
publisher.

82/17. doing good work in a good cause. See 44/20-24, where
Anderson speaks derisively about writing for a "cause." See also
the note to 44/22.

82/21-22. the difficulties of telling a story truly. In the same
section of A Story Teller's Story quoted in the note to 81/16, Anderson also speaks about these difficulties, again using the metaphor of a pregnant woman. The words bracketed and preceded by
an asterisk are words Anderson added to the galley sheets; the
words bracketed without an asterisk are words Anderson or an editor cut from the galleys ("Introduction, " ed. White, pp. xvii-xviii).

> For such men as myself you must understand there is
> always a great difficulty about telling the tale, after
> [*the scent has been picked up]. The tales [*that con-
> tinually came to me]--in the way indicated above--could,
> of course, not become tales until I had clothed them.
> Having, from a conversation overheard or in some other
> way, got the tone of a tale, I was like a woman who has
> just become impregnated. Something was growing inside
> me. [Later,] at night, when I lay in my bed, I could
> feel the heels of the tale kicking against the walls of my

body. Often as I lay thus every word of the tale came
to me quite clearly but when I got out of bed to write it
down the words would not come. (ed. White, pp. 259-
60.)

82/29-30. the way to learn to use the imagination is to use it.
See the note to 44/28-29, which discusses Anderson's theory of the
obligation that a writer has to the imaginative world. See also the
following passage from "Man and His Imagination, " which discusses
the training of the imagination and the importance of an active
imagination in everyday human relations:

> Even if you are not actually practising writers, you can
> employ something of the writer's technique. When you
> are puzzled about your own life, as we all are most of
> the time, you can throw imagined figures of others against
> a background very like your own, put these imagined fig-
> ures through situations in which you have been involved.
> It is a very comforting thing to do, a great relief at
> times, this occasionally losing sense of self, living in
> these imagined figures. This thing we call self is often
> very like a disease. It seems to sap you, take something
> from you, destroy your relationship with others, while
> even occasionally losing sense of self seems to give you
> an understanding that you didn't have before you became
> absorbed. (p. 64.)

83/1. a full rich life. In a letter to an aspiring writer, George
Freitag, written on August 27, 1938, Anderson says: "I have had
a good life, a full, rich life. I am still having a full, rich life. "
In the same letter Anderson also says: "It began to seem to me
that what I wanted for myself most of all, rather than so-called
success, acclaim, to be praised by publishers and editors, was to
try to develop, to the top of my bent, my own capacity to feel,
see, taste, smell, hear" (Letters, ed. Jones and Rideout, pp. 404
and 405).
      Furthermore, it was not only toward the end of his life that
Anderson speaks in this vein. He who often during his lifetime in-
dulged in self-pity wrote to Karl Anderson on February 1, 1922,
telling him about the sales of the Modern Library edition of Winesburg, the third printing of The Triumph of the Egg, and his work
on Many Marriages. He then admits: "And surely few men have
been so blessed of the gods. Now, for a time I have money enough
on which to live and a strong body that does not tire too easily.
I have already had more recognition than I expected to get in a
lifetime" (Letters, Newberry Library, 1922.)

83/1-2. to feel more, see more, understand more. In many
places, in addition to the letter to George Freitag quoted in the
previous note, Anderson speaks about the importance of the development of the senses. See "Man and His Imagination, " p. 40:

> The lives of other humans are, as you all know, the

source materials of the story teller and the story teller
can sometimes be very cruel. He is one who has taught
himself to observe. He wants, for the purpose of his
craft, to develop to the highest possible pitch his own
senses, to constantly see more, hear more, feel more.
He is continually watching others, noting the way in which
people walk, the way they hold their heads.... These
things all have their significance to the story teller. At
his best and when most aware, every movement of the
body of another, the sound of his laughter, the way his
mouth is held in repose and when speaking, the timbre
of his voice, all of these things are full of meaning to
him.

See also a letter that Anderson wrote to Mary Helen Dinsmoor on
June 24, 1938, and which Dinsmoor prints in her thesis, "An Inquiry into the Life of Sherwood Anderson as Reflected in His Literary Works, " p. 67:

You ask what is my philosophy of life, but I am afraid
the answer to that would take too long. I have wanted
to develop, to the highest possible point, my sense of
hearing, of smell, of taste. I have wanted most of all
to develop my ability to enter the lives of others.

See also the statement in Memoirs, ed. White, p. 440: "I had
wanted to tell the story of things seen, felt, tasted, heard, nothing
more. " See, finally, 86/17-23, where Anderson describes the
writing of a story in Harrodsburg, Kentucky, at a time when all
of his senses were "curiously awake. " The whole of Part VII, in
fact, describes three moments of intense and creative awareness.

83/3. "Paper Pills. " See the note to 10/31-32, where the paragraph from "Paper Pills" telling about the sweetness of the twisted
apples of Winesburg is quoted in order to explain Anderson's preoccupation with the themes of loneliness and the grotesque. See
also the note to 83/7-8, where there is a quotation from a letter
from Anderson to Rosenfeld in which Anderson alludes to "Paper
Pills. "
        "Paper Pills" gets its title from the scraps of paper on
which Doctor Reefy writes "thoughts, ends of thoughts, beginnings
of thoughts" (New York: B. W. Huebsch, 1919, p. 20). Doctor
Reefy stuffs the scraps of paper containing his thoughts in his
pockets, and they become round, hard balls. They actually become "Paper Pills" which save him and "the tall dark girl" he
married from the almost universal loneliness of Winesburg. It is
fitting that Anderson should allude to "Paper Pills" in the section
of the "Writer's Book" called "Note--On Saving Ideas. " Doctor
Reefy's practice of writing down his thoughts and then destroying
them prevents these thoughts from turning into "a truth that arose
gigantic in his mind" (p. 20). Unlike the grotesques who parade before the mind's eye of the old writer in "The Book of the Grotesque, "
Doctor Reefy does not make any one truth "his" truth. The old

writer's theory of the grotesque is that "the moment one of the people took one of the truths to himself, called it his truth, and tried to live his life by it, he became a grotesque and the truth he embraced became a falsehood" (p. 5).

83/5-6. so many of our intellectuals are clinging to ideas. Throughout this section of the "Writer's Book" Anderson is speaking against "saving ideas" and "clinging to ideas," not against ideas themselves. See the note to 7/16-17, which shows that the charge of anti-intellectualism leveled against Anderson was at times unjust. There is no doubt, however, that throughout his life Anderson was handicapped by his lack of formal education and by his youthful isolation from the main stream of culture and ideas, a lack and isolation for which his later years never completely compensated. When comparing Anderson to D. H. Lawrence, Irving Howe draws a clear distinction between the intellectual backgrounds of the two men. In his biography of Anderson, Howe says: "Lawrence had a commanding grasp of Western culture when he decided it was not enough, Anderson had only scraps and fragments. Lawrence acted from the strength of secure renunciation, Anderson from the weakness of enforced deprivation" (p. 192).

83/7-8. We are to be saved by communism, or socialism, or fascism. See 79/23-24, where Anderson ironically says that propaganda literature should be dedicated to "the cause," "to the overthrowing of capitalism, the making of a new and better world." Anderson, who spent his youth among the farmers and laborers of a small Midwestern town and his early manhood working in factories and warehouses in other Ohio towns and in Chicago, retained throughout his life his sympathy for the poor and downtrodden. This sympathy led him during the depression years to champion their cause in his writings and to turn more actively toward practical politics. His novel Beyond Desire, published by Liveright in 1932, shows his sincere devotion to the cause of the poor, often unorganized workers, especially in the South. His article "How I Came to Communism," New Masses, VIII (September, 1932), 8-9, gives the motives behind his activities in several communistic causes.

For an analysis of his implications with socialistic and communistic causes, see Schevill, pp. 271-94. Schevill discusses such things as Anderson's participation in the Danville, Virginia, mill strike, which lasted from September, 1930, until the end of January, 1931; his signing, in the spring of 1932, the communistic manifesto, Culture and the Crisis, written by Edmund Wilson and issued by the League of Professional Groups for Foster and Ford, and signed by such other literary men as Lincoln Steffens, John Dos Passos, Theodore Dreiser, Newton Arvin, and Malcolm Cowley; and his work, in the summer of 1932, for the "Bonus Army," the Bonus Expeditionary Force which marched on Washington, D.C., asking for a higher bonus for veterans. Anderson consented to lead a group of writers to present in person a protest to President Hoover after the Bonus Army was dispersed by federal troops under the direction of Douglas MacArthur. President Hoover would not

see the writers, and after Anderson left Washington he wrote his
open letter to the President, "Listen, Mr. President," Nation,
CXXXV (August 31, 1932), 191-93. Anderson gives his own interpretation of his part in the Bonus Army protest in Memoirs, ed.
White, pp. 531-32.

Anderson's third and last trip to Europe (see the note to
39/21-22) was to Amsterdam in late August and early September
of 1932 to attend the leftist World Congress Against War. His account of the Congress, "At Amsterdam," appeared in New Masses,
VIII (November, 1932), 11. Because his boat was delayed in its
return voyage, Anderson was not able to attend the meeting held
for the delegates on their return; nor did he attend a meeting on
"War and Culture" in New York in December of 1932. He sent,
however, a statement to be read at the meeting. The statement,
along with his letter to Ida Dailes of the American Committee for
the World Congress Against War, is printed in Letters, ed. Jones
and Rideout, pp. 270-72.

As the depression in the United States declined in vigor and
as Anderson's appreciation for President Franklin Roosevelt and
the New Deal grew, his enthusiasm for communism waned. On
August 10, 1933, Henry Wallace, Roosevelt's Secretary of Agricul-
ture, visited Ripshin and invited Anderson to become one of the
New Deal's public relations writers. Anderson declined the offer,
partly because he knew that it was financially necessary for him to
devote most of his creative energies to the writing of his own
books, and partly because he always felt, when he was most true
to himself, that he was not the kind of writer who could write for
a "cause." He did, however, submit several articles to Today,
described by Raymond Moley, its editor, as "an American political
weekly, independent of, although sympathetic with the administra-
tion" (Schevill, p. 309). The articles that Anderson wrote for
Today are:

> "No Swank," I (November 11, 1933), 23-24; reprinted in
> No Swank;
> "Explain! Explain! Again Explain!" I (December 2, 1933),
> 3;
> "At the Mine Mouth," I (December 30, 1933), 5, 19-21;
> reprinted, with revisions, in Puzzled America;
> "Tough Babes in the Woods," I (February 10, 1934), 6-7,
> 22; reprinted in Puzzled America and The Sherwood An-
> derson Reader;
> "Blue Smoke," I (February 24, 1934), 6-7, 23; reprinted
> in Puzzled America;
> "Price of Aristocracy," I (March 10, 1934), 10-11, 23
> (quoted in the note to 36/21-22);
> "Tom Grey Could so Easily Lead Them," I (March 24,
> 1934), 8-9, 23; reprinted, with revisions, as "A Union
> Meeting," in Puzzled America;
> "New Paths for Old," I (April 7, 1934), 12-13, 32; re-
> printed as "People" in Puzzled America;
> "I Want to Work," I (April 28, 1934), 10-11, 22; last half
> of article reprinted, with revisions, in Puzzled America;

"A New Chance for the Men of the Hills, " I (May 12, 1934),
     10-11, 22-23; reprinted, with revisions, in Scholastic,
     XXVIII (February 1, 1935), 10-12, 27; reprinted as "TVA"
     in Puzzled America and The Sherwood Anderson Reader;
"New Tyrants of the Land, " I (May 26, 1934), 10-11, 20;
     reprinted with revisions, in Puzzled America;
"Virginia Justice, " II (July 21, 1934), 6-7, 24; reprinted as
     "Justice" in The Sherwood Anderson Reader;
"Jug of Moon, " II (September 15, 1934), 6-7, 23; reprinted
     in Memoirs, ed. Rosenfeld;
"Young Man from West Virginia, " III (December 1, 1934),
     5, 23-24; reprinted as "They Elected Him, " in Puzzled
     America;
"Sherwood Anderson Goes Home, " III (December 8, 1934),
     6-7, 23; reprinted, with revisions, as "Night in a Corn
     Town, " in Puzzled America;
"Northwest Unafraid, " III (February 12, 1935), 8-9, 22-23;
     reprinted, with revisions, as "Olsonville, " in Puzzled
     America;
"War of the Winds, " III (February 23, 1935), 8-9, 20; re-
     printed, with revisions, as "Revolt in South Dakota, " in
     Puzzled America;
"Nobody's Home, " III (March 30, 1935), 6-7, 20-21;
"Valley Apart, " III (April 20, 1935), 6-7, 22-23;
"Give Rex Tugwell a Chance, " IV (June 8, 1935), 5, 21;
"Broadwalk Fireworks, " V (November 9, 1935), 6-7, 19.

Anderson's book of essays, Puzzled America, represents the culmination of much of his writing during this time. Its publication
in 1935 can be taken as the date of the end of his active interest
in communism and its causes. For a discussion of Anderson's
place among other socially concerned novelists of the 1920's and
'30's, see Robert L. Rothweiler, "Ideology and Four Radical Novelists: The Response to Communism of Dreiser, Anderson, Dos
Passos, and Farrell" (unpublished Ph. D. dissertation, Washington
University, 1960).
     Finally, see Anderson's statement in Memoirs, ed. White,
p. 156:

> If, in later life, I was sometimes to be called a "red, "
> even a communist, which, of course, I never was, it was
> because every working woman I saw reminded me of my
> mother, coming into our little frame house on a winter
> day, after hanging a wash out on the line, her clothes
> frozen to her body.

See also Anderson's letter to Edward H. Risley, Jr., the Harvard
undergraduate who sent him his B. A. thesis, "Sherwood Anderson,
the Philosophy of Failure, " in 1938. Anderson explains to Risley:

> It is true that in '31 and '32, when I went about a
> good deal in industrial cities, when I saw American work-
> ing men eating out of garbage cans, etc., I got pretty

wrought up. I think it must have been during those
years that I got what of the red label has been pasted
on me.

. . . .

Frankly, I don't think you can trust the Communists,
and, as for yourself, I would a thousand times rather
suggest that you trust your own natural reactions.

. . . .

This I know, that Dreiser, one of my real friends, is no
more a Communist than I am, and, only a few weeks
ago, I had a note from Dos Passos that went a good deal
further than I have here in saying, "To hell with them."

. . . .

[P.S.] And all of this doesn't mean that I am not,
heart and soul, for anything that I think will bring to an
end the dominance of business in American life. I don't
at all mind being canned [?called] "red." I just object
to the Communists trying to herd me into their camp.
(Letters, ed. Jones and Rideout, pp. 395-96.)

In regard to Anderson's attitude toward fascism, see the
three versions of a letter from Anderson to Paul Rosenfeld in the
Sherwood Anderson Papers at the Newberry Library. Three times,
first on August 4, then on August 5, and finally on August 14,
1936, Anderson attempted to write a frank letter to Rosenfeld explaining his position in regard to the rights of the artist, the rights
of the worker, and his attitude toward fascism. At the top of the
August 14 typed version of the letter, Anderson penciled in hand
the words, "Not sent. Too smug." The following quotation is
from this August 14 letter as printed by Jones and Rideout. It is
interesting to see that in this letter Anderson alludes to "Paper
Pills," implying that Rosenfeld was taking the "truth" of fascism
too much to heart:

When you were here with us, there was almost constantly talk of Fascism and Communism, and it seemed
to me that you had got hold of something, an idea difficult to put into words.
It had to do with the obligation of the artist, let's say
to the tradition. At any rate, Paul, I gave myself credit
with having known always what you were talking about.
But, Paul, as you talked, as you made little remarks,
I kept thinking of a story I once wrote. I called it
"Paper Pills."
You will remember that a year or two ago you took
me to task because, in carelessly signing a certain manifesto [Culture and the Crisis], I betrayed the central
meaning of the artist's life. I probably deserved what I
got for signing something without reading it, largely
through trust in the political and social keenness of Edmund Wilson.
Paul, I have been wondering this summer if you do not
go pretty far the other way, and I have even, from many

remarks dropped, got at times the impression that your fear and dread of Fascism springs sometimes almost altogether from the fear of what may happen to you as Jew and have even sometimes thought that you might almost welcome Fascism if it suppressed the troublesome workers and gave you security in your own way of living.

. . . .

There seemed to me, Paul, a kind of continual insistence, as though it would give you a kind of pleasure to believe that there exists a whole body of people, for convenience' sake called the proletariat, and that these people were a sullen and ugly folk, existing, as it were, in darkness down below us. I remember a kind of insistence on hatred that you seemed to want to make to cover the impulses of a great world of people.

Then one day when we were walking, you suddenly said, "There is one good thing about Fascism. It ends strikes," appearing thus to welcome the existence of a civilization that would clamp down whole bodies of people into a mold, holding them there for the comfort and security of a few. (Letters, ed. Jones and Rideout, pp. 358-60.)

83/9. it has "a good proletariat angle." See 44/18-19, where Anderson speaks ironically of radical writers who "had turned to the writing of so-called proletariat stories," and 57/10-13, which gives Anderson's attitude toward propaganda literature. Notice also the ironic tone that Anderson uses in the following letter to his mother-in-law, Laura Lou Copenhaver, written in the spring of 1936:

A letter from Perkins of Scribners about Kit [Kit Brandon]. He says, "Extremely interesting, exciting and significant. It tells so much about America. It has plenty of the proletariat angle in it and much more rightly than the proletarians give it. It makes you realize what a strange country America now is." From which, mother, I take it that he is pleased with us. (As quoted in Homage to Sherwood Anderson, 1876-1941, ed. by Paul P. Appel, Mamaroneck, N.Y.: Paul P. Appel, 1970, p. 210.)

83/11. to speak for the proletariat. See a letter that Anderson wrote to Maxwell Perkins of Charles Scribner's Sons on October 6, 1934:

I think that perhaps, for a year or two, I did rather go over to something like a Communist outlook. Now again I am rather uncertain about all that. This attempting to touch off the lives of human beings in relation to the world about them is much more healthy for me. I have no solution. (Letters, ed. Jones and Rideout, pp. 307-308.)

The note to 44/13-14 explains Anderson's attitude towards the "social implication" of his work. In this context see a letter that Anderson wrote to Roger Sergel from Reno in December of 1923:

> As to the social implication of a story, my own mind simply does not work in that channel. My friend Paul Rosenfeld once said I had a deficient social sense. Like yourself I think storytelling worthwhile in itself, for the sake just of storytelling, and one of the things that got me cleverly and beautifully.
>
> . . . .
> Don't you rather think, Sergel, the quality that makes people aware of "social implication" is and should be implicit in good work?
>
> . . . .
> Of course it [Sergel's novel Arlie Gelston] had social implication. What beautiful reality touched to life by an artist's fancy has not? (Letters, ed. Jones and Rideout, p. 116.)

Finally, notice the ironic tone in the article "So You Want to Be a Writer, " Saturday Review of Literature, XXI (December 9, 1939), 13-14:

> You all know, or should know, that nowadays it isn't worth while writing novels about any class other than the proletariat. If you write novels about people of any other class the communists will get you. They'll call you a bourgeois, and then where are you?

83/13. early life was spent among the poor. See the note to 9/17-18, which discusses the poverty of Anderson's youth in Clyde.

83/14. sharpest impressions of life when he is young. See Memoirs, ed. White, p. 109: "For the writer the impressions gained, say in the first twenty years of his life, impressions of events or of people so deeply impressed on the young mind, on the young imagination, are bound to be source material for him all of his life."

83/15-16. Most of my life I have written about small businessmen, workingmen. See two letters that Anderson wrote in January, 1930. He says to Ferdinand and Clara Schevill:

> Really, if I belong to anything, I do belong to the defeated people. I have a notion that labor is defeated right now. Pretty soon, if I am not very careful, I will myself be an old man.
> I ought to give what is in me, for the rest of my life, to my own people.
> That means workers, defeated by Modern America, by the American scheme. (Letters, ed. Jones and Rideout, p. 204.)

To Roger and Ruth Sergel he remarks:

> I have decided that, as I came originally out of the
> laboring classes, and as the laboring people are and al-
> ways have been my first loves, I am going to try a year
> or two of more or less living with them. The most in-
> teresting place in America now is the South. (Letters,
> ed. Jones and Rideout, p. 206.)

83/17-18. the development of the imagination. With these words
Anderson returns to the central idea of Part VI, "Note--On Saving
Ideas, " first explicitly expressed in 83/1-2. See the notes to
23/6-8, 44/28-29, and 82/29-30 for other statements of this central theme in Anderson's artistic creed.

83/29-30. subtile relationships, thoughts passing back and forth,
things thought, not said. These words serve as the epitome of
one of the main themes of Winesburg, Ohio and of some of Anderson's greatest short stories, for instance, "The Egg, " "I Want to
Know Why, " and "Unlighted Lamps."

84/4-5. I do not think that life is ever very dull. When speaking
about the limitations that his own life places upon the artist, Anderson says in "A Note on Realism" in Notebook, pp. 73-74 (reprinted in "Man and His Imagination, " p. 68): "Such men scold at
the life immediately about. 'It's too dull and commonplace to
make good material, ' they declare. Off they sail in fancy to the
South Seas, to Africa, to China. What they cannot realize is their
own dullness. Life is never dull except to the dull."

84/8-9. a continual flow. See the note to 76/2, which discusses
the similarity between Parts V and VI. See also a letter that Anderson wrote to Burton Emmett on June 26, 1928: "I seldom write
things for a purpose or place. I try to let them flow out as they
come into my head" (Letters, Newberry Library, 1928), and the
letter he wrote to Ferdinand and Clara Schevill in October, 1930:
"I came home and went to work. My mind seems clear. It may
be that now I am in one of those clear times of straight flow"
(Letters, ed. Jones and Rideout, p. 224). Anderson also uses the
metaphor of flowing in 38/26, 56/25, 84/9, and 86/30.

84/13-14. real purpose of all this writing is first of all to enrich
the writer. See Sutton's remark in Road to Winesburg regarding
Anderson's "therapeutic" approach to literature (quoted in the note
to 51/19). See also the longer of the two lectures with the Sherwood Anderson Papers in the Newberry Library entitled "America:
A Storehouse of Vitality. " This lecture was written to be delivered
in Portland, Oregon, in July of 1931:

> And here let me point out to you that to the writer
> words are often enough what drink is to the drinker. It
> is to break up the fact of our own isolation we become
> tellers of tales. What we cannot know in the physical

world we carry over into the imaginative world and try
to understand it there.   (p. 9.)

84/14-15. It isn't surely to get fame, recognition.   See a letter
that Anderson wrote to Alfred Stieglitz on June 20, 1925: "I'm not
much worried about my work improving or going off.   What I want
is to do work that will please me a little.   If I can do that, I'll
be happy enough" (Letters, ed. Jones and Rideout, p. 144).   See
also Memoirs, ed. White, p. 546:

> Fame, if you attain any fame, is a deceitful bitch.   It
> gets between you and people.   I have known fellow writers
> who having attained some fame were ruined by it.   They
> began to take themselves seriously, become artificial.
> They lost all touch with the human beings about them.

See also the note to 49/23-24, which comments on Anderson's ambivalent attitude towards recognition and obscurity.   Finally, see
29/23-27, where Anderson speaks about "the mythical thing called
'success.' "

84/16.   Write and throw away again.   See the notes to 53/32-
54/2 and 72/14-15, which explain why Anderson wrote and threw
away, especially between the years 1927 and 1930, when his creative energies seem to have been at low ebb.   See also a letter
that he wrote at the end of 1930; from Marion on December 13 he
tells Charles Bockler:

> Once it was terribly important to me to be producing.
> Now it is just as important to me to be sitting here,
> writing to you, as it would be to write what they call a
> masterpiece.   There is a kind of stillness in me.   I
> should be scared.   In the mood in which I have written
> this year I can sell little or nothing.   I make no money.
> It doesn't bother me.
>   Sometimes I think I am reaching out for something.
> I don't know.   I write and destroy, write and destroy.
> I don't care at all.   I really feel healthy.   (Letters, ed.
> Jones and Rideout, p. 231.)

In Part I, "Prelude To A Story, " Anderson also speaks about
writing and throwing away, even when he is producing his best
work.   See 28/12-17 and their notes, which document the fact that
Anderson wrote, threw away, and rewrote extensively while working
on A Story Teller's Story and "Death in the Woods. "   Part VII, the
last section of the "Writer's Book, " commences with the same
idea: "I have seldom written a story, long or short, that I did
not have to write and rewrite" (85/2-3).

84/17-18.   flow through your body, down your arm, through your
hand.   In speaking of the years when his works were first finding
publishers and when he first started to visit New York, Anderson
says in A Story Teller's Story, ed. White, p. 272:

> My own hands had not served me very well. Nothing
> they had done with words had satisfied me. There was
> not finesse enough in my fingers. All sorts of thoughts
> and emotions came to me that would not creep down my
> arms and out through my fingers upon the paper.

85/1. Note. Part VII, "Note," is printed in Rosenfeld's 1942
Memoirs as "Writing Stories," pp. 341-45. Therefore, "Note" is
the third section of the "Writer's Book" that Paul Rosenfeld printed
in an expurgated form. See the notes to 4/1 and 71/18. See also the Introduction for details on Rosenfeld's editing.

In his biography of Anderson, Schevill reviews Rosenfeld's
edition of Memoirs and mentions both "Writing Stories" and "The
Sound of the Stream," Rosenfeld's title for Part I. As was mentioned in the note to 61/1-3, Schevill says that the total effect
created by Memoirs is the "creation of myth," and then continues:

> The symbols expand and grapple for meaning in all sig-
> nificant areas of American experience; economic in such
> chapters as "Money! Money!" and "Bayard Barton," po-
> litical in "The Capture of Caratura" and "I Become a Pro-
> tester," psychological in "I Write Too Much of Queer
> People," and aesthetic in "Writing Stories." If the Mem-
> oirs is less complete and integrated than Winesburg, it
> gains by its greater exploration of the nature of myth.
> All of these diverse mythological elements reach their
> climax in the chapter called "The Sound of the Stream."
> (p. 349.)

"Note" discusses the writing of three short stories: an unnamed story written in Harrodsburg, Kentucky, "I'm a Fool," and
"The Man's Story." It is a discussion of the "glorious moments"
when a short story is written in one absorbing burst of awareness
and inspiration, although Anderson, when he began the manuscript,
had intended to write about the difference between the short story
and the novel (89/26-29 and 91/19-21).

85/3. have to write and rewrite. See the note to 84/16.

85/3-5. single short stories of mine that have taken me ten or
twelve years to get written. Anderson makes a significant revision
in the manuscript in this sentence. The manuscript reads: "There
are single short stories of mine that I have taken me ten or twelve
years to get written." The change from active to passive voice
helps convey one of the central tenets of Anderson's theory and
practice of short story writing. If, as he says at 85/27-28, a
short story "is an idea grasped whole as one would pick an apple
in an orchard," the writer of the short story has to labor, sometimes for ten or twelve years, to grasp the idea. The writer
does not actually take ten or twelve years to write the story, but
the story sometimes takes ten or twelve years "to get written."
See 28/14-18, where Anderson also uses the passive voice in
speaking of writing short stories: "Some of my best stories have

been written ten or twelve times, and there is one story, 'Death
in the Woods,' a magnificent tale, one of the most penetrating
written in our times, that was ten years getting itself written."
See also the note to 15/20-21, which comments on Anderson's unusually frequent use of the passive voice.

85/5. It isn't that I have lingered over sentences. See 28/12-13,
where Anderson says: "I have never been one who can correct,
fill in, rework his stories." The note for these lines explains in
what respect the statement is true and in what respect it is not
true.

85/7. Gertrude Stein. Karl Anderson was the first to introduce
Sherwood to the writings of Gertrude Stein. He brought Sherwood
a copy of Tender Buttons, published in 1914, when he was living
in the boarding house at 735 Cass Street with "The Little Children
of the Arts" and writing the Winesburg stories. Later Sherwood
was also to read Stein's Three Lives. Sherwood speaks about the
great influence that Gertrude Stein had on his writing in A Story
Teller's Story, ed. White, pp. 260-63. The section commences:

> How significant words had become to me. At about
> this time an American woman living in Paris--Miss Ger-
> trude Stein--had published a book called Tender Buttons
> and it had come into my hands. How it had excited me.
> Here was something purely experimental and dealing in
> words separated from sense--in the ordinary meaning of
> the word sense--an approach I was sure the poets must
> often be compelled to make. Was it an approach that
> would help me? I decided to try it. (pp. 260-61.)

When Sherwood went to Europe in 1921 he met Gertrude
Stein. He renewed his acquaintance when he returned to Europe
in 1926-27, and he and Gertrude Stein enjoyed a lasting friendship
until Sherwood's death in 1941.

85/9-10. She spoke, I think, of passionate sentences. In The
Autobiography of Alice B. Toklas, Gertrude Stein writes: "Gertrude Stein contended that Sherwood Anderson had a genius for using sentence to convey a direct emotion, this was in the great
american tradition, and that really except Sherwood there was no
one in America who could write a clear and passionate sentence"
(Selected Writings of Gertrude Stein, ed. by Carl Van Vechten
[New York: Random House, 1946], p. 180). Rosenfeld in his edition of Memoirs, p. 341, omits this sentence.

85/12-13. "I can make myself miserable enough." Elizabeth
Prall Anderson's Miss Elizabeth, pp. 76-77, contains a surprising-
ly similar passage: "Sherwood could not endure adverse criticism.
He once asked me to look through his reviews, only showing him
the ones that were favorable. He said he made himself miserable
enough without having others do it for him."

85/14-15. I have asked her to show me only the more favorable criticisms. Mrs. Eleanor Anderson in an interview at Ripshin on July 17, 1970, told the editor that Sherwood also asked her to go over the criticisms of his work and show him only the favorable ones. Sherwood's attitude toward criticism, however, was always ambivalent. See 47/1-3, where he says that his passion has always been to pay as little attention to criticism as possible. The note to 47/3 documents this ambivalent attitude.

85/16. days of misery, of black gloom. See 65/11-15 and 74/23-26, which also speak of "failures" (65/15) and "black gloom" (74/24). The note to 65/11-12 documents some of Anderson's periods of depression.

85/20-21. I am best at the short story. See 31/30-31: "I have had a profound effect on the art of short story writing." See also the surprising statement, for Anderson, of 81/18: "The novel is the real test of the man." See also the notes to these passages.

85/24. admit they have never read anything else. Anderson was fond of repeating this statement. See, for example, his letter to George Freitag written on August 27, 1938:

> Critics who had ignored or condemned the book [Winesburg] now praised it.
> "It's Anderson's best work. It is the height of his genius. He will never again do such work."
> People constantly came to me, all saying the same thing.
> "But what else of mine have you read since?"
> A blank look upon faces.
> They had read nothing else of mine. For the most part they were simply repeating, over and over, an old phrase picked up. (Letters, ed. Jones and Rideout, p. 406.)

See also his statement in Memoirs, ed. White, p. 297:

> There would be a woman who would come up to me saying that she thought my Winesburg the best thing I'd ever done. It is so tactful telling a man of fifty-five that a book done when he was thirty-five contained his best work.
> I would get a little sore when that one was sprung on me.
> "What other and later books of mine have you read? Name them. I dare you."

85/25. an opinion that is no doubt sound. In an interview at the Newberry Library on June 5, 1969, Mrs. Eleanor Anderson told the editor that Sherwood always thought of himself as a story teller, that he preferred his short stories to his novels, and that he thought his greatest contribution to American literature was in the field of the short story.

His critics and biographers generally agree with this opinion. In 1927 his biographer Cleveland Chase said: "It is in no way surprising that Anderson should find his most complete expression in the short story.... This often reiterated belief of his that only moments of 'awareness' are important is much more conducive to the episodic treatment of the short story than to the cumulative continuity of the novel" (p. 32). Also in 1927 Vernon Louis Parrington in Main Currents in American Thought, III (New York: Harcourt, Brace and Company, p. 371), said that Anderson's artistic talent was "limited in scope to episodic crises--hence his better stories short." In 1952 his erstwhile friend Van Wyck Brooks in The Confident Years (New York: E. P. Dutton and Company, p. 500), spoke about "Sherwood Anderson, the admirable teller of tales who should never have attempted to write his ineffectual novels." One of the best summaries of Anderson's position in relation to the novel and the short story is in Maxwell Geismar's Introduction to Sherwood Anderson: Short Stories, p. xi:

> There is, to be sure, a certain kind of curious logic behind the notion that Anderson wrote one great book and then quietly faded away. It makes some sense if you follow his record through the mid-twenties--and ignore the books he wrote in the thirties. It makes sense, perhaps, if you deal only with his novels, which are generally poor, and completely ignore the fact that he was a natural-born short-story writer, completely as original in this genre as he was unsuited for the novel form. Anderson's later tales are different from the Winesburg tales and the other early volumes, but no less good--perhaps even better.

85/26-27. passionate interest. In his edition of Memoirs, p. 341, Rosenfeld changes this expression to "passion." In The American Short Story (Minneapolis: University of Minnesota Press, 1961), Danforth Ross, when discussing Sherwood Anderson, states: " 'The short story,' he once said, 'is the result of a sudden passion' " (p. 30). Ross evidently is quoting from Rosenfeld's edition of the Memoirs.

85/27-28. It is an idea grasped whole as one would pick an apple in an orchard. See the note to 80/22. See also the quotation from "Paper Pills" cited in the note to 10/31-32. Anderson says that the story of Doctor Reefy "is delicious, like the twisted little apples that grow in the orchards of Winesburg" (p. 19).

When commenting on the manner in which Anderson wrote the Winesburg stories, Malcolm Cowley in his Introduction to the Viking Compass edition of Winesburg (1960, p. 13) comments: "All the stories were written rapidly, with little need for revision, each of them being, as Anderson said, 'an idea grasped whole as one would pick an apple in an orchard.' " Although he gives no source, Cowley is quoting from the "Writer's Book," either directly from the manuscript or from the section called "Writing Stories" in Rosenfeld's edition of Anderson's Memoirs, p. 341.

85/28-29. All of my own short stories have been written at one
sitting. In his writings Anderson sometimes says that certain
stories were written at one sitting, but it would be hard to prove
that "all" were written in this way. What Anderson probably is
referring to in this passage is the fact that the final version of a
story was usually written in one burst of creative energy when, in
definitive form, the idea was "grasped whole. "
       The stories that Anderson explicitly claims to have written
"at one sitting" are "Hands, " "I'm a Fool, " and "The Man's Story. "
In regard to "I'm a Fool, " see 88/19 to 89/24 and their notes; in
regard to "The Man's Story, " see 89/30 to 92/6 and their notes.
In regard to "Hands, " see the note to 12/16, which quotes a typescript in Box 2 of the "Memoirs" manuscripts, and Memoirs, ed.
White, pp. 237 and 352-53. Finally, see the note to 28/12-13,
which quotes William Phillips in regard to the composition of
"Hands. "

85/30. these glorious moments. See the note to 74/29, which
comments on "these rich glad times" when Anderson worked well
"under strange enough circumstances" (85/29-30). In the remainder of Part VII Anderson explicitly refers to these moments in
87/14, 88/6, 8, 9-10, and 19, 89/22, and three times on p. 91.
Anderson seems almost obsessed with the idea that only during
these moments of creative awareness can he do good work. See
also A Story Teller's Story, ed. White, p. 232, where, in speaking about his repudiation of business in Elyria in 1913, he remarks:

> It was not until long afterward I came to the conclusion
> that I, at least, could only give myself with complete
> abandonment to the surfaces and materials before me at
> rare moments, sandwiched in between long periods of
> failure. It was only at the rare moment I could give
> myself, my thoughts and emotions, to work and some-
> times, at rarer moments, to the love of a friend or a
> woman.

85/31. these pregnant hours. See A Story Teller's Story, ed.
White, p. 223. The context is again, as it was in the quotation
given in the previous note, the decisive days prior to Anderson's
departure from Elyria and business: "And being this thing I have
tried to describe, I return now to myself sitting between the walls
of a certain room and between the walls of a certain moment, too.
Just why was the moment so pregnant? I will never quite know. "

86/2. the little town of Harrodsburg in Kentucky. The present
editor has not been able to identify the story written in Harrodsburg, Kentucky. The story, however, may be "The New Englander, " for, as shown in the note to 54/10-11, Anderson in A Story
Teller's Story, ed. White, p. 155, speaks about one of his "rich
and fine spots" when he wrote "The New Englander" in a railroad

station in Detroit. Anderson's memory very easily could have
confused Detroit and Harrodsburg.

There is, also, among the Anderson Papers in the Newberry
Library, a typewritten copy of a fragment of one of Anderson's
stories. The fragment is dated December 15, 1916, and the story
begins: "He was an old man." Before it abruptly breaks off at
the end of page 3, the fragment tells of Tom, seventy-five, who
cures warts, and his crippled wife of thirty. The fragment, therefore, seems to be an early draft of the story "Nobody Laughed, "
first published in The Sherwood Anderson Reader and labeled there
"1939, unpublished." It is possible that the first draft of this
story was written in 1916 and the final draft only in 1939. The
opening scene of the story is laid in "the railroad station in a
small Kentucky town." The original of the fragment is housed in
the Hi Simon Papers in the University of Chicago Libraries.

If Anderson is mentioning the writing of his stories in Part
VII in chronological order, and if, with the exception of "Nobody
Laughed, " the stories were published in the order in which they
were written, either "Nobody Laughed" or "The New Englander"
would have been written before the two stories which are mentioned
by name. "The New Englander" was first published in the Dial for
February, 1921; "I'm a Fool, " in the Dial for February, 1922; and
"The Man's Story, " in the Dial for September, 1923.

86/3. when I was still a writer of advertisements. According to
Memoirs, ed. White, pp. 201-202 (see the note to 48/15), and according to the letters in the Sherwood Anderson Papers, 1916-1922,
Anderson's advertising business occasionally brought him to Kentucky. For example, see a letter written to Waldo Frank sometime in the spring of 1918: "Plan your trip out here so that you
will be sure to be in the West during the last week in April. I
have to go to Kentucky that week and you and Tennessee can go
along" (Letters, Newberry Library, 1918).

86/4. I was at a railroad station. In A Story Teller's Story, ed.
White, p. 154, Anderson speaks about the fact that he can write
amid great physical discomfort:

> I had so trained myself to forget my surroundings that I
> could sit for hours lost in my own thoughts and dreams,
> or scribbling oftentimes meaningless sentences in a cold
> room in a factory street, on a log beside some country
> road, in a railroad station or in the lobby of some
> large hotel, filled with the hurrying hustling figures of
> business men, totally unconscious of my surroundings.

86/23. all of your senses curiously awake. See the quotations in
the note to 83/1-2, which speak of the importance of the life of the
senses. See also "Notes Out of a Man's Life" in Notebook:

> Tales are everywhere. Every man, woman and child
> you meet on the street has a tale for you....
> When I had been working well there was a kind of in-

> sanity of consciousness. There may be little nerves in
> the body that, if we could bear having them become sen-
> sitive enough, would tell us everything about every per-
> son we meet. (p. 183.)

86/27-28. I called it the land of the Now.   The editor could not
find any poem of Anderson's called "The Land of the Now." Perhaps Anderson is referring here to the prose poem originally published in Double Dealer, III (February, 1922), 64-67, under the
title of "A New Testament," and reprinted in his second book of
verse, A New Testament (New York: Boni and Liveright, 1927),
under the title of "The Thinker," pp. 64-71.   In this poem Anderson says in part:

> I have a passionate hunger to take a bite out of the now--
> the present.   The now is a country to discover which, to
> be the pioneer in which I would give all thought, all
> memories, all hopes.   My ship has but skirted the shores
> of that country.   What is growing there?   I would take a
> bite out of the present.   I would consume it quite.   I
> would live my life in the present, in the now only.
> (p. 68.)

Anderson also speaks of the Now at 74/19, 87/15, and 91/23.

86/29-30.   How the words and sentences flow, how they march!
See the note to 38/26.

87/14-15.   for this moment, for this glorious peep I am having
into the land of the Now.   See the notes to 85/30 and 86/27-28.

88/19-20.   I was in a big business office, surrounded by many
people.   With this sentence the section in Part VII that speaks
about writing "I'm a Fool" commences.   In Box 2 of "Memoirs"
manuscripts in the Newberry Library there is a four-and-a-half
page fragment entitled "I'm a Fool." This fragment is not printed
in either Rosenfeld's or White's edition of Memoirs.   Basically it
recounts the same tale of writing "I'm a Fool" as told in the
"Writer's Book," and in the two versions that are included in
Memoirs, ed. White, pp. 122-23 and 432-33.   The manuscript
reads in part:

> There are such moments that come occasionally--
> rarely to writing men.   I was one morning in the adver-
> tising office where I worked for years.   Something hap-
> pened to me.   I had been given an assignment.   There
> was a series of advertisements to be written.   What it
> was all about I can't remember....
> I went to my desk, sat down.   Men and women were
> passing up and down past my desk.   Some of them spoke
> to me and I answered.   Why, I dare say that the boss,
> the head copy man, came to me.   He would have seen
> me writing furiously.   I never did learn to write with

any skill on a typewriter.   Perhaps he cautioned me
about the series of advertisements I was presumed to be
writing....
    Interruptions of that sort, constantly going on as I sat
writing the story "I'm a Fool."
    It didn't matter.   I was far away.

88/25.   the work in which I was presumed to be engaged.   In a
letter to Waldo Frank written on September 15, 1917, as well as
in the "Memoirs" manuscript quoted in the previous note, Anderson tells about the way his imagination was at work while he was
presumed to be writing advertisements:

> Now that I am back at my desk in the city and in the
> midst of all the clatter of things I am having an experi-
> ence that is always a delight to me.   The thing is some-
> thing that I am always being reminded of and always for-
> getting.   It is this--that I always work better and most
> freely when conditions for working are the worst.
>   I don't know that I clearly understand the reason for
> this but believe I do.   In a business office such as ours
> the mental conditions are at the very worst.   Men are
> occupied with matters so trivial and so very unimportant
> that their minds run about in little crazy circles.   In
> self defense one is compelled to create and sustain in his
> own mind a world of people who have significance.   Day
> by day as he goes on this created world becomes a thing
> more definite.   It comes to have height, breadth and
> thickness....
> . . . .
>   I am beginning again to live in a wonderful world.
> Things march in long processions past me.   I wake and
> sleep and dream in a world full of significance.   All the
> weary trivialities with which my hours in the office are
> occupied count as nothing.   (Letters, Newberry Library,
> 1917.)

88/26.   in a blue funk.   In Memoirs, ed. White, in Anderson's
first account of writing "Hands," he says that he came home to
his Chicago rooming house on a winter night "in a blue funk" but
that soon the mood changed and he wrote "Hands," his "first authentic tale" (p. 237).

89/3-4.   wrote the story "I'm a Fool."   Twice in the printed edition of Memoirs, ed. White, Anderson tells how he wrote "I'm a
Fool" in his Chicago advertising office.   On p. 122 he speaks about
writing the story after he had been given "an assignment to write
certain advertisements of pills to cure people's bound up bowels."
See 47/20-48/8, where Anderson describes his disgust when asked
to use his abilities in the writing of this kind of advertisement.
On p. 432 of Memoirs he says that he was asked to write advertisements, not for a cathartic, but "for the manufacturer of commercial fertilizer."

89/4. It is a very beautiful story. In the two accounts of writing
"I'm a Fool" in Memoirs, ed. White, Anderson also has high praise
for this story which is generally acknowledged as one of his finest.
On p. 123 he says that it is a story "to be translated in languages
all over the world" (see 23/14-15 and its note); on p. 433 he says:
"It is a grand story, one of the great stories of our literature."
In a letter to Van Wyck Brooks written in the summer of 1923,
however, Anderson has some reservations about "I'm a Fool." To
Brooks he wrote:

> I think also that "I'm a Fool" is a piece of work that
> holds water, but do you not think its wide acceptance is
> largely due to the fact that it is a story of immaturity
> and poses no problem? After all, isn't it, say, Mark
> Twain at his best, the Huckleberry Finn Mark Twain?
>
> In the same book [Horses and Men] there is a story,
> "There She Is--She Is Taking Her Bath" [see the note to
> 30/24-25], I would like you to read. And then the story
> called "The Man Who Became a Woman" and "The Man's
> Story."
>
> One doesn't want to go on always with the childlike
> feeling for surface, not just that.   I suppose this is my
> quarrel with you, which isn't a quarrel because I love
> you and you have done so much for me, cleared so many
> paths for me.   I mean, I presume, that I do not want
> you to like best of my things the things easiest to like.
> (Letters, ed. Jones and Rideout, p. 102.)

Critics who praise "I'm a Fool" include:

> Horace Gregory, ed., The Portable Sherwood Anderson
>   (New York: The Viking Press, 1949), p. 26;
> Fred B. Millett, Reading Fiction (New York: Harper and
>   Brothers, 1950), pp. 101-103;
> Danforth Ross, The American Short Story (Minneapolis:
>   University of Minnesota Press, 1961), pp. 30-31;
> Claude Simpson and Allan Nevins, eds., The American
>   Reader (Boston: D.C. Heath and Company, 1941),
>   p. 862.

89/22-24. The moments, the hours, in a writer's life of which I
am here trying to speak seem very real to me. The end of the
second account of the writing of "I'm a Fool" in Memoirs, ed.
White, also alludes to the mystery that surrounded its composition
and the relative unimportance of the circumstances of its composition.   The creative moment of intense awareness is the important
thing: "But why did it come at that moment and in that place? In
what year or month did it come? How does it matter?" (p. 433.)

89/26-27. I had intended, when I began to write, to speak of the
great gulf that separates the two arts. Unfortunately Anderson,
neither here nor in any of his writings, is able to articulate what
he sees as the essential difference between the short story and the

novel. He is a creative artist, not a theorist, and he cannot
translate into theory what he instinctively understands and practices as an artist. He can give two descriptive definitions of the
short story in 80/22 ("The writing of the short story is a kind of
explosion") and in 85/27-28 ("It is an idea grasped whole as one
would pick an apple in an orchard"); and he can recognize the importance of his work in the short story form in 26/9-10 (Winesburg is "one of the greatest [books] of our times"), in 31/30-31
("I have had a profound effect upon the art of short story writing"),
and in 85/20-25 ("I am best at the short story ... an opinion that
is no doubt sound"). Anderson comes nearest to articulating a
theory of short story writing in 80/22-30. This passage, however,
ends with the statement: "The actual physical feat of writing
either a long or a short novel is another matter"; but the "other
matter, " the real difference between short story writing and novel
writing, is never explained. This sentence, therefore, is very
much like the two statements in the "Writer's Book" where Anderson admits that he is unable to pinpoint the essential difference
between the short story and the novel: the passage from 89/24 to
29 (see especially 89/25-26: "writing of the long story, the novel,
is another matter") and the passage from 91/19-21 ("I had started
here to speak of the relationship of the story to the novel but have
been carried away").   These passages are also similar to Anderson's statement in a letter written to Robert Morss Lovett in the
spring of 1924: "One does not go from the novel to the short tale
for any reason but that some themes offer themselves for long, involved treatment, others for direct, simple treatment" (Letters,
ed. Jones and Rideout, p. 123). Disappointingly, however, Anderson goes into no more detail about these themes. It is also disappointing to hear him say in the "Writer's Book": "It is not for
nothing that we honor the novelists above the simple story tellers.
The novel is the real test of the man" (81/17-18).
        Although we are forced to say that Anderson could never
arrive at a satisfactory theory regarding the essential difference
between the short story and the novel, he can lay claim to an outstanding accomplishment: the creating of a wholly new art form in
American letters. In "Waiting for Ben Huebsch" in Memoirs, ed.
Rosenfeld, p. 289, he says:

> I have even sometimes thought that the novel form does
> not fit an American writer, that it is a form which had
> been brought in.   What is wanted is a new looseness;
> and in Winesburg I had made my own form.   There were
> individual tales but all about lives in some way connected.
> By this method I did succeed, I think, in giving the feel-
> ing of the life of a boy growing into young manhood in a
> town.   Life is a loose flowing thing.

89/30.   There was the day in New York City. With these words
Anderson starts the account of the third of the "glorious times in
the life of the writer of short tales" (89/28-29), the time when he
wrote "The Man's Story. "   The story is not mentioned by name
until 90/32. "The Man's Story" and three other stories are men-

tioned at 54/10-11, where Anderson recounts a friend's praise of
these stories and of his house at Ripshin.

In Memoirs, ed. White, Anderson tells how he used a building remembered from his youth as the setting for "The Man's
Story." Cora was a young woman with whom he had a love affair
when he was a laborer in Chicago. In Memoirs he says: "There
is a story of mine, in the book called Horses and Men, the tale
itself called 'The Man's Story,' in which I have used, as nearly as
I could remember it, just the setting of Cora's place" (pp. 159-
60).

89/31-90/1. I have spoken of how long it sometimes takes to
really write a story. See 82/21-23, where Anderson says it is
foolish to save ideas but that "when men speak of the difficulties
of telling a story truly, getting at the real meat of a story, that
is another matter." See also 90/32-91/1 and its note.

90/8. The friend was Mr Stark Young. In Memoirs, ed. White,
pp. 434-35, Anderson tells the same story about writing "The
Man's Story" in Stark Young's New York apartment as he tells
here in the "Writer's Book." Another very similar account is in
Elizabeth Prall Anderson's Miss Elizabeth, pp. 51-52. Stark
Young, the New York drama critic and author, was a friend of
Anderson's from the early twenties to the end of his life.

90/28. as I wrote hour after hour. In 57/3-7, where Anderson
alludes to the writing of "The Man's Story" without naming it, he
says: "I had written for ten hours" (57/3). In the account of
Memoirs, ed. White, he says: "I had begun writing at eight in
the morning and I wrote until five in the evening" (p. 435). See
also 91/4, where Anderson says it was "in the late afternoon"
when the story was finished.

Rosenfeld in his edition of "Writing Stories" in Memoirs,
pp. 344-45, supplies the words "I remember that" before "as I
wrote hour after hour."

90/32-91/1. For three, four, five years I had been trying to
write it. See 28/17-18, where Anderson says that "Death in the
Woods" was "ten years getting itself written," and 85/3-5, where
he says: "There are single short stories of mine that have taken
me ten or twelve years to get written." In regard to "The Man's
Story," see also 89/31-90/1 and its note, as well as 90/13-14,
where Anderson says: "There is this tale, Stark, that I have for
years been trying to write."

91/6. Mr Ralph Church. Anderson met Ralph Church in Paris
during Anderson's trip to Europe in the winter of 1926-27. Church
was then a student of philosophy at Oxford University. Anderson
speaks of their Paris days together in Memoirs, ed. White,
pp. 271-73 and 464-65. Anderson and Church started correspond-
ing regularly when Anderson returned to the United States in 1927;
when Church returned he became professor of aesthetics at Cornell University.

91/9-10. sheets of my story thrown about the room. See 57/3-4,
where Anderson speaks about "throwing the sheets on the floor as
I filled them."

91/16. moments that bring glory into the life of the writer. Anderson says much the same thing in a letter to his son John, then
an art student in Paris. The letter was probably written in April,
1927, and Anderson tells John that he had started a letter to him
but then put it aside to work on his book:

> I have perhaps written 2[, 000] or 3, 000 words since
> then. Now I am tired, and my hands are shaky. It is
> still raining, harder than ever. I shall have to take a
> drink of moon to write to you at all.
>   What I want to say is something about the delight that
> may finally come to you in such moments of work. You
> may come to get out of canvases what I get out of sheets
> of paper.
>   I presume it is the power of losing self. Self is the
> grand disease. It is what we all are trying to lose.
>   I think the reason I want you to be an artist, have an
> artist's viewpoint, is just because such times compensate
> for so much else.
>   . . . .
>   I presume that is why, loving you as my son, I want
> you to be an artist. I don't really give a damn whether
> you succeed or not. (Letters, ed. Jones and Rideout,
> pp. 167-68.)

91/17. get fame. In addition to the end of the letter to his son
John quoted in the previous note, see also 26/20-21, where Anderson says: "after the years of writing, some fame got," and
84/13-15: "the real purpose of all this writing is first of all to
enrich the writer. It isn't surely to get fame, recognition." See
also the notes to 49/23-24 and 84/14-15.

91/19-21. I had started here to speak of the relationship of the
story to the novel but have been carried away. This sentence is
omitted by Rosenfeld in his edition of Memoirs, p. 345. Apropos
of Anderson's inability to speak of this relationship, see 89/26-27
and its note.

91/23. into the land of the Now. See 74/18-19, 86/26-28, and
their notes.

91/32. a beautiful, a significant story and now I am drunk. See
Memoirs, ed. White, p. 435: "Stark, I am drunk now but, before
I got drunk, I wrote oh such a beautiful story."

92/2-3. At least at the moment, my story, written thus, seemed
very beautiful to me. Rosenfeld omits this sentence from his edition of "Writing Stories" in Memoirs, p. 345. See the note to
54/11, where Mrs. Eleanor Anderson is quoted as saying that

Sherwood always said that his favorite story was "The Man's Story."

92/5. half mystic wonder. See 27/2-3, where Anderson speaks
about his "experimental, half mystic verse." See also Thomas K.
Whipple in Spokesmen: Modern Writers and American Life (New
York: D. Appleton and Company, 1928; Berkeley and Los Angeles:
University Press, 1962), who says:

> [Anderson] recognizes the mystical element in love of
> every sort, and he ranks love of creative work and sexu-
> al love first. The theme of sex is thus treated in Many
> Marriages, and in the most enigmatic and most unusual
> of his tales, and also the most avowedly mystical, "The
> Man's Story" in Horses and Men. I do not understand
> this story, but so far as I can decipher a meaning it is
> that through the love and possession of one woman a man
> may attain to a similar kind of union with the whole
> world. If sometimes one is tempted to demur at what
> seems Anderson's obsession with sex, one must remem-
> ber that sex is for him a key to a larger experience.
> (p. 136.)

TEXTUAL APPARATUS

All significant changes introduced by Anderson into the manuscript of the "Writer's Book" and all significant changes introduced by the editor into the present edition are listed below according to page and line number. The Introduction, Section V, "The Present Edition and Its Procedures," explains the kinds of manuscript revisions and editorial changes that are not considered significant enough to be included in the Textual Apparatus. A complete record of all deletions, corrections, and additions made by Anderson, as well as of all the changes made by the editor, can be found in "The 'Writer's Book' by Sherwood Anderson: A Critical Edition," unpublished Ph.D. dissertation, Loyola University of Chicago, 1972.

2/1-6   the only typewritten page in the manuscript

2/4   Trilena White] Trillina Wjite

2/6   feels] fee.s

3/3   indentation not in manuscript; by a ve canceled after
         Written

4/3   indentation not in manuscript; a canceled before years;
         some interlineated; s interlineated at end of year;
         or two canceled after years

4/14   period and quotation mark canceled after stories; that
         spoils the sale." interlineated

4/17   thus canceled before this

5/8-9   say ten canceled before thousand; about ten interlineated

5/21   I canceled before a man; to me interlineated after come;
         to my house. canceled after evening.

5/25   there canceled before to his town

5/32-6/1 an canceled before excited; a tense interlineated; tense
         canceled before mood

6/3   worst] read worse

6/10   certainly. canceled after said.

6/13   comma changed to period after talking; He interlineated
            before talked

6/25   comma canceled after invented

7/9   too canceled before unpleasant

7/24   here canceled after write; that night canceled after
            talked

7/26   wept canceled and cried interlineated

8/10   These the sentences I had begun saying to myself.
            interlineated in a different ink

8/19   also had canceled before disappeared; has interlineated

8/23   says canceled after he; seems to be saying interlineated

8/25   here canceled after involved

8/26   it interlineated after put

8/27   put interlineated after all

8/30   everything after window. is canceled; the long cancella-
            tion reads:

                        And, oh, how I needed it.
                              x   x   x
                        I was at a bar, in the city, drinking with my
                        friend, the agent.
                            "You sent me that outline.   It was splendid.
                        What did you not ink it in?"

9/13   indentation not in manuscript

9/28   somewhe canceled after got

11/6-7   often canceled before sometimes

11/25   the canceled after where

11/30   facing it,] period canceled after facing it

12/14   rings canceled before under; patches interlineated

12/18   evening, she comes down the stairs] evening she comes
            down the stairs,

12/21   three;] three

13/17   resturant canceled after with the; waitress interlineated

13/25   [us] others] we others

14/2   presently ...] presently.

14/9   them] read her

14/15   In a city] ... In a city; house, where] house where,

14/31   windows] s interlineated

15/12   woman with bare feet] woman, with bare feet,

15/16   dugs] lugs

15/17   horse] horse,

16/12   have,] have

16/18   her] he

16/25   hailed] hailed,

16/28   recognized] read recognizes; him ...] him ..,

16/30   comma changed to period after men; it canceled after
          men; of canceled before by

16/31   changing,] changing

16/32   becomes] becomes,

17/1   dreams] dreams,

17/7   a canceled before narrow; the interlineated

17/22   voice, but,] voice period canceled but,

18/11   quotation mark canceled after dark.

18/13   often,] often; the canceled before such

18/16   went] went,

18/26   it.] its.

19/18   curtain] curtain,

19/29   feeli canceled before impulse

20/13   could] could,

20/15   quotation mark canceled after this

21/12   You canceled and He interlineated before might

21/20   confessed to me canceled before talked to me; of inter-
           lineated after talked to me

22/13   indentation not in manuscript

22/21   period canceled after remember

22/26   woman] wom

22/28   babes] babe

22/29   by canceled before in

23/4   up canceled before those; those of us] those of up

23/5   dream?] dream.

23/19   week, tw canceled before day

23/28   American interlineated before writer

23/29   certain, at present,] certain at present

24/18   be thousands] the thousands

24/30   fr canceled before and pencils

25/16   being] read to be

25/21   indentation not in manuscript

25/27-28   coming? My Winesburg, Ohio] coming, (my Winesburg
           Ohio

25/31   thousand;] thousand

25/32   published] published,

26/1   parenthesis canceled after dollars. Anderson thus can-
           celed the parenthesis that closes the parenthetical
           clause begun in line 5. The editor has omitted both
           parentheses.

27/11   sheep] sheep,

27/12   stream rolling over rocks,] stream, rolling over rocks

28/22   period changed to comma and quotation mark canceled
         after life

28/27   now ..."] now."

29/21   al canceled after have

29/23   but for us] but that, for us

29/24   success, but] success, but that

29/25   "success"] success

30/10-11 come: so many pounds] come, so many pound

30/22   another?" And] another?" and

30/23   wire] wire,

30/24   story,] period canceled after story

30/28   rights,] period canceled after rights

31/3   fellow,] period canceled after fellow

31/6   that he] that, while he

31/20   innocent;] innocent,

31/32   have canceled before more

32/1   ask] asks

32/25   period canceled after off; the editor has supplied a
         semicolon

34/17   He canceled before first Do

34/20   business";] business",

36/20   destroyers;] destroyers

36/28   take; but--"You had better take one, "] take but, "you
         had better take one",

36/32   drink canceled before drug

37/8   twenty-two ...] twenty-two,

37/21   lines] could possibly be read as lives

37/32-   Emerson ... we] Emerson, with whom, when we; town
38/1   ...] town,

39/1-2   heads of cabbage] heads of cabbages; Halloween] the
            holloene

39/11   I can canceled before my eye

39/15-16   eighteen ...] eighteen, ; and canceled before or; six-
            teen? ...] sixteen,

39/19-20   rather ... to write,] inserted down the right-hand mar-
            gin

39/24   myself? ...] myself.,

40/13   Winesburg, Ohio.] Winesburg Ohio, to her.

40/25   know, that having, long ago, seen] know that, that hav-
            ing, long ago, seen,

41/1-2   on the edge of canceled and near to interlineated after
            You are

41/5   paintings;] paintings,

41/7-8   ago, I painted,] ago I painted; of canceled before when

41/10   at odd moments and canceled before when

41/29   indecipherable word canceled and mother interlineated
            after her; some] (Some

41/31   who] Who

42/2   is] read are

42/7   all of interlineated before the; men and interlineated
            after the; past;] past,

42/20   and canceled and but interlineated after woman

42/21   al canceled before whole; quickly;] quickly

42/27   in which] is which

42/28   lying;] lying,

42/29   two periods canceled after fetch the doctor.

43/4   unreal;] unreal,

43/13   talent who had once been my friend,] talent, who had
            once been my friend

43/15   life; and] life and,

43/24   who,] who; success] success,

43/25   American stag canceled before New York; who,] who;
            had canceled before having

44/12-13   also canceled before were also

44/16   after A manuscript has "If I go to Hollw indented on a
            separate line and then canceled

45/1   indentation not in manuscript

45/6   yourself canceled after accuse

45/8   being in California, interlineated after Hollywood,

45/9   studioes;] studioes,

45/10   a grea canceled before a hallway

45/25   your canceled before their

46/3   thousand of words] read thousand words or thousands of
            words

46/10   about;] about

46/14-15   and doing it interlineated after others; hundred dollars."]
            there is a period and quotation mark after hundred
            and then dollars.' is written in very close to hundred.'

46/20   and rus canceled after stars; swift running] read swift-
            ly running

46/21   streams;] streams

46/22   an open door into interlineated after through

46/24   room,] room

47/5   them--] them; to get a fare dea canceled before after

47/21   constipated;] constipated

48/11   fakery] fakiness

49/3   enough" ...] enough, "

49/11   day;] day

49/26   that, if] read that perhaps

49/28   false canceled before often false

50/16	worst] worse

50/16   worst] worse

50/31   sing] singing

50/32   Hill to the Poor-House. "] hills to the Poor House. "

51/2   father's father] fathers' father

51/3-4   lived--precariously] lived precariously

51/5   if it had not happened] read it had happened; life,] life

51/6   rich] rich,

51/7   years when] years, when,

51/8   manufacturer,] manufacturer

51/11   man] man,

52/7   life canceled before art

52/9   danger canceled before contradiction; th canceled before us

52/10-11   life;] life, ; are really all canceled and a comma and our books, interlineated after produce

54/4   st canceled before sit; the top of interlineated after on

54/6   moonlight] read moonlit

54/10   two canceled and three interlineated after named

54/19-20   feet] feet, ; stairways] stairway

54/22   world dictated] world, dictated

54/28   forgotten--] forgotten

54/32   Winesburg, Ohio, and one day had got] Winesburg Ohio and, an day, had got,

55/1-2   all th canceled before the names

55/12   period canceled after book; the editor has supplied a comma

56/21   road] road, ; and by a creek canceled after road,

56/22   do canceled before going

57/12   basis] bases

57/13   professors--] proffessors,

57/14   joy] indecipherable word, perhaps jole, and a comma

57/16   of the real st canceled after people

57/18   gone;] gone,

57/30   period canceled after sounds; the editor has supplied a
             comma

58/11   to wh canceled before with whom

58/17   other,] other

58/18   home in canceled after walked

59/3   John Emerson] Jane Emerison

60/10   was a joy] has a joy or possibly has a jole

60/22   my canceled and the interlineated before bathroom

60/25   sleepily;] sleeplily

60/30-31   of women interlineated and on us canceled after millions

61/3   me;] me

61/4   morning,] morning; that] that,

61/5   along,] along

61/6   to the black] so the black; creek] creek,

61/17   story of their own interlineated between own and lives

61/18   only canceled and merely interlineated after pen

62/30   fell] read fall

65/8   bit] lit

65/15   failures; and very often] failures and very often,

65/25   I hav canceled after know.

65/26   indentation not in manuscript

67/24   He began canceled before When

68/10-11   "Agnes, " and then "dear Agnes, " and finally] Agnes and
             then dear Agness and finally,

68/22   youth canceled before own boyhood

69/12   baker blocks,] Baker blocks

69/19   he told her] to told her

70/5   indentation not in manuscript

70/24   it, "] manuscript has either a period or an exclamation
           mark after it

71/16   does demad mand some control canceled before when

74/32   period canceled after best; the editor has supplied the
           semicolon

76/2   indentation not in manuscript

76/18   begin] read begins

76/22   it:] it.

76/23   He canceled after the first Heavy

76/24   poem:] poem.

76/26   indentation not in manuscript

78/13   say canceled before recall

79/2   rapidly canceled after speaking

79/13   in canceled before he; wr canceled before puts

79/15   comma and in canceled after want

80/7   Sauk Centre] read Gopher Prairie

80/10   grey] grew

81/28   yourself;] yourself

82/14   of canceled and to interlineated after talking

82/23   matter;] matter

84/1   quotation mark canceled after evening.; manuscript has
           indentation and quotation mark before I notice

85/2   indentation not in manuscript

85/4   I canceled before have taken

85/22   Very well. canceled before And

86/5   it--] it

86/16   wa canceled before were; to canceled before live;
           chickens] chicken

86/22   passing] passion

86/27   land] land,

87/22   sixteen ...] sixteen

87/28   seem] read seems

87/29   house] house,

88/6   in canceled after man,

88/17   houses,] house,

88/19   indentation not in manuscript

88/29   shall canceled and will interlineated before have

89/14   in low canceled before with

89/24   I am, to be sure,] I am to be sure

89/28   glorious] glories

91/19   times] time

91/27   two br canceled before two men

91/31   asked;] asked

92/2   least] least,

SELECTED BIBLIOGRAPHY

I. UNPUBLISHED WORKS OF SHERWOOD ANDERSON

Sherwood Anderson Papers. Deposited in the Newberry Library, Chicago. 16, 718 items in 144 boxes. Letters, clippings, photographs, royalty statements and autographed and type-written works of Anderson. Fragments, notes, and tenta-tive sketches for short stories. Arrangement in four sec-tions: (1) outgoing letters, arranged chronologically; (2) in-coming letters and material relative to Anderson, arranged alphabetically; (3) works by Anderson, arranged alphabetical-ly; and (4) appendix: (a) art work, (b) development project, (c) dust jacket collection, (d) photographs, (e) reserved boxes, and (f) sealed boxes.

Smyth County News, 1927-1929. Microfilm of Smyth County News. The Newberry Library, Chicago. The material Anderson wrote for the Marion Democrat is identical with the materi-al he wrote for the Smyth County News.

"What Say." Smyth County News, July 7, 1932. Microfilm of Smyth County News, Archives, Virginia State Library, Richmond.

II. PUBLISHED WORKS OF SHERWOOD ANDERSON

A. FULL-LENGTH VOLUMES

Alice and The Lost Novel. London: Elkin Mathews and Marrot, 1929.

The American County Fair. New York: Random House, Inc., 1930.

Beyond Desire. New York: Liveright Publishing Corporation, 1932.

Beyond Desire. Introduction by Walter B. Rideout. New York: Liveright Publishing Company [1961].

Dark Laughter. New York: Boni and Liveright, 1925.

Dark Laughter.   Introduction by Howard Mumford Jones.   New
         York: Liveright Publishing Company [1960].

Death in the Woods.   New York: Liveright, Inc., Publishers,
         1933.

Hello Towns!   New York: Horace Liveright Publishing Inc., 1929.

Home Town.   New York: Alliance Book Corporation, 1940.

Horses and Men.   New York: B. W. Huebsch, Inc., 1923.

Kit Brandon.   New York: Charles Scribner's Sons, 1936.

Many Marriages.   New York: B. W. Huebsch, Inc., 1923.

Marching Men.   London: John Lane, The Bodley Head, Ltd.,
         1917.

Mid-American Chants.   London: John Lane, The Bodley Head,
         Ltd., 1918.

The Modern Writer.   San Francisco: The Lantern Press, Gelber,
         Lilienthal, Inc., 1925.

Nearer the Grass Roots.   San Francisco: The Westgate Press, 1929.

A New Testament.   New York: Boni and Liveright, 1927.

No Swank.   Philadelphia: The Centaur Press, 1934.

Perhaps Women.   New York: Horace Liveright, Inc., 1931.

Plays: Winesburg and Others.   New York: Charles Scribner's
         Sons, 1937.

Poor White.   New York: B. W. Huebsch, Inc., 1920.

Poor White.   New York: The Modern Library, 1926.

Poor White.   With an Introduction by Walter B. Rideout.   A Vik-
         ing Compass Book.   New York: The Viking Press, 1966.

Puzzled America.   New York: Charles Scribner's Sons, 1935.

Sherwood Anderson's Memoirs.   [Edited by Paul Rosenfeld.]   New
         York: Harcourt, Brace and World, Inc., 1942.

Sherwood Anderson's Memoirs: A Critical Edition.   Newly Edited
         from the Original Manuscripts by Ray Lewis White.   Chapel
         Hill: The University of North Carolina Press, 1969.

Sherwood Anderson's Notebook.   New York: Boni and Liveright,

1926.

A Story Teller's Story. New York: B. W. Huebsch, Inc., 1924.

A Story Teller's Story. Preface by Walter B. Rideout. A Viking
    Compass Book. New York: The Viking Press, 1969.

A Story Teller's Story: A Critical Text. Edited with an Introduc-
    tion by Ray Lewis White. Cleveland: The Press of Case
    Western Reserve University, 1968.

Tar: A Midwest Childhood. New York: Boni and Liveright, 1926.

Tar: A Midwest Childhood: A Critical Text. Edited with an In-
    troduction by Ray Lewis White. Cleveland: The Press of
    Case Western Reserve University, 1969.

The Triumph of the Egg. New York: B. W. Huebsch, Inc., 1921.

Windy McPherson's Son. New York: John Lane, 1916.

Windy McPherson's Son. Rev. ed. New York: B. W. Huebsch,
    Inc., 1921.

Windy McPherson's Son. Introduction by Wright Morris. Chicago:
    The University of Chicago Press, 1965.

Winesburg, Ohio. New York: B. W. Huebsch, Inc., 1919.

Winesburg, Ohio. Introduction by Ernest Boyd. New York: The
    Modern Library [1922].

Winesburg, Ohio. Introduction by Malcolm Cowley. Viking Com-
    pass Book. New York: The Viking Press, 1960.

Winesburg, Ohio: Text and Criticism. Edited by John H. Ferres.
    The Viking Critical Library. New York: The Viking Press,
    1966.

B. COLLECTIONS

Homage to Sherwood Anderson, 1876-1941. Edited by Paul P. Ap-
    pel. Mamaroneck, N.Y.: Paul P. Appel, Publisher, 1970.

Letters of Sherwood Anderson. Selected and Edited with an Intro-
    duction and Notes by Howard Mumford Jones in Association
    with Walter B. Rideout. Boston: Little, Brown and Com-
    pany, 1953; New York: Kraus Reprint Company, 1969.

The Portable Sherwood Anderson. Edited, and with an Introduction,
    by Horace Gregory. The Viking Portable Library. New
    York: The Viking Press, Inc., 1949.

Return to Winesburg: Selections from Four Years of Writing for a
    Country Newspaper.   Edited with an Introduction by Ray
    Lewis White.   Chapel Hill: University of North Carolina
    Press, 1967.

Selected Short Stories of Sherwood Anderson.   Edition for the
    Armed Services, Inc., 1945.

The Sherwood Anderson Reader.   Edited, with an Introduction by
    Paul Rosenfeld.   Boston: Houghton Mifflin Company, 1947.

Sherwood Anderson: Short Stories.   Edited and with an Introduction
    by Maxwell Geismar.   American Century Series.   New York:
    Hill and Wang, 1962.

C.   ADDITIONAL ARTICLES

"Introduction."   Free and Other Stories by Theodore Dreiser.
    New York: Boni and Liveright Publishers, 1918.

"Man and His Imagination."   The Intent of the Artist.   Edited by
    Augusto Centeno.   Princeton: Princeton University Press,
    1941.

"On Being Published."   Colophon, Part I (February, 1930), 4.

"Price of Aristocracy."   Today, I (March 10, 1934), 10-11, 23.

"The Situation in American Writing: Seven Questions (Part II)."
    Partisan Review, VI, Number 5 (Fall, 1939), 103-105.

"So You Want to Be a Writer?"   Saturday Review of Literature,
    XXI (December 9, 1939), 13-14; condensed in Reader's Di-
    gest, XXXVI (January, 1940), 109-11.

"Why Men Write."   Story, VIII (January, 1936), 2, 4, 103, 105.

III.   SECONDARY MATERIAL

A.   BIBLIOGRAPHIES

Gozzi, Raymond D.   "A Bibliography of Sherwood Anderson's Con-
    tributions to Periodicals, 1914-1946."   Newberry Library
    Bulletin, Second Series, Number 2 (December, 1948),
    pp. 71-82.

Sheehy, Eugene P., and Lohf, Kenneth A., compilers.   Sherwood
    Anderson: A Bibliography.   Los Gatos, Calif.:   Talisman
    Press, 1960.

Tanselle, G. Thomas.   "Additional Reviews of Sherwood Anderson's

Work." Papers of the Bibliographical Society of America, LVI (1962), 358-365.

White, Ray Lewis, compiler. Checklist of Sherwood Anderson. A Charles E. Merrill Checklist. Columbus, Ohio: Charles E. Merrill Publishing Company, 1969.

B. BIOGRAPHIES OF ANDERSON

Anderson, David D. Sherwood Anderson: An Introduction and Interpretation. American Authors and Critics Series. New York: Holt, Rinehart and Winston, Inc., 1967.

Burbank, Rex. Sherwood Anderson. New York: Twayne Publishers, Inc., 1964.

Chase, Cleveland B. Sherwood Anderson. New York: Robert M. McBride Company, Inc., 1927.

Fagin, Nathan Bryllion. The Phenomenon of Sherwood Anderson. Baltimore: The Rossi-Bryn Company, 1927.

Howe, Irving. Sherwood Anderson. New York: William Sloane Associates, 1951.

Schevill, James. Sherwood Anderson: His Life and Works. Denver: University of Denver Press, 1951.

Sutton, William A. Exit to Elsinore. Ball State Monograph Number Seven. Muncie, Indiana: Ball State University, 1967.

_____. Road to Winesburg: A Mosaic of the Imaginative Life of Sherwood Anderson. Metuchen, N.J.: The Scarecrow Press, Inc., 1972.

Weber, Brom. Sherwood Anderson. Pamphlets on American Writers, Number 43. Minneapolis: University of Minnesota Press, 1964.

C. FULL-LENGTH VOLUMES

Anderson, Elizabeth, and Kelly, Gerald R. Miss Elizabeth: A Memoir. Boston: Little, Brown and Company, 1969.

Bates, Herbert E. The Modern Short Story: A Critical Survey. London: Thomas Nelson and Sons, 1945.

Bridgman, Richard. The Colloquial Style in America. New York: Oxford University Press, 1966.

Brooks, Van Wyck. The Confident Years: 1885-1915. New York:

E. P. Dutton and Company, 1952.

Cargill, Oscar. Intellectual America: Ideas on the March. New
    York: The Macmillan Company, 1941.

Duffey, Bernard. The Chicago Renaissance in American Letters:
    A Critical History. East Lansing: Michigan State College
    Press, 1954.

Gilmer, Walker. Horace Liveright: Publisher of the Twenties.
    New York: David Lewis, 1970.

Hansen, Harry. Midwest Portraits: A Book of Memoirs and
    Friendships. New York: Harcourt, Brace and Company,
    1923.

Hatcher, Harlan. Creating the Modern American Novel. New
    York: Farrar and Rinehart, 1935.

Hicks, Granville. The Great Tradition. Rev. ed. New York:
    Crowell-Collier and Macmillan, Inc., 1935.

Hoffman, Frederick J. Freudianism and the Literary Mind. 2nd
    ed. Baton Rouge: Louisiana State University Press, 1957.

Kramer, Dale. Chicago Renaissance: The Literary Life in the
    Midwest, 1900-1930. New York: Appleton-Century, 1966.

Kazin, Alfred. On Native Grounds: An Interpretation of Modern
    American Literature. New York: Harcourt, Brace and
    Company, 1942.

Lewis, Sinclair. Cheap and Contented Labor: The Picture of a
    Southern Mill Town in 1929. United Feature Syndicate, Inc.,
    1929.

_____. Main Street. New York: Harcourt, Brace and Com-
    pany, 1929.

Maugham, W. Somerset. Of Human Bondage. New York: George
    H. Doran Company, 1915.

Mott, Frank Luther. A History of American Magazines. Vol. IV.
    Cambridge, Mass.: Harvard University Press, 1957.

O'Brien, Edward Joseph. The Advance of the American Short
    Story. New York: Dodd, Mead and Company, 1923.

_____. The Best Short Stories of 1915 and the Yearbook of the
    American Short Story. Boston: Small, Maynard and Com-
    pany, 1916-1925; New York: Dodd, Mead and Company,
    1926-1933; Boston: Houghton Mifflin Company, 1934-1941.

_____. The Dance of the Machine: The American Short Story
    and the Industrial Age. New York: The Macaulay Company,
    1929.

O'Connor, Frank. The Lonely Voice: A Study of the Short Story.
    Cleveland and New York: The World Publishing Company,
    1962.

Orton, Vrest. Dreiserana: A Book about His Books. New York:
    The Chocorua Bibliographies, 1929.

Parrington, Vernon Louis. Main Currents in American Thought.
    Vol. III. New York: Harcourt, Brace and Company, Inc.,
    1927.

Peden, William. The American Short Story: Front Line in the
    National Defense of Literature. Boston: Houghton Mifflin
    Company, 1964.

Pfeiffer, Karl G. W. Somerset Maugham: A Candid Portrait.
    New York: W. W. Norton and Company, Inc., 1959.

Quinn, Arthur Hobson. American Fiction: An Historical and Cul-
    tural Survey. New York: D. Appleton-Century Company,
    Inc., 1936.

Ross, Danforth. The American Short Story. Pamphlets on Ameri-
    can Writers. Number 14. Minneapolis: University of
    Minnesota Press, 1961.

Smith, Arthur H. An Authentic History of Winesburg, Holmes
    County, Ohio, Including A Winesburg "Who's Who." [Chi-
    cago: n. p., 1930.]

Spaeth, Sigmund. A History of Popular Music in America. New
    York: Random House, 1948.

Spratling, William. File on Spratling: An Autobiography. Intro-
    duction by Budd Schulberg. Boston: Little, Brown and
    Company, 1967.

_____. Sherwood Anderson and Other Famous Creoles: A Gal-
    lery of Contemporary New Orleans. Drawn by Wm. Sprat-
    ling and Arranged by Wm. Faulkner. New Orleans: Pub-
    lished by the Pelican Bookshop Press in Royal Street New
    Orleans [1926].

Stein, Gertrude. The Autobiography of Alice B. Toklas. Selected
    Writings of Gertrude Stein. Edited, with an Introduction
    and Notes by Carl Van Vechten. New York: Random House,
    1946.

Swanberg, William A. Dreiser. New York: Charles Scribner's

Sons, 1965.

Trilling, Lionel. The Liberal Imagination: Essays on Literature
    and Society. New York: The Viking Press, 1950.

Walcutt, Charles Child. American Literary Naturalism, A Divided
    Stream. Minneapolis: University of Minnesota Press, 1956.

Wells, H. G. The Country of the Blind and Other Stories. Lon-
    don: Thomas Nelson and Sons, [1911].

West, Ray B., Jr. The Short Story in America: 1900-1950.
    Chicago: Henry Regnery Company, 1952.

Whipple, Thomas K. Spokesmen: Modern Writers and American
    Life. New York: D. Appleton and Company, 1928; Berke-
    ley and Los Angeles: University Press, 1962.

White, Ray Lewis, ed. The Achievement of Sherwood Anderson:
    Essays in Criticism. Chapel Hill: University of North
    Carolina Press, 1966.

Why Sinclair Lewis Got the Nobel Prize. Address by Erik Axel
    Karlfeldt, Permanent Secretary of the Swedish Academy, at
    the Nobel Festival, December 10, 1930; and Address by
    Sinclair Lewis before the Swedish Academy, December 12,
    1930. New York: Harcourt, Brace and Company [n.d.].

D.   PERIODICAL LITERATURE

Anderson, Karl James. "My Brother, Sherwood Anderson." Sat-
    urday Review of Literature, XXXI (September 4, 1948), 6-7,
    26-27.

Dell, Floyd. "How Sherwood Anderson Became an Author." New
    York Herald-Tribune Books, XVIII (April 12, 1942), 1-2.

_____. "On Being Sherwood Anderson's Literary Father."
    Newberry Library Bulletin, V (December, 1961), 315-21.

Dreiser, Theodore. "The Early Adventures of Sister Carrie."
    Colophon, I, Part 5 (1931), [n.p.].

Frank, Waldo. "Emerging Greatness." Seven Arts, I (November,
    1916), 73-78.

_____. "Vicarious Fiction." Seven Arts, I (January, 1917),
    302.

Homage to Sherwood Anderson. Story, XIX (September-October,
    1941).

Joselyn, Sister M. "Some Artistic Dimensions of Sherwood Anderson's 'Death in the Woods.'" Studies in Short Fiction, IV (Spring, 1967), 252-59.

Phillips, William L. "How Sherwood Anderson Wrote Winesburg, Ohio." American Literature, XXIII (March, 1951), 7-30.

_____. "Sherwood Anderson's Two Prize Pupils." The University of Chicago Magazine, XLVII (January, 1955), 9-12.

Rosenfeld, Paul. "Sherwood Anderson." Dial, LXXII (January, 1922), 29-42.

Sherwood Anderson Memorial Number. Newberry Library Bulletin. Second Series, Number 2 (December, 1948).

Sherwood Anderson Number. Shenandoah, XIII (Spring, 1962).

Taylor, Welford Dunaway. "Sherwood Anderson." Virginia Cavalcade, XIX (Spring, 1970), 42-47.

E. UNPUBLISHED THESES AND DISSERTATIONS

Cole, Janice Ellen. "Many Marriages: Sherwood Anderson's Controversial Novel." Unpublished Ph. D. dissertation, University of Michigan, 1965.

Crist, Robert Lenhart. "Sherwood Anderson's Dark Laughter: Sources, Composition, and Reputation." Unpublished Ph. D. dissertation, University of Chicago, 1966.

Dinsmoor, Mary Helen. "An Inquiry into the Life of Sherwood Anderson as Reflected in His Literary Works." Unpublished M. A. thesis, Ohio University, 1939.

Harvey, Cyrus J. "Sherwood Anderson's Natural History of Winesburg." Unpublished B. A. thesis, Harvard University, 1948.

Hilton, Earl Raymond. "The Purpose and Method of Sherwood Anderson." Unpublished Ph. D. dissertation, University of Minnesota, 1950.

Miller, William Vaughn. "The Technique of Sherwood Anderson's Short Stories." Unpublished Ph. D. dissertation, University of Illinois, 1969.

Nemanic, Gerald Carl. "Talbot Whittingham: An Annotated Edition of the Text Together with a Descriptive and Critical Essay." Unpublished Ph. D. dissertation, University of Arizona, 1969.

Phillips, William L. "Sherwood Anderson's Winesburg, Ohio: Its

Origins, Composition, Technique, and Reception." Unpublished Ph. D. dissertation, University of Chicago, 1949.

Risley, Edward H.   "Sherwood Anderson, the Philosophy of Failure." Unpublished thesis, Harvard University, 1938.

Rothweiler, Robert L.   "Ideology and Four Radical Novelists: The Response to Communism of Dreiser, Anderson, Dos Passos, and Farrell." Unpublished Ph. D. dissertation, Washington University, 1960.

Sutton, William A.   "Sherwood Anderson: The Formative Years (1876-1913)." Unpublished Ph. D. dissertation, The Ohio State University, 1943.

F.   PERSONAL INTERVIEWS

Anderson, Mrs. Eleanor, of Marion, Virginia.   At the Newberry Library, Chicago, on June 5, 1969.

_____.   At Ripshin Farm, Grayson County, Virginia, on July 16-17, 1970.

Anderson, John, of Chicago, Illinois.   At the Newberry Library, Chicago, on July 23, 1970.

Greear, David, of Marion, Virginia.   At Ripshin Farm, Grayson County, Virginia, on July 17, 1970.

G.   PERSONAL LETTER

Barker, Ruby Sullivan, of Roanoke, Virginia.   Letter of August 24, 1970.

INDEX